"Respectfully
D. B. Beardsley

HISTORY of HANCOCK COUNTY

[OHIO]

FROM ITS EARLIEST SETTLEMENT TO THE PRESENT TIME

TOGETHER WITH REMINISCENCES OF PIONEER LIFE,
INCIDENTS, STATISTICAL TABLES, AND
BIOGRAPHICAL SKETCHES

BY

D. B. Beardsley

FINDLEY. O.

HERITAGE BOOKS
2015

HERITAGE BOOKS
AN IMPRINT OF HERITAGE BOOKS, INC.

Books, CDs, and more—Worldwide

For our listing of thousands of titles see our website
at
www.HeritageBooks.com

A Facsimile Reprint
Published 2015 by
HERITAGE BOOKS, INC.
Publishing Division
5810 Ruatan Street
Berwyn Heights, Md. 20740

Entered according to act of Congress, in the year 1881, by D. B. Beardsley, in the office of the Librarian of Congress, at Washington

Originally published Springfield, Ohio: Republic Printing Company, 1881

Copyright © 1989 Heritage Books, Inc.

DEDICATION
To the memory of the brave men and women, who, forsaking home, friends, and the comforts of civilization, emigrated to this county, and by their self-sacrificing industry and untiring perseverance, laid broad and deep the foundation of our present prosperity, and left to their descendants so rich a heritage, this book is respectfully dedicated.

— Publisher's Notice —
In reprints such as this, it is often not possible to remove blemishes from the original. We feel the contents of this book warrant its reissue despite these blemishes and hope you will agree and read it with pleasure.

International Standard Book Numbers
Paperbound: 978-1-55613-188-2
Clothbound: 978-0-7884-8827-6

PREFACE.

In presenting this volume to the public, I do so with much hesitation, and embarrassment. Making no pretensions to being an author, and this book being the result of an accident as it were, I ask from the reader a kindly consideration, and generous criticism. Some eight years ago, I, for my own amusement, furnished to the press a series of articles entitled "Our Early Settlers," in which I endeavored to truthfully detail some of the many reminiscences of pioneer life in this county. As these articles progressed, they had the merit of attracting some attention, especially from the old settlers, who took the matter in earnest, and steps were taken to form a Pioneer Association, which resulted in the formation of such a society. At the meetings and re-unions of this Association papers appropriate to the occasion were prepared and read by myself and others. I was then requested by many of the old frontiersmen, for whom I have the profoundest respect, as well as by many of the descendants of those who had "gone home" to prepare and have published a history of the county.

Upon this earnest solicitation, and with a due appreciation of the labors and responsibilities of the undertaking, I consented. The work has been one of great labor and research, of continual inquiry and thought. And now, with the assistance I have received from many kind friends, who have cheerfully furnished all the information in their power, when requested, and by the courtesy of the various county officials to whom I have applied for permission to examine the records, and their assistance in such examination, this work is completed, and offered for your amusement and possible instruction.

There is no pretence in its preparation to rhetorical flourish, choice phrases, or finish of diction, but I have endeavored to

"Tell a plain, unvarnished tale,"

in a plain homelike manner. Of course absolute verity can not be claimed for all here related. But I do claim that there is nothing herein written, which has not the sanction of either the public records, or of the best recollection of those who were actors in the scenes related, or of those who had them directly from these actors, hence this work is as nearly a truthful history in all its parts, as is possible, under the circumstances. Nothing has been introduced by way of embellishment, at the expense of truth. The arrangement of the work may be somewhat desultory, but this does not interfere with its historical value, or understanding, and may be a source of relief to the reader.

CONTENTS.

CHAPTER I.—Before the Organization of the County..................... 9
CHAPTER II.—First Organization of the County........................... 23
CHAPTER III.—Independent Organization of the County.............. 27
CHAPTER IV.—General Description of the County. Its Soil and Products 33
CHAPTER V.—Relating to a Few First Things in the County......... 38
CHAPTER VI.—Early Appraisement and Assessment of Property.. 45
CHAPTER VII. - First Jail and First Court House........................... 52
CHAPTER VIII.—Early Courts. First Judges. First Juries.......... 58
CHAPTER IX —The Country Shoemaker. The Schoolmaster. Log Rolling 69
CHAPTER X.—First Roads and Bridges... 73
CHAPTER XI.—County Records. First Census. General Election 1828.. 80
CHAPTER XII.—An Incident. General Muster............................... 85
CHAPTER XIII.—Railroads.. 90
CHAPTER XIV.—Common Schools... 97
CHAPTER XV.—Some Other Things of Interest............................. 101
CHAPTER XVI.—Our Associates in the General Assembly of Ohio, in Senatorial and Representative Districts.................................. 106
CHAPTER XVII.—Matters of Interest in Brief Paragraphs........... 114
CHAPTER XVIII.—Murders and Murder Trials.............................. 120
CHAPTER XIX.—The Deer Lick. Plum Orchard. Johnny Appleseeds.. 131
CHAPTER XX.—Present Court House. New Jail. Infirmary...... 136
CHAPTER XXI.—Early Sports. Corn Huskings. House Raisings. Grain Threshing and Cleaning... 143
CHAPTER XXII.—Our Judicial Associate Counties and Judges...... 146
CHAPTER XXIII.—Hancock County in the War.............................. 151
CHAPTER XXIV.—Hancock County Agricultural Society............. 164
CHAPTER XXV.—County Officers... 167
Statistical Tables.. 169
Table of Distances 173
Land Surveys... 175
Allen Townships.. 180
    Van Buren... 192
Amanda Township.. 194
    Capernaum 200
    Vanlue... 200
Blanchard Township... 205
    Benton... 214

Contents.

Louisville	215
Big Lick Township	217
Freedom	225
West Independence	225
Cass Township	228
Frankford	230
Delaware Township	236
Mt. Blanchard	242
Eagle Township	246
Martinstown	250
Findley Township	254
Findley	269
East Findley	274
North Findley	276
Industries of Findley	316
Churches	331
Schools	341
Benevolent Societies	345
Newspapers	350
Hotels	362
Banks	365
Fire Department	367
Maple Grove Cemetery	369
Jackson Township	372
North Liberty	379
Liberty Township	382
Madison Township	395
Williamstown	402
Arlington	402
Marion Township	404
Orange Township	412
Pleasant Township	421
Olney	426
McComb	427
Portage Township	430
Lafayette	439
Union Township	441
Rawson	448
Cannonsburg	450
Cory	450
Van Buren Township	453
Washington Township	457
Risdon	466
Arcadia	466
Social Statistics	470

BIOGRAPHICAL.

Alspach, George W...................250	Engle, Jacob...........................211
Algire, Rev. Geo.......................423	Eckles, John...........................234
Barnd, John..............................190	Elder, Josiah 238
Baldwin, David M...................207	Fishel, Michael.......................208
Burman, John..........................231	Ford, John T...........................356
Bonham, Robert......................261	Fountain, Wm.........................389
Byal, John................................261	Folk Nicholas..........................444
Beardsley, Barna....................263	Goode, Judge P. G.................149
Baldwin, Dr. W. H..................298	George, Peter...........................196
Blackford, Price......................299	Gilbert, Aquilla........................196
Byal, Henry..............................307	Goit, Edson, Sr........................315
Bishop, Henry.........................351	Glessner, Lewis......................353
Brown, Henry..........................352	Glessner, Wm. L....................353
Balsley, A. H............................358	Huff, Abraham......................... 61
Boylan, Rev. John..................388	Hardy, John.............................189
Bright, Major............................406	Hughes, Owen........................211
Blakeman, Charles.................424	Hedges, Joshua......................260
Burns, James...........................443	Hamilton, John P....................260
Burket, George........................443	Henderson, Wm. L.................308
Burket, Jacob...........................444	Henderson, F...........................311
Biggs, Rev. Richard................445	Hollabaugh, A. M...................353
Carson, Dick............................211	Hurd, Robert............................399
Chamberlain, Job, Sr..............259	Howard, Samuel 436
Carlin, Squire...........................300	Johnson, Joseph.....................434
Cory, Judge D. J.....................311	Jordan, Charles E...................465
Coffinbury, J. M.......................357	Karn, Ezra................................232
Comer, Isaac...........................389	Kilpatrick, Wm.........................423
Cusac, Daniel..........................390	Kalb, John................................423
Cooper, Judge John...............435	Lake, Asa M............................238
Cramer, Philip.........................442	Lamb, Henry........................... 303
Church, William.......................463	McKinnis, Judge Robert......... 60
Dukes, Richard........................206	Moffit, Thomas........................208
Dukes, Louis, Sr.....................206	Moore, John.............................223
Dukes, John.............................207	McAnnelly, Moses..................224
DeWolfe, Eli G.........................360	Moreland, Wm.........................260
Davis, William..........................410	Morrison, J. H..........................303
Dalley, Henry L........................416	Mungen, Wm...........................351
Dulin, Sandford F....................431	McKinnis, Philip.......................391
Ensminger, George................191	Martz, Napoleon B.................400

Biographical.

Miller, William B................480
Marvin, Willam, Sr...............409
McKinley, John...................415
McConnell, J. T..................418
Moorehead John...................431
Morris, Mahlon...................432
Moorehead, Samuel................438
Newell, Hugh.....................309
Newell, Joseph...................377
O'Neal, Charles W................297
Potter, Judge E. D...............148
Powell, Rev. John................210
Parker, Jonathan.................294
Patten, Dr. David................308
Poe, Jacob.......................388
Rollor, Judge Wm.................225
Reightly, Mathew.................260
Rawson, Dr. Bass.................296
Rosenburg, B. F..................352
Ralston, Alpheus.................376
Rickets, Andrew..................399
Reed, John.......................432

Shoemaker, John..................224
Sampson, Levi....................376
Showalter, Levi..................448
Taylor, Washington...............188
Thompson, Thomas.................195
Taylor, William..................313
Treece, George...................378
Thomas, Lewis....................406
Todd, Benjamin...................422
Thompson, John...................431
Vickers, James...................233
Vance, Wilson....................292
Van Emon, Rev. Geo...............389
Wilson, Judge Ebenezer............61
Walters, John....................251
Wilson, James H..................305
Watson, Richard..................388
Williams, John W.................399
Welty, Christ....................39 /
Wiseley, Allen...................406
Wade, Weuman.....................442
Wiseman, James G.................463

HISTORY

—OF—

HANCOCK COUNTY.

CHAPTER I.

BEFORE THE ORGANIZATION OF THE COUNTY.

I NEED only remind the reader, that as a part of Ohio, Hancock County was a part of that great "North-west Territory," ceded by Virginia to the United States Government, and which territory has since been carved up into States, which have rose to the first rank in this Union of States, none of which are more prominent than our own beautiful Ohio. Her military chieftains are no less prominent that her statesmen, and the highest judicial honors of the nation have been conferred on more than one of her distinguished sons. Every citizen of this free Republic, is proud that he is an American, and we may be excused for the feeling of pride, that in addition to being an American citizen, we are also a native "Buckeye."

Of course not much, if anything, was known of this wild region, perhaps not even of its existence, except by the Indians, until about 1812, or during our second war with Great Britain. In common with all the great west, this was an unbroken wilderness, and far from civilization. June 21, 1785, a treaty was concluded at Fort McIntosh, with the Wyandotte, Delaware, Chippewa and Ottowa Indians, by which the boundary line between the United States and the Wyandotte and Delaware nations, was declared to begin " At the mouth of the river Cuyahoga and to extend up said river to the Portage between that and the Tuscarawas branch of the Muskingum; thence down the branch to the crossing place above Fort Laurens; thence westerly to the Portage of the Big Miami which runs into the Ohio, at the mouth of which branch the fort stood which was taken by the French in 1752; thence along said Portage to the Great Miamee or Omee (Maumee) river, and down the south side of the same to its mouth; thence along the south shore of Lake Erie to the mouth of the Cuyahoga river where it began." In this boundary Hancock County was included.

In 1796 Wayne County, Ohio, was established, including all the north-western part of Ohio, a large tract in the north-eastern part of Indiana, and the whole Territory of Michigan. As late as 1816, this, with the counties of Hardin, Wood and some others, was embraced in Logan County, Bellefontaine being the county seat. It was not until after 1805, that by treaties with the Indians, all the country watered by the Maumee and the Sandusky and their tributaries, was acquired by the United States.

The first white settlement in the territory now embraced within the limits of Hancock County, so far as we have any authentic account, was made at the present site of the town of Findley, in about the year 1815. It is possible, however, and indeed, we have a tradition to that effect, that a man by the name of Thorp or Tharp, came here with the

First White Settlement.

soldiers, who occupied Fort Findley in the war of 1812–15, and remained here after its evacuation, and either lived alone, or with the Indians. Not much, however, is known or remembered of him.

The first white family settling here, was that of Benjamin Cox. Upon their arrival, nought but an unbroken forest, save in the immediate vicinity of the old Fort, greeted them. Indians and wild beasts roamed the woods. No neighbors within many days journey perhaps. All was new, all was solitude, and it must have been a most trying time for that one lone family. After making this their home for a few years, the family removed to Wood County, where some of them are still living. On their removal, one of the daughters acted as an interpreter between the whites and the Indians, she having a knowledge of the language of both the Wyandotte and Ottowa tribes, who frequented this part of the country.

But not long did they remain here alone. Others, through a spirit of adventure, or restless desire for new scenes, came and formed settlements. Emigrants were attracted by the richness of the soil, and the abundance of game. Or perhaps with imaginations reaching out to the future, they pictured to themselves the exceeding loveliness, and fruitfulness of the lands, when redeemed from the wilderness, and were constrained to make this their abiding place.

True it is, that from whatever motive they were actuated, they came here and formed settlements, cleared up the forests, built themselves cabins and roads, and laid the foundations, deep and permanent, for our present great prosperity and wealth, and transmitted to their children a rich and beautiful inheritance.

About the middle of June, 1812, the army, under Gen. Hull, left Urbana, Champaign County, Ohio, and passed north through the present couuties of Logan, Hardin, Hancock and Wood, over what was known during, and after the war, as "Hull's Trail," into Michigan. This army cut a road through the unbroken wilderness, uninhabited except by hostile Indians and wild animals.

On this route they built Fort McArthur, on the Scioto River in Hardin County, and Fort Findley, on the Blanchard River, in Hancock.

In the same summer (1812) General Edmund W. Tupper, of Gallia County, enlisted about one thousand men for six months service, mainly from Gallia, Lawrence and Jackson Counties, who, under orders of General Winchester, marched from Urbana north by "Hull's Trail" to the foot of the Maumee Rapids. The enemy attacked Tupper's forces, but were driven off with considerable loss. They then returned to Detroit, and the Americans, under Tupper, returned back to Fort McArthur.

The Fort at Findley was erected by Col. James Findley, under orders from Gen. Hull, and was named in honor of the Colonel. It was a stockade of about fifty yards square, with a block house at each corner, and a ditch in front. It stood on the south bank of the Blanchard River, just west of the present iron bridge, and was used as a depot for military stores.

The Fort was garrisoned by a company under the command of Captain Arthur Thomas, who lived at King's Creek, three miles from Urbana. So far as known, there were no battles fought at Fort Findley, and garrison duty was no doubt monotonous and irksome. But little to excite or amuse the men, they no doubt longed for peace

Adventure of Col. William Oliver.

and a release from duty, that they might again join their families.

Colonel William Oliver, late of Cincinnati, left Fort Meigs, on the Maumee River, about 8 o'clock on a dark and stormy night, during the war, in company with a Kentuckian, on an errand of importance to Fort Findley. They had proceeded but a short distance on their perilous journey, through the wilderness, surrounded with enemies, when they unexpectedly came upon an Indian camp, around the fires of which the Indians were cooking their suppers. So near had they got to the camp, that the noise of their approach alarmed the savages, who at once sprang to their feet and ran towards them. Oliver and his companion reined their horses into the branches of a fallen tree. The horses, as if conscious of danger, as were their riders, remained perfectly quiet, and the Indians passed around the tree without discovering them. At this juncture, the daring messengers put spurs to their horses and dashed forward into the woods, through which they passed to the Fort, where they arrived safely, but with the loss of their clothing, which had been torn from them by the brush through which they had passed—their bodies bruised and lacerated. Nor were they a moment too soon in their arrival, for the Indians, enraged at their escape, had pursued them so closely, that. Oliver and his companion had scarcely been admitted into the Fort, when their pursuers made their appearance on the opposite side of the river. After giving vent to their disappointment at the loss of the scalps of the *pale faces*, in hideous yells, they very wisely retraced their steps toward the Maumee, on the lookout for some unsuspecting but less fortunate white man.

After the close of the war, Captain Thomas' company

returned to Urbana. On their journey home, the Captain and his son lost their horses, and separated from the rest of the company in search of them.

They encamped at the Big Spring, near Solomonstown, about five miles from Bellefontaine, and the next morning were found murdered and scalped. Their bodies were taken to Urbana by a deputation of citizens.

In connection with this account of the fate of Captain Thomas, I will give a copy of a letter received by me from one who speaks knowingly of the matter, and although he is unknown to me, yet I have no doubt but his statements are correct, and as a matter of history, are of great interest. But to the letter:

MARION, IOWA, Dec. 6, 1875.

D. B. BEARDSLEY, Esq.;—DEAR SIR:—I saw in a sketch of the early history of Hancock County, Ohio, as read by you at the Second Annual Pic-nic and Reunion of the Pioneers of your county, published in the Findley Jeffersonian, an account of Captain Arthur Thomas and son, that was killed by the Indians at the Big Springs, some five miles from Bellefontaine, and thinking I might furnish you an item or two, concluded to drop you a line. My father was stationed at a block-house called Menary, about two miles north-west from Bellefontaine, there being a small company of soldiers, I think commanded by Lieut. John Kelly. The object seemed to be to guard and keep in bounds some pet Indians that the Government had in care, and was furnishing supplies through an Agent by the name of McPherson.

On the morning after the murder of Thomas and son, word was brought to the company, and a deputation s sent out after them. among whom was my father (John

Rathbun) and when they reached the spot, and found them in the broiling sun, being scalped, and the blood oozing from their heads, he thought it the most sickening sight he ever beheld; and made him declare vengeance against the tawny tribe. pet or no pet. He always said that it was the pets that done the deed, for as they were returning with the men to the block-house, three of the half-breeds came in sight armed and painted, contrary to orders. The horsemen took after them, and succeeded in stopping them, but the Commander would not let the Post Guard come up in shooting distance, tor he knew there would have been three red-skins less in double quick.

The officers let them go with some good promises on their part, not to be found there arrayed again. After reaching the block-house, they (the Thomas') were put into the hands of the citizens, that conveyed them to their homes and final resting place, as you have it recorded. At Roundhead there was a large village of those pets or friendly Indians, as they were called, and an order was sent out from the Post, to have them come in on a certain day, but the day came and none made their appearance; the second day none. The third day a deputation started after them, but they met them in squads coming in. They were old men, women and children, all the warriors had gone to fight for the British, except a few young men that had charge of affairs. When they reached the village, all had left but one, and he dodged out of sight in a moments time. About all that was accomplished, was to show that while we were taking care of their families, the warriors were fighting against us.

Time passed on, the war ended, and when I reached my fourteenth year, I went to visit an uncle that lived on what was called the Block-house farm. The house was in rather a dilapidated condition, the roof off and half the upper story had been removed. It brought to mind many incidents that I had heard my father relate thirty-six years ago. I left the place of my nativity and settled in what was called the Black Hawk purchase, or Iowa. Had not been here long before I heard of the Thomas family having settled at Cascade, where the son of a brother of the Captain, and son alluded to, owned a fine mill property, and in the course of some three years I went to his mill, where I saw the whole family, the widow, her son and three or four daughters, all married except the widow. She never married, or at least not to that time. Thomas sold his mill and went further west, and I have lost sight of him. I always like to cherish in memory those who have suffered in their country's cause.

But I will close.

Yours in Pioneer Friendship,

NELSON RATHBUN.

The Lakes, and Greers, and Elders, and Hamlins formed a settlement at the present site of Mt. Blanchard, in one of the most beautiful and fertile portions of the county. And today, around the town of Mt. Blanchard, are some of the most valuable farms in the county.

Wilson Vance, and Carlin, and Hamilton and Johnston and the Chamberlains, with others, formed the settlement of Findley and vicinity, and in casting their lots here, they were not disappointed, in the fertility of the soil, in the natural advantages of the location, or in their estimate of the future of the town.

The McKinnis, the Poes, the Fishels and other kindred spirits, formed a settlement down the river from Findley, in a most beautiful part of the county, and it was not long until these families of hardy stalwart men and women were known for their hospitality and bravery.

Moreland and Helms and a few other families form settlement in the south part of the county, where their industry and energy enabled them to soon open up the country, and where they resided many years, respected by all who knew them, for their honesty and fair dealing.

A little later along perhaps, a settlement was formed still further down the river than was the McKinnis settlement, by the Dukes brothers, John, Richard and Lewis, and by the Moffitts, and the Downings, and Groves, and Davis. These men, all farmers, were fortunate in the selection of their lands, and to-day there is not a richer region of country in north-western Ohio than is this same Dukes settlement. Farms of unsurpassed loveliness; acres of most productive lands, bordering on the Blanchard River on either side; first-class farm buildings; lands in the highest state of cultivation, all tell of the industry, economy and good managament of these broad acres.

Todd, and Kalb, and Algire and other families settled at or near the site of the village of McComb. These families, true pioneers, made for themselves homes, and where was one unbroken wilderness, now stands the prosperous village of McComb. And a few of these first settlers, these frontiersmen of half a century ago, are still alive, and look with just pride upon the results of their labor.

And as it is in all new countries, so here the bold emigrant bought his land, built his cabin, and then addressed himself to the more serious business of reclaiming the lands, and making for himself and his family a home.

At this time no one thought of any law but that of doing to others, as they would others should do to them, and of dealing honestly with all men, of fulfilling every promise, of redeeming every pledge, of rendering to his neighbor, without hope of fee or reward, that assistance which was necessary. But of course this state of affairs could not last long. The time would come when these settlements must be organized into political divisions, and when rulers must be elected. Not so much perhaps by reason of any real necessity, on the part of the inhabitahts, but because the state had some claims on the people. For the protection it threw around them, it must be paid, and hence taxes must be levied and collected, and the rights of the people must be respected, and this could not be done without officers, and officers must be paid for the time they devoted to the public good, so the county must be organized, and of this organization we will speak in the next chapter.

But before doing so I deem this the proper place to relate an interview I had with a daughter of Benjamin Cox, spoken of before as the first white settler in the county. In the summer of 1880, I visited Mrs. Eberly, the daughter before spoken of, at her home about one mile east of Portage, Wood county, and spent a few hours in conversation with her, and from her learned many incidents of the earliest history of the county. But I will give the substance of what she said to me in the shape of a narrative, and as nearly in her own words as I can. I was warmly received by Mrs. Eberly and her worthy husband, who seemed to be delighted in talking over the wild scenes of fifty years ago.

MRS. EBERLEY'S NARRATIVE.

I am the daughter of Benjamin Cox, and was born in Green County, Ohio, in 1806, and when about nine years old, my father removed with his family to Findley, in Han-

Mrs. Eberley's Narrative.

cock County. Our family was the first white family to settle in that county. My sister Lydia, born in 1817, was the first white child born in that county. We lived in a hewed log house, located where the brick residence of the late Wilson Vance now stands, on the south bank of the river, and on the east side of Main street. When Mr. Vance came to the place, we had to move into a log cabin a little east of the hewed log house, into which Mr. Vance took his family.

My father was engaged in farming--if the cultivation of a small tract of cleared land surrounding our cabin could be called farming—and keeping a public house. Shortly after we came to the place, Hamilton, Moreland and Slight came. Some other families came in, stayed a short time and then left. For to be candid about it, Findley was not then a very inviting place, whatever it may now be. There were two or three block-houses, and some pickets, the remains of Ft. Findley, standing when we came. The Ottowa Indians made frequent visits to the place, as it was stated that they were in some way related to the Wyandotts.

Before we left Findley, the Morelands, Hamiltons, Slights, Chamberlains, Frakes, McKinnis, Simpsons, Vances and Rileys had moved to the county. Hamilton and some others had started a settlement above the town, and Frakes and the McKinnis' below the town. I was at that time too young and too busy to make the acquaintance of many of these persons. But I shall never forget Susy Frakes—as she was called—the wife of Nathan Frakes. Many a day did I spend with them in their cabin on the river side, and I thought Susy the best woman I ever knew, kind-hearted, almost to a fault, hospitable and intelligent.

Mrs. Riley was perhaps the first white person who died in the county. She had been sick with the chills and fever, and had called in the services of a Mr. Smith, a Kentuckian, who pretended to be a druggist, and who gave her medicine which was so effective that she was soon a corpse. So sudden was her decease that it was suspected that a mistake had been made, either in the medicine or in its administering. It was said at the time that Smith had forbidden her to drink water, but such was her intense thirst that she prevailed on two little girls who were left to watch with her, to bring her some, of which she drank freely, and very shortly afterwards was found dead. Of course her sudden death was attributed to the drink of water.

I was but a girl when Vance came to Findley. The first mill in the county was built whilst we were there. Mrs. Vance had gone to Urbana just previous to the birth of their first child, and Mr. Vance's sister, Bridget, came to keep house for him, but had been with him but a short time when she was attacked by the ague. I then went to live with them, and not only cooked for the men who were digging the mill race, and boarded at Vance's, but I even worked in the race. My mother, my sister and myself gathered the stalks of nettles which grew on the river bottoms below the town, from which we stripped fiber enough, that on being dressed like flax, was spun and woven into linen to the amount of forty yards, and was made into clothing for the family.

At one time We-ge-hah, or Tree-top-in-water, son of In-op-qua-nah, a Wyandott chief, became sick, and the Indians believed him to be bewitched by a bad spirit, and sent to Towa-town for Big Medicine to exorcise the spirit. My mother did not like the Indians very well, and never went amongst them much. On this occasion, however, when the Indians sent out their invitations for the great pow-wow my mother received one. It was after much persuasion on the part of my father, and with the understanding that I should accompany her, that she finally consented to attend. When we arrived at the place of meeting, which was a log house a little west of where Judge Cory now lives, we found a few Indians assembled. The Big Medicine and his interpreter occupied the center of the room. The lights were extinguished. The tom-tom was beaten and a great noise and hub-bub was made. The lights were again set to burning, and after a short silence refreshments were passed around. During this time my mother and myself having been seated in the circle which was formed around the room, clung closely together, not a little frightened at the performance.

The sick man got no better. Big Medicine declared that the young chief was bewitched, and that the witch lived in Browntown, near Detroit, and that the sick man had a bunch of hair in his breast, blown there by the witch, and he must cut it out. He went into a tent alone with the young man, and afterwards produced and exhibited a knot of bloody hair which he pretended to have taken from the breast of the sick man. He said, however, that just as likely as not the old witch would find out that he had taken it out, and blow it back again, and if he did the young chief would die. The witch no doubt did so, for the young man died. The disease of which he died was no doubt the consumption.

I am now seventy-four years old. I have seen some very hard times, but I have never seen the time that I was not happy and contented.

I have not visited Findley but once since I left there in 1825, and that was about twenty years ago. There is but one person now residing in Findley that I remember to have been there during our stay, and that one is Job Chamberlain. When we first came to Wood County, I lived for some time in the family of Squire Carlin, who then resided there."

My visit to Mrs. Eberley was a very pleasant one, and she is a very pleasant old lady, having the appearance of a well preserved person of not more than sixty years.

CHAPTER II.

FIRST ORGANIZATION OF THE COUNTY.

ON the 12th day of February, 1820, the General Assembly of Ohio, with Allen Trimble as President of the Senate, and Joseph Richardson as Speaker of the House, passed an "Act for the erection of certain counties named therein." In that Act we find the following reference to Hancock county, "* * * * * fifth, to include townships, one and two, south, and one and two, north, in the ninth, tenth, eleventh and twelfth ranges, and to be known by the name of Hancock County."

Section 2 of the same Act provides, "That the counties of Hancock, Henry, Putnam, Paulding and Williams shall be attached to the county of Wood."

The following order was made by the Commissioners of Wood County on the 4th of March, 1822: "Ordered by the Board that the township of Waynesfield, within the jurisdiction of the county of Wood, be co-extensive with the boundaries of Wood and Hancock, and to include the same."

The territory thus included in one township, is now divided into two counties, which counties are sub-divided into thirty-six townships, any one of which perhaps to-day has a greater population than had the two counties of Hancock and Wood at the date of that order.

The following order was made by the Commissioners of Wood county on the 28th day of May, 1823:

"Ordered further, that so much of the township ot Waynesfield as is included in the unorganized county ot Hancock, be set off and organized, and the same is hereby organized into a township by the name of Findley, and that the election for township officers be held on the first day of July, A. D., 1823, at the house of Wilson Vance, in the said township."

The first record of the township we have is that of the election of April 5th, 1824, at which election Job Chamberlain, William Moreland and Jacob Poe were Judges, and Matthew Reighly and Wilson Vance clerks, who certify that there were *eighteen* votes cast, and that Job Chamberlain, Wilson Vance and Jacob Poe were elected Trustees, Matthew Reighly, Clerk; Wilson Vance, Lister (Assessor); Philip McKinnis, Constable; John Hunter and John Gardner, Fence Viewers; Robert McKinnis and William Moreland, Overseers of the Poor; and Job Chamberlain, senior, Treasurer.

A search of the records of Wood County for a duplicate of the taxable property of Hancock County fails to disclose any prior to the year 1826.*

In the year 1826 there were twenty-six tax-payers in the county, and the value of taxable personal property was about two thousand dollars. The total tax was fifty-six dollars and twelve cents. In 1827 there were fourteen tax-payers, the largest of whom was Elnathan Cory, and the total tax was fifty dollars and twenty-nine cents.

Not much labor in auditing that duplicate, and not a very fat salary for collecting it. An Assessor might have some trouble in finding the property, but he would certainly not have much trouble in making his report to the Auditor.

---
*See Chapter VI for earlier duplicate, found since writing the above.

Dependence on Wood County.

The people of the county, at that day were not rich, certainly in this world's goods. Their capital was their strong arms and willing hands, and their wealth was their honesty, contentment and indomitable pluck.

During these years of dependence on the protection of Wood County, and the inconveniences of transacting public business, so remote from home, if it was counted an inconvenience by the pioneers, which we very much doubt, emigration was flowing into the county in a steady, if not a rushing stream. Settlements were being formed all over the county, and farms were being opened in every direction. Neighbors were getting closer than a day's journey of each other. Ministers of the Gospel had already visited the locality, and had formed religious societies. So much had the population increased that the county had outgrown its township clothes, and now asked to be advanced to a separate county organization, and to be entitled to all the privileges and conveniences incident thereto. Wood County had also increased in population, and so much territory was cumbersome to it, and the people of that county were willing to release their guardianship of Hancock, and allow her to try the experiment of taking care of herself. The General Assembly of Ohio said "Let it be done."

During this transition state, as it were, from 1820 to 1828, the authorities had very little trouble in preserving the peace, and protecting the lives and property of the people, as all the early settlers were intent on building themselves homes, and felt in all its force the necessity of each one living an orderly and peaceable life. This quietude was occasionally disturbed by some inroad of the red-man, but against these foes, the instinct of self-preservation did not ask the intervention of law and law officers to repel them. Each man considered himself in duty bound to aid in the general defense, without the formality of an election, as one of the public guardians.

CHAPTER III.

INDEPENDENT ORGANIZATION OF THE COUNTY.

ON the 21st day of January, 1828, the General Assembly of Ohio, passed an Act entitled "An Act to organize the County of Hancock" of which Act the following are some of the provisions:

"SEC. 1. That the County of Hancock as heretofore laid off, and the same shall be, and is hereby organized into a separate and distinct County, and suits and prosecutions which shall be pending, and all crimes which shall have been committed within said County of Hancock previous to its organization, shall be prosecuted to final judgment and execution within the County of Wood, in the same manner they would have been, had the County of Hancock not been organized; and the Sheriff, Coroner and Constables of Wood County, shall execute within the County of Hancock, such process as shall be necessary to carry into effect such suits, prosecutions and judgments; and the Treasurer of Wood shall collect all such taxes as shall have been levied and imposed within the County of Hancock previous to the taking effect of this Act."

"SEC. 2. That all Justices of the Peace, and Constables within the said County of Hancock shall continue to execute the duties of their respective offices, in the same manner as if the County of Hancock had remained attached to the County of Wood."

History of Hancock County.

"SEC. 3. That on the First Monday of April next, the legal voters within the County of Hancock shall assemble within their respective Townships, at the place of holding elections, and shall elect their several County Officers, who shall hold their offices until the next annual election. This Act shall take effect from and after the First day of March next."

In accordance with the provisions of this Act, the voters of Hancock County met in Findley, (there being but one Township in the County) and proceeded to hold an election.

The following is a copy of the Poll Book, Tally Sheet and abstract of that election, verbatim:

"Pool book of the Election held in the township of finley county of hancock, on the seventh day of Aprile in the year of our lord one thousand eight hundred and twenty eight. Abram Huff, Wilson Vance, Mordica Hammond, Judges. John C. Wickham, Edmun S. Jones, Clerks for county officers of this Election were severally sworn as the law directs, previous to their entering on the duties of their respective offices. Of this election were severally sworn as the law directs previous to their entering on the duties of their respective offices.

Number and names of Electors.		Number and names of Electors.	
1	Ephriam Elder	12	Amos Beard
2	Asher Wickham	13	Mordica Hammond
3	Samuel Sargent	14	Bleuferd Hambleton
4	Thomas Slight	15	Don Alonzo Hamlin
5	William Hackney	16	John Elder
6	John P. Hamilton	17	Joseph Slight
7	Henry George	18	George W. Simkins
8	Thomas Thompson	19	Miner T. Wickham
9	Joseph Sargent	20	Nathan Frakes
10	Abram Huff	21	Thomas Wingate
11	Peter George	22	Wilson Vance

First Electors.

Number and names of Electors.		Number and names of Electors.	
23	Joseph Johnson	49	Chaples D. Smith
24	Thomas Chester	50	Robbert McKinnis
25	William Wade	51	John Shoemaker
26	John C. Wickham	52	John Boid
27	Josiah Elder	53	Charles McKinnis
28	John Huff	54	James Hendricks
29	Jesse Hewitt	55	Abel Tanner
30	John Long	56	Jacob Moreland
31	Daniel Hamblin	57	George Shaw
32	Sampson Dildine	58	Asa Lake
33	Asa M. Lake	59	William Greear
34	Reuben W. Hamblin	60	Sqire Carlin
35	George Swagart	61	Simeon Ransbottom
36	John Jones	62	Benjamin Chandler
37	William Moreland, jr.	63	John Tullis
38	John Taylor	64	James McKinnis
39	John Fishel	65	William Moreland
40	James Beard	66	David Gitchel
41	Godfrey Wolford	67	John Simpson
42	Edwin S. Jones	68	John Travis
43	Selden Blodget	69	Joseph Dewitt
44	Job Chamberlin	70	Philip McMinnis
45	John Gardiner	71	Mathew Reighly
46	Robbert Macully	72	Joshua Hedges
47	Jacob Poe	73	Reuben Hale
48	Ebenezer Wilson	74	Isaac Johnson

TALLY SHEET.

Names of persons voted for and for what office, containing the number of votes for each candidate.

Sheriff.	Reuben Hale, lllll lllll lllll lllll lllll lllll llll No. 34
	Don Alonzo Hamlin, lllll lllll lllll lllll lllll lllll lllll llll No. 39
Coroner.	Isaac Johnson, lllll lllll lllll lllll lllll lllll llll No. 34
	Thomas Slight, lllll lllll lllll lllll lllll lllll lllll ll No. 37
	John Boid, lll No. 3
	Job Chamberlin, lllll lllll lllll lllll lllll lllll l No. 31
Commissioners.	Charles McKinnis, lllll lllll lllll lllll lllll lllll lllll No. 35
	Godfrey Wolford, lllll lllll lllll lllll lllll lllll lllll lllll lllll lllll lllll
	John P. Hambleton, lllll lllll lllll lllll lllll lllll lllll lllll l No. 41
	John Long, lllll lllll lllll lllll lllll lllll lllll llll No. 39
	lllll lllll llll Godfrey Wolford continued No. 74
Assessor. Treas. Auditor	Mathew Reighly, lllll lllll lllll lllll lllll lllll lllll lllll lllll lllll lllll llll No. 59
	Joshua Hedges, lllll lllll lllll lllll lllll lllll lllll lllll lllll lllll lllll ll No. 57
	John Long, lllll lllll lllll lllll lllll lllll lllll No. 35
	William Hackney, lllll lllll lllll lllll lllll lllll lllll llll No. 39

Certificate of Election.

We do hereby certify that Reubin Hale had votes for Sheriff, 34, and Don Alonzo Hamlin for Sheriff 39.
John Boid, for Coroner, had 3 votes.
Isaac Johnson, 34 votes.
Thomas Slight, 37 votes.
Job Chamberlain, had 31 votes for Commissioner.
Charles McKinnis had 35 votes.
Godfrey Wolford had 74 votes.
John P. Hambleton had 41 votes.
John Long had 39 votes.
Mathew Reighly, had 59 votes for Auditor.
Joshua Hedges, had 57 for Treasurer.
John Long had 35 votes for Assesser.
William Hackney had 39 votes.

ATTEST

ABRAHAM HUFF,
WILSON VANCE, } Judges of Election.
MORDICA HAMMOND

J. C. WICKHAM,
E. S. JONES, } Clerks.

On examining the Poll Book of the Election for County Officers, we do find that the following candidates were elected:

DON ALONZO HAMLIN, Sheriff.
THOMAS SLIGHT, Coroner.
GODFREY WOLFORD,
JOHN LONG, } Commissioners.
JOHN P. HAMBLETON.
MATHEW REIGHLY, Auditor.
JOSHUA HEDGES, Treasurer.
WILLIAM HACKNEY, Assesser.

Clerk and Justices present,

WILSON VANCE, Clerk, pro tem.
JOSHUA HEDGES,
WILLIAM HACKNEY, } Justices of the Peace.

There were no Public Buildings in the county at that time; and we have no information as to where the offices were held, in what building or part of the town. Tradition has it, that the Treasurer's Office was in his hat, or at least that is where he carried the tax duplicate for convenience sake, as he resided in the country. He was thus ever ready with his duplicate to receive moneys of the unfortunate tax payers, at any time or place they chanced to meet. Whether this legend be true or not, the fact that the tax duplicate could have been carried in the hat of the Treasurer without any inconvenience to the wearer will not admit of serious doubt.

We are not told as to where the other officers kept their books, but as they were not of any greater volume than those of the Treasurer, they might have been disposed of in the same way.

The county is now under an independent organization, and fully officered and prepared for business, in which happy condition we will leave it for the present, and turn our attention to some of the general characteristics of the country.

CHAPTER IV.

GENERAL DESCRIPTION OF THE COUNTY. ITS SOIL AND PRODUCTS.

HANCOCK County was named in honor of John Hancock of Revolutionary fame. It originally contained 368,640 acres of land, but upon the formation of Wyandotte County in 1845, 28,800 acres were struck off of Hancock and became a part of the new county.

This county is in the north-west part of Ohio, and in what is known as the Maumee Valley. It is bounded on the north by Wood County, on the east by Seneca and Wyandotte, on the south by Hardin, and on the west by Putnam. The soil is varied, mostly black loam, mixed with sand on a limestone base. There is scarcely a foot of soil in the county, but is susceptible of cultivation, and adapted to the production of almost any crop known in the temperate zone. The soil is not of that character which is adapted to and produces but one kind of cereal, but is just as productive of wheat as of corn, of grass as of vegetables. In most parts of the county the soil is deep and lasting, and does not require much assistance from fertilizers. The river and creek bottoms, though subject to occasional overflows, are especially productive, whilst the high lands yield scarce less bountiful crops.

The county is well watered, (in fact at times too well watered). The Blanchard fork of the Auglaize River passes through it. Having its source in Hardin County, it enters this county in the south-eastern part, at nearly the center of the south line of Delaware township, running nearly north through that and Jackson and Amanda, and to near the center of Marion, when from that point it runs in a westerly course through Marion, Findley, Liberty and Blanchard townships, to the Putnam County line. The most northern curve of the river is in section seven, Liberty township.

The Shawnee name of this river was Sho-po-quo-to-kepe, or Tailor river. It was so called from the fact that Blanchard, after whom it was named, was by occupation a tailor.

This river formerly furnished sufficient water power for running mills, almost the entire year, but as the country has improved, lands became drained, creeks cleared of fallen timber and other obstructions, the supply of water is only sufficient for such purposes for a few months in the year.

The early settlers were enabled to supply themselves, from the river, with an abundance of choice fish, but now by reason of the many obstructions placed in the river in the shape of mill-dams, but few fish are caught, and they only of an inferior quality. Wild game was also very abundant, but since the settlement of the county it has almost entirely disappeared. The wild honey bee, that advance courier of civilization, led the settlements of the white man, and the pioneers were well supplied with its sweet labor.

There are but few springs of water in the county, but water of a good quality may be easily obtained, in most places, by sinking wells from six feet to thirty feet in depth. The water, in consequence of the almost universal presence of limestone, is highly impregnated with lime, and is what is called "hard water." The river and creeks furnish an abundance of good limestone, used only, however, for making lime, of which article a very fine quality is pro-

Timber and General Characteristics.

duced, and for building foundation and basement walls, not being of a quality suitable for other building purposes.

The timber consists of the different varieties of the oak, and ash, walnut, poplar, beech, elm, maple—both hard and soft—buckeye, linn, hackberry, honey locust, wild cherry and mulberry. There was a very great quantity of walnut, ash and poplar, which woods are now most valuable, but which at the early settlement were of little or no value except for making rails for fencing, and aside from that they were regarded as a very nuisance. Now no timber grows but is of some value and in great demand, and at this day the timber on any ordinarily wooded tract of land is of more value than the land is after the timber is removed.

At the time of the first settlement of the county, it was an unbroken wilderness, densely covered with rank vegetation. A part of what is now Big Lick township was a wet prairie, covered with a luxuriant growth of grass, but the ground was so wet and soft that it was almost impassable.

The face of the country is generally level, and much of it is appropriately called "flat land." The borders of the river and creeks are in many places broken, but in no place can they be said to be hilly. Enough declination towards the water courses to make drainage easy and cheap. No hills, no swamps, no lakes, no deserts, but the entire county is adapted to agricultural purposes.

In the north part of the county there is a tract of land ranging from one mile to two miles in width, and about ten miles in length from east to west, known as "the wild-cat thicket." It has its beginning in the western part of Portage township, and crosses Allen and Cass, terminating in the western part of Washington township. Prior to the settlement of that part of the county this tract of land was covered with a dense undergrowth, the larger timber having all been blown down by a hurricane, it is supposed, which passed over it, no one knows when. Indeed, from its then appearance, the entire body of timber, both large and small, must have been prostrated by the violence of no ordinary storm, and the present growth of timber dates since that period. Many of the older inhabitants well remember the look of desolation which was here presented—trunks of forest trees, decayed and decaying, an almost impenetrable thicket of bushes and wild vines, all believed to be, and possibly was inhabited by wild cats, and other dangerous animals. Hence, the name of "Wild Cat Thicket."

The course of the storm must have been from west to east, as the trunks of the fallen trees lay in that direction, with their tops to the east. The land in this thicket, in its wild state, is low and wet, but when reclaimed by proper drainage is very productive.

In the south-western part of the county, in Orange township, there was quite an extensive cranberry marsh, which for years after the settlement of the county, was considered valueless almost, and certainly entirely so for farming purposes. But as the country became settled, and farms were opened up on the borders of this marsh, making gradual encroachments upon it, the attention of the land owners in the vicinity was called to it, and now by a system of drainage under the supervision of the county officials, it has all been reclaimed, and is rich beyond measure. Thus demonstrating, as before observed, that all parts and all portions of the county are susceptible of remunerative cultivation.

Productions of the County.

The productions of the county are varied, not confined to any one product, but adapted to all. The principal crops are wheat—and in this cereal we are numbered the fourth county in the State. Indian corn is produced in all parts of the county and has always been regarded as a standard crop. Oats of a good quality are produced in great quantities. Barley and rye are cultivated to some extent, but not being so readily marketed as wheat, not much attention is paid to their raising. Flax has become an article of great demand, and much attention is being paid to its cultivation, both for the value of the fiber as well as of the seed, there being both a flax mill and linseed oil mill in the county. Buckwheat of course commands some attention from the farmer, as people could not very well do without their "Buckwheat cakes" for breakfast. Irish and sweet potatoes are easily cultivated, and yield most abundantly. Indeed all kinds of vegetables yield a most bountiful harvest. Fruits of almost all kinds can be found in all parts of the county. Apples are the surest crop. Peaches, although a never failing crop in the early days of the county, may now be considered an almost entire failure. Small fruits are usually a good crop, but occasionally complete failures happen.

In some parts of the county farmers meet with difficulty in tilling the soil, in consequence of the cropping out of the limestone formation. But the perfect adaptation of such lands to wheat raising, and the enormous crops produced fully compensate for the extra trouble.

Tables of Agricultural Statistics found elsewhere in this work, will exhibit the wealth and prosperity of the county, as a farming and stock raising locality.

CHAPTER V.

RELATING TO A FEW FIRST THINGS IN THE COUNTY.

AN examination of the Poll Book of that first election, held in April, 1828, discloses the fact that Squire Carlin is the only man now living in Findley, of all those who then voted. The names of Judges Huff, Hammond, McKinnis and Wilson, George Shaw, Josiah Elder, Wilson Vance, Jacob Poe, Joshua Hedges, Asa M. Lake, Nathan Frakes and many others appear, all of whom, after having provided a goodly inheritance for their children, have passed away. Squire Carlin, Joseph Johnson, Peter George and perhaps a few others of that old 74 still live in our county, a link connecting the past with the present of our history. They have lived to see the wilderness disappear before the march of civilization, and beautiful farms, commodius buildings and thriving villages spring into life all over the county. To see railroads and telegraph lines, and all the modern improvements introduced amongst us. And others still, such men as James McKinnis, John Fishel, Edmund S. Jones and Joseph DeWitt after a residence of many years in the county, again took up the line of march westward, and became the pioneers of other states.

The first church edifice erected in the county was the "Dukes' Meeting House," in Blanchard township. It was built and owned by the Methodist Episcopal Church.

First House of Worship.

The building was of hewed logs, and its dimensions were thirty-two feet long and twenty-eight feet wide. The roof was of clap-boards, a kind of roofing very much in use at that time, and were kept in their places by poles laid on each course of boards. The openings between the logs were chinked with wood, and daubed with mortar, the then prevailing style. The pulpit and seats were of rude construction. The seats were simply benches without backs, and the pulpit of unpainted boards. The building still stands, and although not now used as a house of worship, still to many who are now living it is surrounded with cherished memories. Many, very many, who in that early day met in that house for worship, have passed away. The pulpit in that old church has been occupied by such ministers as Bigelow, Finley, Thompson, Wilson, Gurley, Allen, Heustiss, Conway, Hill, Runnells, Breckenridge, Delany, Biggs and a host of other pioneer Methodists, whose names are familiar, not only in our own county, but all over Western Ohio. But they have nearly all gone to their reward, and their works do follow them.

Humanity, civilization, good society, and all that goes to make us a great people, owe to these self-sacrificing, earnest, unselfish, devoted servants of their Master, a debt which can never be repaid, except by a practice of the precepts they taught, and in a defense of their memories.

As early as the year 1822, the Rev. James Gilruth, a Methodist minister, and who died but a few years ago, preached in Findley. In an interview with him but a short time before his death, and whilst he was here on a visit to his daughter, Mrs. Frederick Didway, he stated that in 1822 he left his home in the east and came west for the purpose of entering lands. He first visited the land office at Bucyrus, Ohio, and there obtained a plat of Government lands not taken up in the District. He made his way into Hardin County, passing through old Ft. McArthur. But not being able to suit himself in that region, he turned north towards Findley. After leaving Ft. McArthur, he did not see a dwelling house until his arrival in Findley, which was in the month of April.

As soon as it became known that a preacher had arrived, he was waited upon by some of the citizens, and requested to preach for them. This he readily consented to do, and an appointment was made and circulated to the different settlements. Father Gilruth said he had a very attentive congregation, and as large an one as he could expect, and indeed it was said at the time, by those in attendance, that almost every man and woman in the county was present. This sermon was undoubtedly the first ever preached in the county.

The late Rev. Adam Poe, also of the Methodist Church, was led to suppose that he preached the first sermon in the county, and related the following incident connected with it. He and another young minister on their way from the Maumee River to the South, stopped at Findley over night, and as a matter of course were solicited to preach. Poe consented to do so. They had put up at the tavern kept by Wilson Vance, had their horses cared for and ate their suppers, after which they went to the place of meeting, which was in a log school house near where the depot of the C. S. & C. Railroad is now located. The two Missionaries had but a single dollar between them, and as it would require all that to pay for their suppers and the care of their horses, and no one inviting them home with them, they slept in the school house that night, and the next morning, after paying their bill at the tavern, they rode to the next settlement, a distance of several miles, before getting breakfast. It is not at all strange, after such an experience, that Poe and his companion should conclude that they were the first to bring good tidings to this benighted people.

The first school house in the county was built in Findley, and the first school was taught by John C. Wickham, who was long a resident of the county. As there has been very decided improvement in the architecture and conveniences of this class of buildings, it will not be uninteresting, perhaps, to the young people, at least, to describe one of these ancient seats of learning, and as a specimen "brick," I will briefly describe one with which I was most familiar, but which fairly represents a majority of the primitive school houses of the county.

It stood some rods from the public highway—did the one I refer to—built so perhaps, that the attention of the scholars might not be attracted to passers-by, but more, I suspect, for the reason that its location was at a place less liable to be inundated by the floods. It was built of round logs, and was chinked and daubed in the most approved style. Its dimensions were certainly not more than fifteen feet square. It was covered with clapboards, nailed on with weight-poles. The height between the floors was about six feet. Nearly the entire north side was occupied by a huge fire-place—stoves were not then invented—with an outside chimney built of sticks and mortar. On the south side was a door—and the only one in the building—made of unplaned boards, which creaked on its massive wooden hinges, and by the way they were the only massive things about the building. The older boys said that the door and fire-place were placed opposite to each other for convenience in bringing in the logs of wood for the fire, which they protested were drawn in through the fire-place by a yoke of oxen, and the oxen were then unyoked and driven out at the door. But I think this could not have been true, for no little boy or girl ever saw such a performance. The lower floor was of split logs, or puncheons, a kind of lumber much in use at that time, as it was manufactured without the assistance of saw-mills, and the upper floor was of clap boards, laid loosely on the round joists. Windows almost the entire length of the two ends of the building, admitted the light. These windows were just ten inches in height, and the writing-desks were placed immediately beneath them. In lieu of window-glass, these windows were filled with paper well oiled to protect it from the weather. The writing-desks were long boards supported by wooden pins inserted in the walls at proper angles, for that purpose. The seats were slabs procured at the saw mill, supported by wooden legs, and always elevated high enough from the floor to prevent the feet of the smaller scholars from touching, thus making it impossible for them to be noisy with their feet, an arrangement satisfactory to the teacher no doubt, but dreadfully uncomfortable for the little boys and girls. We were perched upon these seats of torture eight hours each day, with nothing at our backs, and the same under our feet.

A Primitive School House.

The external surroundings of this primitive academy were not so disagreeable. True, in the winter season, when not frozen, we had an over abundance of water, but when frozen we had an almost boundless skating rink. In the summer season it was a very pleasant place. Just in the rear of the house and used as a playground, was a most beautiful grove, cool, shady and inviting. Only a few rods from the house ran the river, with its cool waters, and the old mill, with its huge wooden wheel, splashing and battling in the flood, seemed to laugh at us little prisoners shut up in the hot school room, and bid us run away from teacher, and school and books, and join it in its sport.

The boys and girls of that day knew nothing of the modern improvements in school houses, school books, and school conveniences. The school year consisted of three months of school in the winter for the larger pupils, and a three months term in the summer for the smaller ones. No blackboards, no geographical or astronomical apparatus, no changing text books every term. Orthography was taught from the old American and United States spelling books. The Introduction to the English Reader, the English Reader, and the Sequel to the English Reader, the New Testament and the Life of Washington were the principal readers. Pike and Daball furnished the Mathematics and Olney and Kirkham the Grammar and Geography.

With all these inconveniences and want of what would now be deemed indispensable necessities, quite a passable education was obtained at these schools. No scholar was then allowed to idle away his time, if it were possible to prevent it. The substance, the real business of imparting and obtaining an education, actuated both teacher and pupil. But little attention was paid to forms; provided a pupil got a fair understanding of that which he was studying, the way, the formula, was not of so much anxiety to the teacher. Good wholesome instructions in deportment as well as the sciences were made a part of the duty of the teacher. Pupils were under their care not only in the school room, but on the way to and from school as well, and woe! to the urchin who was guilty of passing a man or woman on the road, without a bow or courtesy. No brawling on the road, no impertinence to strangers, no profane language, no tale-bearing. The conduct of the pupils was as much the concern of the teacher as was their studies. I fear, with all our present boasted superiority in school appliances, that we have gone backwards in this matter of "good manners," and that the youth of to-day would suffer by comparison with those of that early day.

CHAPTER VI.

EARLY APPRAISEMENT AND ASSESSMENT OF PROPERTY.

THE proceedings of the County Commissioners on the 1st day of June, 1829, show the following entry:
"Don Alonzo Hamlin made his return of assessment of chattle property, and land property subject to taxation in Hancock County, which was examined and accepted, and the said Assessor presented his account for his labor in assessing the property of the county, which was accepted, and which was nineteen dollars and seventy-five cents."

There was but one Assessor in the county, and his duty appears to have been to value both real and personal property. In December of the same year we find this entry: "The Auditor presented his account, and was qualified to the same, ordered that the said Auditor be allowed twelve dollars and twenty-five cents for his services, and that said Auditor be paid the sum of ten dollars for extra services up to and including this day."

In June, 1831, the Commissioners and Auditor, as a Board of Equalization, ordered that the valuation of lot No. 16 be reduced from eighty-five dollars, to forty dollars; and lot No. 1 was then, as now, occupied by Squire Carlin, as a residence, to be valued at five hundred dollars, including buildings.

A search of the records of Wood County failed to show a tax duplicate of this county, prior to 1826, but upon information received from Judge Whitely, I learned that Chief Justice Waite had in his possession a copy of the tax list for 1824. I thereupon addressed a letter to the Judge to which I received the following reply:

TOLEDO, OHIO, July 11, 1881.

DEAR SIR:—I take pleasure in sending you a copy of the paper to which Judge Whitely refers. The original is in the office of the Auditor of Wood County.

Truly yours,
M. R. WAITE.

I give a copy of that list, as sent by the Judge.

List of all the Taxable Property in the Township of Findley:

	Proprietors Names.	Horses above 3 years old.	Neat cattle above 3 years old.
L	Asa Lake,	2	11
M	Charles McKinnis,	2	4
M	Henry McWhorter,	2	10
P	James Patterson,	0	7
P	Jacob Poe,	1	5
W	Joseph White,		2
H	John P. Hamilton,	2	2
G	John Gardner,	2	4
H	John Hunter,	1	8
C	Job Chamberlin,		5
S	John Simpson,	2	1
G	John Gardner, jr.	1	3
M	Jacob Moreland,		4
B	Michael Beck, taken in from lady,	2	2
M	Philip McKinnis,	1	6
S	Thomas Slight,	1	4
T	Thomas Thompson, taken in from lady,	1	5
M	William Moreland,	1	3
V	Wilson Vance,	1	4
C	Elnathan Cory, given in by Wilson Vance,		15

Real and Personal Property.

I certify the above to be a correct list.
WILSON VANCE,
Lister of Findley Township, Wood County, Ohio.
Endorsed Taxable property, Findley Township, 1824.

The Amount of tax on each animal was fixed by the Auditor, the tax being a specified sum on each, and not a per cent., as at the present day. No animals under three years of age were taxable. The Township of Findley, it will be recollected, embraced the whole county, at this date.

In 1826, as the Records of Wood County—to which we were then attached—comprising one township—shows that the tax in this county was *Fifty-six dollars* and *seventeen cents*. In 1829, the earliest tax list found, after the independent organization of the county, the value of the taxable property of the county, as returned, was *sixteen thousand six hundred* and *one dollars*, and included in the then townships of Findley, Delaware and Amonda, the only organized townships in the county, and the assessment included both real and personal property. The tax assessed upon the valuation was *one hundred* and *seventy-two dollars* and *forty-four cents*.

In 1829, there was but four thousand seven hundred and seventy-five acres of land subject to taxation in the county, and this was valued at eight thousand one hundred and eighty-six dollars, not more than an average farm is now worth. Of this taxable land, two thousand nine hundred and sixty-nine acres was in Findley; thirteen hundred and seventy-four in Delaware, and two hundred and fifty-two in Amonda Township. Our Amonda Township friends will perhaps be mortified to know that their lands were valued much lower than were the lands in the other townships, and yet it was no doubt some consolation to know that they paid but *four dollars* and *thirty cents* tax on land.

In 1829, there was returned by the Assessor *ninty-three* horses, valued at three thousand seven hundred and twenty dollars. *Two hundred* and *seventy-nine* cattle, valued at three thousand one hundred and sixteen dollars.

From these few illustrations, we may see from what small beginnings the early settlers began life in this new country.

In the year 1830, the salary of the County Assessor was fixed at twenty-three dollars and thirty-seven and a half cents, and that of the Auditor at forty dollars.

On the 3d day of April, 1834, William L. Henderson was appointed appraiser of real estate for Hancock County.

The tax levy for 1829 for county purposes, was seven and one half mills on the dollar. For 1830, it was seven mills. For 1831, it was seven mills. For 1832, it was five mills. In 1833, for county purposes, seven and one-quarter mills, and for road purposes, two mills.

In June, 1831, we find a Record of the County Board of Equalization. Present, John P. Hamilton and Charles McKinnis, Commissioners; Don Alonzo Hamblin, Assessor, and Thos. F. Johnston, Auditor. It was ordered "That Lot 16 (Patterson's Corner), appraised at eighty-five dollars, shall be reduced to forty dollars. That L. & B. Rawson, Physicians income, be two hundred and fifty dollars. That Lot 15, (Newell's Main st.) be entered on the duplicate at forty dollars. That Lot 85, (Commercial House) be entered on the duplicate at one hundred dollars. The capital of S. & P. Carlin, merchants, be entered on the duplicate at one thousand dollars."

At the session of the Board of Equalization in 1834, it was "Ordered that the south part of north-east fraction, in name of John Cambell, with a grist and saw-mill thereon, appraised at twelve hundred dollars, be, by this Board, appraised at nine hundred dollars." (Now Carlin's Mills.)

"Also, that the east half of south-west quarter of Section eleven; Township two South Range eleven, with grist mill, (G. S. Fohl's Mill,) be appraised at five hundred dollars."

"Also, the east half of north-west quarter, Section 12, in the name of S. & P. Carlin, (now a part of the town of Findley,) be appraised at six hundred dollars."

"Also, that the east part of south-east quarter of fractional Section thirteen, Township one north, Range ten east, in the name of James Gilruth, (now Didway farm,) be appraised at four hundred dollars."

"Also, that Lot No. 3, in Findley, in the name of Wm. Taylor, (now Davis Opera House) be appraised at three hundred dollars."

For the present condition of the county as to amount, valuation, assessment and taxation of the property of the county, the reader is referred to the statistical tables in another part of this work. By a comparison of those tables, with the statements made in this chapter, the reader will find that whilst our wealth has increased at a wonderful and gratifying rate, that our taxes have not in the least been slow to accumulate in the same wonderful ratio. Business, wealth, prosperity, security in person and property, cannot be enjoyed in this or any other county without pay. A study of these tables will engage the attention of every tax payer, and very likely more than one will exclaim: "Where does all the money go to." Look around you; see your public buildings; your bridges; your roads, all costing money, for your answer.

History of Hancock County.

Table showing the value of Real and Personal Property, with rates of taxes thereon, and amount of taxes assessed, from 1829 to 1879, inclusive, as prepared by Elijah Barnd, Esq., Deputy Auditor:

Year.	Value lands.	Town lots.	Personal.	Total.	Amount tax.	Rate per $1000.
1829	$8186		$4116	$12302	$172.44	$14.01
1830	8836	$6867	4940	20643	290.52	14.22
1831	10252	7622	6560	24434	371.74	15,22
1832	13150	9698	7350	30198	451.20	14.95
1833	18210	11210	9400	38820	720.50	18.56
1834	25115	14169	43102	82386	1028.39	12.48
1835	64008	27788	56798	148594	1854.07	12.47
1836	76305	36035	71526	183521	1588.73	8.64
1837	99140	42127	80351	221618	3110.42	14.48
1838	129464	43781	83404	257850	3480.62	13.49
1839	289085	57656	102990	448733	5967.56	13.29
1840	435366	58041	115032	608439	9797.08	16.10
1841	564904	21537	131649	724990	10206.53	14.00
1842	710861	29645	143102	879708	12950.77	14.72
1843	718462	30722	157004	906188	14010.10	15.46
1844	726553	34299	167384	928236	15141.86	16.31
1845	683118	34942	179302	897362	13597.55	15.15
1846	989475	38747	169636	898158	14164.27	15.77
1847	1702775	126286	373450	2196511	18452.43	8.40
1848	1714415	128262	422952	2265629	21470.63	9.32
1849	1725879	146479	480720	2553078	23650.00	10.05
1850	1742281	166749	495715	2404745	29266.48	12.17
1851	1761815	178719	564015	2504549	23754.37	9.49
1852	1781169	190186	660915	2832237	27458.07	10.05
1853	1815798	205144	1183108	3204050	27575.10	8.39
1854	3130089	334642	1290453	5164184	31881.29	6.17
1855	3262391	388075	1800709	5511175	36386.51	6.60
1856	3332921	417837	1626651	5347424	37163.18	6.74
1857	3371183	431588	1633350	5466127	44131.00	8.73
1858	3414565	455805	1645772	5516142	51059.63	9.25
1859	3457013	469056	1558498	5485167	53251.81	9.70

Taxes of Hancock County. 51

1860	1479230	429769	1670258	6579257	60534.38	9.20
1861	4485720	458400	1805635	6779785	86554.84	12.76
1862	4501953	460668	1620532	6583153	74023.23	11.24
1863	4517907	465055	1844167	6827186	80007.43	11.71
1864	4535434	481480	2130700	7147674	121464.29	16.90
1865	4547977	491899	2168838	7208754	148218.46	20.56
1866	4560746	512990	2520937	7594673	134258.37	17.66
1867	4605265	540368	2352421	7498054	141193.94	18.68
1868	4634728	551285	2442677	7628790	135588.90	17.77
1869	4670313	581623	2585511	7832447	143282.18	18.29
1870	4991422	595788	2478659	7765869	158055.52	20.35
1871	8044485	832940	2516893	11394318	131715.29	11.55
1872	8068679	873122	2880963	11822764	153906.15	13.01
1873	8201120	902163	3177257	12180432	182701.51	14.90
1874	8192268	907029	3146215	12245512	172510.64	14.08
1875	8235058	944851	3149012	12328921	188406.22	15.28
1876	8255709	1006684	3269956	12532349	194153.35	15.49
1877	8295426	1029185	3232652	12557263	195389.15	15.56
1878	8330166	1053334	3086815	12470915	205449.17	16.47
1879	8369655	1062210	2906973	12338838	189494.47	15.35

CHAPTER VII.

FIRST JAIL AND FIRST COURT HOUSE.

AS shown by the records in July, 1830, the Commissioners of the county determined to build a Jail, for the safe keeping of criminals, and ordered that said jail should be "*Sixteen* feet wide, and twenty-four feet long, with a partition in the center. The timber to be white oak, twelve inches square, with two doors and three windows." The jail was built on the Public Square, and situate about midway between the present Court House and "old white corner Store." With this location it seems that some of the citizens of the county were not well pleased, for in December of the same year, it is recorded that a petition was presented by sundry citizens of Hancock County, praying for the removal of the jail from the public square in the town of Findley. But the Commissioners rejected the petition, thinking no doubt that the sight of such an institution would have a restraining effect upon the somewhat wild community. Many of the readers of this history will remember the old log jail on the Public Square. They will doubtless remember, too, that as a place of safe-keeping for prisoners, it was but a trifle better than the open street. I quite well remember that it was not a formidable looking structure, and that it had neither beauty or strength to adorn it. The prisoners used to amuse themselves by burning down the door, or removing the iron bars from the windows, and after escaping, report themselves to the Sheriff, who would conduct them back to the place from whence they came. But the old log jail, like many other things of its day, has long since passed away, giving place to a structure, more in keeping with the wants of the county, and affording the better security of the prisoners, and this in its turn has been replaced by a structure magnificent in its proportion, and secure in its construction.

Prior to 1831 the courts had been held in the old log school house, but now increased business demanded increased facilities for its transaction. The minds of the people had been prepared for a building such as was needed, and the financial condition of the county was such as to permit its erection. Whereupon the County Commissioners at their December session in 1831, ordered, "that advertisements be posted up in three public places, for constructing, putting up and furnishing a frame in the village of Findley, etc.," and here I may be pardoned for copying at length from the records, to show not only the kind of building intended to be erected, but as also showing the degree of exactness in which the plans and specifications were intended to be placed before competitors for the contract. I say intended, for a careful perusal of the specifications will show a degree of ambiguity not intended by the Commissioners. But to the record. "The building to be *twenty-four feet* by *thirty-six feet*, two stories high. Lower story to be nine feet in the clear, and the upper story eight and a half feet in the clear. Lower story to have a hall or entry eight feet wide, through the center, with good partitions on either side of planed boards. The one end to be divided by a partition through the center, dividing it into equal parts. A good substantial flight of stairs to be put up in the entry. One front door, one back door to said entry, both to be of panelled doors, the front one to have four lights over it. Four twenty-light windows in front, and two back of twenty lights each in lower story, and five twenty-light windows in front in upper story and three same size back. Glass to be eight by ten, and well puttied in. The upper story to be ceiled with three-quarter boards, planed, tongued and grooved. A good joint shingle roof to be put on. The building to be underpinned with a good, rough stone wall, laid in lime and sand mortar, raised eighteen inches above the surface. With plain door into each room, all the doors to be hung with three-inch cast iron butts, the lower floor to be laid out of white ash boards, not to exceed six inches in width. The upper floor to be of white or blue ash boards of the same width; both floors to be tongued and grooved, and joints broken, and well nailed. The sills, posts and sleepers of the frame to be of white oak, the studding not to exceed two feet from center to center, joists same distance apart. Good sufficient locks on all the doors, and plain latches and handles. Plain eavetroughs and cornise. The front to be weatherboarded with poplar, plained, and the remainder with black walnut, rough. A washboard and chairboard up stairs and down, a plain bannistering to the stairs, together with substantial bannistering at the top of the stairs."

The Commissioners met on the 16th day of January, 1832, the time appointed for opening the bids for the above work. Two proposals were handed in—one from Mathew Reighley for seven hundred and fifty dollars, and one from William Taylor, Frederick Henderson and Jonathan Parker

The First Court House.

for seven hundred dollars, which last was accepted, and I infer that the work was well and satisfactorily done, and accepted by the Commissioners, although there is no record of that fact.

In June, 1833, the Commissioners met and received proposals for plastering the Court House, when the bid of Parlee Carlin was accepted, the price, hewever, was not named. Whereupon, Parlee Carlin entered into a bond to lath and plaster the several rooms in the Court House in a durable and workmanlike manner, and complete the same by the first of November next. This job too, was no doubt completed according to contract and accepted by the Commissioners, although the records are silent on the subject.

The building was erected on the southwest corner of Main and Putnam streets, the site now occupied by the "Wheeler Block," and was used as a Court House, school house and church until the completion of the present Court House in 1841. The old Court House has since been removed to the south part of Main street, just north of the First Presbyterian Church, and is occupied by Jacob Carr and family as a residence. After having served as a Court House it was for many years used as a hotel.

The County Commissioners were very solicitous about the good usage and the authorized occupancy of this new structure, and passed not a few orders touching the matter, and prescribing the terms on which it could be occupied.

In March, 1833, the Commissioners met "and examined the Court House, and accepted it." At their December session, 1834, it was "ordered that the Auditor do cause to be erected in the Court House a suitable seat for the Court. Also that he do procure two sets of chairs for the Court room."

History of Hancock County.

At the session of December, 1836, "Ordered that all religious societies be prohibited from holding meetings in the Court House after the 1st day of January, 1837." This was rather rough on the churches, and I have been unable to find a reason for the order.

But the authorities soon relented, if indeed they ever attempted to enforce the order, for at their very next session, that of March, 1837, the records show this action: "Ordered that the Presbyterian Church and the Methodist Episcopal Church, of the town of Findley, each pay into the Treasury of Hancock County the sum of seventy-five cents per month for the time they occupy the same, for the use of the Court Room for religious purposes, to commence from this date."

At the same session it was "Ordered that the Directors of School District, No. one, in Findley township, pay into the County Treasury at the rate of *Eleven* dollars for six months, for the use of the Court Room for a district school."

Finally, at the session of the Commissioners held in March, 1840, it was "Ordered that the Auditor of the county of Hancock offer the lot that the old Court House stands on, including said building, at public sale, one third of the purchase money in hand, the balance in two equal annual payments, on the third Saturday of May next, advertising the same thirty days previous to the day of sale." The property was sold to one Jacob Barnel.

Thus ended the use of said building for legal purposes, for the county had outgrown so small a temple of Justice, and had already erected, or had in process of erection the present Court House, which, however shabby and inferior it now seems, was at the time of its building regarded as a massive structure, and in beauty and finish, was regarded a triumph of architectural skill. Now it is regarded as being entirely too old fogyish for our present wants, as well as wholly inadequate for the proper transaction of the necessary business of the county.

CHAPTER VIII.

EARLY COURTS—FIRST JUDGES—FIRST JURIES.

THE early history of our Courts is one of interest. We learn from the recorded proceedings, the simplicity of such courts, their cheapness, and the promptness with which business was transacted. Under the Constitution of Ohio, adopted in 1802, the Judicial power of the State, both in law and equity, was vested in a Supreme Court, in Courts of Common Pleas for each County, &c. Sec. 3 of the Constitution provided: "That the several Courts of Common Pleas shall consist of a President and Associate Judges. There shall be appointed in each county, not more than three, nor less than two Associate Judges, who during their continuance in office shall reside therein."

These Judges were appointed by a joint ballot of both Houses of the General Assembly, and held their office for the term of seven years, if so long they behaved well. Such were the provisions of the Constitution, and when Hancock became a separate and distinct County, three of her citizens were honored with the appointment of Associate Judges.

In March, 1828, Abraham Huff, Robert McKinnis and Ebenezer Wilson were appointed by the Legislature. We find the record of their first meeting, or the first court held in the county: "At a special court begun and held in the town of Findley on the 14th of March, in the year of our Lord, one thousand, eight hundred and twenty-eight, pres-

The First Courts.

ent, Honorables Abraham Huff, Robert McKinnis and Ebenezer Wilson, Judges of and for the County of Hancock, and State of Ohio, and proceeded to appoint a Clerk, pro tem., and after consideration, appointed Wilson Vance, and gave him the following certificate of his appointment in the following words and ffgures, to-wit: 'Know all men by these presents, that we, Abraham Huff, Robert McKinnis and Ebenezer Wilson, Associate Judges, in and for the County of Hancock, have this day met at the school house in the town of Findley, in said county, and after consultation and deliberation, have proceeded to appoint by living voice, Wilson Vance, Esq., of said county, Clerk, Pro tem., at Findley, this 14th day of March, 1828.'

      ABRAHAM HUFF,
      ROBERT MCKINNIS, } Associate Judges.
      EBENEZER WILSON,

The vote stood, ayes *two*, nays *one*. Mr. Vance was sworn into office by Judge McKinnis."

The office of Clerk, was held by Mr. Vance as clerk pro tem., under the provisions of Sec. 7, Art. 3, of the Constitution of 1802, which recited: "That each Court shall appoint its own Clerk, for the term of seven years, but no person shall be appointed Clerk except pro-tempore, who shall not produce to the Court appointing him a certificate from a majority of the Judges of the Supreme Court, that they judge him to be well qualified to execute the duties of the office of Clerk to any Court of the same dignity, with that for which he offers himself." There is a litle sprinkling of "civil service reform" in that.

The first Judicial officers of the county deserve more than a passing notice. Many who are now living, and who had an acquaintance with them, can no doubt bear witness to their fidelity to business, and their fairness in the discharge of their duties, and to their unsullied character as men.

Judge Robert McKinnis was born in Butler County, Pennsylvania, and removed from thence to Ross County, Ohio, and from thence, in 1822, he came to Hancock, where he at once became one of the leading spirits of the then new settlements in the county. Judge McKinnis married before his emigration to Ohio, and was surrounded by a grown up family when he came to this county. He was of Scotch-Irish descent, and combined the frankness of the Scotchman, with the warm jovial hearted Irishman.

Not only was the Judge himself a noted man, but his sons, of whom there were four, Charles, Philip, James and John, were men who were trusted by the early settlers with positions of responsibility, which positions were always filled with intelligence and honesty. Charles was one of the first Commissioners of the County, a position which at that time, was one of peculiar importance. The affairs of a new county were to be put in shape, all the conflicting interests of rival settlements to be harmonized, public buildings and public business were to he looked after. To safely and successfully manage, and control all these with economy, and to the best interests of a poor struggling population, required discrimination, decision and patience. Mr. McKinnis did not fail in these qualifications.

Judge McKinnis was the owner of a good farm in Liberty Township, on the south bank of the Blanchard, and lived to enjoy the fruits of his toil. In after life, and when quite advanced in years, he made several trips to the far west, some of his children having removed there, going and returning alone in his wagon. He died at a ripe old age, loved and respected by all who had his acquaintance.

First Judges.

Judge Ebenezer Wilson came to the county in 1826, and settled in Liberty Township, on the farm on which his son Joseph now resides, where he continued his residence until his death. Of the Judge, it can be said that as a man, he enjoyed the respect and confidence of his neighbors to an unlimited extent. That he filled the office of Associate Judge, with intelligence and honesty, is evidenced by the fact that he held the office for two terms—fourteen years—a greater length of time than did any other. The Judge was one of the Pioneers of the Presbyterian church, and was noted for his exemplary life. He had a large family of children. who like the Judge, were social, good natured people. The Judge lived long enough to reclaim from the wilderness, and enjoy the blessings of one of the handsomest farms in the county, to see those who had come to the wilds of the county with him, peaceably enjoy the fruit of their labor, and he had the good fortune to retain to the last the esteem and friendship of his old pioneer associates.

I have not been able to ascertain at just what time Judge Abraham Huff came to the county, but it was a very early period in its history. There seems to be but little known of his history by those living. I have learned this much, however, from some of his old acquaintances, that he was an honorable, straight forward man, of good strong common sense, and was an upright, intelligent Judge. He was a man of poor bodily health, and left the county at an early day, and went to the State of Missouri, in hopes of regaining his health, in which he partially succeeded, but he has been dead many years.

The first Court of Common Pleas held in the county, was the June term 1828, and the following is a complete record of the term.

History of Hancock County.

"At a Court of Common Pleas begun and held in the town of Findley, in and for the county of Hancock, in the State of Ohio, on the third day of June, in the year of our Lord eighteen hundred and twenty-eight. Present, the Associate Judges, Abraham Huff, Robert McKinnis and Ebenezer Wilson, the Presiding Judge not being present. Don Alonzo Hamlin, Sheriff, Wilson Vance, Clerk *pro-tem.*, Anthony Casad was appointed by the Court to prosecute the Pleas in behalf of the State, for said county for the term of one year, and to be allowed forty dollars for his services."

"Elijah T. Davis was appointed Administrator on the effects of Thomas Wilson, late of Findley township, deceased. Joshua Hedges and Squire Carlin were accepted as his sureties, bonds given in the sum of Five Hundred dollars. Joshua Hedges, Jacob Poe and Charles McKinnis were appointed appraisers of said effects. On application ordered that the citizens of Welfare—now Delaware—township have leave to elect one Justice of the Peace. One Justice of the Peace was appointed for Amanda township. The Court appointed Wilson Vance Recorder of Hancock County for the term of seven years, and the Court adjourned without day.

ABRAHAM HUFF."

The first Grand Jury was composed of the following named persons: Joseph DeWitt, John P. Hamilton, Jacob Poe, Asa Lake, Charles McKinnis, Reuben Hales, Mordica Hammond, William Wade, John Boyd, Henry George, William Moreland, James McKinnis, William Taylor, Edwin S. Jones and John C. Wickham. The foreman was William Taylor.

The First Petit Jury.

The first Petit Jury summoned was as follows: John Beard, Joseph Johnson, John Huff, William Moreland, jr., John Tullis, John J. Hendricks, Thomas Thompson, James Pettis, and there being no business for a Jury they were discharged without filling the panel. Rachel Wilson was appointed guardian of Rebecca and Jane Wilson, minor children of Thomas Wilson, deceased. Rebecca was eight and Jane one year old. When grown up Rebecca became the wife of John Reed, of Liberty township, and Jane the wife of George L. Poe, of Allen township.

On application, a license was granted to William Taylor to vend merchandise at his residence in Findley, until the first day of April next, he to pay into the Treasury *two dollars* and *twenty-five cents* for said license.

At the November term of the Court it "Appearing that there was no business before the Grand Jury, they were discharged." At the same term William Taylor was appointed Surveyor of the county, and the Clerk ordered to certify the same to the Governor. William Taylor, William Hackney and Mordica Hammond were appointed examiners of common schools. It was "Ordered by the Court that there be allowed to the Clerk of the Court the sum of *ten dollars* each year, to be paid one half at each term of Court." Seven years Clerk of the Court for the magnificent sum of *seventy dollars.*

A special session of the court was held on the 19th day of March, 1829, for the purpose of granting letters of administration on the estate of John Patterson. William Taylor was appointed. Mr. Patterson was a brother of the wife of Mr. Taylor.

At the April term, 1829, Judges Huff, Wilson and McKinnis were present, also Sheriff John C. Wickham, Clerk

Wilson Vance and Prosecuting Attorney Anthony Casad. The Grand Jury, the second one called and empanneled in the county was as follows: Robert Long, Amos Beard, Thomas Cole, John Shoemaker, Rueben W. Hamblin, Samuel Sargeant, William J. Greer, Robert Elder, John Hunter, Isaac Johnson, Nathan Frakes, Rueben Hales, Jacob Foster, William Moreland, jr., Nathan Williams. The foreman was William J. Greer. Due notice having been given, William Taylor was licensed to keep a tavern at his house in Findley, by paying five dollars. The Grand Jury, at this session, found a bill of indictment, the first ever returned in the county.

The first case on the civil docket was that of Robert Elder and wife against Asa Lake and wife for slander. Damages claimed, five hundred dollars. The action was brought at the November term, 1828, Abel Rawson, Plaintiff's Attorney. A judgment was rendered for the defendants, and the plaintiffs ordered to pay the costs, taxed at *two dollars* and *twenty-two cents*. Such a cost bill as that would not go very far towards paying the costs of a slander suit in these hard times, neither would it make the officers of the court either rich or happy.

At the April term, 1830, the case of Henry McWhorter against Samuel Sargeant and Abraham Huff was tried before Ebenezer Lane, President Judge, and Judges Wilson and McKinnis, Associates. The action was upon note of hand, and amount claimed four hundred dollars, and one hundred dollars damages. I give only the finding of the court. "Now comes the plaintiff by Mr. Godman, his Attorney, and the defendant being three times solemnly called came not, but made default. It is therefore considered that the plaintiff recover of said defendants the sum of $237.83,

Division of Findley Township.

his debt aforesaid, together with his damages assessed by the court at one cent, and his costs of suit to be taxed at $3.30.

The case of State of Ohio against Thomas Slight was tried before a jury composed of Joshua Hedges, Vanrensalear Hancock, John Elder, Seldon Blodgett, Sampson Dildine, James McKinnis, Wm. DeWitt, Josiah Elder, Thomas F. Johnson, Asa M. Lake, Asa Lake and Mathew Reighly. Verdict, guilty. Second trial allowed, case finally dismissed.

Perhaps no cases tried in the county excited more interest at the time than those in which John P. Hamilton and Charles and Philip McKinnis figured. The facts as I have them are as follows:

Charles McKinnis and John P. Hamilton were both County Commissioners, and a petition had been presented to the Board, praying for the division of Findley township, which then included all the western part of the county.

To this proposition McKinnis, and perhaps his immediate constituency, were opposed, as it struck them off from Findley.

At the session in which the matter was to be determined, McKinnis after coming to town was attacked with the ague, and consequently was not able to meet with the Board, and whilst the ague was shaking him, Hamilton and the other Commissioner passed the act dividing the township. This was done no doubt, without any intention of discourtesy or insult to McKinnis, but as it came up in the regular order of business. But it seems that McKinnis did not so regard it, for when the matter came to his ears, he was terribly enraged, as he believed they had purposely taken advantage of his absence to pass the obnoxious order.

As soon as he was able to be on the street, meeting Hamilton, and considering him the prime mover in the matter, he at once proceeded to revenge himself by giving Hamilton a severe whipping, according to the usages of warfare, practiced amongst gentlemen at that time. Philip McKinnis happening in town and hearing that his brother Charles and Hamilton had been in a fight, and knowing that Charles was sick, took it for granted that he had been worsted in the fight. Well aware that a fight between two full grown men meant business, and that whoever got whipped was badly whipped, he in his impetuous manner, and without stopping to inquire who had the best of the fight, started out to find the man whom he supposed had taken an undue advantage, and meeting Hamilton, without further ceremony pitched into him, and repeated the dose which Charles had administered. Thus by mistake Hamilton got two dressings, for had Philip known that Charles had come out first best in the fight, or even that he had been the aggressor, and got whipped in a fair fight, he would not under any consideration have interfered.

The matter came before the Grand Jury, and bills of indictments were found against the McKinnis brothers. The indictments were found by the following named Grand Jury: William Moreland, George Flenner, Squire Carlin, Asa Lake, John Bashore, Jacob Foster, John Hunter, Edwin S. Jones, John Beard, Don Alonzo Hamblin, Asher Wickham, Joshua Powell, Isaac Johnson, Joseph Sargent and Bass Rawson. The record says that to the indictment the defendants say they are guilty, and throw themselves on the mercy of the court. The sentence pronounced by the court against Charles McKinnis was: "And, thereupon, it is considered and adjudged by the court, that said McKinnis pay a fine of *one dollar*, and the costs of suit, taxed at $2.24, and that he stand charged until the sentence of the court is complied with and be in mercy." The case against Philip was disposed of in the same way.

John P. Hamilton, in September, 1829, by T. C. Powell, his Attorney, brought suit against Charles McKinnis for damages sustained by him in the assault and battery, claiming five hundred dollars damage.

The declaration (or petition as it would now be called), recites that: "The said Charles on the first day of September, 1829, at Findley, in the County of Hancock, with force and arms made an assault upon the said John, and then and there, with a certain stick, and with his fists, gave and struck the said John a great many violent blows and strokes, on and about his head, face, breast, back, shoulders, arms, legs and divers other places of his body, and, also, then and there with great force and violence, shook and pulled about the said John, down onto and upon the ground, and then and there violently kicked the said John, and gave and struck him a great many other blows and strokes, by means of which said second premises he, the said John, was then and there greatly hurt, bruised, wounded and became and was sick, sore and lame."

It will perhaps, be well enough to remember that the lawyers of that day, in drawing up papers, put in everything that actually did happen, and for fear of accidents, they then put in everything that might have happened. If the said Charles was guilty of inflicting even a tithe of the injury on the said John, with which he was charged, the fine of one dollar, although that was a large sum of money at that day, was a very cheap punishment.

The case was tried to a jury composed as follows: Josiah Elder, Don Alonzo Hamblin, Robert L. Strother, Joseph Egbert, Joshua Powell, Nathan Williams, William J. Greer, John J. Hendricks, Mordica Hammond, Peter George, Thos. Thompson and William Moreland. Verdict, guilty. Damages assessed at seventy-five dollars.

Suit was also brought against Philip McKinnis, and a judgment for thirty-five dollars recovered.

Anthony Casad, of Bellefontaine, Ohio, was appointed Prosecuting Attorney of the County, at the munificent salary of forty dollars. Amongst the names of Attorneys practicing in the courts at that day, and for many years subsequently, we find those of Casad, Godman, Powell, Goit, Hall, Bates, Morrison, O'Neal, Coffinberry, Patterson, May and Rawson.

In 1835, Robert L. Strother and John W. Baldwin were appointed Associate Judges, in place of Huff and McKinnis, Judge Wilson being reappoined. Judge Baldwin held the office but a short time, and upon his resignation, Major Bright was appointed.

In 1842, John Ewing, Mordica Hammond and William Roller were appointed, and they were succeeded by Michael Price, John Cooper and Gamaliel C. Brandel, and with them the race of Associate Judges became extinct, as the Constitution of 1851 abolished the office. The people of the county were very fortunate in the appointment of Judges, as all were, at least, of the best citizens of the county.

CHAPTER IX.

THE COUNTRY SHOEMAKER—THE SCHOOLMASTER—LOG ROLLING.

IN the early settlement of the county, an absence of mercantile and manufacturing establishments made it exceedingly inconvenient, and at times almost impossible to obtain the necessary articles of clothing. A very large portion of the early settlers were preparing to engage in agricultural pursuits, and hence mechanics and artisans were in demand, and the supply was of the less skillful class. At that time the country shoemaker—and almost every settlement contained one—was a very necessary appendage to a well regulated neighborhood. His mission and duty was to go from house to house in the neighborhood, and make up sufficient foot wear for the whole family. Each farmer or head of a family, would purchase leather enough, both sole and upper, to supply each member of his family with a pair of shoes, good heavy water proof ones, none of your cotton cloth, consumption soled articles—shoes made for service, rather than for ornament. The shoemaker was then engaged to work up the stock. He had no shop furnished with counters, shelves and drawers, well stored with manufactured work, indeed it frequently happened that he had no abiding place, but like the country school-master, boarded around.

He went from house to house, carrying with him his *kit* of tools, would take his seat by the side of the huge fire-place, and then to the wonder and astonishment of the young members of the community, would measure, and cut, and shape, and make shoes enough for the whole family. When finished, he would pack up his *kit* and go to the next. His annual visits were looked for with interest by the little ones who, when he had come, would gather around him, watching with open eyed wonder, the putting together with wax end and peg, the homely but serviceable shoe. And how they enjoyed his story telling and his songs. The coming of the shoemaker was one of the events not to be forgotten.

The pioneer, after he had prepared his clearing ready for logging—as it was called—would invite his neighbors to come and assist him in rolling the logs into heaps ready for burning, and no one who was invited would neglect to attend, unless for the best of reasons. When the log-rollers had assembled on the ground, they selected two or more of their number as Captains, and by choice made by the Captains would divide themselves into parties, and apportion an equal amount of work to each party. The party who first cleared the ground, was declared winner and entitled to the first "smile" from the little brown jug, and a seat at the first table. A clearing with a score or more of men thus engaged in a friendly contest, was rather a lively place.

But on occasions of this kind, the good wife, not to be outdone by her man, would quietly put the patch-work quilt in the frames, and invite the wives and daughters of the log rollers to come in and help her. Thus, whilst the men and boys were busy in the fields, the women and girls were equally busy with needle. After supper, whilst the girls were engaged in washing the dishes, and setting the house

Log-Rolling and Quilting.

in order, the men found recreation in feats of running, wrestling and jumping. Candles, or the dry hickory-bark torch were lit at dark, and the rural violinist, that is, the *country fiddler* makes his appearance, takes his seat on a table, tunes up his instrument, when "choose your partners" was in order. Away goes the music and away go the dancers, often much more energetic than graceful. "French four," "money musk," "Scotch reels," interspersed with jigs and regular break downs. None of your now fashionable waltzes, polkas, schottish, and fancy cotillion, in which the whirling and turning, and everlasting swinging, is enough to give the spectator the delirium tremens.

The pioneer boys and girls danced to the music of such good old healthy tunes as the Fisher's Horn Pipe, Devil's Dream, Arkansaw Traveller and Col. Johnston. Whilst the young people were thus engaged, the older ones occupied themselves in smoking and rehearsing the gallantries and exploits of their younger days, occasionally joining in the dance, just to show the young folks how they used to do, you know.

But to the still younger ones, the most interesting part of a log-rolling and quilting was the supper, for they were sure to get an extra piece of Johnny Cake, and a piece of pumpkin pie, after which they were generally willing to go to bed; but willing or unwilling, they went, as their room was much more desirable than their company.

Fifty years ago there were but few school buildings in the county, and they were of the rudest sort, but small and rude as they were, they were deemed sufficiently large to accommodate all who would attend school. There was not a very great demand for school marms, nor were the expenses of keeping up a school three months in the year, very heavy. Although the school buildings were cheap, and perhaps shabby in appearance, and the accommodations for the pupils the poorest, and the qualifications of the teachers far from first-class, yet with a determination on the part of teachers, and pupils, and parents, that the time should be well improved, the community progressed in intelligence. As the population increased, each settlement had its log school house, not built perhaps, by taxation, but the free gift of the honest patrons, who met, cut the logs, carried them together, erected the building, completed it by covering with clap boards and weight poles, chink and daub the cracks, put in the rude benches, the paper windows, and employ the first man who came along, qualified to teach spelling, reading, writing and arithmetic as far as the single-rule of three, and who was willing to board around, sent their children to school and were happy.

Thus our forefathers did not forget that the peace, and safety, and prosperity, and happiness of every community depended upon the intelligence of its members. Did not forget that vice in all its forms, was sure to attend ignorance and superstition. Hence, the first building erected in a settlement, was a school house. In those days the country school master ranked next in importance to the circuit preacher, and as he went boarding around he was welcomed to the best seat by the fireside, and the choicest viands at the table, and was regarded by the patrons of the school as the embodiment of wisdom, and by the younger members of the family as the embodiment of power, for well they remembered the birch rods sticking up in the walls of the old school house, and with what expertness he could wield them.

CHAPTER X.

FIRST ROADS AND BRIDGES.

AT the June session of the Commissioners, in the year 1829, "A petition being presented by sundry citizens of Hancock County, praying for a county road, commencing at the county line at John Smith's farm, running thence a north-westerly direction to John Longs, in Section one, thence to cross Blanchard Fork at or near John J. Hendricks, thence to run down the river to the mouth of the three mile run, thence the nearest and best direction to Findley, which was granted, and John Huff, John J. Hendricks and William Moreland were appointed viewers, and William Taylor, Surveyor." On the 16th of September the Commissioners met in special session to receive the report of the viewers of said road. Report received and the road established. This road is the one now known as the Findley and Vanlue road, which crosses the river at the farm of Richard Hall.

In August, 1830, the County Commissioners met for the purpose of apportioning the amount of the *three per cent.* fund on the several state roads, and the record says: "Whereupon it is agreed on by said Commissioners that the aforesaid amount of money appropriated, shall be laid out on the following roads, to-wit: The road leading from Bellefontaine to Perrysburgh, and the road leading from

Upper Sandusky through Findley to Defiance, which work is to be performed in cutting out said roads, thirty-two feet wide, all timber twenty inches in diameter, and clearing the ground of all timber."

A petition was presented to the Commissioners July 28th, 1831, signed by numerous parties, "Humbly representing that it would conduce much to the public convenience if a county road was established between the following points, to-wit: Beginning at the west end of Main Cross Street, in the village of Findley (at a point where West street crosses Main Cross street, at the residence of Mrs. Dr. Detwiler,) thence on the nearest and best route to Solomon Foglesong's improvement on Toway Creek, thence on the nearest and best route in direction of Toway Village, (now Ottowa, Putnam County,) to the county line." As this is now one of the leading as well as one of the best roads in the county, I will give the report of the viewers in full.

"Gentlemen: We, the undersigned viewers, met at the time and place appointed in your order of December last, and after being qualified as the law directs, proceeded to view the ground as therein set forth. Surveying and making a line as we proceeded, having always a regard to the nature of the ground, and at the same time paying particular attention to have no more angles in the survey, than what could not possibly be avoided. We found it impossible, however, to take the line to the immediate point at Foglesong's. We went as near to it, notwithstanding, as the nature of the ground would admit, which was satisfactory to the petitioners. And we can assure you, the whole line (with the exception of a part of the first mile leaving Findley, which was unavoidable,) is on as good ground for a road as we know of any where in this region of country. We also be-

First Roads.

lieve it will, when opened, be a road of general utility, both to the immediate neighborhood and the public in general.

Respectfully submitted,
THOMAS F. JOHNSTON,
ISAAC BAKER."

March 5th, 1832.

After these followed the location and opening up of the Tiffin, Port Clinton, New Haven, Lima and other important roads. In fact, for the first ten years after the organization of the county, the principal part of the business of the Board of Commissioners, was to receive petitions for, and confirm reports of reviewers and surveyor of county roads. Such has been the desire of the people, and the acts of the Commissioners, that we have now public highways running by and bordering on almost every farm in the county, thus affording to all an easy and convenient means of communicating with his neighbors.

The records of Wood County, recite that the "Road from Fort Meigs, or the foot of the Rapids of the Miami of the Lake (Maumee), to Bellefontaine, opened December 11th, 1829." This is the road now known as the Perrysburg and Bellefontaine state road, which crosses the county from north to south, and divides it into two almost equal parts. This road was laid out on and near "Hull's Trail."

The Commissioners of the same county, on the 6th day of June, 1826, "Ordered that four hundred dollars of the road fund be appropriated for Hancock County, to be expended on the Urbana road in said county." This road was the Perrysburg and Bellefontaine road.

The first roads in the county, were for years scarcely more than blazed paths through the woods. Very many places would have been utterly impassable had it not been for a system of bridging, then extensively indulged in, known as corduroy. This was a kind of rail road in which the position of the ties and rails on an ordinary rail road were reversed. That is, the ties were laid lengthwise and the rails crosswise. But as timber was abundant, and not much attention was paid to the smoothness of the road, they were not so very expensive.

The County authorities, and the citizens for many years contented themselves by bridging the smaller streams and water courses, wherever absolutely necessary, and then only with a temporary structure, barely answering the purpose of its building, without a thought of bridging the river. So impossible of completion, seemed such an undertaking, and so immense an amount of money was supposed to be necessary, that no one dared mention such a project.

In 1841, when it was seriously contemplated to build a bridge across the river at Findley, it was deemed of so much importance, that this order was made: "Ordered that the Auditor instruct the Assessors to take the vote of the people as to the propriety of laying a tax of eight hundred dollars for building a bridge across Blanchard River in Findley."

How the voters of the county decided the matter does not appear by the records, but the inference is, that they "seconded the motion," for in March, 1842, the following resolution was passed by the County Commissioners: "*Resolved*, That the Auditor receive proposals for building two bridges across Blanchard River, one at Findley, and the other at the crossing of the Findley and New Haven State road, (known as the Marvin Bridge,) until the first day of April next, agreeable to the plans now in this office, as submitted to the Commissioners, one half the pay in January, 1843, and the other half in one year thereafter."

First Bridge at Findley.

On opening the bids, at a special session, January 7th, 1843, for the completion of the extension of the bridge across the river at Findley, it was found that James Robinson was the lowest bidder, and the contract was awarded to him.

The records do not give the names of the contractors, nor the price paid, except as we find in the proceedings of the Commissioners at a special session in March, 1843, when it was "Ordered that the Auditor of Hancock County, Ohio, inquire into the cause why the bridge across the Blanchard Fork of the Auglaize River, at Findley, is not completed agreeable to contract by S. Carlin and H. Eaton, and if no good cause is shown, institute a suit against said contractors, and employ counsel if necessary."

June 1, 1843, the Commissioners "Ordered that the Auditor of Hancock County enter a suit against the contractors of the bridge at Findley, by the first of July next, if the same is not by that time finished to the satisfaction of the Commissioners."

It is fair to presume that the bridge was finished to the "satisfaction of the Commissioners," as there is no record of a suit being brought. The bridge was a wooden structure, known as a trestle bridge, the superstructure being supported by wooden trestles, placed, perhaps twenty feet apart. The finish was of the plainest kind, only ordinary railing, no cover, no paint.

In 1850, the contract for a new and better bridge across the Blanchard, was let to Jesse Wheeler, William Klamroth and Edwin B. Vail, for the sum of fifteen hundred dollars. It too, was a wooden structure, but of a different plan, and whilst it was more pretentious in appearance, it was also a much more substantial piece of work. It consisted of two spans, being supported at the ends, by massive stone abutments, with a pier in the centre, of the same material. The sides were elevated—being a truss bridge—and inclosed, and the whole covered with a shingle roof. There was but a single track for wagons, with a foot path on either side. The bridge when finished and opened for travel, was regarded as a superb piece of work.

But in time, this structure wore out, and decayed, and the business and travel of the county demanded a better bridge. One that would not only answer the purpose for which it should be intended, but which would also be an honor to the county, and an ornament to the county seat.

In 1872, the old bridge was sold, torn down and taken away, and the Canton Iron Bridge Company, under contract with the County Commissioners, erected the present beautiful and substantial Iron Bridge, at a cost to the county of about thirteen thousand dollars.

Previous to the building of any of these bridges, the river was crossed by canoes, when too high to drive teams across.

In 1839, John Byal, Aquilla Gilbert and Daniel Fairchild, Commissioners, at their March session: "Ordered that there be appropriated for building a bridge across Eagle Creek, at what is now called the Upper Ford, or where the Melmore and Findley State road crosses the creek, the sum of *ten dollars*, provided, there is a good and sufficient bridge erected thereon before the first day of November next." This bridge was to be built where the Sandusky street bridge now is. What would our friends in East Findley, and in the eastern part of the county say to a ten dollar bridge at that place now. But they must remember, that when this order was passed, that the place designated for the bridge, was a considerable distance out in the country.

Bridges.

In 1845, the sum of nine hundred and forty dollars was expended in the county for bridges. Numerous bridges, wooden structures, were built across the river at various times, and were gradually replaced by other and better structures, until now there are not less than thirteen good, substantial bridges spanning the Blanchard River within the limits of the county. Besides these, there are scores of smaller iron and wooden structures spanning the numerous creeks and water courses. The value of these bridges, is quite considerable, and their conveniences to the population cannot be estimated.

CHAPTER XI.

COUNTY RECORDS. FIRST CENSUS. GENERAL ELECTION 1828.

THE early records of the county are in a very imperfect condition, not having been kept with that care, and in a form which would outlive the times in which they were made. Kept for the most part in small books, poorly made, or on scraps of paper, poorly preserved, much of our early history is lost beyond hope of recovery. Much that was recorded, has by the carelessness of those who had them in charge, been mutilated to such an extent as to be almost unintelligible, and much has been entirely destroyed.

The greatness of a country depends, perhaps not so much upon the extent of territory, as upon its population, wealth and intelligence. and the progress made in these in Hancock County during the last half century is a matter of interest, and pride as well, perhaps, to my readers.

I have been unable, in my researches, to find a report of the population of this county previous to 1830, that being the year in which the first federal census was taken after the organization of the county. We might, by the usual method, estimate the population in 1828 from the vote polled in that year. As we have already seen, the first election held in the county after its separate organization, took place on the first Monday in April in that year, at

First and Last Census.

which election there were *seventy-four* votes cast. Now counting the population at five times the number of voters, we have three hundred and seventy as the entire population, which number is no doubt very nearly correct.

At this date there were perhaps not more than a half dozen settlements—as they were called—iu the county. One at Mt. Blanchard, one at Findley, one at McKinnis, and one perhaps in the south part of the county. Of course there were a few families residing at other points in the county, but they were regarded as a part of one or the other of these principal settlements, for all were neighbors then who lived within a day's journey of each other.

Two years later, when the census of 1830 was taken, there were eight hundred and thirteen persons in the county. Of that number four hundred and fifty-one were white males, and three hundred and fifty-one were white females, and there were three males and six females colored. Of the total number, only two hundred and fifty-two were above the age of twenty-one years. One hundred and fifty-five males, and one hundred and forty-seven females, about three-fourths of the entire population, were under the age of twenty. The population then of the county in 1830 was eight hundred and thirteen, and in 1880, just fifty years after, it was twenty-seven thousand three hundred and forty-three.

The census of 1830 does not give the number of acres of improved lands, and value of buildings in the county. We may, however, well conclude that but little had been done as yet towards subduing the wilderness, for even an hundred good stalwart pioneers could make but little headway against nature, which had been at work for centuries, and that farms or clearings were few and far between. As to buildings, I presume there was not a frame or brick building in the county, outside of Findley.

Long before church buildings were erected, the missionary—ever mindful of the Master's work—came, and for the time being the rude cabin of the frontiersman, or the log school house, were the church edifices, in the advanced settlements. Here too, in these primitive buildings, were held the Sabbath Schools, the meetings of which were as anxiously looked for, and as highly enjoyed as are our more modern schools. Church services were frequently held in the woods, under the cool shade of the forest trees, "God's First Temples." Such meetings were known as campmeetings, because those attending erected tents in which to reside during the continuance of the meeting.

This style of meeting was then a necessity, as there were no buildings of sufficient capacity to hold the congregations, and not ministers enough to supply the different settlements with services, hence, they came together in large bodies, and had the advantage of the ministrations of a number of preachers.

These meetings were conducted with the utmost decorum, with services at stated hours, and rules governing the little community in such a manner that all might enjoy their coming together. This style of services is practiced to a great extent even in this day, though there exists no such necessity as at that early date. With the abundance of houses of worship, and ministers of the gospel, the holding of them meets with much disfavor by very many good Christian men and women, as they are too generally visited by the wicked to avail themselves of an opportunity of showing their inate cussedness.

The first settlers, situated as they were in the midst of an

First General Election. 83

Indian country, cut off by many miles of forest, from the outside world, naturally felt their dependence on each other It would have been the extreme of folly in them to have allowed differences and dissensions to have crept in and divided them, and guarding against that, there was a feeling of friendship between them, stronger than the fear of Indians, and which lasted longer.

There was not that constant desire to gain wealth for its own sake, that *fifteen per cent.* feeling, that effort to reach *respectability* through the medium of fine clothes, that desire to build themselves up by pulling others down, that jealousy of another's prosperity, that envy of another's success, which has unhappily sprung up amongst their children, and which has been so destructive of that genuine happiness, which they enjoyed.

At a general election held October, 14, 1828, the second held in the county, there were *seventy-seven* votes cast, of these Allen Trimble received forty-four, and John W. Campbell thirty, for Governor. A certificate signed by Joshua Hedges and William Hackney, two Justices of the Peace, and Wilson Vance, Clerk, certifies that for Congress Joseph Vance had *thirty-one* votes and John Alexander had *forty-two* votes. For State Senator Asa Sandford had *twenty-nine* votes and David Campbell had *thirty-two* votes. For Representative Samuel M. Lockwood had *fifty-four* votes. Samuel Lockwood had *one* vote. The following named persons were elected County officers: Commissioners, John Long, John P. Hamilton and Charles McKinnis, their comqetitors being William J. Greer, Mordica Hammond and Godfrey Wolford. Sheriff, John C. Wickham, beating Squire Carlin. Thomas Slight was elected Coroner over Reuben W. Hamblin. For Treasurer Edwin S. Jones beat Joshua

Hedges, and for Auditor William Hackney had a majority of *four* over Mathew Reighly, and Don Alonzo Hamblin had a majority of *twenty-eight* over Edwin S. Jones for Assessor.

CHAPTER XII.

AN INCIDENT. GENERAL MUSTER.

AN anecdote, which is vouched for by persons now living, is told of Wilson Vance and Philip McKinnis, two of the pioneers of the county, and who have both been dead for some years. The story illustrates, not only the honor of the early settlers, but also shows the light in which they regarded an agreement.

In consequence of the want of flouring mills in the county, flour and other bread stuffs had to be procured from distant and more favored settlements. Urbana, Perrysburg and Sandusky City were the principal points visited. On one occasion Vance and McKinnis, who were warm friends, had occasion to go to Urbana for provisions, each with his own team of oxen. Everything went along smoothly until they arrived at Mud Fort, near the south line of the county, on their return. From that point there were two roads leading to Findley, one of which roads Vance wanted to take, but McKinnis objected, and desired to travel the other. They were in a dilemma, neither wanting to yield the point, and yet both compelled to travel the same road as a protection against the savages, as well as to assist each other in case either team should get *stalled* in the mud.

After a heated discussion of the matter for some time, and not being able to agree, McKinnis proposed this novel compromise. They should take the road indicated by Vance with the understanding that if either of the teams stalled before reaching Findley, that Vance should submit to a whipping from McKinnis, but that if they did not stall, that he—McKinnis—would submit to a whipping from Vance, for insisting that they should take the other road. The whipping to be done with the ox-whip. To this Vance agreed.

They then started, with Vance in the lead. In this way they travelled until they had almost reached Findley, without meeting with any mishap, and McKinnis began to shrug his shoulders, and had made up his mind that Vance had beaten him for once. But Vance's team suddenly halted, having failed to touch solid bottom in one of the mud holes, so common at the foot of Chamberlain's Hill. Nor could they with all the whipping and coaxing expended on them by Vance, extricate the wagon, and with a rather solemn countenance, McKinnis was called on to assist. He readily consented, and with the help of his team, Vance's wagon was soon placed on solid ground again. Now came McKinnis' time, and insisting on the contract, Vance accepted the situation as gracefully as possible, while his opponent, who had fairly won, laid on the ox-gad right lively.

A general muster in the olden time was an event of no small importance, especially to the younger portion of the population. For months before the annual parade, people began preparing to attend. The soldiers were busy in repairing and polishing up their old flint-lock muskets, those who were fortunate enough to have one. The commissioned officer was busy studying up his words of command, and brushing up his regimentals. The farmer, who always had an eye to business on such occasions, was carefully cultivating his melons, and vigilantly watching them to see that

General Muster.

no thieves should break through and steal them. Everything seemed to be so arranged that general musters and ripe melons both came at the same season of the year, and we boys could never quite decide whether general muster came in water-melon time, or whether water melons came just when general musters were ripe. The thrifty house wife was gathering up the eggs and laying by the butter, for she intends going to town on training day, and with the proceeds of her produce, buy a little tea for her next quilting, and an extra bit of muslin for a new cap.

The grown up girls—now called ladies—were busy making dresses, for their beaux had been over and invited them to go to town on muster day, and had offered them a seat on the horse behind them, and the small boys were carefully getting and keeping all the pennies they could, for when they went to militia muster—and had they not industriously picked up brush in the clearing and pulled weeds in the corn-field all summer under the promise that they should go?—they expected to invest their savings in ginger-bread and candy.

When the long looked for day came, the farmer hitched up his ox-team, took his wife and little ones in his wagon, together with his melons, and butter, and eggs; and the beaux on horse back with their sweethearts behind them on the same horse, with their rifles on their shoulders, wended their way to the county-seat, the place of general rendezvous. Here almost the entire population of the county was assembled. Officers in blue coats, brass buttons, red sash, monstrous epauletts, and broad swords, mounted on the stately plow horse, cavorting up and down the street, the terror of anxious mothers, in danger themselves of broken necks, and to the admiration of small boys. Oh! but wasn't it gay?

George Washington in all his glory was never arrayed like one of these militia officers, and we doubt if he ever felt half so important. The men by companies, some armed with rifles, but more with sticks and mullein stalks, marched and counter marched, and performed evolutions not now laid down in the regulations. They were formed into lines, into circles, into hollow-squares—a great deal more hollow than square. There were the Findley Rangers under the command of Capt. Lape, arrayed in Aaron Baker's uniform. The Captain, I believe, still survives the dangers of those troublous times. The Rangers were dressed in uniforms of green, profusely trimmed with yellow tape. There were the Van Buren Rangers commanded by the now venerable Col. Wall, with uniforms of green, trimmed with red, marching to the music of fife and drums. There were other companies, clothed every man according to his taste, or comfort, or ability. But the "Light Horse Company," commanded by Capt. John Byal, was to us boys the very highest military achievement. To see the men mount and dismount, to face and right face, was to us truly wonderful. True the evolutions were not performed as rapidly and as gracefully as Phil Sheridan would have done, but then what does he know about cavalry mustering on farm horses.

Under the direction of Gen. Bell, Col. Byal and other field and staff officers, the companies were put through their facings until noon, when they were dismissed for dinner. After dinner the fun commenced, in the shape of running, jumping, wrestling, pitching horse-shoes, drinking and fighting. The few groceries in the town were places of lively interest, and a good gingerbread and small beer business was done.

General Muster.

Each company had its fighting man, a much more economical and comfortable plan than keeping up a whole fighting company, and he was expected to whip any and every man who dared offer an indignity to the company or any member thereof; and it was a very dull day, indeed, if there were not as many fights as there were companies on parade. After these amusements, and the wounded had been properly cared for, those who were not disabled in the engagement, and could walk, were marched to the green on the river-bank—now the circus ground—for "Grand Review," or dress parade. Here they were inspected by the General in command who sat on his horse, "grand, gloomy and peculiar," under the shade of his umbrella, whilst the heated warriors marched solemnly and silently by. Tired, foot-sore, and hungry, they were discharged until the next mustering day. These veterans can now well quote the stanza;

"Oh! were you ne'er a militia man,
And did you never train?
And feelthat swelling of the feet
We hope to never feel again."

CHAPTER XIII.

RAIL ROADS.

AT a special session held April 26th, 1839, the County Commissioners "Ordered that we, the Commissioners, agree to subscribe one hundred shares, amounting to one hundred thousand dollars, to the capital stock of the Bellefontaine and Perrysburg Rail Road, and that in our incorporate capacity, we will place our signatures to the books of the company for that amount.

JOHN BYAL,
DANIEL FAIRCHILD, } Com."

With all our wealth and population, at the present, no such liberal terms towards any rail road project would be entertained by our Commissioners.

At the same meeting, for it seems that the Commissioners meant business, it was ordered "That we appoint a special Commissioner to negotiate the loan on the credit of the county, in the City of New York, or elsewhere, at a rate of interest not to exceed six per cent. per annum," and it was "Ordered that Parlee Carlin be delegated our special agent, [to ne]gotiate the loan of one hundred thousand dollars which [we h]ave this day subscribed to the capital stock of the [Belle]fontaine and Perrysburg Rail Road Company."

[Th]us ends the history of this rail road, so far as this [coun]ty is concerned. Like an innumerable number of such projects, it ended in talk, and futile resolutions and orders.

In 1845, the rail road fever again broke out in the county, and the Commissioners went earnestly to work to make some

The First Rail Road.

project a success. They were not wholly disappointed, for they set on foot a movement, which finally resulted in the building of the Findley Branch of the Mad River and Lake Erie Rail Road, as it was then called.

On the 4th day of March, 1845, George Shaw, Peter George and John Lafferty, Commissioners, issued a proclamation to the qualified voters of Hancock County to vote at the election on the first Monday of April, 1845, for or against a proposition to subscribe to the capital stock of the Mad River and Lake Erie Rail Road, and that the Auditor have said proclamation published in three newspapers published in Findley, until the April election. The returns of said election was made and counted and certified as follows:

Washington Township,	For	6.	Against,	135.
Amanda	"	" 30.	"	87.
Jackson	"	" 40.	"	50.
Cass	"	" 31.	"	83.
Findley	"	" 243.	"	4.
Eagle	"	" 67.	"	39.
Van Buren	"	" 6.	"	36.
Union	"	" 121.	"	4.
Pleasant	"	" 44.	"	2.
Big Lick	"	" 55.	"	26.
Delaware	"	" 1.	"	121.
Marion	"	" 107.	"	5.
Portage	"	" 65.	"	61.
Liberty	"	" 120.	"	5.
Madison	"	"	"	64.
Orange	"	" 17.	"	41.
Blanchard	"	" 102.	"	1.
Totals,		1055.		784.

History of Hancock County.

On the 11th day of April, 1845, the Commissioners, in their corporate capacity, subscribed to the Capital stock of the Mad River and Lake Erie Rail Road Company, twelve hundred shares, of fifty dollars a share, making in all, the sum of sixty thousand dollars. Wilson Vance, William Taylor, John Patterson and William L. Henderson were appointed agents to meet with the Railroad Company, and they were authorized to employ a special messenger to go to Perrysburg to get the bonds printed in a neat manner, at as reasonable a compensation as they can agree upon.

On the 22d of April, 1845, the Commissioners, in special session, issued bonds for the sum of thirty thousand dollars, payable to the Mad River and Lake Erie Rail Road Company, as first payment of sixty thousand dollars subscribed. At the June session of the Commissioners, John Ewing and Jacob Barnd were added to the Rail Road Commissioners.

On the 11th day of September, 1845, the County Commissioners subscribed three hundred shares, amounting to fifteen thousand dollars, in addition to the sixty thousand dollars already subscribed. At the same time, Squire Carlin was appointed Rail Road Commissioner in place of Jacob Barnd, deceased.

On the 19th day of August, 1846, the Mad River and Lake Erie Rail Road Company accepted the subscription of seventy-five thousand dollars, and agreed to build the road. On the 22d day of September, 1846, the Commissioners of the County appointed John Ewing, John Patterson and Hiram Smith Commissioners to manage the construction of the road.

The road, however, was not completed and put in operation, until the latter part of December, 1849. This road, commencing at Findley, takes a south-easterly course,

Dayton and Michigan R. R.

through Findley, Marion and Amanda Townships, to Carey, Wyandotte County. It crosses the Blanchard River in Marion Township. This road is about sixteen miles in length, and was originally constructed on a cheap plan. The iron rails were simply strap iron, or flat iron, as it was termed, laid on stringers, placed lengthwise on the road-bed. In this condition it remained for many years, always paying large dividends to the company, but furnishing very inferior accomdations to the county.

Finally, however, by an arrangement entered into, between the officers of the road and the County Commissioners, the company agreed to and did repair the road, lay the track with "T" rails, and build a passenger house at Findley. The road now is in first class condition, except the rolling stock, which, as a general thing, is such as is deemed unfit for use on the main line, and of course is of a very unsatisfactory quality.

In 1853, at the time the Dayton and Michigan Rail Road project was under consideration, it was supposed, and perhaps promised, that Findley should be one of the points on the route, and our people became enthusiastic over the matter. In July, 1853, the Commissioners of the County subscribed one hundred thousand dollars to the capital stock of the company. A preliminary survey was made of the line, and we felt reasonably sure of the road. In this we were disappointed. The management, for some reason, selected a route farther west, missing our county entirely, and thus ended this rail road project, so far as Hancock County was concerned. The road was built on a line further west, and has proved a paying investment, a good business road, but no more so than it would have been, had the route through our county been chosen. And the road would have been of immense advantage to us.

About this time, and perhaps not until after it was definitely settled that we were not to have the Dayton and Michigan Road, a project to build a road from Fremont, in Sandusky County, to Union City, a town on the line of Ohio and Indiana, by way of Findley and Lima began to be agitated. Henry Brown, Esq., then Editor of the "Hancock Courier," of Findley, taking the lead in the matter, and setting forth in glowing terms the advantage to be derived from such a line of road. Finally the matter took form, and a Company was organized, and chartered under the name of the "Fremont and Indiana Rail Road Company," to construct a road from Fremont, Ohio, to Union City, on the Indiana line, by way of Findley and Lima. A survey of the route was made, which was decided to be practicable. Subscription books were opened, and stock readily subscribed. The principal stock-holders in Findley, were Judge Corey, S. and P. Carlin and Bass Rowson. Judge Corey and Squire Carlin were Directors. After much delay, caused by the difficulty in collecting subscriptions, and inability to procure iron, the road was not completed to Findley until 1861. About this time, the company became embarrassed, and the road was sold. The purchasers organized a new company, under the name of the "Fremont, Lima & Union Rail Road Company," and this company, in 1865, consolidated with the Lake Erie & Pacific Rail Road Company, under the name of the Lake Erie & Louisville R. R. Company, but the road was not completed and operated to Lima until the winter of 1873, perhaps. From that time until 1878, the road was operated, most of the time, in the hands of a Receiver.

Lake Erie and Western R. R.

At this time, however, some shrewd eastern capitalists seeing the advantage of such a line, bought the road, and at once set themselves to work to develop its resources. They extended the line from Celina, in Mercer County, Ohio, to Muncie, Indiana, thus making good western connections, also connecting with Chicago. The name of the road was changed to that of Lake Erie & Western, the better to express its intentions. Connections were sought and obtained with St. Louis. The road was extended from Fremont to Sandusky City, on Lake Erie, and to-day this is regarded as a "Trunk Line," and its business has brought it well up to the front.

This road enters the county at Fostoria, in Section one, Washington Township, thence runs a south-west direction, passing through the Townships of Washington, Cass, Marion, Findley, Liberty, Eagle, Union and Orange, crossing into Allen County, at Bluffton. There is about twenty-five miles of the road in Hancock County, and its business at Findley and other points, amounts to many thousands of dollars.

The citizens of McComb and vicinity, having been several times disappointed in their expectations of the completion of the Continental Road, which had been graded through their town, conceived the idea of building a line of road to intersect the Dayton & Michigan at Deshler, about eight miles distant, went to work earnestly in the matter, and having made satisfactory arrangements with the Dayton & Michigan, organized a company to construct the McComb and Deshler Railroad. The work was pushed rapidly forward, and the road completed in January, 1881. About four miles of this road is in Hancock County.

The old Continental line has been bought up by eastern

capitalists, and under the name of the New York, Chicogo & St. Louis Railway, is being pushed forward to completion. This line runs directly across the northern tier of towships, and when completed, will have about twenty-five miles of road within Hancock County.

CHAPTER XIV.

COMMON SCHOOLS.

WE cannot give even the approximate cost of the schools of the county a half century ago, or the number of youth within school age. We can very safely conclude, however, that the number of the one, and the amount of the other was not large. The schools at that early day were supported by subscription, and not by money raised by taxation. It is not probable that the costs of the school was very great, as we now count the cost. The school buildings were the rude log cabins, as rudely furnished, and the teachers were of very limited acquirements, and of but little experience in the management of schools. The books used were in very many instances utterly unfit for the use of children as text books in schools. There was no system, and very little method in conducting these schools, and perhaps, the only wonder is that pupils learned anything at all, or that the schools were not a positive evil, instead of a benefit.

Yet under all these difficulties, and want of almost every thing intended to render the school life of the pupil not only bearable, but attractive, much, very much progress was made in the acquirement of a common school education. Indeed many, and in fact almost all the older men and women of the county, never had other than just such training.

But such was the perseverance and the determination of the boys and girls of that day in the pursuit of knowledge under so many discouraging surroundings, that the education thus obtained, has enabled them to go successfully through life, managing their own affairs, and in many instances those of the public as well, with intelligence an success.

A great change has transpired. The friends of popular education have been able to frame and put into successful operation, a common school system, which for universal good, is second to that of no other State in the Union. Free schools—common schools—such as the intelligence of Ohio men have brought into existence, and such as Ohio laws foster and protect, have done more to make us a great, prosperous and happy people, than any other blessing bestowed upon us.

Hancock County has not been slow in appreciating this fact, and in availing herself of the present and lasting benefits which attend it. This is fully proven by a glance at the school statistics relating to this county. And no surer indication of our prosperity can be produced than that which becomes evident in an examination of these statistics. For it is not possible that a community, which so generally avails itself of the provisions of so good a law, should be other than prosperous and happy.

In 1880 the enumeration of youth of school age, in the county, was nine thousand, two hnndred and ten (9,210), or about forty per cent. of the entire population. Of this number seven thousand, seven hundred and forty-eight were enrolled in the different schools of the county, during the school-year.

To accomodate this small army of boys and girls, there

Schools and their Cost.

are one hundred and forty-nine school buildings, containing one hundred and seventy-five school rooms. The cost of these buildings is put down at one hundred and eighty-five thousand dollars ($185,000). For the instruction of these children there were one hundred and seventy-six teachers employed, at a cost of thirty-eight thousand, two hundred and ninety-four dollars and ninety-eight cents ($38,294.98). The total receipts of school money during the year was ninety-six thousand, nine hundred and seventy-seven dollars and seventy-one cents, and the total expeuditures were fifty-six thousand, eight hundred and four dollars and sixty-eight cents.

Large as these amounts really are, what is that compared with the intelligence which is diffused? What is that compared to the preparing of the young for useful and law-abiding citizens? What is that compared with the comfort and happiness that may attend each individual recipient, if properly used.

Hancock County has good reason to be proud of her two hundred school buildings, of her well regulated school rooms, in many instances furnished with the most approved school apparatus, and all the modern appliances which tend to make the acquirement of an education a pleasure rather than a task. These incipient colleges—the poor man's colleges—are scattered all over the county, but conveniently accessible to all. Places where the children of the poor can meet on an equality with the children of the rich, where all may have an equal opportunity of mastering a common school education, without money and without any other price than that of industry and close application.

Yes, the common school system of Ohio is fraught with innumerable blessings, designed as it is for the benefit of all who see proper to avail themselves of its provisions. It is not perfect, perhaps, but may the hand of no quack Legistor ever be laid upon it to mar its present fair proportions, and fasten upon it the foul sores of political legislation. May no change ever be allowed, except a change for the better.

CHAPTER XV.

SOME OTHER THINGS OF INTEREST.

UNDER the old judicial system of the State, Administrators of the estates of deceased persons were appointed by the Associate Judges of the County, and upon the decease of an individual seized of an estate, it was necessary to call a special session of the court, in order to appoint an Administrator. This was certainly very inconvenient, and at this day would be very expensive.

The first record we find of such a session of court in this county, was one held on the 19th day of March, 1829, at Findley, by Judges Huff, McKinnis and Wilson. At that time, William Taylor was appointed Administrator of the estate of John Patterson, deceased. His sureties were Job Chamberlain, sr., and John Boyd. The whole amount of money coming into the hands of the Administrator from the sale of both real and personal property, was $869.50, quite an estate for that early day, and Mr. Patterson was regarded as one of the wealthy men of the county.

In looking over the items of the settlement, we find the administrator has a credit of two dollars, for two days services as administrator. This was certainly a novel way of getting pay for such services, to say nothing of the very moderate charge made. The attorneys, for procuring sale of land, and advsing in the settlement of the estate, were allowed five dollars. No doubt the heirs and the creditors of the estate in those days received larger dividends, than many of that class do at the present.

The first will recorded, was probated in March, 1830, and in this day of brevity in such matters, it may be of interest to mention the introduction to this will as it appears on record, which we will do, omitting the name of the testator.

"In the name of God, Amen. I * * * * * of Hancock County, State ef Ohio, being sick and weak in body, but of sound mind, memory and understanding, (praised be God for it,) and considering the certainty of death, and the uncertainty of the time thereof, and to the end I may be better prepared to leave this world whenever it may please God to call me home, do therefore make and declare this my last will and testament in manner following, (that is to say) first and principally I commend my soul into the hands of Almighty God, my Creator, praying for free pardon, and remission of all my sins, and to enjoy everlasting happiness in the Heavenly Kingdom through Jesus Christ my Savior. My body I commit to the earth, at the discretion of my executor hereafter named."

Then follows the several items of the will all as properly, and at the same time as specifically expressed, as is the foregoing. Indeed, in looking over the records of wills of that day, we are impressed with the certainty of the language of every bequest. No ambiguity, no looseness of expression on which a law suit might hinge, no possible chance for litigation and fat fees. No wasting of the estate in determinig the intentions of the party, but all is plain and to the point.

In the early history of the county, a noted Wyandotte Chief, known as Sum-un-du-wat, was well known in this county, having made so many incursions here—by almost every man, woman and child in the settlements. He was a christian Indian, brave, generous and kind, and was not only honored by his tribe, but was respected by the pale faces for his honesty and bravery. This noble red man was most foully murdered near Napoleon, in Henry County. The event created a most profound sensation, and for some time there seemed to be danger of an outbreak amongst the Indians, to avenge this most fiendish killing of Sum-un-du-wat, and his daughter and her husband, for they were all three murdered at the same time and by the same men. Without a moment's warning they were slain by those who were receiving their hospitality.

On my visit to the Eberleys, in Wood County, of which I have before spoken, Mr. Eberly, a pioneer of the county, related to me the circumstances of the murder. Mr. Eberly's statement was substantially as follows:

"Sum-un-du-wat, daughter and her husband were murdered near Napoleon, in Henry County, by John Anderson and James Lyons, who lived near Portage, in Wood County. Anderson lived with me at the time. Sum-un-du-wat and party had been in our neighborhood for some days, and Anderson had tried to buy or trade for a favorite dog of the Indians, but without success. He made the declaration that he would have the dog before another week passed. He and Lyons followed the party to near Napoleon, where by the direction of one John Ellsworth, who resided about six miles west of Portage, they committed the bloody murder. They got all the money of which Sum-un-du-wat was possessed, which Snake-bone and other Chiefs, declared was about six hundred dollars; also, seven ponies, a lot of furs and dogs. They returned to the house of Lyons, a little west of Portage, where they concealed the ponies and all of the dogs, except the favorite one, which Anderson appropriated as his own, and although the dog was seen in his company, no one suspected that he had obtained it other than by fair means.

"In the excitement after the murder, one of the ponies escaped from the boys, and wandered to the camp of Snake-bone and his party. On being followed it returned to the place where the murdered Indians lay. The alarm was given, and Snake-bone and his party followed the trail to Portage, where they found and arrested Anderson and Lyons.

"The former was at church in the village. The Indians surrounded the building and captured him as he came out. The prisoners were conducted to Napoleon, where a preliminary examination was had, and the parties were commited to jail, but afterwards made their escape, and were never punished. At the trial, Anderson turned States evidence, and related the story of the murder. He stated that they stayed with the party three days before they met with a favorable opportunity to commit the hellish deed. When the Indians arrested Lyons, they found all the dogs belonging to them, under the floor of Lyon's house. The boys said that Ellsworth induced them to commit the murder, and after it was done, advised them to let him have the money until the excitement should pass over, and then they would divide. But the old scoundrel took the money and fled the country.

"Sum-un-du-wat was about sixty years of age. Snake-bone, in his endeavors to find the murders, wat three days and nights on the trail, and such were his exertions, that he broke down from their effects, and died shortly after."

It was thus that another crime was committed towards a people, who were as often a friend as an enemy. It was but another exhibition of that devilish disposition, possessed by some, to cruelly treat the weak and unprotected, to shield themselves behind a general feeling of hostility towards a people, and commit acts of persecution and murder even, on individuals, who are entitled to, and deserve the greatest consideration at their hands. No one could truthfully point to a single act of cruelty or hostility by Sum-un-du-wat towards any white man, on the contrary, he had been the friend of the whites, and had rendered them many valuable services.

CHAPTER XVI.

OUR ASSOCIATES IN THE GENERAL ASSEMBLY OF OHIO, IN SENATORIAL AND REPRESENTATIVE DISTRICTS.

THE reader will remember that from the organization of the county in 1820, preliminary only, until the time of its separate and independent organization in 1828, we were attached to, and for all municipal purposes were a part of Wood County. This being the fact, then in the name of Wood County, in the following list of Senators and Representatives up to 1828, will be included Hancock County.

The following table shows with what counties we have been connected, both in the election of State Senators and Representatives to the General Assembly of Ohio.

In 1821, the Senatorial District of which we were a part was composed of the counties of Champaign, Clark, Logan and Wood. Senator, James Cooley.

Representative District—The counties of Logan and Wood. Representative, John Shelby.

In 1823, Senatorial District—The counties of Logan, Clark and Wood. Senator, George Fethian.

Representative District—The counties of Logan and Wood. Representative, John Shelby.

In 1824, Senatorial District—The counties of Logan, Hardin and Wood. Senator, Robert Young.

Representative District—The counties of Logan, Hardin and Wood. Representative, John Shelby.

Senators and Representatives. 107

In 1825, Senatorial District—The counties of Miami, Shelby, Allen, Logan, Hardin and Wood. Senator, Robert Young.

Representative District—The counties of Logan, Hardin and Wood. Representative, John Shelby.

In 1826, Senatorial District—The counties of Miami, Shelby, Logan and Wood. Senator, Daniel M. Workman.

Representative District—The counties of Logan, Hardin and Wood. Representative, John Shelby.

In 1827, Senatorial District—The counties of Miami, Logan, Shelby and Wood. Senator, Daniel M. Workman.

Representative District—The counties of Logan and Wood. Representative, John Shelby,

In 1828, Senatorial District—The counties of Sandusky, Seneca, Wood and Hancock. Senator, David Campbell.

Representative District—The counties of Sandusky, Seneca, Wood and Hancock. Representative, Samuel M. Lockwood.

In 1829, Senatorial District—The counties of Sandusky, Seneca, Wood and Hancock. Senator, David Campbell.

Representative District—The counties of Sandusky, Seneca, Wood and Hancock. Representative, Samuel M. Lockwood.

In 1830, Senatorial District—The counties of Sandusky, Seneca, Wood and Hancock. Senator, David Campbell.

Representative District—The counties of Sandusky, Seneca, Wood and Hancock. Representative, Josiah Hedges.

In 1831, Senatorial District—The counties of Huron, Sandusky, Seneca, Wood and Hancock. Senator, S. M. Lockwood.

Representative District—The counties of Sandusky,

Seneca, Wood and Hancock. Representative, Henry J. Harmon.

In 1832, Senatorial District—The counties of Huron, Sandusky, Seneca, Wood and Hancock. Senator, Daniel J. Tilden.

Representative District—The counties of Seneca, Sandusky, Wood and Hancock. Representative, James L. Everett.

In 1833, Senatorial District—The counties of Huron, Sandusky, Seneca, Wood and Hancock. Senator, Daniel Tilden.

Representative District—The counties of Seneca, Sandusky, Wood and Hancock. Representative, James L. Everett.

In 1834, Senatorial District—The counties of Logan, Hardin, Hancock, Union and Madison. Senator, Samuel Newell.

Representative District—The counties of Sandusky, Seneca, Crawford and Hancock. Representative, James Hubbard.

In 1835, Senatorial District—The counties of Madison, Union, Logan, Hardin and Hancock. Senator, Samuel Newell.

Representative District—The counties of Seneca, Sandusky, Wood and Hancock. Representative, James Hubbard.

In 1836, Senatorial District—The counties of Madison, Union, Logan, Hardin and Hancock. Senator, Samuel Newell.

Representative District—The counties of Sandusky, Seneca, Wood and Hancock. Representative, W. B. Craighill.

Senators and Representatives.

In 1837, Senatorial District—The counties of Hancock, Lucas, Wood and Henry. Senator, John E. Hunt.

Representative District—The counties of Hancock, Seneca and Wood. Representative, W. B. Craighill.

In 1838, Senatorial District—The counties of Lucas, Wood, Henry, Hancock, Van Wert, Allen, Shelby and Hardin. Senator, Curtis Bates.

Representative District—Sandusky, Seneca and Hancock. Representative, Samuel Treat.

In 1839, Senatorial District—The counties of Lucas, Wood, Henry, Hancock, Van Wert, Allen, Shelby and Hardin. Senator, Curtis Bates.

Representative District—Seneca, Sandusky and Hancock. Representative, John Welsh.

In 1840, Senatorial District—The counties of Hancock, Wood, Lucas, Henry, Williams, Paulding, Putnam, Van Wert, Allen, Hardin and Shelby. Senator, John E. Hunt.

Representative District—Hancock, Sandusky Seneca, Wood and Ottowa. Representatives, Moses McAnnelly and Amos E. Wood.

In 1841, Senatorial District—The counties of Seneca, Sandusky, Wood, Ottawa and Hancock. Senator, John Goodin.

Representative District—Seneca, Wood, Hancock and Ottowa. Representatives, Amos E. Wood and George W. Baird.

In 1843, Senatorial District—The counties of Seneca, Sandusky, Wood, Ottawa and Hancock. Senator, Moses McAnnelly.

Representative District—Seneca, Sandusky, Hancock, Wood and Ottawa. Representatives, Wm. B. Craighill and Samuel Waggoner.

History of Hancock County.

In 1844, Senatorial District—The counties of Sandusky, Seneca, Hancock and Crawford. Senator, Amos E. Wood.

Representative District—Wood, Lucas, Hancock and Ottowa. Representative, Elijah Huntington.

In 1845, Senatorial District—The counties of Lucas, Wood, Hancock and Ottawa. Senator, Charles W. O'Neal.

Representative District—Hancock, Wood, Lucas and Ottowa. Representative, Lyman Parker.

In 1846, Senatorial District—The counties of Hancock, Lucas, Wood and Ottowa. Senator, Jesse Wheeler.

Representative District—Wood, Lucas, Hancock and Ottowa. Representative, John McMahan.

In 1847, Senatorial District—The counties of Hancock, Lucas, Wood and Ottowa. Senator, Jesse Wheeler.

Representative District—Wood, Lucas, Hancock and Ottowa. Representative, Emory D. Potter.

In 1848, Senatorial District—The counties of Lucas, Henry, Wood, Hancock, Sandusky and Ottowa. Senator, James Myers.

Representative District—Hancock and Wyandotte. Representative, M. C. Whiteley.

In 1849, Senatorial District—The counties of Seneca, Hancock and Wyandotte. Senator, Joel W. Wilson.

Representative District—Hancock and Wyandotte. Representative, M. C. Whiteley.

In 1850, Senatorial District—The counties of Seneca, Hancock and Wyandotte. Senator, Michael Brackley.

Representative District—Hancock and Wyandotte. Representative, Henry Bishop.

In 1852, Senatorial District—The counties of Hancock, Wood, Lucas, Putnam, Fulton and Henry. Senator, William Mungen.

Representative District—Hancock. Representative, Henry Bishop.

In 1854, Senatorial District—The counties of Hancock, Wood, Lucas, Fulton, Henry and Putnam. Senator, Samuel H. Steedman.

Representative District—Hancock. Representative, John F. Perkey.

In 1856, Senatorial District—The counties of Hancock, Wood, Lucas, Fulton, Henry and Putnam. Senator, W. S. Lunt.

Representative District—Hancock. Representative, Parlee Carlin.

In 1858, Senatorial District—The counties of Hancock, Wood, Lucas, Fulton, Henry and Putnam. Senator, Josiah N. Wescott.

Representative District—Hancock. Representative, John Wescott.

In 1860, Senatorial District—The counties of Hancock, Wood, Lucas, Putnam, Fulton and Henry. Senator, George Laskey.

Representative District—Hancock. Representative, John Wescott.

In 1862, Senatorial District—The counties of Hancock, Wood, Lucas, Fulton, Henry and Putnam. Senator, Charles M. Godfrey.

Representative District—Hancock. Representative, Wm. Gribben.

In 1864, Senatorial District—The counties of Lucas, Wood, Hancock, Fulton, Henry and Putnam. Senator, James C. Hall.

Representative District—Hancock. Representative, Parlee Carlin.

In 1866, Senatorial District—The counties of Putnam, Lucas, Hancock, Fulton, Henry and Wood. Senators, Parlee Carlin and James C. Hall.

Representative District—Hancock. Representative, Isaac Cusae.

In 1868, Senatorial District—The counties of Wood, Lucas, Hancock, Fulton, Henry and Putnam. Senators, James C. Hall and Abel M. Cory.

Representative District—Hancock. Representative, Isaac Cusae.

In 1870, Senatorial District—The counties of Fulton, Lucas, Wood, Hancock, Henry and Putnam. Senator, Abel M. Cory.

Representative District—Hancock. Representative, A. B. Shafer.

In 1872, Senatorial District—The counties of Putnam, Henry, Fulton, Lucas, Wood and Hancock. Senators, D. W. H. Howard and Hanks P. Gage.

Representative District—Hancock. Representative, Chas. Oesterlin.

In 1874, Senatorial District—The counties of Henry, Putnam, Hancock, Wood, Lucas and Fulton. Senators, E. D. Potter and W. A. Tressler.

Representative District—Hancock. Representative, Wm. M. McKinley.

In 1876, Senatorial District—The counties of Hancock, Wood, Lucas, Fulton, Henry and Putnam. Senators, Charles J. Swan and T. P. Brown.

Representative District—Hancock. Representative, Alex. Phillips.

In 1878, Senatorial District—The counties of Lucas,

Hancock, Wood, Putnam, Fulton and Henry. Senators, David Joy and James B. Steadman.

Representative District–Hancock. Representative, Henry Sheets.

In 1880, Senatorial District—The counties of Henry, Lucas, Fulton, Wood, Putnam and Hancock. Senator, W. A. Wilkins.

Representative District—Hancock. Representative, W. H. Wheeler.

I am indebted to Hon. W. H. Wheeler for nearly all of this chapter.

CHAPTER XVII.

MATTERS OF INTEREST, IN BRIEF PARAGRAPHS.

AT a session of the Court of Common Pleas, in and for the County of Wood—Hancock being then a part of said county—the court being held at Maumee, in 1820, "Wilson Vance was appointed Surveyor of Wood County."

At a session of the same court, held in May, 1822, "Wilson Vance was licensed to keep a tavern in Findley for one year. The court fixed the price at five dollars per annum."

At the October term, 1824, of said court, the following entry was made on the court records: "The Commissioners appointed to establish the seat of Justice in the County of Hancock, in the State of Ohio, report that they have selected the town of Findley, in said County of Hancock, as the most suitable site for the seat of Justice of said county, as per their report on file in the office of the Clerk of this Court."

This Commission was appointed under the provisions of the Act of the General Assembly, as follows:

"*Resolved*, By the General Assembly of the State of Ohio, that John Owens, of the County of Champaign, Alexander Long, of the County of Logan, Forest Meeker, of the County of Delaware, be and they are hereby appointed Commisioners, to locate and fix the seat of Justice, in and for the County of Hancock, February 2d, 1824."

I find this record under the date of January, 1825: "Fin-

First Marriages.

ley, January 11th, 1825. This is to certify, that on the second day of September, in the year 1824, Samuel Kepler, of Williams County, and Rachel McKinnis, of Hancock County, were legally joined in marriage by me, a Justice of the Peace, in and for the County of Hancock, and Township of Finley. Given under my hand,

WILSON VANCE, J. P."

This was, undoubtedly, the first marriage in the county. At all events, it is the first of record in both Hancock and Wood Counties. Mrs. Kepler, who was one of the parties in interest, is still living. Many of her relations are residents of this county.

It might be of interest in this connection to give the dates of some others of these old-time weddings—matters of quite as much importance at that day—simple as were the ceremonies, and plain as were the accompaniments, as are the gorgeous displays made on such occasions at the present day. But to the record:

May 4th, 1826, Jacob Moreland and Sarah Poe, by Robert McKinnis, J. P.

September 14th, 1826, Asa M. Lake and Charlotte Greer, by Joshua Hedges, J. P.

March 12th, 1827, William Moreland and Julia Chamberlain, by Joshua Hedges, J. P.

August 24th, 1827, Sampson Dildine and Sarah Highland, by Joshua Hedges, J. P.

November 1st, 1827, John Gardner and Susan Moreland, by William Hackney, J. P.

December 20th, 1827, Philip McKinnis and Susan Dukes, by Joshua Hedges, J. P.

When we are told that many of these parties went miles through the forests, traveling the narrow paths—for roads there were none—on horseback, bride and groom both on same horse—all alone perhaps, in search of the man of law, who was authorized to say the words, that would make them one (?) and that afterwards a home must be hewn out of the forests, and that life—even married life was real—we can easily imagine that there were no extended wedding tours, no idle honeymoons, no rounds of gaiety—except, perhaps, the country dance at the infare, as it was called. And yet they lived, and loved and prospered. They enjoyed life, always looking on the bright side.

"On the 4th day of June, 1832, Thomas F. Johnston, Auditor, resigned, and the Commissioners appointed Joseph C. Shannon to fill vacancy. Johnston, late Auditor, was allowed forty dollars for extra services."

At the session of the Commissioners held in December, 1831, they sold to Rev. Peter Monfest, lot number 105, (first lot east of Commercial House,) and lot number 148, (now owned by John L. Downing,) for forty-three dollars and twenty-five cents, payable on the first day of April 1832.

The Commissioners, at their December session, in 1834, appointed Parlee Carlin, Recorder of Hancock County, until the next annual election in October.

The records are silent as to the causes which made it necessary to appoint a Recorder.

The first case of contested elections, of which we have notice, in the records of the county, is the one indicated in the following notice, which seems to have been served on the Clerk of the Court:

"To the Clerk of Hancock County. You are requested to withhold the returns of the election of Union Township, wherein Wenman Wade was elected Justice of the Peace, and the election is contested, and said contest is to be tried on the 13th of September, 1838.

WM. ROLLER.
Associate Judge."

The Commissioners of Wood County, at their session in December, 1820, ordered that the "Road from Ft. Meigs, or the foot of the rapids of the Maumee of the Lake, to Bellefontaine, be opened."

And at their session March 4th, 1822, this order was made: "Ordered by the Board that the Township of Waynesfield, within the jurisdiction of the County of Wood, be co-extensive with the boundaries of Wood and Hancock, and to include the same."

June 6th, 1826, the Commissioners of Wood County, "Ordered that four hundred dollars of road fund be apportioned to Hancock County, to be expended on the Urbana road, in said county."

The first order for printing so far as the records show, was made at the December session, 1836, of the Commissioners, and reads thus: "Ordered that Jacob Rosenberg print sixteen hundred county orders, for sixteen dollars, in Hancock County orders, to be issued when the orders are struck."

It was also ordered at the same session, "That a warranty deed be made to Jacob Foster and Daniel Foster for in-lot No. 64; also, to William Taylor, for in-lots numbered 8 and 156."

It appearing that no record of land entries in the county had been kept in any of the county offices, and the County Commissioners believing such a record a necessity, we find in their proceedings, in 1839, this entry: "It was ordered that some suitable person go to each of the Land Offices in this Land Office District, and procure a duplicate of all lands entered in the county up to this date, with the names of the original enterers, the date of entry, the description, quantity, township and range, was ordered to be set up to the lowest bidder at public outcry. Whereupon, the same being cried in the presence of the Commissioners, it was cried off to Jacob Rosenberg, he being the lowest bidder, for the sum of thirty-nine dollars."

We find another order for county printing, this time, June 7th, 1842, and in this, as in the former one, the Commissioners fix the price. It was "Ordered that the Auditor of Hancock County, have the receipts and expenditures of said county, published in the Courier, providing he can get it done at the rate of $87\frac{1}{2}$ cents per square, in a condensed form, if not, have it posted up as the law directs."

We have about this time a recorded specimen of how easy, and how quickly, an officer may resign, when he makes up his mind so to do. That the officer in question was in earnest no one doubted, and his resignation was accepted. "To Aquilla Gilbert, George Shaw and Andrew Rickets, Commissioners of Hancock County, Gentlemen: I hereby resign to you my office of Auditor of Hancock County, Ohio. You will therefore now consider said office vacant from this moment.

Yours with respect,
W. L. HENDERSON."

As soon as the Commissioners could recover from their sudden surprise, and comprehend the full meaning of the letter, they proceeded at once not only to receive the resignation so suddenly thrust upon them, but also to fill the vacancy, which they did by appointing James H. Barr until the first day of March next ensuing.

Court House Bell.

The Commissioners, on the 3d day of March, 1846, authorized Frederick Henderson to procure a suitable bell for the Court House, the original cost of which should not exceed two hundred and fifty dollars, and have the same placed in the cupola of the Court House.

In July, 1830, the Commissioners "Ordered the sale of cutting out the road—Bellefontaine to Perrysburg, and Findley to Defiance—thirty-two feet wide. All timber twenty inches in circumference to cut out, and the ground to be cleared of all timber."

CHAPTER XVIII.

URDERS AND MURDER TRIALS.

ALTHOUGH no less than six men have been indicted and tried for the crime of murder, in some form or other, in this county, yet no one has ever been convicted of or suffered the extreme penalty of the law for murder in the first degree. In other words, no one has ever been legally hanged in Hancock County. Some of the cases seemed to be of the most aggravated kind, but by some defect in the law, or in the judgment of the jury, no verdict was ever rendered, calling for capital punishment. The county has now been organized for more than sixty years, and but six trials have been had for murder, three of which have occured within the last eight years.

In 1846, a horse was stolen in Hardin County, and the thief was pursued through this county, several persons here joining in the chase. Amongst them was John Parish, who resided in Williamstown, in this county. Parish was a powerfully built man, brave as a lion, and resolute in any undertaking. At Van Buren the thief was overtaken, and so hard pressed was he, that he left his horse and took to the fields, about a mile beyond that village. Parish at once dismounted and pursued him. Overtaking him in the field, he closed in with him, finally overpowering him. He then gave the signal for the others to approach, but while doing so, the thief pulled his revolver and shot him dead, and made his escape. Afterward a man who gave his name as Benjamin F. Dulin, was arrested, charged with being the murderer. After laying in jail for some months, he had a preliminary hearing before the Associate Judges of the Common Pleas Court. A large number of witnesses were present from Lake and Geagua Counties, in the interest of the prisoner, and he succeeded in proving an alibi and was discharged. It was, however, pretty generally believed that Dulin was the murderer. The prosecution was conducted by the late Abel F. Parker, who was then Prosecuting Attorney, assisted by Aaron H. Bigelow. The prisoner was defended by Judge M. C. Whiteley and Wm. M. Patterson. The real murder, if Dulin was not, was never known.

WILLIAM FOSTER.

At the November term of court, in 1856, William Foster, who lived in Jackson Township, was indicted for murder in the second degree, for the killing of his son, Andrew. The facts in the case, as related by Judge Whitely, who defended Foster at the trial, were about these: Foster was of weak mind, irritable, and easily influenced by others. He had married a second time, the mother of Andrew being dead. The boy was about fifteen years old, and he and his step-mother could not agree, and all misconduct, or supposed misconduct of the boy, was reported to his father, who became excited, and without inquiry, would punish the boy severely. It seemed that the boy was possessed of a morbid appetite, apparently, his hunger was never appeased. He would get up in the night, even, and seek food.

On one occasion, some food, which had been prepared the night before, was found to have been taken during the night. Its loss was charged to Andrew, and his father in a rage, made an assault upon him. The boy was afterwards found terribly bruised, and injured in loins and back. From these wounds he afterwards died, and his father was arrested, indicted and tried for the killing.

Judge Whitely says that it did not certainly appear on the trial, just who did inflict the wounds, as some evidence tended to show that the step-mother had also taken a part in the assault. At the April term, in 1856, the following jury were empannelled, before whom Foster was tried: Lower Walters, William Moffat, Peter Byal, Benjamin Dudley, Richard Wall, Samuel Ramsey, Hugh Boyles, Samuel Knowlen, Perry Edgington, John Boyles, Samuel Huffman, Eli Paxon. Verdict, *Manslaughter*. Sentence, five years in the Penitentiary at hard labor. After about two years service, Foster died.

The trial was conducted on the part of the State by William Gribben, Prosecuting Attorney, assisted by William Mungen, the defense by M. C. Whitely and Andrew Coffinberry.

In 1868, there lived in Findley, a man by the name of Adam Conkle, whose wife was not of the Mrs. Ceaser kind—above suspicion--and it was alleged that she had been frequently visited by one James Winnell, a young man employed about the offices in the court house, as copyist. He was almost a stranger, and but little known of him, other than that he was a dissipated rough.

These visits coming to the knowledge of Conkle, he warned Winnell not to come near his house, nor to hold any communication whatever with his wife, on penalty of being killed. Winnell, whilst on one of his sprees, in April, 1868, visited the residence of Conkle, who then resided in the frame building on east Main Cross street, adjoining the residence of James Robinson. Being apprised of his visit, Conkle immediately hurried home, and on ascending the stairs, found Winnell and his wife in a room together. He of course, highly excited, commanded Winnell to leave, who no doubt being afraid of bodily harm, seized a cavalry saber which chanced to be in the room, assaulted Conkle, drove him from the room, and made his escape down the stairway. Thereupon Conkle seized a loaded shotgun standing in the hal and gave pursuit. Winnell fled across the lot in the rear of the house, crossed into the alley known as Hyatt's Alley, down which he made his way towards Main street, hotly pursued by Conkle. When about two hundred feet east of Main street, Winnell being closely pressed, turned upon Conkle, with the saber which he still retained, when Conkle fired at him, the charge entering near the left temple, causing instant death.

Conkle gave himself up, and after a Coroner's inquest was held on the body of Winnell, had a preliminary hearing before E. T. Dunn, Esq., who held him to answer to the Grand Jury, in a bond of $1,500.

In October, 1868, the following named Grand Jury, to-wit: Isaac Davis, B. Finch, Job Phillips, Adam Roth, J. H. Wilson, Robert Crawford, Washington Martin, John Henry, L. C. Groves, John Reed, Henry Bowers, John Palmer, Eli Paxon, Samuel Creighton, and G. W. Galloway, returned a true bill of indictment for murder in the second degree.

The trial was had in November, 1868, before Judge James Pillars and the following jury: Aaron Cole, Jacob Groul, Jacob Thompson, Frederick Ernst, Samuel Mosier, Joseph Helms, Joseph Morrell, A. S. Beek, Henry Bayless, Jacob H. Loehr, Washington Eaton and Jacob Harris. The defense was that the prisoner, at the time of killing, was acting in self-defense, having been attacked by Winnell with a deadly weapon. Verdict of the jury, *not guilty.*

The prosecution was conducted by William H. Anderson, now of North Baltimore, who was then Prosecuting Attorney, assisted by A. B. Shafer. The defense was conducted by Henry Brown, J. F. Burket and A. Blockford, of Findley, and W. V. Layton, Wapakonetta. A great number of witnesses were examined, and the case was closely tried, but the verdict was generally regarded as a just one. Conkle left the county at once, and has been lost sight of. The woman in the case, also left, before the day of trial, and has never returned.

The town was shocked on the morning of Febrnary 3d, 1873, by the report that Jacob Gartee, a young man about twenty years of age, and whose parents resided in the town, had deliberately and in cold blood, murdered Nicholas Bensing, residing on the farm of M. D. Shafer, Esq., just east of town, on the Tiffin road. Sheriff Henry and Coroner Karst, accompanied by Marshal Ruhl, had already, during the night, been informed of the murder, it having occurred early in the evening of the 2d of February, and were on the spot, and before daylight of the 3d, had the murderer under arrest.

The facts, as they were afterwards developed, were substantially these: Gartee had been in the employof Bensing for some time, chopping wood, and boarded in the family. On the night of the murder, having armed himself with a single barreled pistol, he gave notice at the supper table, that he was going into town. Mrs. Bensing, the wife of the murdered man, gave him a letter to mail, and he started, but instead of going directly to town, he concealed himself in the log barn in which the chickens were kept, where by causing an alarm amongst the chickens, he induced Bensing to approach, to ascertain the cause, and when within a few feet of him, placed the pistol between the logs and fired, striking Bensing in the breast, who retreated a few steps, fell and expired just as his wife, who had been alarmed by the report, could reach him. Gartee then ran down the lane, and across the fields, to the Tiffin road, near the residence of Wm. Snyder, and thence to town.

After remaining in town a short time, he started to return to Bensing's, but was met on the road by a messenger, who informed him of Bensing's death, and a request that he return to town, and inform the friends of the murdered man. Gartee returned with the friends, and the officers having become convinced that Gartee was the murderer, boldly charged him with the crime, which he admitted, and pointed out the place where the pistol was secreted. He was immediately arrested and lodged in jail.

Ugly rumors were afloat that the wife of the murdered man, was perhaps, a party to the crime, and the fact that the prisoner and the murdered man were good friends, and had no quarrel, and there being no apparent cause for the commission of so cold blooded a murder, gave some color to the truth of these rumors. At the preliminary examination held before D. B. Beardsley, J. P., which was a most rigid one, so far as Mrs. Bensing was concerned, no evidence sustaining the theory of her guilt was found. Gartee was committed without bail, for the crime of murder.

On the 28th of May, 1873, the Grand Jury, to-wit: Geo. Heck, David Lee, William Howard, Alfred Davis, Adam Stineman, Jackson Currie, Simon Bushong, Anthony Huntington, Joseph Fleck, Elias Wilson, J. C. Brown, Eliab Hassan, A. J. Bushong and Henry D. Taylor, returned an indictment of murder in the first degree,

The case came up for trial, on a plea of not guilty, before Judge Pillars, and a jury as follows: William Hartman, Peter Hosler, Michael Glauner, David Bish, Alexander Phillips, J. L. Hartman, Jacob Bushong, Daniel Hoy, Charles S. Kelley, John Boyles, Henry Shuler and L. D. Smith. The trial began on the 29th day of July, and occupied about ten days. The plea for the defense was insanity. The prosecution was conducted by Prosecuting Attorney George F. Pendleton, and W. H. Anderson, and the prisoner was defended by Henry Brown and M. D. Shafer. Verdict of the jury, "Murder in the Second Degree." The prisoner was sentenced to the penitentiary for life, at which place he died in less than a year from the time of his sentence.

Orange Township, and all that part of the county, was thrown into a state of the wildest excitement, on account of the death by poison, of Mrs. Malissa Charles, wife of John Charles, on the 6th day of June, 1876. This excitement was intensified when it was known that Isaac B. Charles, a brother of the husband of the deceased, had been arrested, charged with the crime of murder. At the preliminary examination, before W. M. McKinley, Esq., as well as on the final trial, the circumstances connected with the case, were about as follows:

Mrs. Charles had made bread from flour purchased shortly before at Ada, O., and the family partaking of it, became suddenly sick, eleven of them in all, and Mrs. Charles died from its effects. The prosecution had two theories regarding the matter. One was, that the flour, after being purchased at Ada, had remained in the wagon standing in an alley, while the family were at dinner, and that whilst there, the sack had been opened by the prisoner, and poison introduced, which showed its presence in the bread.

The other theory was that the poison—arsenic—had been placed in the yeast crock at the house of the murdered woman, by Isaac B. Charles, whilst on a visit to the family, and that the poison had been obtained from a quantity purchased by John Charles, husband of the woman, for the purpose of killing rats, and left in the room where the yeast crock stood, which was a kind of up ground cellar.

The cause for the poisoning—for there appeared no apparent one—was said to be found in the fact that, Isaac B. Charles, having formerly been Treasurer of the village of Ada, and about to become a defaulter, made use of a large sum of money belonging to the estate of his father, of which estate he was the administrator, and now that a settlement was to be made, formed the plan of murdering, by poison or otherwise, all who stood between himself and the balance of his father's fortune, and that the poisoning of this family was but the first step in the plan.

An indictment for "Murder by Poison" was found on the 21st of October, 1876, by William Bright, Noah Spitler, S. M. F. Bâme, W. H. Todd, John Wyant, Augustus Hortzie, A. S. Beck, Isaac Cooper, S. B. Leonard, G. W. Ernst, William Russell, D. D. McCahon, Henry Rudisell, David Bibler and Hugh Fellers. After much delay, and the interposition of a number of motions, the case was finally tried in January, 1877, before Judge Pillars, and a Jury, on general plea of "Not Guilty." The Jury were Thomas H. Taylor, Hugh McConnell, Abraham Overholtz, Oliver Powell, John Haddox, William Anderson, Isaac Davis, E. C. Palmer, Frederick Mack, Joseph Wilson, John Reed and John

Cusae. Verdict, "Guilty of Murder in Second Degree." The prosecution was ably conducted by Henry Brown, Prosecuting Attorney assisted by Frank H. Dougherty, of Kenton, and W. H. Whitely, of Findley, and the defense was stubbornly made by A. Blackford, J. F. Basket and J. H. Smick, of Ada. Charles was sentenced to the Penitentiary for life, where he is now serving his sentence.

In 1877 there lived in the village of Benton, Henry K. Nott and Frank H. Knapp, both physicians, and both in practice. Unfortunately there had sprung up bad feelings between the two, the result, no doubt, of professional jealousy, and the over officious meddling by friends of both parties, and although a great amount of brave talk and loud boastings, as to what would be done, accompanied by ugly threats, yet no one could believe that much else than a war of words, or at the farthest, a little round at fisticuffs would be the result. Imagine the consternation which spread over the village, when the astounded inhabitants realized that Dr. Knapp had in broad day light shot Dr. Nott to death, in one of the streets of the village.

Dr. Knapp was at once arrested, taken before John Bergman, Esq., who at once remanded him to the jail of the county to await the action of the Grand Jury. Intense excitement prevailed, and the friends of the two unfortunate men took sides, and for a time society was so torn up, that almost everybody in the village, or who came to it, were regarded with suspicion by one side or the other. The killing was done on the 15th day of November, 1877, and the court being then in session, a special Grand Jury were duly impanneled on the 5th day of December, composed of William Anderson, D. J. Cory, Henry Byal, Moses Louthen, J. C. Garnett, Frank Karst, sr., B. F. Kimmens, William Mc-

Kinnis, Daniel Buck, Henry N. Cronninger, John Markel, Samuel Moyer, A. J. L. Hartman, Charles E. Jordan and Abraham Yerger, who returned a verdict of "Murder in the First degree."

Upon this indictment the defendant was tried on a plea of "Not Guilty," the defense being that the shooting was done in self-defense, claiming that the murdered man had made an assault on the defendant, just previous to the shooting, and that he had fired two shots at the defendant, intending to kill him, and that to save his own life the defendent did the shooting which killed Dr. Nott. This the prosecution denied, and alleged and sought to prove, that at the time of the shooting, and just previously thereto, there had been no quarrel, no meeting in fact between the parties, but that the defendant had gone to the lower end of the village, procured a gun, came back, sought out his victim, whom he found on a side street, approached him unperceived, and without notice, deliberately shot him, from the effects of which Dr. Nott immediately expired. Upon these declarations the cause was tried before a Jury, empanneled after all the motions and objections known in criminal practice were made and overruled, Judge Pillars presiding. The Jury were A. J. Nunamaker, James Stafford, George Biggs, G. W. Rinehart, A. C. Warden, Ephraim Leiber, William Vance, J. P. Lee, John Adams, H. H. Alban, David Comer and P. H. Powell. After a trial which lasted twelve days, and arguments covering three days more, the jury returned a verdict of *Not Guilty*. Prosecuting Atttorney Henry Brown and E. T. Dunn conducted the prosecution, and A. Blackford and M. D. Shafer managed the defense.

Such is the history of murders and murder trials in this county, and it is to be hoped that this will forever complete that history. In these cases, as in all others, there was of course a diversity of opinions as to the guilt or innocence of the parties, and the characters of the murdered men did not pass without severe criticism in some instances. The only regret of every good citizen is that the records of our otherwise fair county should be compelled to record such monster infractions of the law.

There were a few other indictments found for felonies of the kind treated of in this chapter, but parties were never put on trial under the indictments. In 1854, Philemon P. Pool was indicted for an assault with intent to kill. Samuel Ramsey was indicted for stabbing Nicholas Oram with intent to kill. Dr. R. J. Haggerty was indicted for the killing of Dr. Mansfield at Mt. Blanchard, and Levi Chain was indicted for the killing of his son Jerry at Findley, by stabbing him with a pocket knife. All these cases were disposed of on pleas for less offences.

CHAPTER XIX.

THE DEER-LICK—PLUM ORCHARD—JOHNNY APPLESEEDS.

ABOUT two and a half miles west of Findley, on the north side of the river, and on the farm now owned and occupied by Richard M. Watson, was a "Deer Lick," or spring, impregnated with salt, which was a favorite resort, as well for the timid deer, as for the roaming red man. To this spring the deer were attracted, and near it the hunter had erected his look-out high up in the trees upon which he would seat himself, and patiently wait for the appearance of the unsuspecting game, and the first intimation the doomed animal had of the presence of danger, was the crashing of a bullet through its brain.

Eight miles down the river from Findley, and on the north bank, is the "Plum-Orchard," or "Indian Green," and "Indian Burying-Ground." The timber was removed from a considerable tract of land, and there are still to be seen the remains of earth-works, running parallel with and a short distance from the river. They seem to have been thrown up as a protection against an attack by water, or by land from the opposite side of the river. In the rear of these fortifications, was the Indian burying-ground, flanked on the north by a heavy and dense forest.

The number of fruit trees found already growing in different parts of the county by the first settlers, was evidence of the visits of "Johnny Appleseeds," as he was familiarly called. This eccentric individual was regarded as a religious enthusiast, of the Swedenborgian persuasion, who acted as a kind of missionary amongst the Indians, and who, in his perambulations through the wilderness, planted the seeds of the different kinds of fruits, so that in many places in the county, there were fruit trees in great numbers, and some of them already producing fruit, at its first settlement.

The writer hereof remembers having seen "Johnny" in the year 1839 or 1840, perhaps the last time he ever visited the county. He was at that time quite an old man, and did not appear to have a very great quantity of this world's goods. He was regarded as an intelligent, harmless, but slightly demented man. At all times sociable, but eccentric, full of pleasant story, and good advice, after his fashion, he was always made welcome by the pioneers.

A short time since I read an article in the Cleveland Leader, by a correspondent at Mansfield, Ohio, in which allusion was made to this man, and whilst it seems to me, that it is a rather exaggerated account of his appearance, and peculiarities, I am tempted to re-produce it here, for I am sure that any incidents connected with the life and history, of this, to us almost unknown being, until he made his appearance here—or rather until the first settlers made their appearance, will be of interest to the older readers at least.

The writer of the article alluded to and which is entitled, 'Men of Function. The Notables who have made the city of Mansfield a stopping place," says: "There is still another character who assists in making Mansfield, and Richland County of some historical consequence. Years ago, among the forests in this neighborhood, tramped a half nude specimen of humanity, a regular "Old Mortality" in some respects, whom the straggling settlers knew as 'Johnny

Appleseeds.' Protected from the winter blasts, and summer storms, by nothing save a coffee sack, he traversed the whole of Central and Eastern Ohio, time and again, planting appleseeds as he went.

"He was first seen in Ohio in 1801, and with him an old blind horse, drawing in an aged and infirm wagon, a quantity of appleseeds. These seeds he planted in Eastern Ohio, along the banks of riveis snd creeks. Returning to Pennsylvania, Johnny disposed of his steed and equipments, and gathering up several bushels of seeds at the cider presses in Western Pennsylvania, he started for Ohio with them on his back. For years he kept on in the even tenor of his way, starting orchards all over this part of the state, but when emigrants from other states began to pour in and take up the land in Ohio, poor Johnny found his occupation gone, amd taking up his coffee sack, moved into Indiana, where he continued to plant appleseeds for some time, when death overtook him, and he was laid away in a country church yard, a few miles from Fort Wayne.

"His name was John Chapman, and it is thought he was born in Massachusetts. He was a regularly constituted minister in the Swedenborgian Church, and always carried with him several books on pious subjects, which he would leave with a settler whom he thought needed spiritual bracing up. During the coldest weather, he refused to wear shoes, and upon one occasion, when forced to accept a pair from a kind hearted farmer, he came to Mansfield, which was then but a small village, and gave them to a poor family, who were going west. When he first came to Ohio, he accepted the cast off clothing of the settlers, but afterwards became convinced he was getting too proud and worldly, and finally he adopted the coffee sack suit, in which he died.

"His head was protected from Old Sol's smiles, by a tin pan, which was also used as a culinary utensil, when he was overtaken by hunger in the woods. He believed it a sin to tread upon a worm, or eat flesh of any kind, hence he never took turkey on Thanksgiving, or fish during Lent. His wounds he would sew up with a red hot iron, and then apply the juice of certain weeds to cure the burns.

"His appletrees he sold to the settlers, and if they were, too poor to pay him, he would give them a receipt in full up to date. He was a small wiry man, with black eyes, and long unkempt hair and whiskers. He has left several monuments of his good deeds, in the shape of huge appletrees, near this city, which still continue to bear fruit and protect the weary and foot sore traveller from the scorching sun of summer."

After the advent of Johnny into our county, he dressed as other men, poor men, shoes and all, and I have never heard of his selling, or demanding a price for his appletrees.

Of this eccentric man, Henry Howe, in his valuable work, "Historical Collections of Ohio," says: "At an early day there was a very eccentric character, who frequently was in this region. His name was Jonathan Chapman, but he was usually known as 'Johnny Appleseeds.' He was supposed to be originally from New England, and had imbibed an uncontrolable passion for rearing and cultivating apple trees from the seed. He first made his appearance in western Pennsylvania, and from thence made his way into Ohio, keeping on the outskirts of the settlements. He planted his seeds in spots of cleared ground, and on the banks of the streams.

"When the settlers began to flock in and open up farms, Johnny was ready for them with his trees, which he either gave away, or sold for some trifle, as an old coat, or any other article of which he could make use. His personal appearance was as singular as his character. He was a small, chubbed man, quick and restless in his motions and conversation. He wore his hair and beard long, and had a sparkling black eye. He lived the roughest life, and often slept in the woods. He went barefooted, and often travelled miles through the snow in that way. In religious belief, he was a follower of Sweedenborg, leading a most blameless life. Wherever he went, he circulated Swedenborgian works. He was careful not to injure any animal, and thought hunting morally wrong.

"This story is told of him, as illustrating his kindness of heart. On one cool autumnal night, whilst lying by his camp fire in the woods, he observed that the musquitoes flew in the blaze and were burnt. Johnny thereupon brought water and quenched the fire, afterwards saying: 'God forbid that I should build a fire for my comfort, that should be the means of destroying any of His creatures.'

"At another time, he made his camp fire at the end of a hollow log, in which he intended to pass the night, but finding it occupied by a bear and her cubs, he removed his fire to the other end, and slept on the snow in the open air, rather than disturb the bear. (I think I would have done the same thing. Au.)

"An itinerant preacher was holding forth on the public square in Mansfield, and exclaimed: 'Where is the barefooted christian travelling to heaven?' Johnny, who was lying on his back on some timber, taking the question in its literal sense, raised his bare feet in the air, and shouted: 'Here he is!'"

CHAPTER XX.

PRESENT COURT HOUSE—NEW JAIL—INFIRMARY.

IN a former chapter I have spoken of the old frame Court House, and the old log Jail, which did good service in their time, but had to give way to more suitable buildings, and whatever of interest connected with them remains only as a memory. The fact that the county has built three jails and but two Court Houses, is perhaps not a very flattering commentary on the morals of the county, unless we remember that our people failed to put up substantial jails, a mistake which was not made in the building of a Court House.

As early as 1837 the project of building a new Court House was agitated, and in that year action was taken by the County Commissioners to its speedy erection. At their June session of that year it was "Resolved that the Commissioners of the county will borrow the sum of ten thousand dollars for the purpose of building Public Buildings in Findley." It was also at the same session "Ordered that the Auditor shall give notice in the Findley Courier, that proposals will be received on the 4th day of July next, at the Auditor's office in Findley, to make 200,000 good brick to build county buildings in Findley," and "Ordered that a draft or model shall be drawn of a Court House suitable for the county, at the expense of the county."

There is no record as to whom the contract for the building was let, or to whom let, or at what price, when to be finished, or how constructed. We can only guess at the time of the letting of the contract, and it must have been in the same year, or very early in 1838, as we shall presently see by the record. All agree, however, that the contract was let to John McCurdy, and that he was the builder.

At the meeting of the Commissioners in April, 1838, it was "Ordered that William Taylor receive the Surplus Revenue Fund from the Treasurer of said fund, and pay over the same to John McCurdy on the contract of the Court House, provided the interest be allowed until the first of June, 1838, for the amount so advanced."

The present Court House—the building of which was contracted for with the said John McCurdy, is of brick— then a wood roof—now metal—and surmounted by a wooden cupola, with spire and lightning rod. In front are four massive wooden columns, one either side of the rotunda or entrance, and one at each corner. The Court Room occupies the entire first floor except the rotunda and stair way, and the Sheriff's office, which are in front. This Court Room was originally finished in the plainest manner, with plain benches, plain platform for Judge's seat, and only benches for Jurors. It is now, however, made much more comfortable and convenient by successive additions, and improvements in furniture and interior arrangement.

The upper story is occupied by the different county officers, whose rooms are arranged on either side of a wide hall running the entire length of the building. The building stands in a park, which occupies an entire square on the west side of Main street, and the location is a commanding one. This structure answers the purpose for which it was built, but is sadly out of place as a representative of the wealth and public business of the county.

In December, 1838, the Commissioners "Ordered that Jacob Barnel, Esq., be and he is hereby appointed to receive funds from the fund Commissioners of the county, to pay over the same to John McCurdy, on the contract entered into by the County Commissioners with John McCurdy, for building the Court House."

In December, 1839, the Auditor of the county was "Ordered to procure all the receipts of John McCurdy given for monies received by him, and file the same in his office, and open an account with the said McCurdy in a book to be procured by him for that purpose. Also to ascertain the amount due him, and exhibit the same to the Board at its next session."

At the same meeting it was "Ordered that John McCurdy put, construct, erect and finish a partition wall up stairs, or in the upper story of the said Court House, across the present hall with a door therein, so as to cut off any communication with the Jury room." No tampering with the jury was intended to be possible.

In 1841 the Auditor was ordered to employ some suitaable person to make one dozen chairs for the use of the Court House, and benches for the jury rooms.

It seems that there was some trouble, or at least delay in the completion of the building, for in June, 1841, it was "Ordered that if the Court House in Findley is not finished by the 15th of August next, the Auditor put the bonds in the hands of Edson Goit, Esq., to commence suit thereon." And in July, 1842, it still being unfinished, it was "Ordered that the Auditor will have suit brought against John McCurdy, by the first of September next, providing the contract for finishing the Court House should not be completed by that time."

Present Court House.

In June, 1843, the Sheriff was directed to be careful and not have the Court House abused by public gatherings and Justice's Courts. So great were the differences between the Commissioners and McCurdy, and so impossible of amicable adjustment, that the matters in dispute were submitted to arbitration, and at an extra session in July, 1843, we find the Commissioners directing the Auditor to enter upon the journal the amount of arbitration in the case of John McCurdy vs. the Commissioners.

In March, 1846, it was "Ordered by the Commissioners that Frederick Henderson be, and he is hereby authorized to procure for said county, as soon as practicable, a suitable bell for the Court House, the cost of which shall not exceed two hundred and fifty dollars." The bell was procured and put in place.

It is impossible to tell from the records the cost of the buildings, and it is a matter of recollection only fo those who remember the incidents connected with it. Elijah Barnel, Esq., who was Auditor of the county for two terms, and who is perhaps as well informed in the matter as any man now living, says that the building cost about eleven thousand dollars.

Thus, through much contention and many disappointments, and not a few threatenings of law suits, was the building completed, and occupied by the several county officers, with a feeling that we had about as magnificent a county building as could be found anywhere.

JAILS.

Feeling the necessity of a secure place for prisoners the Commissioners in December, 1851, ordered "That the Auditor cause a notice to be published in the two papers published in Findley, to receive sealed proposals for building a jail in said county. Said jail to be let on the 9th day of January, 1852." At that date the contract was let to Thomas McCrary for the sum of four thousand seven hundred and forty-three dollars.

The contract was entered into January 15th, 1852, and the building completed the same year. It was built on Lot No. 58, on the west side of the Park. The structure was of brick and stone, so put together, that it was thought to be impossible for any one to escape, and yet, in later years especially, it seemed no trouble for those inside to make their escape.

But this, too, has been superseded by the present magnificent building on corner Main, Cross street and the Park. This edifice includes Sheriff's residence, a two story brick, with basement, finely ornamented with stone, and tastefully finished on the interior, in the rear of which are the cells, entirely of stone and iron, and constructed in the most secure manner. The whole premises are a credit to the county, and were erected at a cost of something over twenty-five thousand dollars. The lot on which the building stands cost $5,000, the contract for the building was let for $17,264, and to this must be added the cost of grading, fencing, etc.

The necessity of the county making some provision for the care of the poor, other than letting each township look after its own, and have them distributed throughout the county at a great expense, had long been acknowledged, and the propriety of purchasing lands and erecting thereon suitable buildings for an Infirmary, had been pretty generally discussed, especially in those townships in which the care of the poor had become burdensome. Accordingly the Commissioners ordered that the question of building an Infirmary should be submitted to the voters of the county

County Infirmary.

at the April election in 1867. This was done and the following is the vote for and against, in each township:

Township		For		Against
Washington Township,	For	151.	Against,	26.
Big Lick	"	51.	"	41.
Amanda	"	21.	"	95.
Delaware	"	86.	"	43.
Jackson	"	126.	"	16.
Marion	"	164.	"	0.
Cass	"	78.	"	15.
Allen	"	20.	"	90.
Portage	"	147.	"	7.
Liberty	"	33.	"	81.
Findley	"	712.	"	5.
Eagle	"	19.	"	119.
Madison	"	104.	"	2.
Van Buren	"	1.	"	72.
Orange	"	156.	"	6.
Union	"	139.	"	8.
Blanchard	"	91.	"	16.
Pleasant	"	202.	"	4.

The proposition having carried by a large majority, the Commissioners thereupon caused the following notice to be published in both the county papers for one week. "Citizens living from three to eight miles from the county-seat, and wishing to sell their lands for this purpose, will send their proposals to the Auditor within due time."

In May, 1867, they purchased the present farm of Geo. Heck, paying therefor the sum of seventeen thousand, one hundred dollars. The farm is in Liberty township, bordering on the east line of the township, and on the south side of the river, about two and a half miles from Findley as the road goes. It is a most beautiful location, being on quite an eminence, overlooking the river and the splendid farms on the opposite side. The land is very fertile and yields most abundant crops.

In March, 1868, the Commissioners contracted with John Shull, a builder and contractor, for the erection of a suitable building. The building is of brick, four stories high, including basement, which is eight feet in heighth, the first story eleven feet in the clear, and the other stories ten' feet each. All covered with a metal roof. The contract price for the building was $12,393.

Our county has an Infirmary which will favorably compare with any in the State, and its management has always been in the interests of the county, and the comfort of the unfortunate inmates.

CHAPTER XXI.

EARLY SPORTS — CORN HUSKINGS — HOUSE RAISINGS — GRAIN THRESHING AND CLEANING.

EVERY pioneer was of necessity a hunter. Not that he followed the business for amusement alone, but for the reason that much of his subsistence, and his safety, and that of his property depended upon his skill and vigilance with the rifle. Hence it was, that almost every man and boy, and a great many women and girls were accomplished shots, and many a leisure hour did they while away in friendly competition with their trusty rifles, and proud was the champion of his laurels thus honorably won.

Not the least pleasant of the gatherings of these early settlers, were the corn huskings. Sometimes the corn was husked just as it had been cut and shocked in the field. At other times it was all gathered at one place, either on a fine grass plot, or on the barn floor. It was usually divided into equal parts, and the husking party was also divided under captains. The company who first completed the task was declared the victor.

If these husking bees were in the barn, the women and children would frequently assist. These husking bees were usually held when the moon was at its full, so that there would be sufficient light.

In the mean time the women-folk of the party were engaged in cooking and preparing supper for all. And such suppers! None of your ice cream—strawberry—jelly cake—weak tea affairs, but instead, the yellow corn cake, juicy venison, luscious turkey, and occasionally a slice or two of bear steak.

So popular was this sport—for in that light was it regarded—that not unfrequently an entire crop of corn was husked in one night, and without any expense to the owner, other than the furnishing supper for the workmen, for which he considered himself amply repaid in the amount of fun which he would have.

Another source of pleasure, although mixed with hard work, was the house-raisings. In this, as in log rollings and corn huskings, the participants were divided into companies, each under the lead of a captain. To each was assigned the raising of one side and one end of the cabin. Each of these parties chose two of the most active and expert ax-men to carry up the corners, as the logs were raised to the proper place.

A good deal of skill, and a mechanical eye was required by these corner men, as a very slight mistake in making a notch too shallow, or too deep, or out of a straight line, might loose the whole corner. So expert became many of these men—and they were found in every settlement—that they were enabled to notch and place the logs almost as rapidly as they could be raised to their place on the building.

The grain was not threshed by machinery driven by steam, as now, but was either beaten out by the old fashioned swingle or flail, or tramped out by horses or oxen. When threshed it was separated from the chaff by a fanning mill made of two men and a linen sheet, the grain being slowly poured from a measure at an elevation, passed in front of this mill, which was kept constantly in motion; the chaff was blown away, the grain falling to the floor. A rather slow, but sure way of getting clean grain, and resorted to by the early settlers for the reason that modern fanning mills were then unknown.

The men did not have all the sport, no more than they did all the work. Quilting bees were no less a source of pleasure and enjoyment to their wives. All the good dames in a neighborhood would assemble around the patch-work quilt, and with stitch and gossip while away the time pleasantly, and around the well-laden tea table rehearse the scenes of their girl-hood days.

Strong, active, athletic sports had a great charm for these backwoodsmen. Running foot races, jumping, wrestling, pitching quoits or horse shoes, lifting weights, and like manly exercise best pleased them. Some of their feats of jumping and racing would do credit to a troup of modern athletes. And the ease with which they could "ring the meg" with a horse shoe at twenty-five or thirty yards was astonishing. With such exercises as these, their muscles became hardened, their limbs were developed, and their endurance put to the test.

Horse racing was also a favorite amusement with some. The swiftness of a race was not regarded as of much moment, the simple fact that two horses would make a race, no matter how slow it was, would be sufficient to draw a crowd, and the pleasure in the amusement seemed to be just as keen, as if they had been witnessing some of the feats of modern high-flyers.

Because of the isolated condition of the settlements, and the almost unceasing toil of all, any social gathering was hailed with pleasure, and enjoyed to the fullest extent.

CHAPTER XXII.

OUR JUDICIAL ASSOCIATE COUNTIES AN JUDDGES.

IN 1830, the Judicial Circuit to which we belonged, was composed of the counties of Huron, Richland, Delaware, Sandusky, Seneca, Crawford, Wood, Marion, Hancock Henry, Williams, Putnam, Paulding and Van Wert. Ebenezer Lane was the Circuit Judge, but having just been elected to the Supreme Bench of the State, was succeeded by David Higgins.

Knapp, in his "History of the Maumee Valley," says that Judge Higgins, in his "Memoirs of the Maumee Valley," relates the incident of a voyage from Findley to Perrysburg, by way of Defiance, in the good "Piroque Jurisprudence." "A countryman," says the Judge, "agreed to take our horses to Perrysburg by land. We purchased a canoe, and taking with us our saddles, bridles and baggage, proposed to descend the Blanchard Fork, and the Auglaize Rivers to Defiance, and then to Perrysburg. Our company consisted of Rudolphus Dickenson, J. C. Spink, Count Coffinberry, myself and a country man, whose name I forget. The voyage was a dismal one to Defiance, through an unsettled wilderness of some sixty miles. Its loneliness was only broken by the intervening Indian settlements at Ottawa, where we were cheered lustily by the Tohwa Indians, as would be a foreign ship at New York."

The General Assembly of Ohio, in 1838-39, by enactment, created the Thirteenth Judicial Circuit. This embraced ten counties, but out of that territory the counties of Defiance, Auglaize and Fulton, have since been erected. These ten counties were Seneca, Wood, Henry, Williams, Paulding, Putnam, Van Wert, Allen, Hardin and Hancock.

Judge Higgins was succeeded in the old Circuit by Ozias Bowen. But Emery D. Potter was elected Presiding Judge, and held the office until 1844, when he resigned to take his seat in Congress, He was succeeded as Judge by Myron H. Tilden.

Judge Potter still resides in Toledo, and but a few years ago represented the District of which we are a part, in the Ohio state Senate.

On the 19th of February, 1845, the 16th Judicial Circuit was formed, embracing the counties of Shelby, Mercer, Allen, Hardin, Hancock, Putnam, Paulding, Van Wert and Williams, and Patrick G. Goode, of Sidney, was elected Presiding Judge. This was the last of the Circuit Judges.

Under the Constitution of 1851, the counties of Wood, Seneca, Hancock, Wyandotte and Crawford formed a sub-division of the Second District, and Lawrence W. Hall, of Bucyrus, was elected Common Pleas Judge. After one term of five years, he was succeeded by Machias C. Whitely, of Findley. Judge Whitely was re-elected in 1861, the sub-division then being the counties of Wood, Hancock and Putnam. In 1856, Seneca having been placed in the sub-division, George E. Seeney, of Tiffin, was elected an additional Judge.

In December, 1866, Hancock, Seneca and Wood being joined in one sub-division, Chester R. Mott, of Upper Sandusky, was elected Judge, and served one term. In 1868,

James Pillars, of Tiffin, was elected, and in 1871, Crawford and Marion Counties having been added to the District, Abner M. Jackson, of Bucyrus, was elected an additional Judge, but after serving a short time, he resigned, and Thomas Beer, also of Bucyrus, was elected to fill vacancy. At the expiration of Judge Pillars' term, Henry H. Dodge, of Perrysburg, (present incumbent,) succeeded him, and in 1879, Hardin County having been attached to this District, John McCauley, of Tiffin, was elected an additional Judge.

A brief sketch of these men, or some of them at least, although not residents of the county, will perhaps be appropriate here, as they were actors in the early history of our county.

Hon. Emery D. Potter is said to have been the first lawyer who opened an office in Toledo, and that he is the last of his early professional contemporaries, and is yet a citizen of Toledo.

He was born in Providence County, Rhode Island, the son of a farmer in limited circumstances. At the age of two years, Judge Potter was taken by his parents to Otsego County, New York, then a wilderness. Mr. Potter entered the office of Hon. John A. Dix and Abner Cook, jr., at Cooperstown. After having completed an academic education, and there diligently pursued the study of the law, until he was admitted to practice in the Supreme Court of the State.

In the fall of 1835, he emigrated to Toledo, a place as he then thought, opening a good field for a young practitioner. After a successful practice of four years, he was, in February, 1839, elected Presiding Judge of the Thirteenth Judicial Circuit.

Judge Goode.

In 1843 he was nominated and elected to Congress by a handsome majority. In 1847 he was elected to a seat in the Ohio House of Representatives. In 1848 he was again elected to Congress. In 1875, Mr. Potter was elected to the Ohio Senate from the Thirty-third Senatorial District.

In 1845, Patrick G. Goode, of Sidney, was elected Presiding Judge of the Sixteenth Judicial Circuit. Judge Goode was an honest, upright man, an impartial Judge and a christian gentleman. He was very punctilious in the preservation of the dignity of the court, and the courtesies of the bar. Pettifogging and undignified conduct, and vulgar language were his horrors. After holding court all day, he would not unfrequently preach at night, as he was a minister in the Methodist Episcopal Church.

It is told of Judge Goode, that while holding court in Mercer County, in 1847, he met a juryman who was rather too smart for him. A case had been tried, and just a few minutes before the regular dinner time, had been given to the jury, and the court had adjourned until after dinner. Within a few minutes, one of the jurymen, Cyrenius Elliott by name, entered the room at the hotel, where the Judge was seated. The Judge was surprised, and exclaimed: "What are you doing here? Have the jury agreed?" "Jury agreed," hissed Elliott, "you must be a simpleton to ask the question. You must understand, Pat Goode, that I don't believe much in the divine right of Kings, or in the infallibility of courts, when run by such men as yourself. Your right way would have been to let us have our dinner before sending us to the jury-room, knowing as you must, if you have good sense, that jurors have stomachs and bowels as well as judges and lawyers."

At another time the Judge was holding court in Findley,

when the late John H. Morrison opened an address to the jury, with this declaration: "May it please the court, by the perjury of witnesses, the ignorance of the jury, and the corruption of the court, I expect to be beaten in this case." The Judge turned to the counsel and inquired: "What is that you say, Mr. Morrison?" The latter replied: "That is all I have to say on that point," and proceeded with his argument.

At another time, a man of bad repute, made application to the court for license. The court considered the proposition, and Judge Goode announced that the application was refused. Mr. Morrison, much excited, arose and addressed one of the Associate Judges: "Judge Ewing, is that your decision?" An affirmative answer was given. "Judge Price do you concur in this decision?" "Yes." Morrison was about to put the same question to the other associate, when Judge Goode inquired: "Mr. Morrison, what are you doing?" Morrison replied, "Why, I am polling the court, your honor."

I have these reminiscences from H. S. Knapp's History of the Maumee Valley, a very valuable work.

CHAPTER XXIII.

HANCOCK COUNTY IN THE WAR.

THE part which the gallant volunteers of Hancock County took in the war for the suppression of the Rebellion, deserves a much more extensive notice than I am able to write, or for which there would be sufficient space in this work. I shall, therefore, have to content myself by giving a brief account of the brave boys, assuring my readers that no better soldiers were found, than the boys from Hancock. They went cheerfully wherever duty called them. They never flinched under fire. They never retreated unless ordered to do so. They endured all the hardships of marching, fighting, and of rebel prisons, and more than five hundred of them laid down their lives without a murmur, that the country might live. Loyal, patriotic, they left father, mother, wife, children, all that was dear to them on earth, all that makes life pleasant, and went forth at the call of danger, and for four long weary years, endured the hardships of one of the most stupendous wars on record: went forth, some to die in battle, some to die in hospitals, some to die in rebel prisons, others to come home, with a leg or an arm missing, maimed for life, others with wounds rendering them almost helpless, others with ruined health, broken constitutions, to linger on for a few years, and at last sink into a premature grave. Such is the fate of those who engage in war. Such was the fate of many of the gallant boys who went from Hancock, and whose memory is enshrined in the hearts of the people.

A whole volume might be written commemorative of their many deeds. Such a volume should be written. In this work, however, I can only speak of organizations and aggregates. And even in this brief sketch I will no doubt overlook some, for many of our boys went elsewhere and enlisted, or being temporarily absent from the county at the breaking out of the rebellion, enlisted at the first opportunity, without first returning home. Of such of course I can not speak only in general terms.

21ST OHIO VOLUNTEERS.

In the three months service, this county furnished three full companies of men, under Capt. Jome Wilson, Capt. Geo. F. Walker, and Capt. K. Henry Lovell. The company under command of Capt. Wilson was further officered by 1st Lieut. D. M. Stoughton, and 2d Lieut. Geo. Foreman. That under command of Capt. Walker had as 1st and 2d Lieuts., M. D. Shafer and J. E. Stearns. And that under Capt. Lovell had as Lieuts., Joshua S. Preble and J. J. Thrap. The late Col. J. M. Neibling was Lieut. Col. This regiment was organized at Camp Taylor, near Cleveland, on the 27th day of April, 1861.

The service of the regiment was in West Virginia, under Gen. J. D. Cox. They were engaged in the fight at Ripley, and also at Scary Creek. The companies from this county did not loose a man in any of the engagements. On the way home to be mustered out, Eli S. Reed, Quarter Master of the Regiment, died at Cincinnati. The Regiment was mustered out August 12, 1861, at Columbus, Ohio.

On the 19th of September it was again re-organized for

three years, and went into camp at Findley, Ohio, where it was mustered into service. In this service J. M. Neibling was again appointed Lieut. Col., but in December, 1862, he was promoted to the Colonelcy, which position he held until his discharge, by reason of losing his right arm at New Hope Church, on the 28th of May, 1864. In the three years service, Hancock County had four Companies. Co. A, Capt. D. M. Stoughton, who was promoted to Major, and in December, 1863, was promoted to Lieut. Col., which position he held at the time of his death, in November, 1864, from wounds received at the battle of Chickamauga. Co. B, Capt. Geo. F. Walker, who was afterwards promoted to Major. Co. E, Capt. Isaac Cusae, who was promoted to Major, and mustered out with the Regiment at the close of the war. Co. F, Capt. H. H. Alban, who was honorably discharged at the close of the war. The Lieutenants of Co. A were J. A. Williams and Geo. Foreman; of Co. B, Wm. Vance and Joseph E. Sternes; of Co. E, James Porter and Simon B. Webber, and of Co. F, John C. Martin and Alex. A. Monroe.

During the time this Regiment was in the field, a great number of its members were promoted to Captains and Lieutenants. It bore the name of "Fighting Regiment," having been engaged in as many, and as severe battles, as was any other Regiment in the service. This Regiment accompanied Sherman on his celebrated march to the sea, and was present at the "Grand Review" in Washington City, May 26, 1865, and was mustered out of service at Louisville, Ky., and finally paid off and discharged at Columbus, Ohio, July 28, 1865. This Regiment made a record during the war, for bravery, good discipline, and persistent fighting, of which the members are justly proud.

There were perhaps, from the organization of this Regiment for three years service, until discharged, in the four companies from this county, not less than six hundred men.

31ST OHIO INFANTRY.

This Regiment was commanded by Col. M. B. Walker from its organization until the muster out at the close of the war. Col. Walker volunteered from this county, and took with him in the service quite a number of Hancock county boys. This Regiment made a good record, was with Sherman to the sea, was at the Grand Review at Washington, was mustered out at Louisville, Ky., and paid and discharged at Columbus, Ohio. I have no means of knowing the exact number of Hancock boys in this Regiment, but there were perhaps not more than thirty.

49TH OHIO INFANTRY.

This was Gen. W. H. Gibson's Regiment, he being its first Colonel, and was organized at Tiffin, O. In this Regiment Hancock County had one Company, under command of Capt. A. Longworthy, and Lieuts. S. F. Gray and J. W. Davidson. Lieut. Gray was afterwards successively promoted to Captain, Major, and Lieut. Colonel, and was, I believe, in command of the Regiment at muster out. This Regiment did as much marching, was in as many engagements, and suffered as many hardships, as any in the service in the South-west. Their gallant Colonel was ever ready by word and act to make them comfortable, and always led in an engagement. His loyalty, patriotism and eloquence seemed to inspire the men, and they were under his leadership willing to undertake any expedition.

They suffered incredible hardships in their winter march, to the relief of Burnside at Knoxville. Almost naked,

Hancock County War Record. 155

without shoes, and rations exhausted, the brave fellows did not grumble. On their return from this expedition they were called upon to re-enlist, and right nobly did they respond. Many of the Hancock boys won and received promotion.

On the 13th of July, 1865, this Regiment was ordered to Texas, where they suffered the hardships of a campaign of four months, after nearly all the other troops were discharged. The Regiment was mustered out of service Nov. 30th, 1865.

The whole number of men on the rolls of this Regiment was fifteen hundred and fifty-two. Eight officers were killed in battle and twenty wounded, (six of them mortally.) Of the privates one hundred and twenty-seven were killed in battle, seventy-one were mortally wounded, one hundred and sixty-five died from hardship and disease, and seven in rebel prisons. Six hundred and sixteen were discharged on account of wounds or other disability. Of these Hancock furnished her full proportion. There were perhaps not less than two hundred men from this county in the 49th, and every boy who survives, is proud that he was a member of this famous Regiment.

57TH OHIO INFANTRY.

This Regiment was organized at Camp Vance, at Findley, Ohio, in September 1861. Co. B was made up of men from Hancock and Seneca Counties. Co. F and Co. G from Hancock, and Co. H from Hancock and Seneca. Wm. Mungen, of Findley, was first Colonel. Dr. W. D. Carlin was Surgeon, James Wilson was Capt. of Co. F, John B. May of Co. G. By promotions Hiram E. Henderson, John W. Wheeler, Daniel Gilbert, Squire Johnson and George

Trichler became Captains, and Squire Johnson was promoted to Major. The Lieutenants from this county at the formation of the Regiment were Co. B, Daniel S. Price; Co. F, H. E. Henderson and John Adams; of Co. G, Edmund W. Firmin; of Co. H, John W. Wheeler; of Co. I, Daniel Gilbert, and of Co. C, Oliver Mungen.

This Regiment very soon after its organization, and before it had become accustomed to camp life, marching, or military tactics, was to join the army of the Tennessee. Going immediately into a different climate, exposed to hardships, it suffered terribly from sickness, and on the 6th of April, 1862, less than six months from the time it broke camp at Findley, only four hundred and fifty men were fit for duty. From the time the Fifty-seventh shelled the rebel works at Chickason, Alabama, in April, 1862, until they were finally discharged, they were almost continually in the front, and took part in the skirmishing and fighting in these four dreadful years. At Pittsburg Landing, at Corinth, at Hamburg, at Pea Ridge, at Camps Six and Seven, at the Russell House, at Morning Sun, at Wolf Creek, at Chickason Bayou, at Arkansas Post, at Clay Plantation, at Haine's Bluff, at Raymond, at Champion Hills, at Vicksburg, at Mission Ridge, and at numerous other engagements, it was always in the van, and received the first fire of the rebels. In all these places the Regiment behaved well, and did herself great credit.

The boys from Hancock were amongst the bravest of the Regiment, and are proud of the achievements of the old Fifty-Seventh. This Regiment was discharged and paid off at Camp Chase, O., on the 25th of August, 1865. The Fifty-Seventh travelled by railroad, steamboat, and on foot, more than twenty-eight thousand miles, and of the one

Hancock County War Record. 157

thousand five hundred and ninety-four men on the muster rolls, there were only four hundred and eight-one alive at the muster out. In all there were perhaps five hundred men from this county in the Fifty-Seventh.

65TH OHIO INFANTRY.

This Regiment was in what was called Sherman Brigade, raised at Mansfield. Joshua S. Preble, of McComb, was Captain of Co. H, and in his company were quite a number of men from this county. The Hancock boys of course acquitted themselves as become true soldiers, in the many engagements in which they participated, from their first fight at Pittsburg Landing, under Gen. Garfield, until the final battle at Nashville. They were ordered to Texas in June, 1865, and did garrison duty at San Antonio until December 1865. They were then ordered to Columbus, O., to be mustered out, and paid, being perhaps the last Ohio Volunteers to be discharged.

87TH OHIO INFANTRY.

This was one of the three months regiments, and Hancock had one company therein, under the command of Capt. Sam. Huber and Lieuts. Philip Ford and Christopher Keasy. The Rev. Geo. D. Oviatt, of Findley, was Chaplain. On the 12th of June, 1862, the Regiment had orders to repair to Baltimore, at which place they were assigned to a camp under command of Col. Banning. In July they had orders to report to Col. Miles at Harper's Ferry. At the siege of that place by Jackson's men, they were surrendered to him, although their term of enlistment had expired. They were however immediately paroled, and returned home and were mustered out at Columbus, on the 20th of September, 1862.

99TH OHIO INFANTRY.

Of this Regiment, Co. C, Capt. O. P. Capell, and Lieuts. C. G. Barnel and Robert B. Drake, and Co. F, Capt. J. A. Bope, and Lieuts. James Harsh and W. C. Kelley, were from Hancock. Albert Longworthy was the 1st Colonel, and Dr. J. T. Woods was Surgeon. This Regiment left Camp Lima August 31st, 1862, with an aggregate of one thousand and twenty-one men, under orders to report at Lexington, Ky. Severe marching and hot weather occassioned so much sickness, that when the Regiment moved forward to take part in the battle of Stone River, only three hundred and sixty-nine men, two field officers, seven line, and three staff officers were fit for duty. In courage and discipline this Regiment was not found wanting, as their acts at Rocky Face Ridge, Kenesaw Mountain, Pine Mountain, Atlanta, Jonesboro, Lovejoy, and many other engagements, demonstrated. During almost the entire Atlanta campaign they were under fire daily. At Nashville it was consolidated with the Fiftieth Ohio, forming one Regiment. The men were mustered out at Salsbury, N. C., and discharged and paid at Camp Dennison, O., July 17th, 1865. Hancock furnished perhaps three hundred men in all for this Regiment.

118TH OHIO INFANTRY.

This Regiment went into camp at Lima, in August 1862. Co. H was from Hancock, and was officered by Capt. Samuel Howard and Lieuts. Darius Pendleton and M. B. Patterson. In September, only eight companies being then full, it was ordered to Cincinnati to assist in repelling the threatened invasion of Kirby Smith. Here the ninth company joined it, and the Regiment was mustered in. Their first engagement was at Mossy Creek, where after a desperate charge, the rebels under Generals Martin and Armstrong, were driven back with a loss to the One Hundred and Eighteenth, of forty killed and wounded.

Whilst in East Tennessee, the Regiment subsisted for six months on quarter and half rations, and endured great privation. On the afternoon of the 14th of May, 1864, they participated in a charge on the enemy's works at Reseca, and out of three hundred men actually engaged lost one hundred and sixteen in less than ten minutes. Such was some of the desperate fighting of this Regiment, and it was continued at Dalton, Pumpkin Vine Creek, Kenesaw Mountain, and at Atlanta. Such was the fatality in this Regiment, that at no time after June 1st, did it number over two hundred and fifty men, and at one time it was reduced to one hundred and twenty.

During one hundred and twenty-one days they were within hearing of hostile firing every day but one, and for sixty consecutive days it was under fire, sixty different times. About one hundred and fifty of Hancock's brave boys participated in the fortunes of this gallant Regiment.

133D OHIO INFANTRY. N. G.

In this Regiment of one hundred-day men, this county had a company under the command of Capt. James Walternire and Lieuts. Jacob Romich and Jefferson Darrah. This Regiment did duty around Washington City, and at Bermudae Hundred. Whilst at work on the fortifications at Fort Powhattan, it was so very unhealthy that over three hundred of this Regiment were on the sick list at one time.

134TH OHIO INFANTRY. N. G.

A company of men from this county belonged to this

Regiment, and were under the command of Capt. Miles Wilson. The Regiment was ordered to Cumberland, Va., May 7th, 1864, and from there proceeded to White House, on the Pamunky, by way of Washington City, but before dis-embarking at White House, were ordered to City Point. On June 17th, they had an engagement with the enemy at Fort Walthall, during the assault on Petersburg, and the men displayed great courage under fire. For seventy days this Regiment formed a portion of the advanced line operating on Richmond. The Regiment was mustered out at Camp Chase, August 31st, 1861.

161ST OHIO INFANTRY. N. G.

One company from Hancock County, under command of Capt. Geo. Foreman and Lieut. H. B. Green, was a part of this Regiment, which was mustered into service at Camp Chase, May 9, 1864, and was immediately ordered to Cumberland, Md. The operations of this Regiment were confined to the Shenandoah Valley. Five companies of this Regiment made a march from Lynchburg to Webster, in charge of sick, prisoners, and wagon and ambulance train, a distance of nearly five hundred miles. At Maryland Heights, they were engaged two days in a lively skirmish with the enemy. On the 2d of September, 1864, the Regiment was mustered out at Camp Chase.

192D OHIO INFANTRY.

This Regiment was organized at Camp Chase, and one company from this county, under command of Capt. Moses Louthan, formed a part. They started for the field in March, 1865. They marched through Charleston, Va., and under orders on the 3d of April, they moved before daylight to relieve a Regiment picketing the Shenandoah River.

Hancock County War Record. 161

This was accomplished by noon of that day, without loss. This Regiment was stationed for some time at Stevenson Station and Jordon Springs.

This Regiment was in high favor for its very excellent drill, and discipline. They were paid off and discharged on the 6th of September, at Columbus.

12TH OHIO CAVALRY.

This Regiment was recruited in September and October, 1863, and went into camp at Cleveland. During the winter of 1863-64 one half of the Regiment did guard duty on Johnson's Island. This county had one company in this organization, with Capt. A. A. Monroe and Lieut. E. N. Flaiseg. This Regiment did duty in Tennessee and North Carolina, and aided in the capture of Jeff Davis. They were discharged at Columbus, in November, 1865.

1ST OHIO HEAVY ARTILLERY.

This Regiment was joined with the 117th Ohio Infantry, and on the 2d day of May, 1863, the Regiment (117th) was ordered to be changed into the First Heavy Artillery. The Artillery Regiment was then recruited up to the full maximum of twelve companies, with an aggregate of eighteen hundred and thirty nine men, including officers. The principal field of operations of this Regiment was in East Tennessee, and they took part in nearly all the battles in that section. They were in almost constant action against the guerrillas under Vaughn and Debrill. Our county had one company in the Artillery commanded by Capt. Joshua S. Preble and Lieuts. Ebenezer Wilson and John Foreman.

INDEPENDENT SHARP SHOOTERS.

Capt. Campbell Dougherty, and Lieuts. James Waltemire and James Cox, joined this organization with a company of

Hancock County boys. This company ("H") was in the following engagements and skirmishs: Tuscumbia Bridge, Danville, Miss., Blackland, Rienzi, Jumpertown, Miss., Hatchie River, Booneville and Whitesides Farm. They also took part in the Atlanta campaign, in the Sixteenth Army Corps, of McPherson's Army.

In this campaign they were engaged in no less than thirty encounters with the enemy, between the 8th of May and the 5th of September, 1864. They were with Sherman in his march to the sea, and were paid off and discharged at Camp Dennison.

In addition to the several commands already named, our county was represented in many other organizations, not only of this, but of other States. A few of our patriotic colored citizens went into the Fifty-Fourth and Fifty-Fifth Mass. Colored Regiments. Every branch of the service had representatives from Hancock. Every grade of soldier, from the humble private in the ranks, who did the marching and fighting, to the Brigadier General, who did the planning and commanding, had her full share of representation by our boys. It is estimated that not less than two thousand as brave, as loyal men, as ever went forth to defend their county, marched out of old Hancock at the signal of danger, and that more than one-third of that number laid down their lives on the altar of their country—died that their country might live. Hancock County is justly proud of her war record, justly proud of her noble sons who went forth to battle for right, and she jealously cherishes the memory of her fallen braves, whose deeds are recorded in their hearts. May their example ever keep alive a burning love of country in the hearts of the living.

I have thus briefly, and imperfectly, given a statement of

ours in the war, a history that ought to be written, and when written, the recital of the gallantry, the patriotism, the sufferings, the achievements, the heroism, of our brave men in that four dreadful years, would fill a volume. If, in my sketch I have overlooked any who should have been mentioned, or have did injustice to any one, my excuse is ignorance of the matter, together with want of time and space to do the subject justice.

CHAPTER XXIV.

HANCOCK COUNTY AGRICULTURAL SOCIETY.

ON the 30th day of August, 1851, a number of the farmers and other friends of agriculture, met at the Court House in Findley, having for their object the organization of an Agricultural Society. Aaron Hall, Esq., now a resident of Michigan, but for many years an active member and officer of the Society, was chosen President, and Robert Coulter, Secretary. Little else, however, was done at this meeting, other than to discuss the propriety of such an organization, and to adjourn until the first Saturday in October following.

At the meeting in October Judge Strother presided, and Henry Brown acted as Secretary. A constitution was adopted and officers elected as follows: President, Judge John Cooper; Vice President, Judge R. L. Strother; Secretary, William Taylor; Treasurer, Judge D. J. Cory, and John Dukes, Aaron Hall, Wm. Yates, Henry Lamb, John Moore, John Lafferty and Alex. Phillips, a Board of Managers.

Amongst the names of members recorded at that meeting, in addition to those already named, are these of Hiram Cox, A. P. Byal, Jesse Ford, Edson Goit, Elijah Barnel, James Elsea, Wm. Mungen, Samuel Howard, Chas. Oesterlin, Abner Leonard, Samuel Kemble, Allen Wisely, S. R. Gray, J. H. Wilson, S. Carlin and Aaron Baker.

The Society held its first *Fair* on the 15th day of Octo-

Hancock County Agricultural Society. 165

ber, 1852, on rented grounds, north of the river, on what is now known as Bruner's brick yard. Mr. Henry Brown, as Secretary, says in his report, "That the attendance was very large," The premiums awarded amounted to *ninety-nine dollars and twelve cents*.

In 1858 the idea of purchasing, or permanently leasing grounds on which to hold the annual exhibitions of the Society, was broached at a meeting of the members of the Board, and Dr. Oesterlin, I. N. Teatsorth, W. C. Cox and R. S. Mungen were appointed a committee to " view sites, and receive proposals for the purchase or lease of grounds on which to hold Fairs, and to report to the Board of Officers the result of their labors, at their next meeting, for their action thereon."

At that same meeting officers were elected as follows: Israel Green, President; A. P. Byal, Vice President; S. F. Gray, Secretary; A. M. Hollabough, Treasurer; and A. W. Strother, E. Karn, William Vance, William Martin, A. Leonard, A. F. Parker, Aaron Hall, John Moore, Daniel Alspoch, David Fox, Baker Hales and A. Hodge, Managers.

On the 9th day of February, 1868, the Board met and accepted the proposition of J. H. Wilson for the sale of eight acres of land adjoining East Findley, at one hundred dollars per acre, payable in three annual payments.

The interest and attendance at the Fairs of the Society so increased that it became necessary to look around for more extensive grounds, to accommodate the patrons of the Society.

Accordingly at a meeting of the Board in October, 1867, G. W. Galloway, John Markel and C. L. Turley were appointed a committee to receive bids for the sale of the old Fair Grounds and to report at the next meeting.

In July, 1868, the whole matter was referred to A. W. Frederick, John Markel and C. L. Turley. The old grounds were sold to Samuel Hoxter, and the Society purchased of Timothy Russell twenty and one half acres of ground just south of town, to which was afterwards added five acres, purchased of John Powell. Mr. Galloway was appointed to superintend the improvements of the grounds.

The Society now owns twenty-five and one half acres of ground, in a most beautiful location, which with the improvements, are worth at least *ten thousand dollars*, and their annual exhibitions are surpassed by none in the State.

The present officers are A. P. Byal, President; Ezra Karn, Vice President; Henry Greer, Treasurer; D. B. Beardsley, Secretary; and David Downing, Chester Cook, Isaac N. Teatsorth, Rufus R. Hartman, James M. Van Horn, George Wilson, John Cusae, Isaac W. Marshall, John M. Moreland and Jackson Robbins, Managers.

County Officers. 167

CHAPTER XXV.

COUNTY OFFICERS.

NAMES of officers of the county since 1828, with the date of election or appointment of same:

Date.	Sheriff.	Clerk.	Auditor.	Recorder.
1828	Don Alonzo Hamlin.	Wilson Vance.	Mathew Reighley.	W. Vance.
1829			Wm. Hackney.	
1830	John C. Wickham.		Thos. F. Johnson.	
1832	Joseph Johnson.		Jos. C. Shannon.	
1834	Christian Barnel.			
1835			Edson Goit. (app.)	
1836		W. H. Baldwin	C. W. O'Neal.	
1838	Jacob Rosenberg.		W. L. Henderson.	J. Barnel.
1842	Elisha Brown.	W. Henderson	Jas. H. Barr.	
1844	Alonzo D. Wing.		Jas. S. Ballentine.	Jno. Adams
1846	Absalom P. Byal.		Wm. Mungen.	
1847				Paul Sours.
1848	Thomas Buckley.	A. P. Byal.		
1850	James Robinson.		Elijah Barnd.	
1853				I J Baldwin
1454	Wm. M. Yates.	W. W. Siddall.	Henry Brown.	
1855	D. D. McCahan, (act)			
1856	J. M. Neibling.		Aaron Howard.	
1859				A Stineman
1860	C. B. Wilson.		Henry Sheets.	
1863		Jas. Dennison.		
1864	D. D. McCahan.		Solomon Shafer.	
1865				L. Robinson
1867	A. Yerger. (act.)			
1868	Samuel Myers.	Peter Pifer.	John L. Hill.	
1871				P. Kemerer.
1872	J. L. Henry.			
1873			G. S. Mosher.	
1874	Samuel Myers.			
1875		S. W. Preble.		
1876	Parlee C. Tritch.			
1877			Jos. R. Kagey,	J Gutzinler.
1878		H.H.Louthon.		
1880	C. B. Hall.		Jos. R. Kagey.	J Gutzinler.
1881		H.H.Louthon.		

History of Hancock County.

Date.	Prosecutor.	Commissioner.	Treasurer.	Surveyor.
1828	Anthony Cusad.	John Long.	Edwin S. Jones.	Wm. Taylor.
		J. P. Hamilton.		
		C. McKinnis.		
1830		M. Hammond.	Squire Carlin.	W L Henderson
1831		R. L. Strother.		
1832	Edson Goit.			
1833		John Rose.		
1834		John Byal.		
		Jno. L. Carson.		
1835		Wm. Taylor.		
		Darius Smith.		
1837		Aquilla Gilbert.		
1838	Jacob Barnd.	Dan'l Fairchild.	Edson Goit.	Joel Pendleton.
1839		George Shaw.		
1841	Jude Hall.	Andrew Rickets.		
1842	A. F. Parker.		Levi Taylor.	
1843		Peter George.		
1844	W. M. Patterson.	John Lafferty.	Wilson Vance.	
1845		Wm. Taylor.		
1846	A. F. Parker.		Mahlon Morris.	
1847		W. W. Hughes.		
1848		Thomas Kelly.		
1849		Elias Cole.	L. Taylor. (app.)	
1850	John E. Rosette.		Sam'l Howard.	
1853		Jacob Bushong.		
1854	Wm. Gribben.	Wm. Davis.	Benj. Huber.	G. W. Powell.
1855		John EcKinley.		
1857				Joel Pendleton.
1858	Edson Goit.	John Graham.	Wm. Vanlue.	
1859	J. A. Bape.	Isaac Cusac.		
1861	H. Brown. (app)	J Bushong.(app)		
1862		John Cooper.	Benj. Huber.	
1863		Wm. Taylor.		
1864		D. W. Engle.	Sam'l Spitler.	
1867	W. H. Anderson			
1868		W. M. Marshall.	H. B. Wall.	
1869		Sam'l Creighton		
1870		Jos. Saltzman.		
1871	G. F. Pendleton		H. Sheets. (app.)	
1872		J. D. Bishop.	Benj. Huber.	
1874		Jno. Edgington.	Peter Hosler.	
1875	Henry Brown.			Edwin Phifer.
1876		R. W. Moore.		
1878		Louis Luneack.	Sam'l Howard.	
1879	A. B. Shafer.	R. W. Moore.		
1880		B. B. Powell.		
1881	A. B. Shafer.	A. S. Beck.		

PROBATE JUDGES.—James H. Barr, Nathaniel E. Childs, James H. Barr, Alfred W. Frederick, Gamaliel C. Barnel, Samuel B. Huffman, Sylvester J. Siddall.

STATISTICAL TABLES.

TABLE showing the number of school houses in each township, and their value, together with the value of school house sites, as far as could be ascertained.

Townships.	No.	Value of Lands.	Value of Buildings.	Total.
Allen.	7	$129	$6140	$6266
Amanda.	8	240	3100	3340
Big Lick.	10	129	4150	4279
Blanchard.	10	185	5275	5460
Cass.	6	120	2950	3070
Delaware.	7	185	3015	3200
Mt. Blanchard.	1	300	3600	3900
Eagle.	9		2400	2400
Findley.	7	360	2400	2460
Borough.	4	3800	41400	45200
Jackson.	8		6400	6400
Liberty.	8	240	1560	1800
Madison.	8	350	3110	3460
Marion.	6	50	2900	2950
Orange.	9	189	4900	5089
Portage.	6	100	2440	2540
Pleasant.	8		2255	2255
Union.	10	260	8600	8860
Van Buren.	6		2150	2150
Washington.	10		4300	4300
Fostoria.	1			15000
Totals.	149	$3637	$112045	$136382

History of Hancock County.

Table showing the No. of acres of land and value, and value of town lots.

Township.	Acres of Plow land	Acres Meadow&pas're.	Unsettled and Wood land.	Total Acres.	Value.
Allen.	7712	1673	5894	15280	$390056
Van Buren.					1345
Amanda.	10078	2885	4787	17750	509582
Vanlue.					7260
Big Lick.	7999	5996	9038	23033	633433
W. Independence.					2600
Blanchard.	13108	2207	7559	22874	617834
Benton.					9060
Cass.	6089	2470	6809	15368	452078
Delaware.	8406	4579	7197	20182	482340
Mt. Blanchard.					9640
Eagle.	10108	4461	8023	22592	560310
Findley.	6630	3304	3765	13999	669040
Borough.					492190
Jackson.	7744	4294	6775	18813	448504
Houcktown.					1690
Martinstown.					480
Liberty.	8812	1191	4985	14978	428270
Madison.	5707	2854	6522	15083	334920
Arlington.					3280
Williamstown.					1230
Marion.	6822	3595	4921	15338	443821
Orange.	6658	6215	10058	22951	494751
Portage.	6625	2646	6174	15443	386575
Pleasant.	8173	1867	13138	23178	444297
McComb.					13650
Union.	10650	3934	7626	22210	527782
Cannonsburg.					560
Rawson.					2925
Mt. Cory.					2774
Van Buren.	6450	2809	6120	15379	355970
Washington.	11156	4413	6919	22488	741390
Arcadia.					6360
Fostoria.					29320

Value of Buildings.

Table showing value of buildings in each town and township:

Township.	Value of Houses.	Value of Mills.	Other Buildings.	Total.
Allen.	$28662	$2200	$23656	$54418
Van Buren.	5220		1535	6755
Amanda.	25800	1800	19570	47170
Vanlue.	23900	6500	3400	33800
Big Lick.	34856		22644	57500
West Independence.	5850	600	9156	15606
Blanchard.	31266	1206	15986	48452
Benton.	7780		1400	9180
Cass.	33727	1400	20132	55259
Delaware.	24630	2800	17800	45230
Mt. Blanchard.	11080	3000	26520	40600
Eagle.	28090	1520	20730	50340
Findley.	67240	4900	30850	102990
Borough.	399110	13300	20900	430310
Jackson.	23842	800	20595	45237
Martinstown.	150		200	350
Houcktown.	4090		575	4665
Liberty.	26200	3100	17600	46900
Madison.	14660	500	10140	25300
Arlington.	1890			1890
Williamstown.	1210	300	120	1630
Marion.	26350	1200	21400	48950
Orange.	29708	273	15575	45556
Portage.	33940	600	21650	56290
Pleasant.	30876	3582	18124	52582
McComb.	21510	2500	1060	25070
Union.	31000	2000	17904	50904
Cannonsburg.	1855	400	250	2505
Rawson.	5995	700		6695
Mt. Cory.	5512		800	6312
Van Buren.	27150	1150	30760	59060
Washington.	79310	2900	31060	113270
Arcadia.	18280	4000	2320	24600
Fostoria.	29780	1400	2250	33430

Table showing number and value of churches in the county, with the value of lands thereto belonging so far as could be ascertained.

Township.	No.	Value of Lands.	Value of Buildings.	Total value.
Allen.	5	$149	$2850	$2999
Amanda.	8	210	5000	5200
Big Lick.	9	345	5600	5945
Blanchard.	6	105	4750	4855
Cass.	2	50	4000	4050
Delaware.	7		5400	5400
Eagle.	5		1750	1750
Findley.	2	60	400	460
Borough.	10	8200	63500	71700
Jackson.	7		6850	6850
Liberty.	4	80	1600	1680
Madison.	3	200	780	980
Marion.	4	44	3100	3144
Orange.	7	76	3800	3876
Portage.	3	34	1800	1834
Pleasant.	3	30	770	800
Union.	11	228	10050	10278
Van Buren.				1740
Washington.	7		8400	8400

Table of Distances. 173

Table of distances of towns and Post offices in the county.

	Arlington.	Arcadia.	Benton.	Cannonsburg.	Cory.	Deweyville.	Findley.	Hassan.	McComb.	Mt. Blanchard.	North Liberty.	Oak Ridge.	Portage Centre.	Rawson.	Van Buren.	Vanlue.	West Fostoria.	West Independence.	Williamstown.
Arlington.	0																		
Arcadia.	17	0																	
Benton. 1	11	17	0																
Cannonsburg	7	20	6	0															
Cory. 2	9	21	5	2	0														
Deweyville.	18	18	9	15	14	0													
Findley.	10	9	8	11	12	11	0												
Hassan.*	8	24	11	5	20	15	6½	0											
McComb.	16	15	7½	12	13	3	9	18	0										
MtBlanchard	5	15	14	12	21	22	11	13	19	0									
N. Liberty. 3	9	13	12	10	12	18	8	12	16	3½	0								
Oak Ridge.*	14	15	4	10	9	5	8	15	3½	17	14	0							
Portage Cen*	18	12	8½	14	13	5	7	19	3	18	12	5	0						
Rawson.	8½	18	3½	3	3	12	9	7½	10	13	10	7	11	0					
Van Buren.	17	7½	12	17	17	10	7	21	8	17	14	9	5	14	0				
Vanlue.	15	10	17	16	18	21	10	18	19	7	6½	17	17	16	14	0			
W. Fostoria.	22	6	10	26	26	21	15	29	18	20	18	20	17	24	12	13	0		
WIndepen'ce	17	5	19	21	22	21	11	24	18	14	12	18	16	20	12	7	6	0	
Williamstown	4½	21	15	15	11	23	14	7½	22	7	8	18	22	12	21	14	27	20	0

* Post offices.   1. Post office, Benton Ridge.   2. Post office, Mt. Cory.   3. Post office, Houcktown.

HISTORY OF TOWNSHIPS AND TOWNS.

HAVING completed a brief history of the county, I propose to briefly notice the individual organization of the several townships, and characteristics of the several towns. Of course these sketches are incomplete as a full history, and convey only a faint idea of the beginnings of each. But they will serve to somewhat enlighten the attentive reader as to the time and manner, and by whom these several organizations were effected, and of their present condition. All, I presume are interested in any and every thing which pertains to the history of each township, as well as of the general history of the county, and the rise and progress of the several towns, will help to form a correct opinion of our present status. The younger portion of my readers are perhaps in ignorance as to who were the real pioneers of the several parts of the county, and also as to the location even, of the different townships. In these sketches, I have endeavored to give them information on both these subjects. The extent, population and statistics of each is given, and of the towns the different business interests are noted, as well as the churches and schools.

This part of the history of the county will then be of peculiar interest, to the several localities described, as they speak of matters which have come under the personal observation of many who are still living.

LAND SURVEYS.

Land descriptions, as recited in deeds of conveyance, are but imperfectly understood by many, and to some are simply riddles, not easily guessed. In order that they may be comprehended by all, and easily understood, wherever found, I venture a brief explanation.

In order to make correct surveys and locate lands prior to the settlement of the State, or of the formation of counties, or townships, or of the sub-division of townships into sections, the General Government found it necessary to have a certain and fixed point from which townships and ranges should be counted.

The Ohio Survey, to which we belong, was made in 1819 and 1820, after the fixing by the Government of the *first principal Meridian*, as it was called, which meridian commenced at the mouth of the Great Miami River, and running thence north on the line between the States of Ohio and Indiana, to the Michigan line. A line was also established, running east and west on the 49th Parallel of Latitude, and called the base line. This base line runs directly through the center of this county, dividing it into two equal parts, north and south.

Townships were numbered north and south from this base line; those bordering on the line were called township number one—north or south—number two coming next, and so on. The Ranges, which included a township in width, or exactly six miles, were numbered from the principal meridian east, beginning with number one, at the Indiana line, and numbering east. Hancock County is in Ranges nine, ten, eleven and twelve.

You will remember that the act organizing the county of Hancock, provided that it should comprise "townships one and two north, and one and two south, in ranges nine, ten, eleven and twelve, east of the first principal meridian." That is to say, that townships one and two north, and one and two south of the base line, and in range nine, ten, eleven and twelve east of the Indiana line should constitute the county. As these ranges are just six miles wide, the number of the range being given, it is easy to determine the exact distance from the Indiana line east. For example, the first range in Hancock County is number nine, then to the west line of the county there would be eight full ranges, or exactly forty-eight miles from the Indiana line to the west line of the county. The townships being just six miles long north and south, their number determines their distance from the base line.

These townships, in their original form, are just six miles square, and any change in the boundary of an original township, does not effect the range, hence we have in this county some townships which include parts of two ranges. Nor would a change in the boundary of an original township change its number either north or south from the base line. To repeat then, the first row of townships running north and south along the first meridian, or Indiana line, is called Range one east, the second row, Range two, etc., and the first row of the townships on the west side of this county is in Range nine, the second in Range ten, the third in Range eleven, and the fourth in Range twelve. The first row of townships north of the base line, running east and west, are numbered one north, the second row number two north. The first row of townships south of base line is numbered one south, and the second row number two south.

Land Surveys. 177

These townships are divided into sections of one mile square, and numbered from one to thirty-six. The numbers always beginning with number one in the north-east corner of the township, thence west to the line, and then back on the next row of sections, and so on. These sections were divided into halves and quarters. A section comprises six hundred and forty acres, a half section, three hundred and twenty, and a quarter, one hundred and sixty acres. Bearing in mind what has been said, there would be no difficulty in determining the location of the surveys, even though the name of the township was not given.

The rule of the Land Department of the General Government prohibited the Deputy Surveyor, who fixed the boundaries of the townships, from sub-dividing the same into sections. This was done in order that any errors might be detected in the surveys, and to prevent fraud in measurements. The following exhibit will give the dates of the surveys of the townships, and also of the sub-divisions, and by whom made. These surveys are given as they are recorded in the Secretary of State's Office at Columbus, O.

Township one (1) south, Range nine (9) east.—Union. Survey commenced May 23, 1819, by Sylvanus Bourne, D. S. Sub-divided into sections June 4, 1819, by John Collett, D. S.

Township two (2) south, Range nine (9) east.—Orange. Survey commenced May 27, 1819, by Sylvanus Bourne. Sub-divided into sections June 5, 1819, by John Collett.

Township one (1) south, Range ten (10) east.—Eagle. Survey commenced May 8, 1819, by James Holmes, per Alex. Holmes. Sub-divided into sections Aug. 14, 1819, by John Collett.

Township two (2) south, Range ten (10) east—Van Buren

and west half of Madison. Survey commenced May 29, 1819, by Alex. Holmes. Sub-divided into sections July 3, 1819, by John Collett.

Township one (1) south, Range eleven (11) east.—Jackson and west one mile of Amanda. Survey commenced May 31, 1819, by Alex. Holmes. Sub-divided into sections Aug. 17, 1819, by John Collett.

Township two (2) south, Range eleven (11) east.—East end of Madison and a portion of Delaware. Survey commenced June 1, 1819, by Alex. Holmes. Sub-division completed July, 1819, by John Collett.

Township one (1) south, Range twelve (12) east.—Amanda. Survey commenced June 2, 1819, by Alex. Holmes. Sub-division completed Dec. 5, 1819, by Sylvanus Bourne.

This sub-division did not include the Reserve, which was sub-divided in Sept., 1832, by C. W. Christmas.

Township two (2) south, Range twelve (12) east.—Delaware. Survey commenced June 2, 1819, by Alex. Holmes. Sub-division completed Aug. 14, 1819, by Sylvanus Bourne.

Township one (1) north, Range nine (9) east.—Blanchard. Survey commenced May 22, 1819, by Sylvanus Bourne. Sub-division completed Dec. 29, 1820, by J. Wampler.

Township two (2) north, Range nine (9) east.—Pleasant. Survey commenced Oct. 17, 1819, by Samuel Holmes. Sub-division completed Dec. 7, 1820, by J. Wampler.

Township one (1) north, Range ten (10) east.—Liberty and west half of Findley. Survey commenced May, 22, 1819, by Sylvanus Bourne. Sub-division completed Nov. 1820, by J. Wampler.

Township two (2) north, Range ten (10) east.—Portage and west half of Allen. Survey commenced Oct. 15, 1819, by Samuel Holmes. Sub-division completed Dec. 15, 1820, by J. Wampler.

Township one (1) north, Range eleven (11) east.—Marion and east half of Findley. Survey commenced May 24, 1819, by Sylvanus Bourne. Sub-division completed Nov. 6, 1820, by J. Wampler.

Township two (2) north, Range eleven (11) east.—Cass and east half of Allen. Survey commenced Oct. 14, 1819, by Samuel Holmes. Sub-division completed Dec. 23, 1820, by J. Wampler.

Township one (1) north, Range twelve (12) east.—Big Lick. Survey commenced May 24, 1819, by Sylvanus Bourne. Sub-division completed—except Big Spring Reservation—Sept. 21, 1820, by John Glasgow. Big Spring Reservation completed Sept. 22, 1832, by C. W. Christmas.

Township two (2) north, Range twelve (12) east.—Washington. Survey commenced Oct. 28, 1819, by Alex. Holmes. Sub-division completed Oct., 1820, by John Glasgow.

ALLEN TOWNSHIP.

T. 2, N. R. 10 E.   T. 2, N. R. 11 E.
AREA 15,360 ACRES.   POPULATION 1,025.

This township is on the northern line of the county, and was the last township organized in the county. It was formed of territory taken from the townships of Cass and Portage.

On the 3d day of June, 1850, the Commissioners of the county, "Ordered that a new township be erected of the following territory, and called Allen Township. Said territory of Allen to be composed of Sections 5, 6, 7, 8, 17, 18, 19, 20, 29, 30, 31, 32, of township two (Cass) north, Range eleven east, and Sections 1, 2, 11, 12, 13, 14, 23, 24, 25, 26, 35 and 36 in township two (Portage) north, Range ten east.

"Ordered that there be legal notice posted up in the new township of Allen, for the election of the following named officers for said township, to-wit: Three Trustees, one Clerk, one Treasurer and one Assessor."

This township was named in honor of Ethan Allen, of Revolutionary fame, and is bounded north by Wood County, east by Cass Township, south by Findley, and west by Portage Township. The Bellefontaine and Perrysburg State Road runs directly through its centre, north and south.

The first entry of land, in this township, was made on the 25th day of August, 1826, by John Gardner, and was the

First Land Entries.

west half of the north east quarter of section 13. On the 1st day of June, 1829, Nathan Frakes entered the west half of the south-east quarter of section 12, the farm now owned by Sam'l Spitler.

In December, 1828, Major Bright entered the east half of the south-west quarter section 36, and a year later, George C. Collins, of Hamilton County, entered the east half of north-east quarter of section 36.

These entries were followed in 1832 by others, made by Henry Barnel, George Ensminger, Elias Bryan, Wm. Wilkes, Christian Ensperger and others.

The first settlement was made in 1826 or 1827 by Nathan Frakes and one Miller, west of Van Buren, on the farm now owned by S. Spitler, and by Miller on the farm now owned by J. Kempher. In 1827, John Trout, Elias S. Bryan and John Burman came, and they were followed by Christian Barnel, (father of John, Adna, G. C. and Elijah,) who came from Perry County, and located on the Spitler farm, Frakes having purchased and removed to what is now the Infirmary Farm. John Barnel, son of Christian, came in the following year, and is still a resident of the township. He too, moved to the Spitler farm, and his father, with his family, moved to Findley. Then came Charles Baker, of Fairfield, the Ensminger's, of Wayne, Hugh and John Gilchrist, Jos. Howard and others. All of these families settled around and near the site of the present town of Van Buren.

The timber in this township was poplar, walnut, oak, ash, sugar, beech, hickory, &c. Poplar was very plentiful in the south part of the township, but it has nearly all disappeared, as a few years ago it was considered more valuable than any other kind of wood, and was used very largely for building purposes.

The soil in the south part of the township is in part what might be termed a sandy clay. In parts, however, it is almost all clay, whilst elsewhere it is entirely sand. On the north side of the township, between the ridge and Wood County line, it is a black loam, mostly vegetable matter. But all parts of the township are easily tilled and very productive.

The middle branch of the Portage River passes through this township, and is the most considerable stream in that part of the county, and which has water the year around. It passes out of the township at the north-west corner. There are no other runs or creeks in the township, yet there are natural drains in sufficient number, to make all surface drainage necessary.

The first election held within the bounds of the township, was in 1833, at which time both of the townships of Cass and Portage voted. There were then but eleven votes cast. The following are the names of the voters: John Burman, John Trout, Elias S. Bryan, James Wiley, Hugh Gilchrist, John Barnel, Charles Baker, George Ensminger, Michael Ensminger and Peter Hockenberry. Of these eleven, John Barnel is the only one now living. The first election in the present township was held in 1850, in accordance with the order before recited.

The first school house was built in 1836, on the farm now owned by Peter Whetstone. It was of the round log, clapboard roof, huge chimney kind, of course. There are now nine school houses in the township, all brick but one, which is a frame. The enumeration of youth of school age amounts to three hundred and thirty-three.

The first church was built at Van Buren by the Presbyterians, Rev. George Van Emon Pastor. Amongst the first members were Samuel Huntington, John Leader, some of the Mooreheads, of Portage Township, and the Campbells, of Wood County. This organization still exists. There are now four church buildings in the township. One Presbyterian, one Baptist, one German Lutheran, one United Brethren, and all located in the town of Van Buren.

The Baptist church was organized in 1855, and Henry Roder and wife, Samuel Kagry, E. Smith were some of the first members. Previous to the building of the church, services were held at the house of Henry Roder, and as a branch of the Findley church.

The first marriages were those of a Mr. Beeson and Miss Trout; and Francis Rumor and Miss Ensminger. The first death was that of a child of John Trout.

John Burman built a mill on the creek east of Van Buren, at an early day, which was the first built in the township. But as it was propelled by water, and during a great portion of the year the water was so low in the creek, as not to furnish power, the mill was of not much benefit to the early settlers, who had to patronize the Teatserth Horse mill at Findley, or go to Perrysburg, or Sandusky City for flour and meal.

John Barnd, Esq., to whom I am indebted for much valuable information, relates the following incidents:

A very distressing accident occurred at a very early day, in the settlement of this township, by which two persons lost their lives. John Gilchrist and his little son, a boy about twelve years of age, and his brother, Hugh Gilchrist, were out in the night season hunting coon. When about one and a half miles north-west of Van Buren, on the farm now owned by Hugh McMurray, a coon was treed, and it became necessary to cut the tree down in order to get it.

This they did, but before it fell, John and his son took the dog, who was restless, and, to keep him from getting under the tree as it fell, went in the direction the tree was to fall, and at a distance they thought out of reach of the falling tree. When the tree fell, it struck another, which in falling killed the boy outright, and broke the thigh of his father. When Hugh found them, it being in the night season, he could not move them without help, and this was some distance away. Having procured it they took his brother to his home, where he died two days after. John left a wife and five children, all young. They were very poor, and were assisted by the neighbors.

In October, 1833, Mr. Barnd, with a neighbor, went into what was known as the "Wild Cat Thicket," to cut a bee tree, which had been found by Mr. Barnd. At that date wild bees were very abundant, and every pioneer, were he so minded, could always keep his table well supplied with honey. It so happened that in this instance, the bees were in a very large poplar tree, perhaps five feet in diameter. Others besides Mr. Barnd and his friend knew of the tree, for attempts had been made to chop it down, but its great size had been discouraging, and it had been abandoned Mr. Barnd himself had, after examining it, about concluded that there was too much labor in the cutting, for the pay he was likely to get, and had concluded to spare the tree, and lose the honey. Whilst looking up at the bees, busy at work in the body of the tree, he discovered another swarm at work in a large limb still higher up. This, he says, gave him courage for the undertaking, and they two worked with a will until the tree fell. The limb broke off at a distance of about twelve feet from the body of the tree, and at that place honey could be seen. On cutting into the limb at several

Narrative of Mr. Barnd.

places, it seemed to be filled with honey. He and his friend took the buckets they had with them, and filled them from the body of the tree, went home, got their wives, and with them took buckets and tubs, and returned to the tree, where they procured the honey from the limb, which amounted to sixteen gallons.

Mr. Barnd says that when he came to the county, the "Wild Cat Thicket," which extends through this township, was so densely covered with an undergrowth, as to be hardly passable, and although game was plenty elsewhere, it could not get through this thicket. The timber or brush was then quite small. A few large trees only were standing.

Game was very abundant, and the second year that Mr. Barnd was in the township, he killed *forty-five* deer, besides large quantities of smaller game, yet he did not consider himself a hunter, as he had his farm to attend to.

The first frame building erected in the township, was the Presbyterian church, which was built by John Kelley. The first brick building was that of John Trout, on the south of the town of Van Buren. Old Johnny Appleseeds was through this part of the county, and there are still standing several appletrees of his planting, some of which are on the farm of Mr. Barnd.

At a meeting of the Pioneer Association of Hancock County, held a few years ago, Mr. George W. Trout, read a paper, giving an account of the emigration of his father's family to the county, and of some of his recollections of frontier life. I take the liberty of making some extracts from that paper.

Mr. Trout commences by saying that "On November 12, 1828, my father, John Trout, with his family, left Somerset,

Perry County, Ohio, for the regions of Hancock. We passed through Thornville, Newark, Johnstown, Sunbury, Delaware and Marion, thence into the Wyandotte Reserve, where we remained one night, at the house of a widow Walker, a half-breed Indian, formerly the wife of an Indian. Here we had sight of the first Indians we ever beheld. We took dinner and fed our teams the next day, at a tavern in Upper Sandusky, kept by one Armstrong. Mrs. Armstrong was an Indian. We crossed the Tymochtee Creek near the dwelling of John James. From this place we sent back our four horse team, and father and my brother Ephraim proceeded to Van Buren, or rather to the settlement near there, as at that time and for many years thereafter, there was no town, to procure teams to take us the balance of the journey. After procuring the necessary teams, on their return, taking the Indian trail, they cut their way back, by way of the Big Springs. We were eleven days, anxiously awaiting their return. We again took up our line of march, and on the following night, stopped with Peter George, in what was then known as the 'Swamp Settlement.' On leaving Mr. George's, we were told to strike the river as far up as possible on account of high water. This we did, and came to the river at a point called 'Ashery Ford,' but even here the water was so high, that in crossing, it ran into the wagon box. That night we camped in the woods, having failed to reach any settlement.

"The next day, by dint of hard traveling, by a road we had to make as we went, we, at sunset, arrived at the house of a Mr. Powell, about three miles above Findley. On the next day, about noon, we reached the old 'Fort,' passing on the way, a school house, which was a very insignificant log-cabin. There were then but sixteen buildings in the place, and these seemed to have been built in mud and water.

"Though the town was then in its infancy, its people showed, by the generous assistance afforded us in crossing the river, they at least possesed noble hearts. We crossed the river in a 'Pirogue,' and passed the night in a shanty near where Carlin's mill now stands. We still had seven miles to go. Mother, brother John and myself started on foot, and so continued our journey as long as the logs in the way furnished a passage over the water. But presently we reached the end of this natural bridge. Here, luckily for us, a Mr. Foster came to our relief. He took mother on the horse he had brought with him. All that was left for John and I was to wade, and we did wade until we reached Mr. Foster's house. We had by this time become quite cold, for it had snowed the night before.

Having been refreshed by the kindness of Mr. Foster and his family, we continued our journey, urging our cattle through the mud and over the logs, and at last, about the middle of the afternoon, tired out, we arrived at the house of Mr. Miller, on the farm on which Samuel Spitler now resides. In the evening, the balance of our party arrived with the horses, but no wagon. The wagons had got stuck in the mud about three miles back, and the horses were unable to extricate them. It required all the next day to secure the wagons and bring them in, for it was sunset on December 15, when they arrived at the cabin on the hill. These cabins were of the rudest build, and plainest surroundings. On the morning after the first night in our cabin, our first inquiry was, who are our neighbors, and how far are we from any place. We were on the eastern frontier of our immediate neighborhood. Miller, Bryan and Frakes.

living about one half mile to the west of us. Our nearest neighbor on the east, was a Mr. Wade, who lived about eighteen miles distant. On the south, Mr. Foster lived at a distance of about six miles. On the west the nearest settlement was at Fort Defiance, about forty-eight miles away. Twelve miles to the north lived Mr. Haskins.

" Soon after our arrival, the Mr. Miller of whom I have spoken, died, and Mr. Frakes moved to his new home on the river, now the Infirmary farm, which left but two men in the settlement."

Mr. Trout has resided in the township ever since he came to the county, and has witnessed the vast improvements, made here, and the almost unparalleled increase in wealth and population. The wilderness has disappeared, and been replaced by beautiful farms, pleasant homes, comfortable churches and school houses.

WASHINGTON TAYLOR

Was the son of William Taylor, and was born in Bedford County, Pa., July 4th, 1818. Mr. Taylor came to Ohio with his parents in 1824, and located in Richland county, about four miles from Mansfield. Ten years later, Mr. T.'s father died, and in 1836 the family came to this county, settleing first in Portage township. After living in the town of Van Buren a few years, Mr. Taylor, in 1843, moved to the farm on which he now resides. In 1838 he was married to Martha Moorehead, who is still living.

The farm which is owned by Mr. T. is a very valuable one, and beautifully located, with a good brick residence, and commodious farm buildings. His five living children are all near him, and are honest, industrious citizens. After a long life of toil and privations as a frontiersman, Mr. T. is now enjoying the fruits of his labors, in the peaceful companionship of his family, and respect of his neighbors.

JOHN HARDY.

John Hardy was the oldest of a family of five children, and was born in the city of Philadelphia, on the 15th day of July, 1797, and came with his parents to Ohio in 1822, and settled in Stark county. He was married in August 1822, to Martha Orr. In 1832 he came to this county, and took up his residence on the farm now owned by Ezra Karn in Cass township. Mr. H. had entered six hundred acres of land in the county, previous to his removal here. In 1835 he removed to his farm in this township, it being then a part of Portage township, where he resided up to the time of his death, in November, 1860.

Mr. Hardy was a man of strong common sense, and a fair common school education, He was one of the first school teachers in the county, and taught school in the winter seasons, for more than twenty-five years. He was a man of decided opinions, and always had the courage to defend them. With his neighbors, he was noted for his honesty, intelligence and industry, and his counsel and advice were sought by his acquaintances.

Mr. H. was one of the pioneer Methodists of the county, having been a member of that church before his coming to the county, and remained so until his death. His membership in the church covered a period of more than forty years. His house was one of the early preaching places, and the itinerant minister always found a warm welcome at his table and fireside.

He was the father of five children, three boys and two girls, four of whom are living. His eldest daughter, now the widow of John McConnell, resides in Findley. Hannah, the youngest daughter, married the Rev. B. A. Desney, a minister of the Methodist church, has lately taken up her residence in Findley. Joseph O., the oldest son, is now and has been for the past twenty-six years a resident of Pendleton, Ind., at which place he has been engaged in mercantile pursuits. Oliver P. is one of the substantial farmers of Eagle township. Addison, the youngest son, died about five years ago, leaving to his young family, a fine home in Cass township.

JOHN BARND

Came to this county in 1833 from Perry county, his father's family having preceded him the year before. Mr. Barnd had married just previous to his coming here, and being determined to make for his family and wife a home, engaged in the serious business of clearing up the forests with a will, and by his untiring industry, his economy, and intelligent use of the means at hand, he succeeded in surrounding himself with all the comforts of life, and after assisting his children, of which he had a large family, to start in life, has an abundance left for himself and aged wife, who still lives to share the fruits of their united toils, and early deprivations.

No man in the township commands a greater respect from all classes of people, than does Mr. Barnd. Throughout his long life, he has been noted for his honesty and hospitality. Coming to this new country, when neighbors were few and far between, when social enjoyments were almost unknown, and when strangers as well as friends were welcome, Mr. B. always, and on all occasions, displayed the natural goodness of his heart, in extending to all that generous hospitality, for which the genuine frontiersman was noted. He was present and one of the voters at the organization of Portage township, of which this township was a part.

Mr. Barnd was the first Justice of the Peace elected in the new township of Allen, and held the office ten consecutive terms. His discharge of the duties of the office was satisfactory to his constituents, and his decisions were marked with such candor and fairness, that appeals were very seldom made to the higher courts. Mr. Barnd is still living on his old home place, spending his time peacefully and quietly in the company of his family, who are near him. Mr. Barnd has always followed the occupation of a farmer.

GEORGE ENSMINGER

Entered the land on which a part of the town of Van Buren now stands, in 1832, and in 1833 he, with John Trout, laid out the town of Van Buren. Mr. Ensminger followed farming for a livelihood, and was the owner of much valuable land in this township. His descendants have all left the township.

JUSTICES OF THE PEACE.

We here give the names of those who have been elected to this office in the township:

John Barnd—1850, 1853, 1856, 1859, 1862, 1865, 1868, 1871, 1874, 1877.

W. L. Heller—1852.

J. W. McCaughey—1855.

Philip Burman—1861, 1864.

Robert Thornberg—1867, 1870, 1873, 1876, 1879.

G. W. Barnd—1880.

History of Hancock County.

GRAIN CROP AND VALUE OF DOMESTIC ANIMALS IN 1881.

An exhibit of the acreage and products of the grain crop and the number and value of domestic animals, as reported by the Assessor of the township in 1881:

Wheat,	2121	acres.	47,519	bushels.
Oats,	656	"	14,405	"
Corn,	1693	"	72,055	"
Flax,	52	"	511	"
Hay,	786	"	946	tons.
Horses,	509	number.	$24,695,	value.
Cattle,	1103	"	12,630,	"
Sheep,	2836	"	5,273,	"
Swine,	1795	"	4,012,	"

VAN BUREN.

This town was laid out by George Ensminger and John Trout, in December, 1833, and is located on parts of sections twelve and thirteen, in range ten, and sections seven and eighteen, in range eleven, and comprised fifty-three lots. The town is laid out in the form of a cross, with a public square in the center. There were quite a number of large and substantial buildings put up, and nearly all the lots facing on the *square* were built upon. For a time the place assumed considerable importance in trade, but as the country became settled, other towns sprang up, and were fortunate enough to secure rail-roads, and this place gradually lost its prestige, until now it may be safely said to be on the down hill side of life. There are here still some pleasant residences, and a very genial, intelligent population, but business has almost entirely departed. The surrounding country is a rich and well improved agricultural district.

Van Buren.

In June, 1866, upon the petition of thirty of its citizens, this town was incorporated. Daniel Frick was first Mayor, and C. S. Wilkinson, J. H. Loehr, Dr. E. C. Wells, Dr. E. George, A. Mumert and L. P. McCune have succeeded him.

A post office was established here as early, perhaps, as 1836, and the following persons have been Post masters: Dr. Geo. Springer, John Zarbaugh, S. M. Heller, C. S. Wilkinson, L. Michaels, Dr. E. C. Wells, D. Frick, L. J. Hissony, Sol. Zarbaugh, H. C. Hartman, John Lee, Mrs. E. Wells.

The business of the place is transacted by *one* dry goods store; *one* grocery; *one* saloon; *one* steam saw mill; *three* blacksmith shops; *one* wagon shop. There are also *one* Baptist, *one* German Reformed, and *one* United Brethren Church, and *one* Physician. There were one hundred and thirty inhabitants here in 1880.

AMANDA TOWNSHIP.

T. 1, S. R. 11 E. T. 1, S. R. 12 E.
AREA 17,380 ACRES. POPULATION 1,476.

Amanda township borders on the east line of the county, and is bounded north by Marion and Big Lick townships, on the east by Wyandotte county, on the south by Wyandotte county and Delaware township, and on the west by Jackson.

This township was organized in 1828, and beside Findley and Delaware was the only one organized in the first year of our county existence. In the year 1830, at the time of the organization of Marion and Liberty townships, we have mention of Amanda township, for the territory included in this and Findley township was so divided up as to form the four townships of Amanda, Marion, Liberty and Findley. In December, 1831, it was ordered by the Commissioners that "the township of Amanda shall hereafter consist of the original township one south, in Range 12, and sections 34 and 35 in the original surveyed township one north, in the twelfth Range.

This township at the present time, and ever since the formation of Wyandotte county, sections 34 and 35 having been restored to township one north (Big Lick) by act of the County Commissioners, comprises Sections 1, 12, 13, 24, 25 and 36 in township one south, Range eleven east, and

First Entries of Land. 195

Sections 3, 4, 5, 6, 7, 8, 9, 10, 15, 16, 17, 18, 19, 20, 21, 28, 29, 30, 31, 32 and 33 in township one south, Range twelve east.

Thomas Thompson made the first entry of land in this township, on the 25th day of February, 1822, being the east half of the north-west quarter of Section three, and on the 27th day of the same month, the west half of the north east quarter of the same section was entered by Henry McWhorter. In October, 1823, John Brundige entered the north-west quarter of Section thirty-six, and John Smith entered the west half of the south-east quarter of the same section in December of the same year. In the month of March, 1825, Isaac Gifford, of the State of New York, made entry of the east half of the north-west quarter of Section twelve. In 1826, Ira Baker and John Shoemaker made entries. These were followed in 1827 by John Beard, Peter George, Henry George, Abraham Cole and others, and in 1828 by Jesse Gilbert, John J. Hendricks, Andrew Beck and others.

The first settlement in this township was made by Thomas Thompson, in 1824, near the Big Springs, about one mile from the present town of Vanlue, and in 1825 John Huff and William Hackney came. They were followed soon after by James Beard, John Shoemaker, Henry George and Thomas Cole. Very soon after these Peter George, James Gibson, John Hewitt and Aquilla Gilbert settled here. Judge Abraham Huff was also one of the pioneers of this township.

Thomas Thompson was a resident of this township for more than a half century, and was highly esteemed by his neighbors. He was a farmer, an occupation which he followed to within a few years of his death, when old age and infirmities compelled him to desist. He then moved to the village of Vanlue, where he spent his last days in quiet and died regretted.

Peter George, who was known as the "Pioneer land hunter," he having entertained, and guided through the forest of Hancock County, more land hunters and emigrants than any other men in the county perhaps, is still living; And though bent by age and hard labor, is yet cheerful and happy, and loves to recount the experiences of a backwoodsman. Mr. George was County Commissioner for six years.

William Hackney was one of the first officers of the county, and is spoken of elsewhere.

Aquilla Gilbert, one of the first settlers of Jackson, as well as of this township, and who taught the first school in this township, still lives here. Mr. Gilbert has been prominently connected with the affairs of the county almost from its first organization, and has held office in both county and township. He was six years one of the Commissioners of the county, having been elected in 1837. He served as Justice of the Peace for five consecutive terms in Jackson township, and for three terms in Amanda township.

Abraham Huff, as one of the Associate Judges of the county, has been mentioned heretofore.

The first election was held in the township in 1828. The first school house, as stated by Aquilla Gilbert, was built in the Messmore neighborhood, and the first school was taught by Mr. Gilbert. Another opinion, that of J. M. Von Horn, is that the first school house was built near the center of the township, and that the first school in the township was kept in a house on the farm of Uriah Egbert, in about the year 1831, and that one George Smith was teacher. It is not very material which of these gentlemen is correct, for all agree that these two schools were almost, if not quite, cotemperaneous.

There are now eight sub-districts in the township, each one of which has a comfortable school-room. The enumeration of youth is 180 males, and 176 females; total 356 in township, and in the village of Vanlue, special school district, the enumeration is 170.

The first church was built in 1831, in the south part of township, and known as the "Swamp Church." The Lutheran denomination owned it, and amongst the first membership we find the names of Fred. Brenner and wife, Adam Alspoch and wife, John Fenstenmaker and wife, and several members of the Beck family. The first sermon preached in the township was by a Rev. Thompson, an Indian Missionary. There are now in this township eight church buildings, owned as follows: One Methodist Episcopal, one Methodist Protestant, two United Brethren, one Baptist, one German Reformed, one Lutheran and one Disciples.

The timber is principally walnut, ash, oak, elm, hickory, beech, sugar. There were a few places in the township that were but sparsely wooded; notably so a tract in the north-east part known as the fallen timber region, and a portion of the south part known as the swamp.

In the eastern part of the township the soil is clay, mixed with sand and gravel, and when once properly cultivated is very productive. As before remarked, in the south part is what the people here call the "swamp," a strip of land not many rods wide, but extending almost across the township, from east to west, the soil of which is a deep rich vegetable loam, mixed with sand. This tract at the early settlement of this section, was thought to be almost, if not quite wholly worthless. But as agricultural science developed the means by which it might be brought into use, it was found not only possible to reclaim it, but that when so reclaimed, it was unusually productive. The river bottoms of a sandy, gravelly nature, plentifully mixed with the rich deposits of vegetable matter, made by the overflows of the water, of course are easily tilled, and yield most abundantly. In the northern part, as we have before observed, is a tract of about eight hundred acres, known as the "fallen timber," the soil of which is a muck, mixed with portions of clay and sand. This tract was originally very wet, and it is owing to this fact, perhaps, that so much of the timber, especially the larger, had fallen.

The Blanchard River enters this township near the southwest corner of Section twenty-five, runs east to about the center of the section, and then almost directly north through sections twenty-four, thirteen, twelve, and into section one, when it takes a north-westerly direction, leaving the township near the north-west corner. This river furnishes an abundance of water, as well as drainage, for the most part of the township, and is of immense value.

Buck Run, a small and unimportant stream, is the only tributary of the Blanchard, and is important only as a source of drainage. The Big Spring on the land of David Smith, in the north-east part of the township, is most valuable on account of the great volume of water discharged, as well as the excellent quality of the same. This is undoubtedly the largest spring in the county. Such is the amount of water discharged that an abundance is furnished for the watering of stock in all this part of the township.

This is one of the most populous townships in the county, and it is fast becoming one of the wealthiest. Each year sees the better improvement of the older farms, and the reclaiming of new lands; the erection of a better class of farm buildings, and the introduction of the latest improved farming implements. The early settlers came principally from the eastern counties in the State, and their descendants are an active, energetic, and progressive people.

There are two flouring mills, and very good ones too, in this township; one a steam, and the other a water mill.

There have been three Post Offices in this township, but two of them were long since discontinued. The first established was the "Blanchard Bridge," at the house of Aquilla Gilbert, on the Blanchard River. Mr. Gilbert was the first and only Post Master. The office was in existence for many years, and was a great accommodation to the citizens. But villages sprung up in the vicinity, and travel took another route, and the office was discontinued. Shortly after the establishment of "Blanchard Bridge," another office was established near the Richard Hall farm and called "Ashery." Joseph Twining was the first and only Post Master here. This office was long since discontinued for the reason that the necessity for its existence had passed away. The third office was established at Vanlue, of which we will speak in the proper place.

The following named persons have held the office of Justice of the Peace. The date of their election is given.

Thomas Thompson—1829.
John J. Hendricks—1829.
Samuel Gorden—1831, 1834, 1837, 1840, 1843, 1846.
Abraham Karn—1836.
John Thompson—1840, 1843.
William Vanlue—1845, 1848, 1851, 1854.
Aquilla Gilbert—1849, 1852, 1855.
B. A. Etherton—1857, 1860, 1863, 1866.

John Crawford—1857, 1860, 1863, 1865, 1868, 1871, 1874, 1877, 1880.

T. B. Gilbert—1866.

Ira Plotts—1869, 1872, 1875.

B. F. Burnap—1878, 1881.

CAPERNAUM.

The town of Capernaum, which *was* in this township, was laid out by Abraham Huff in March, 1831, on the west half of the north-east quarter of section three, and comprised in all sixteen lots. The land on which the town was located, now belongs to John L. Sheridan, and aside from the fact that it was platted and recorded, the town has no record. The site was probably abandoned before any lots were sold. At least its history is less brief than is that of the city of the plain, for which it was named. It is exceedingly doubtful if any one in the vicinity is able to even point out the site.

VANLUE.

This town was laid out by William Vanlue, Esq., in whose honor it was named, and is on the north-west part of the north-east quarter, and the north-east part of the north-west quarter of section nine. It is located on the line of the Findley branch of the Cleveland, Sandusky and Cincinnati Railroad, ten miles a little south of east of Findley. The town was laid out in May, 1847, and at that time consisted of forty-four lots. In November of the same year the proprietor laid out an addition of fifty lots more.

In October, 1853, S. N. Beach made an addition of fifty-seven lots, and in 1858, he, with others, laid out Beach's second addition of forty-nine lots. Charles Cross laid out an addition of ten lots in 1870.

From the sale of the first lots the town steadily improved, and was a very considerable grain market for a number of years after the completion of the railroad, but of no great importance otherwise.

There are many tasteful and comfortable dwellings, neat fences, shady streets, all giving the place a home-like appearance. The streets have never received that attention from the town authorities which they deserve, and consequently they are frequently in a bad condition. After a few years of great prosperity, the town, as new towns do, slacked up, and stopped progress, came to a stand still, went through a sweat as it were. Business seemed for a time to have forsaken the place. Enterprise too, seemed to have taken its leave. Progress had got stuck somewhere, and everything seemed going to the dogs. But this state of affairs could not last long. The town could not stand still. It must go forward, or must retreat.

In 1866, upon the petition of fifty of the inhabitants, the village was incorporated under the laws of the State. Pursuant to the Act of Incorporation, the first election for village officers was held on the 13th day of April, 1867; Peter Shuck, C. H. Hatch and Jason Lee as Judges, and Ira Plotts and John Dresbach, Clerks. There were thirty votes cast. The following officers were elected: Mayor, Elisha Brown; Recorder, A. Brown; Councilmen, H. Pratt, Ira Plotts, B. A. Etherton, Charles Hatch and A. S. Roberts; Marshal, W. L. Plotts. The following persons have held the offices of Mayor: Elisha Brown, Aquilla Gilbert, Fred Shuler, J. H. Brown, B. F. Burnap, T. B. Gilbert, H. L. Lee.

The population of the village is three hundred and sixty-four, and at present is in a flourishing condition, and promises much improvement.

There is quite a considerable business done in the village, as a list of its business houses will show.

There is one dry goods store, of considerable capital, and in which is kept a supply of the staple articles of merchandise, which are sold at very fair prices. This branch of trade has always been reasonably well represented, sometimes by three or four rival establishments, at the same time.

A grocery and provision store has been lately opened, and is meeting with fair encouragement, and promises not only to be one of the fixtures of the town, but to fill a want long felt in its line.

Daniel Gilbert has for a number of years been engaged in the drug business here, and has an establishment, which for completeness, in everything except extent of stock, is not surpassed by any similar establishment in the county. Here you may find anything necessary to be kept in a country drug store. The building is of frame, and was built expressly for this business.

There are also three saloons, one hotel, one harness shop, one hardware store, with a general stock of goods in that line. This establishment was owned and managed by the late Hon. John Wescott & Son, and had by a course of fair dealing, reasonable prices, and by keeping an assortment of goods, built up a flourishing trade. There is one furniture store, one tin shop, three boot and shoe shops, two barber shops, three dress makers and milliner shops, two blacksmith shops.

The steam grist and merchant mill of Fred Shuler, has no superior in the county as a good flour-maker. This mill was first built about fifteen years ago, and was from the first noted for the fine brand of flour it turned out. Mr. Shuler conducted the business for a number of years, when he sold to a Mr. Vansant, who alter running the mill for a short time, had the misfortune to have it burned down, destroying everything of building and machinery. Not being able to rebuild, Mr. Vansant left the place, when Mr. Shuler again came to the front, and built the present building, completing it with the latest, best and most improved machinery, and now can boast of as good a flouring mill as there is in the county, at least.

There are two steam saw mills, two handle factories, and two planing mills, none of them very large, but all doing a good business.

The English Lutherans have quite a comfortable frame church building, and a good congregation. Some three years ago the United Brethren, who had long had a society here, and a church building, erected a neat frame church, well furnished and comfortable, and have quite a large congregation.

The Methodist Episcopal, the oldest church organization in the town, not to be outdone by her sister churches, recently completed one of the handsomest frame church buildings in the county, furnished with bell, organ, beautiful pulpit, and comfortable seats. They, too, have a large and interested congregation. All of these societies have flourishing Sabbath Schools attached.

The village has a frame school building of three rooms, and boasts of one of the best schools in the county. The enumeration of youth in the district is one hundred and seventy.

A Post Office was established here in 1849, with Dr. W. P. Wilson as Post Master. The successive Post Masters have been as follows; John Wescott, W. P. Wilson, Ira Plotts, W. A. Sponsler and Daniel Gilbert.

The Findley branch of the C. S. & C. Railroad passes through this place, and the town being surrounded as it is by a rich agricultural district, there is quite an amount of freighting business done.

Table exhibiting the number and value of live stock, and the acreage and product of grain, as shown by the return of the Township Assessor in 1881.

Horses, 693 number.	$26,400, value.
Cattle, 1,221 "	13,110, "
Sheep, 2,572 "	4,670, "
Swine, 2,507 "	5,740, "
Wheat, 3,703 acres.	71,162 bushels.
Oats, 376 "	13,422 "
Corn, 2,926 "	133,320 "
Hay, 619 "	705 tons.
Flax, 78 "	496 bushels.

BLANCHARD TOWNSHIP.

T. 1, N. R. 9 E.
AREA 23,040 ACRES.   POPULATION 1,286.

The act of the Commissioners organizing this township, was passed in 1833, in these words: "That original surveyed township number one north, range nine east, shall be known and organized by the name of Blanchard."

In March, 1834, the Commissioners "Ordered that township two north, range nine (Pleasant Tp.) be attached to Blanchard township," but a year later this township was detached from Blanchard and organized into a separate township.

Blanchard is on the west border of the county, bounded north by Pleasant township, east by Liberty, south by Union, and west by Putnam county line. It derives its name from the river of the same name, which passes through it from east to west, dividing it into two almost equal parts.

The first entries of land made in the township were the north half of north-west quarter of north-east quarter of section thirteen, by David Stinson, and the north-east quarter of north-east quarter of same section, by John Veal, both entries being made on the 12th day of August, 1822. On the 19th day of the same month and year, W. A. Johnson entered the south-east quarter of the north-west quarter of section fifteen. On September, 1825, John Hunter took up the south half of south-west quarter of section fifteen, James McClish entered the east half of north-east quarter of section twenty. In 1827, Orlando Moffitt entered west part of south-east fractional quarter of section seventeen, and John Dukes the east half of the north-west quarter of section fifteen, and Henry Epley the east part of the south-east quarter of section eighteen. These entries were followed by others, and a settlement of the township followed close on the entries.

The first settlers in this township were John Hunter and John Chandler, both of Fairfield County, who came here in 1826, and located on the south side of the river, on the farm now owned by Alfred Davis, and known as the old Geo. Shaw farm. The first settlers of this part of the county were in the main from the interior and eastern counties of the State, with a few families from Pennsylvania and New York. These two first families were not long without neighbors, for in 1828, Richard, John and Lewis Dukes, of Franklin County, and Thomas Grove, of Pickaway County, settled on the opposite side of the river, and opened up extensive farms, and erected comfortable buildings. Thomas Groves still lives and occupies the old farm, and in his declining years, is surrounded by broad acres of the richest agricultural lands in the whole county.

Richard Dukes, who but recently deceased, occupied the old homestead, to within a few years of his death, when he removed to Findley, and so situated himself as to enjoy the society of his friends, and obtain the rest from toil, which he so much needed. His last years were peaceful and quiet, in the enjoyment of home and its comforts.

Lewis Dukes, sr., came to this township in 1826, when only about nineteen years of age, and hired out as a farm hand. In a few years, by his industry and frugality, he was able, at the low wages even then paid, to accumulate enough money to enter a tract of eighty acres of land. This he improved, and was enabled as the country improved, to add many acres of valuable lands to it, until he has become one of the wealthiest men in the township. Mr. Dukes has been twice married, but was never blessed with children. He united with the Methodist Church in early life, and has ever since been a consistent member, ever living up to his profession.

Mr. Dukes is of an unassuming nature, never seeking notoriety, and never urging his opinions on others. His industry, tact and economy are proverbial, and his opinions on business matters are clear and forcible. His life has been devoted to agricultural pursuits, in which he been unusually successful.

David M. Baldwin was one of the earliest settlers of the south part of the township, having come from Fairfield County, and settled on lands adjoining the town of Benton. All was a wilderness when he came, and he lived long enough to see one of the finest neighborhoods in the county. Mr. B. was a genial, whole-souled man, ever ready to accommodate to the extent of his ability, and ever ready to resent an insult. For years he kept a tavern, where the weary traveller always found a well laden table. His large family are living near their old home, which is occupied by his aged widow.

John Dukes remained in this township until he became quite well advanced in years, and had witnessed the many changes which occurred, when he disposed of his property and removed to Wood County, where after a residence of several years, he too was gathered to his fathers.

Thomas Moffitt, who with his brothers, William and John, had made their residence here about the time the Dukes' came, after making for himself a home and its comforts, was attacked with the "Western Fever," sold his farm and emigrated to Iowa, or the "Black Hawk Country," as it was called, where he still lives. John and William Moffitt, and McClish, still reside in the township, and are amongst its most substantial men.

Michael Fishel, one of the early residents, only a few years ago sold his farm on the south side of the river, and now resides in the village of McComb. Alfred Davis, another frontiersman, and one of the solid men of the county, owns and occupies a magnificent tract of land on both sides of the river, and takes life calmly. George Shaw, one of the early commissioners of the county, owned a splendid farm here, on which he spent the greater part of his life, and here died and was buried. About the same time came Jeremiah Cocle, David Millham, Sol Foglesong and the Epleys.

These early settlers all chose the independent and honorable occupation of farmers, and well was their choice made, for no richer agricultural lands are to be found in the State, than those which they occupy and cultivate.

These pioneers were hardy, temperate, frugal, energetic and industrious, and deserve their past and present prosperity.

The Dukes' brothers were early and consistent members of the Methodist Church, and friends to, and workers in the Sabbath Schools. The first church building in the county was put up in this immediate neighborhood, and they contributed largely, not only to its erection, but also to sustaining the ministers sent among them. This old log church

Soil and Timber.

still stands on the farm owned by Eli Dukes. Since its day, however, a frame building was erected a little further west, which was used by the same society for a number of years, when about two years ago, it in its turn, made room for a more comfortable and pretentious brick building—indeed one of the finest church edifices in the county. There are now two Methodist Episcopal, two United Brethren, and one Evangelical Church in the township, all good substantial buildings.

The first school house was a log cabin affair, and stood near where the present residence of Thomas Groves stands, and was built in 1830. The first school was taught by John C. Wickham. There are now ten school buildings in the township, and the enumeration of youth is three hundred and eighty-four.

The first marriage was that of John Dukes and Hannah Houchings, the Rev. Thomas Thompson officiating. Two little children of George Shaw were the first deaths.

The soil of this township varies with the locality. Along the river it is a rich sandy loam, mixed with vegetable deposits, made by the overflow of the river. On the south ridge it is a fertile, sandy soil, and between the ridge and the river bottoms, the land is flat and rather wet, but covered by a rich, deep soil of vegetable loam, mixed in places with sand or clay. On the north side of the river, after getting back from the bottoms, the soil is almost invariably clay; good wheat and grazing lands, whilst for the production of corn, the bottom lands are not excelled anywhere.

Oak, ash, hickory, sugar, beech, walnut and poplar, are the principal timbers. Of the latter kind, there were immense amounts, and of the finest quality, but such has been the demand for it, that it has almost entirely disappeared.

This township is well watered by the Blanchard River and Ottowa Creek. The river passes through the township, and furnishes water the whole year around, and also the best of drainage. It is subject to occasional overflows, but does no material damage.

Ottowa Creek rises in section thirty-six, in Union township, runs in a northerly direction, enters Blanchard township in section thirty-six, runs north, thence west, thence in a north-easterly direction, and empties into the Blanchard River in section fourteen. Its distance in the township is about four miles. It is quite a considerable stream, and there have been quite a number of saw-mills along its course, at different times. It furnishes the means of drainage for almost the entire south part of the township.

Shortly after the settlement made on the north side of the river, by the Dukes and others, the Powells, Foglesong, John L. and Richard Carson, Engle, Baldwin, Fishel, Hughes, the Downings, Knepper, and some other families settled in and near the present town of Benton. Solomon Foglesong, and his brother-in-law, Knepper, came there perhaps as early as 1830, and settled on the banks of the "Tawa," as it is generally called. Foglesong, almost the only survivor of the first residents, still lives on the old homestead, but the weight of years is heavy on him, and he may soon be called to follow his early companions. Daniel, William and John Powell still reside in the neighborhood of their first settlement. All have good farms, comfortable homes, and a competency of this world's goods. Jacob, another of the Powell brothers, died a few years ago, from the effects of a cancer, and after years of great suffering.

The Rev. John Powell, who has devoted his life to the ministry of the United Brethren Church, and who not only acquired a good farm by his industry and economy, but within a few years has found a wide reputation as the founder of the Powell Association, and the successful manager of two re-unions of the family, as well as the author of a memorial history of the Powell family, still lives in the quiet enjoyment of his farm, in the south part of the township.

Jacob Engle, the kind, generous, large-hearted Dutchman, as he was called, cleared up and occupied a splendid farm adjoining the present site of Benton, where he lived for years amongst his many friends, until about 1860, when he was called away to meet his reward. Honest, generous to a fault, he was a good neighbor, and a social, genial companion. He left a wife and large family of children, who have since all emigrated to the West, the widow and most of the children being residents of Iowa.

Owen Hughes was one of those honest, up right, cheerful men, that one would expect to find in a new settlement. He lived to a good old age, and died as he had long lived, a consistent member of the church, and a christian man. Most of his children are residents of the county. Mr. Hughes was twice married, but both wives died before he did.

All of my older readers, perhaps, will call to mind Dick Carson, at the bare mention of his name. He was one of the champion fighters of the county. Not that he was quarrelsome, or sought to provoke a fight, but he was one of these powerfully built, muscular men, courageous, sensitive to an insult, and whilst not ill-tempered, especially when sober, he was quick to resent an indignity, or an imputation of his courage or veracity. He was just such a man as every township or county wanted to defend its honor, as it was then the fashion, at a general training, or a country horse race. Dick was just the man for that, as many an unlucky braggart found to his utter discomfiture. But the reader must not suppose from this that Mr. Carson was a rough, a bruiser, or bully. On the contrary he was a good neighbor, a firm friend, and a peaceable citizen. His brother, John L., was at one time Surveyor of the county. The two Carsons and their families emigrated to the west many years ago.

The Downings were of the first settlers, and were a hardy, industrious family, and all became quite well off in course of time. George, David and William were carried off in 1849 by the California Gold Fever, but after a few years toil in that El Dorado, they all returned to Blanchard township, applied themselves to agricultural pursuits, and by industry and economy made great additions to their western earnings.

In after years William moved to Kansas, where he still resides, and has had the honor of representing his county in the State Legislature. He was followed to his new home by his father, old Johnny Downing, as he was familiarly, but respectfully called, and his brother Isaac and family. The old gentleman and Isaac have both died since. George resided in this township until about ten years ago, when he went to Iowa, where he now resides. David still lives in the township, and is not only one of its wealthiest, but one of its most respected citizens. He has a model farm, with one of the finest dwelling houses, not only in the township, but in the county, and commodious and convenient outbuildings. His pecuniary circumstances enable him to devote much time to the breeding and introduction of fine cattle in the county. He has some of the best herds in this part of the State. He deals largely in stock cattle, being quite an extensive feeder. He has been a member of the Board of Managers of the Hancock County Agricultural Society for a number of years, and has devoted much time in making the Society one of the best in the State, and his efforts, and those of his associates, have not been unsuccessful. Mr. Downing has, as he deserves, the confidence of the entire commnuity.

His sons and daughters, of which there are several, are all married, and I believe without an exception, all reside in this and adjoining townships.

This locality, on account of the abundance of fish and game, was one of the resorts of the Indians on their hunting expeditions. And indeed hunting and fishing were not only among the amusements of the whites, but they were works of necessity with them, in order to support themselves. The fish-net and the rifle was a part of the furniture of every well regulated log cabin, and by the skillful use of these, the tables of the pioneer were spread with fish, johnny cake and venison, to which the neighbor and stranger alike were always welcome.

In 1848 a Post Office was established in this township called Oak Ridge. It was first located at the house of William Downing, on the Findley and Defiance State road, north side of the river, and Mr. Downing was the first Post Master. It was an office of no importance, only as it gave to the community in which it was located, mail facilities, and this accommodation has been such as to warrant the continuance of the office to the present time. Mr. Downing has been succeeded by the following persons as Post Masters, viz.: Robert Marshall, Mr. Morris, Mrs. Wm. Downing,

Rezin Cook, David Downing, Eli Dukes and L. C. Groves, present incumbent.

BENTON.

This town situated on the ridge running east and west through the county, and nine miles west of Findley, was laid out in November, 1835, by William Mires, on the east half of the north-west quarter of section thirty-five, and originally composed but thirty-six lots. In 1855, William Powell made an addition of five lots, and in 1867 he made a further addition of eleven lots, and in 1868 he made a third addition of ten lots.

The town was named in honor of the sturdy old Missouri Senator, Thomas H. Benton. The location is a beautiful and healthy one, and is surrounded by a rich and productive agricultural country. The immediate vicinity of the town was settled at a very early day by the Powells—William, Jacob, John and Daniel,—David M. Baldwin, Jacob Engle, Solomon Foglesong, Knepper, Michael Fishel, Owen Hughes and other like enterprising frontiersmen.

The business of the town has never been large, and confined principally to supplying the surrounding country with some of the most necessary articles of trade. Not having as yet any railroad facilities, the town has made but little real advancement.

A Post Office was established here in about 1840, called Benton Ridge, and D. M. Baldwin, William Miller, Philip Ballard, Isaac Sperow, M. Merchant, T. J. Saunders, J. G. Saunders, J. H. Saunders, and H. W. Hughes have held the office of Post Master.

In March, 1875, the town was incorporated for special purposes.

There is now a special school district, owning a comfortable brick school house, and with an enumeration of seventy children.

The Methodist denomination have a fine brick church building, a good congregation, and a flourishing Sabbath School. The Evangelical Association have a frame church building, and an interesting Sabbath School in connection with their congregation.

The business of the town is conducted by *two* dry goods stores, *two* groceries, *one* drug store, *one* saloon, *one* wagon shop, *one* blacksmith shop, *one* plow factory, *one* cabinet shop, *one* hotel. There are *two* physicians located here. A flouring mill and a saw mill are also in operation. The population of the village in 1880 was one hundred and eighty-nine.

LOUISVILLE.

This town was laid out in 1851, by William H. Powell, Daniel Millham and Michael Shearer. The two last named have been dead for many years. The town plat was in the north-west corner of the east half of the north-west quarter of section fourteen, and the north-east corner of the west half of the north-east quarter of section fourteen in township one north, range nine east, and covered forty lots, but I think they were not all sold. The principal streets were Defiance (Main), running east and west, and East, Lima and West streets, running north and south.

The town, however, after a sickly existence of a few years, was finally vacated, and remanded to the several original owners. In its palmiest days, it could boast of a country dry goods store, a school house, and three dwellings. For a year or more John Boylan, an old resident of the township, kept a country store, where the staple articles of the market were on sale in small quantities, but the trade not being profitable, he abandoned the business. Such is the history of the birth, life, and decay of this town of great expectations, and it does not now exist even in name, and scarcely in the memory of the neighborhood. How many hopes were blasted, and how many expectations came to naught in the early decay of this prospective city?

JUSTICES OF THE PEACE.

Thomas Moffitt—1831, 1841, 1844.
John C. Wickham—1835.
John L. Carson—1836.
John M. Radabaugh—1837.
Charles Frost—1838.
Henry Cook—1840, 1843.
Eli Dunning—1846, 1849.
John Boylan—1847, 1856.
Mathew E. Hopkins—1851.
Philip Ballard—1854, 1857.
W. H. Kilpatrick—1857.
George Downing—1857, 1860, 1863, 1866.
Robert Marshall—1860.
Jonn Wortman—1862, 1870, 1878.
Ephriam Mathius—1866, 1869.
Hiram W. Hughes—1869, 1872.
Joseph Thompson—1873.
A. Wittemyer—1875.
W. P. Dukes—1876.
John Bergman—1877.
J. C. Wickham—1880.

BIG LICK TOWNSHIP.

Tp. 1, N.   R. 12, E.

AREA 23,040 ACRES.   POPULATION 1,261.

The Commissioners of the county, at their session of March 7, 1831, after defining the boundaries and extent of Amanda Township, "Ordered that the original survey of township one north, in range twelve east, except sections thirty-four and thirty-five, shall hereafter be known and organized by the name of Big Lick."

At the session of the Commissioners held June 3, 1833, Robert L. Strother and John Rose, Commissioners, being present, the following order was passed: "Ordered that Big Lick Township shall include the whole of the original surveyed township No. one north, in range twelve." Since the passage of that order, the township been has known as an original township of thirty-six sections.

In September, 1821, Henry McWhorter made entry of the west half of the south-east quarter of section thirty-four. This was the first entry of land in the township. In May, 1825, the east half of the south-east quarter of section twenty-seven was entered by John G. Alspach, and September 5, of the same year, Eliza Huff entered the east half of the north-west quarter of section thirty-four. In December, 1828, John Shoemaker made entry of the east half of the south-east quarter of section seventeen. These entries were followed in 1829 by those of John Huff, of the west half of the south-east quarter of section seventeen, of the west half of the north-east quarter of section twenty-one by John Long. In 1830, Henry Hinebaugh, of Fairfield County, entered the north-east quarter of section one, and in the same year, Uriah Egbert took up the west half of the north-west quarter of section nineteen, and about the same time an entry of the west half of the north-west quarter was made by Philip Essex.

William Hackett, of Stark County, William Roller, of Richland, Elijah Brayton, of Crawford, Mary Graham, of Madison, John Graham, William Wiseley and others made entries of land, and became residents of the township.

This township is on the east line of the county, and is bounded on the north by Washington township, on the east by Seneca County, on the south by Wyandotte County and Amanda township, and on the west by Marion township.

The first settler in the township was Samuel Sargent, who made an improvement on the limestone ridge, in the south-eastern part of the township, sometime in 1826. The second person who made a permanent settlement was John Long, who located near the centre of the township the following year. In February, 1829, John Shoemaker settled about three-fourths of a mile west from Mr. Long's. Mr. Shoemaker still lives to recount the hardships and incidents of frontier life. Sargent came from Ross county, and Long and Shoemaker from Fairfield County, this State.

The first township election was held in 1831, at the residence of John Long. The electors present were John Shoemaker, Robert Long, Levi Poulson and Cornelius Poulson. Whilst these men were holding an election and organizing the township, the good Mrs. Long prepared them a dinner of the best in her larder.

Soil and Timber.

Amongst the early settlers here, were the Thomas's the Moore's, the Rollers, the Graham's, the Poulson's, Wiseley and others, some of whom are still living in the township.

The general surface of the land is level, although some parts are undulating. The prevailing soil is clay loam. In the south-eastern part of the township is a sand ridge, and is underlaid with limestone. In that portion of the township is also a marsh or prairie, some fifteen hundred acres in extent, which is entirely a vegetable soil, and largely unreclaimed, except for grazing purposes. It will no doubt all be brought under cultivation in the near future, by the help of drainage. That so much of it has been reclaimed, is largely due to the enterprise and well directed exertions of Judge Cory, of Findley, who owns most of the entire tract.

The timber embraces numerous varieties, among which are white, red and burr oak, blue, black and white ash, beech, elm, hard and soft maple, sycamore, black and white walnut, hickory, basswood and buckeye. A ridge of white oak traverses the township, of such excellence, that shipment of logs have been extensively made to foreign countries.

No streams of water traverse the township of sufficient size to furnish water power. The only stream that maintains a current during the entire year, is the outlet to the marsh or prairie. This sluggish stream takes its size in Seneca County, runs in a westerly direction, and empties into the Blanchard River near Mr. Allen Wiseley's, in Marion Township. There a number of smaller streams, which however, are only water courses in wet weather.

Numerous Sulphur Springs on the farm of Robert Long, near the center of the township, comprise what used to be a famous deer lick, called "Big Lick," from which the township derives its name. Large numbers of deer were killed here by the present owner, and by others. Mr. Long, on one occasion, had secured his seat in a tree convenient to the lick, when a colored man, who had been assisting in driving some cattle from some point farther west, was on his return trip from the east, and night overtaking him, he concluded to camp near the springs. Mr. Long not knowing who he was, and supposing him to be a rival at watching for deer, concluded to frighten him away. Whereupon he made such an unearthly noise, that the poor fellow took to his heels and never stopped until he brought up in the Blanchard River, near Allen Wiseley's. He had so overheated himself as to cause his death soon afterwards. Mr. Long's efforts to have a little fun, turned out quite seriously.

These early settlers were greatly annoyed by gangs of Indian hunters and trappers, who made the neighborhood their rendezvous. Especially was this the case with Mr. Shoemaker, who, more progressive than his neighbors, had secured a grind-stone. The Indians charged upon that grind-stone with their dull tomahawks and knives, until it was literally worn out. They also had a way of trading venison for pork and potatoes with Mrs. John Moore, in which she invariable came out second best. Knowing that the wife was afraid of them, they would make their visits in the abssence of the husband, hence she, in order to get rid of them, would send them to the patch to help themselves. It being the first crop, and not a very large one, Mr. Moore soon discovered that the entire crop had disappeared. Vermin were also destructive upon the corn. The settlers could only protect themselves by the use of the rifle, and if one chanced to be poor shot, he employed some one by the day, who was an expert with the gun. At night, too, it demanded watching, to save the corn from the raccoons.

The surroundings and discomforts of the early settlers here, and the scarcity of even the commonest necessities of life, may be shown in the pioneer life of Mr. John Moore, now an old and much respected citizen of the township, and by the way, one of its most prosperous farmers. Mr. Moore at that time owned one hundred and sixty acres of land, and was perhaps as well fixed as any of his neighbors. He was however, compelled to manufacture all his own furniture.

His first child (A. J. Moore, a resident of this township), was rocked in a sugar trough, made by "Big River," a Wyandotte Chief, and which had been used before the arrival of Mr. Moore in the country, as a sap trough by the Indians. Mr. Moore's first bedstead was made by himself, of ironwood poles. The cords were of bass-wood bark, well interlaced together. No straw was to be had with which to fill the ticks, Mr. Moore thereupon gathered forest leaves sufficient to make a mattress.

Mr. Moore was elected first Supervisor of roads in the township, and had for a district, the north half of the township, eighteen square miles. He superintended the opening of the New Haven road, from the east township line, westward to near the center of the township.

In those days, stock of every description was allowed to run at large in the forest, as all the inclosed land had to be cultivated in order to produce food for man and beast. The damage done to crops by stock running at large, made trouble amongst the people, and a board of fence viewers became necessary. This board were to determine, when called upon, whether or not the enclosure was a sufficient or legal fence.

Accordingly, William Roller, who was noted for his avordupoise, William Moore, who was noted for his diminutiveness, and Richard Bayless, noted for his activity, were chosen as the Board of Fence Viewers. It was then agreed, that any fence which would bear Mr. Roller, and through which Mr. Moore could not creep, nor Mr. Bayless jump over, should be declared a lawful fence.

The first school house in the township was built in 1836— exclusively by voluntary labor—upon the farm now owned by the heirs of James Graham. It was located in the forest a full half mile from any public highway. There were but two sub-districts in the township, at the time. Sometime subsequent to the above date, there was another school house built, about two miles west of the first—on the lands now owned by the heirs of Moses McAnnelly. A fair interest is now taken in the cause of education by the citizens of this township. There are now 413 youth in this township of school age, for the accommodation of whom there are ten school houses.

The first church erected in the township was a hewed log structure, thirty-six feet square, and located on the present site of Enon Valley Church, on the Findley and Tiffin road. It was built in 1844 by the citizens in the neighborhood, mainly, however, by the combined efforts of the Presbyterians, Covenanters and Seceders. The first site selected for the building, was upon Robert Leonard's farm, some two miles south-east from the one subsequently built upon. Rev. R. H. Hollyday, still of Findley, superintended the building of the church.

There are now eight churches in this township. Two owned by the Evangelical denomination, two by the United Brethren, two Methodist Episcopal, one Presbyterian and one Christian Union. Amongst the first church members were Henry Thomas and wife, James Thomas and wife and Andrew Poulson.

The township has been so developed in its resources, as to be one of the richest in the county, In 1880 over 75,000 bushels of wheat was raised; corn, oats and grass are also produced in large quantities.

The Findley and Carey Branch of the Cleveland, Sandusky and Cincinnati Rail Road is the only road of that kind which touches the township, and that runs but a short distance in it.

JOHN MOORE.

Mr. Moore was amongst the first settlers in this township, and came here with his young wife, when all was new, and when energy, industry and good health were the requisites to success. These qualities were combined in Mr. Moore and his brave wife. His strong arm soon opened up a farm, and his house was the stopping place of the stranger emigrant, and at his table was ever found welcome hospitality.

Mr. Moore endured all the hardships of frontier life, and now in his old age, surrounded by his children and grand children, he, in the midst of plenty, the fruits of his own toil, is enjoying life peacefully and quietly. He is one of the largest land owners, as well as one of the wealthiest men in the township. He has always followed the independent life of a farmer, and I believe his children are all engaged in the same business.

Mr. Moore has always been a friend of public schools. His own opportunities for obtaining an education when young has always made him seriously feel his loss, hence he appreciates the blessings of such schools to the rising generations.

MOSES M'ANNELLY

Was one of the prominent men of the county, as well as of this township, coming here at an early day, and being a man of more than ordinary intelligence, he took the lead in the new settlements. He represented this county in both branches of the Ohio Legislature, and was regarded as an honest, upright man. He too was an agriculturalist, and made for himself and family, a pleasant and valuable home. Mr. McAnnelly has been dead a number of years.

JOHN SHOEMAKER

Came from Fairfield County to this township, in February, 1829, having the year previous entered lands in section seventeen. There were but a very few families in the township at that time, among whom were Samuel Sargeant, on the limestone ridge, and John Long in the immediate neighborhood of Mr. S.'s settlement. Mr. Shoemaker was present and assisted at the organization of the township in 1831.

He is still a resident of the township, and is of the very few who came here at that early day. The cultivation of the soil has always been his occupation. Honest, industrious and hospitable he has always commanded the respect of the community. His sterling good sense has always made his advice valuable. He is reaping the fruits of his long years of toil and privation, happy in the consciousness of the unvaried rectitude of his life.

WILLIAM ROLLER,

One of the Associate Judges of the Common Pleas Court of the county, was also a resident of this township. As a Judge, his good common sense, and honesty of action, gave him his very flattering reputation. Honest in his convictions, sympathetic in his feelings, he could hardly err in his decisions, as he was a man of average intelligence and fair common school education. He never abandoned the occupation of a farmer, but succceded in amassing a competency, and leaving a considerable inheritance to his children. He was respected by his neighbors, and was always a friend to those in need. Unostentatious in his private life, and courteous in public, he could not but have hosts of friends.

FREEDOM.

Uriah E. Drake laid out *forty-eight* lots on the east half of the south-west quarter of section nineteen, on the 26th day of October, 1836, and called them the town of Freedom. So far as I can learn, the above is a complete history of the place.

WEST INDEPENDENCE.

George Wyant, Peter Wyant and Henry M. Grose were the proprietors of this town. It is located on the east part of the east half of the north-east quarter of section two, and at present has a population of *one hundred and thirty-four*. The Evangelical Association have a church building, and there is a good, comfortable school house in the village. The business of the place consists of *one* hotel, *one* grocery and provision store, *one* saw mill, *two* shoe shops, *one* physician and *one* blacksmith and wagon shop.

The United Brethren have a neat house of worship, and a prosperous society,

A post office was established here in 1856, with Frederick Reamer as Post Master. Mr. Reamer was succeeded by J. L. Kenower, Jacob Ruth, John Peters, and Wm. Blinn, the present incumbent.

This village had a population of one hundred and thirty-four, in 1880.

Table showing the number and value of live stock. and the number of bushels and acreage of grain in this township, as returned by the Township Assessor, in 1881:

    Horses, 573 number. $30,070, value.
    Cattle, 1417 "   17,090, "
    Sheep, 4975 "   9,050, "
    Swine, 3107 "   5,600, "
    Wheat, 3665 acres.   81,261 bushels.
    Oats, 531 "   16,656 "
    Corn, 2878 "   87,730 "
    Flax, 39 "   680 "
    Hay, 971 "   994 tons.

The following is a list of persons who have held the office of Justice of the Peace in Big Lick Township, with the dates of election:

  Amos Dunken, 1831.
  Levi Poulson—1831.
  James Bright—1835.
  William Roller—1835.
  Robert L. Martin—1836.
  William Williamson—1836.
  Leonard Baumgartner—1838, 1855.
  Moses McAnnelly—1838, 1841, 1844, 1847.

John Graham—1845, 1848; 1851, 1854, 1857, 1860, 1863, 1866.
Charles Henderson—1842.
Jerry Rickets—1850.
James Ruckman—1856.
Fred. Ramer—1859, 1862.
J. P. Edwards—1863, 1866, 1869.
Abraham Mumma—1864, 1867.
Wm. K. Leonard—1867.
Geo. W. Graham—1869, 1872, 1875, 1878, 1881.
J. W. Gibson—1870.
John Newhouse—1873.
Geo. W. Brown, 1877.

CASS TOWNSHIP.

Tp. 2, N.   R. 11, E.

AREA 15,360 ACRES,   POPULATION} 823.

On the 1st day of March, 1833, the Commissioners " Ordered that the original surveyed township number two, in range eleven, be set off into a separate township, politic and corporate, and to be called Cass." Ordered that an order be issued to the voters of Cass, to meet on the first Monday of April, and elect Township Officers.

At the formation of Allen Township in 1850, Sections 5, 6, 7, 8, 17, 18, 19, 20, 29, 30, 31 and 32 of this township were taken to assist in the forming of that township. Hence there are but twenty-four sections in this township at present.

This township was named in honor of Gen. Lewis Cass, of Michigan, and is located on the north border of the county. Bounded on the north by Wood County, on the east by Washington township, on the south by Marion, and on the west by Allen Township.

David P. Day, of Wayne County, O., made the first entry of land in this township, on the 10th day of March 1832, at which time he took up the north-east quarter of section eleven. Two days afterwards, John Franks entered the south-west quarter of section one, and the north half of section ten. Mr. Franks was also from Wayne County.

Timber—Soil—Water.

May 3, 1832, Elam Day entered the east half of the north-west quarter of section twelve, and on the 31st day of the same month, Eleazer C. Fairchild, of Trumbull County, entered the south-west quarter of the south-east quarter of section two, and the west half of the north-west quarter of section twelve. In the same year, entries were made by Andrew W. Page, of Green County, D. Shippy, of Seneca, C. W. Colebaugh, Alpheus Eldridge, James Wood, Samuel McClellan, of Wayne, William Eckles, of Holmes, James Beeson, of Fayette.

The timber of this township is of the varieties known in other parts of the county, such as oak, ash, hickory, sugar, beech, elm, walnut, and poplar. And these several kinds of timber were very plenty.

The soil is of several kinds. On the ridge in the north part of the township, it is a sandy and gravelly soil. Between the ridge and the Wood County line, it is a loam of vegetable formation, whilst south of the ridge there is a mixture of clay with other soils.

The Portage river has its source in this part of Hancock County, and is the only stream of water in this township. Good drinking water, however, is obtained by sinking wells to a no very great depth.

The first school house was built in 1835, and there are now six school houses in the township, and the enumeration of youth of school age in 1880, was 278.

The first church was built in 1843, by the Methodist Episcopal denomination, and was known as the Vickers Church on the ridge. There are now but two church buildings in the township, and they both belong to the Methodist Episcopal.

The first settlements were made in 1833, on sections one, two and three, by E. C. Fairchild, Daniel Fairchild, David P. and Elam Day, James Vickers, John Franks, James Brown, Samuel Harry, and on section twelve, by Charles Eckles, John Welch, George Elliot. On section eleven by John Hardy, Hiram Hulbert, James Woods.

The early settlers here were mostly from the eastern part of this state.

There was a post office established is this township in 1837, and discontinued in 1867. Daniel Fairchild and Jas. Vickers were the only post masters.

The people of this township have always been noted for their steady habits and peaceable disposition. There is much very valuable land in this part of the county, and the farms and farm buildings, for style and comfort, will compare favorably with that of any other township in the county.

The Lake Erie and Western Railroad runs across the south-east corner of the township, and the New York, Chicago and St. Louis road, now in course of construction, passes through the township from east to west.

FRANKFORD.

John Franks laid out the town of Frankford, on the northwest quarter of section ten. The town of seventy-two lots were regularly laid out, with a public square or plaza, in the center. The prospective city, however, only existed in name, and no doubt would long since have been forgotten, had it not been a matter of record. There were, perhaps no lots sold, and the town returned to its original state, that is, cornfield.

Justices of the Peace.

The following named persons were elected Justices of the Peace in this township:
John Payne—1834.
Daniel Fairchild—1835.
David Dorsey—1835, 1838.
John Chaffin—1838.
Andrew R. Brandeberry—1841, 1844.
Alonzo H. Cobb—1841, 1844, 1847.
Joseph Wineland—1847.
Joseph Lash—1850.
Abner Crawford—1853, 1856.
Gideon Smith—1856.
Addison Hardy—1859, 1862, 1865, 1868, 1871, 1874.
Enoch Ross—1862, 1865.
Jacob Steeker—1868, 1871, 1874, 1877.
John L. McKee—1876, 1879.
Samuel Creighton—1847, 1850, 1853, 1859.
Henry Stough—1880.

JOHN BURMAN.

John Burman was born in Luzerne County, Pa., in February, 1783, and came to Fairfield County, Ohio, where he was married to Catharine Fisher. Mr. B. was of Dutch descent. He was a gun-smith by trade, and worked at that business until he came to this county, in 1828, after which time he was a farmer. Mr. B., his father and two brothers were in the service of the United States in the war of 1812, and had head-quartees at Franklinton, opposite Columbus, Ohio. When Mr. B. came to this county with his family he took up his residence in a log cabin on the land on which he occupied up to the time of his death.

Mr. B. was of medium height, and weighed about one

hundred and seventy-five pounds, of strong constitution and robust health, he was well calculated to do battle with the hardships of pioneer life.

In religious belief, Mr. B. was a Lutheran, and was a member of that church many years. He built the first mill in the township. During the first year of his residence here, his was the only family residing in the township. He has four sons and two daughters living. Two of his sons were in the army during the rebellion. Mr. B. died in 1863, and his aged wife survived him about five years.

EZRA KARN

Was one of a family of eight boys and four girls, all of whom attained full age except one, and was born in Washington County, Md., September 16th, 1815. The family removed to Ohio in 1817, and settled in Holmes County, then on the frontier, with only a few log cabins, and plenty of wild beasts. In 1836 Mr. Karn came to Hancock County with his family, and settled in this township, on the farm now owned by P. C. Redfern.

Again the family became frontiersmen, the country being new, and but sparsely settled, and without roads or markets. Here the Karn's had as neighbors, John Hardy, Hiram Hulbert, Daniel Fairchild, John Franks, John Eckles and James Vickers.

In 1839 Mr. Karn married Miss Elizabeth Albertson, and commenced at once to make for himself a home. He cleared up two farms, and by his industry and perseverance, succeeded in surrounding himself and family with the comforts of a beautiful home. Mr. K. had a family of eight children, all now living but one. Mrs. Karn died in May, 1880, after a long and useful life. Mr. Karn has the confidence of his neighbors and acquaintances, for his sterling honesty and good common sense. He has been a member of the Lutheran Church for about forty years, and his life has been consistent with his profession.

Mr. Karn has always been a farmer, a progessive farmer, one whose experience and advice have been of advantage to his neighbors. For many years he has been an officer of the Hancock County Agricultural Society. He was one of the very first members of this society at its organization in 1852, and has ever since lent his influence and aid to its building up, and its present success is largely due to his continual labors in its behalf. He is now and has been for four years Vice President of the Society.

JAMES VICKERS

Was born in England, and came to this country in abont 1825, and settled in Wayne County, Ohio. In 1833, he made his way to this county, and commenced his labors on the farm now owned by his son James A. No man in the township was more generally respected, than was Mr. Vickers. Conscientious, honest, temperate and hospitable, kind to all, a friend to the poor, and always ready to render assistance to the weary emigrant. His house was the home of the Methodist itinerant, and here were held the services of the church, until a suitable building for the purpose was erected on his land. To the building of this house and the sustaining of the minister of the church, he was a liberal contributor. Mr. Vickers was a farmer, and by the aid of his good wife and his family, which was a large one, he always had an abundance. He died in 1867, lamented by the entire community. His wife survived him until 1881.

JOHN ECKLES.

The subject of this sketch was born in Westmoreland County, Penn., on the 25th day of April, 1795, and resided in that State until 1836. In 1819 Mr. Eckles married Esther Booth, with whom he lived up to the time of her decease in 1862. His ancestors were from Ireland. He, during his whole active life, followed the occupation of a farmer. He is a man of strong will and of very decided opinions, and is not easily swerved from his purposes.

In 1836, with his wife and four sons, he emigrated to this township. He purchased two hundred and twenty acres of land on the ridge, between Fostoria and Van Buren, principally of John Franks, sr., and went boldly to work clearing up a farm, and he succeeded in making one of the very best on the ridge. The country was new, no markets, no roads, no neighbors scarcely, and the family endured all the hardships incident to new settlements. Mr. E. united with the Presbyterian Church in early life, and was one of the first members of that church at Van Buren. He is quite active for a man of his age, yet the weight of years is sensibly felt by him, but his former habits, and his early industry, enaable him to now live a quiet, peaceful life, free from toil or privations.

Statistics of Grain and Stock.

Statistical table showing the acreage and bushels of grain and the number and value of live stock, as returned by the Township Assessor, to the County Auditor in 1861.

Wheat,	2,502	Acres.	52,668	Bushels.
Oats,	489	"	15,416	"
Corn,	1,674	"	57,675	"
Flax,	16	"	137	"
Hay,	628	"	740	Tons.
Horses,	439	number.	$18,565,	Value.
Cattle,	1,019	"	10,735,	"
Sheep,	2,295	"	4,343,	"
Swine,	1,551	"	3,764,	"

DELAWARE TOWNSHIP.

Tp. 2, S., R. 11, E.   Tp. 2, S., R. 12, E.
Area 19,200 acres.   Population 1,456.

In the year 1828, the territory now included in this township was organized and named Welfare. We find this record of the proceedings of the County Commissioners, under date of June 1st, 1829; "Agreeable to the petition of sundry citizens of Welfare township, in Hancock County, the name of Welfare is changed to that of Delaware, and to be known as such."

I have not been able to ascertain why the township was originally called Welfare, nor do the records disclose the reason for changing to Delaware. The township no doubt owes its present name to the fact that the Delaware tribe of Indians made this part of the county a favorite resort.

This township now includes sections 1, 2, 3, 4, 9, 10, 11, 12, 13, 14, 15, 16, 21, 22, 23, 24, 25, 26, 27, 28, 33, 34, 35, 36, in township 2 south, range 11 east, and sections, 6, 7, 18, 19, 30 and 31 in township 2 south, range 12 east. It is located in the south-east corner of the county, and bounded on the north by Amanda and Jackson townships, on the east by Wyandotte County, on the south by Hardin County, on the west by Madison township. It contains thirty sections of land.

Asa M. Lake made the first entry of lands in this town-

First Settlement.

ship on the 12th day of December, 1822. The tract entered was the west half of the north-west quarter of section 1.

In 1823 entries were made in the following order as to dates; Michael Buck, west half of the north-east quarter of section 2, Curtis Berry, east half of north-east quarter of section 2, John Brundige, the south-west quarter of section 1, W. J. Greer, east half of north-west quarter of section 1, John Rose, east half of south-west quarter of section 14, William Davis, east half of north-west quarter of section 14. Then followed entries by David Augustus, Marquis Lafayette Plumb, Levi Edgington and others in 1826, and by Josiah Elder, Godfrey Wolford and others in 1827.

The first settlement made in this township was by Asa M. Lake in the year 1822. Mr. Lake built a log cabin on a parcel of ground now owned by Michael Treece, and in the limits of the village of Mt. Blanchard. The parcel of land had been used by the Indians as a burying ground. Many skeletons and relics have been dug up, and even to the present day they are to be found. Mr. Lake was one of the very earliest settlers of the county. He entered and settled on the west half of the north-west quarter of section 1. This tract was on the east side of the Blanchard River, and is now occupied in part by the village of Mt. Blanchard.

Amongst the first settlers of this township were Asa M. Lake, Josiah Elder, the Hamlins, one of whom—Don Alonzo—was one of the first county officers, the Wolfords, of whom Godfrey was one of the first Commissioners of the county, and the Greers.

The settlement here was perhaps the very earliest in the county, next to that at Findley. Don Alonzo Hamlin was the first Sheriff of the county, and was also County Assessor. Godfrey Wolford was Coroner of the county, and was also County Commissioner I believe, and Asa M. Lake was one of the first Justices of the Peace in the county.

The lands in this township were mostly purchased by emigrants from the south-eastern counties of Ohio. A few, however, were from Pennsylvania and Virginia. This was a full township of thirty-six sections until the formation of Wyandotte County in 1845, when one tier of sections on the east side were taken to help form that county.

Asa M. Lake, who first came to the county in 1822, resided here to the time of his death. He was a fair specimen of the class of men who first emigrate to a new country, hardy, industrious and honest. He succeeded in building up for himself and children a home in one of the richest sections of our county, and lived long enough to see a thriving village built up on the very lands he had redeemed from the wilderness, and peopled with an intelligent and energetic population, supplied with schools and churches and other appliances of civilization.

The red-man, who had been his early companion, had long since been removed westward, and herds of domestic animals taken the place of the wild.

Josiah Elder, whose parents came to this part of the county almost simultaneously with the Lakes, after spending an honest, active lifetime, almost, in the township, died a few years ago, on the old homestead. Mrs. Henry Helms, a sister of Mr. Elder, related to me, a few years ago, the incidents connected with her wedding day, in that long ago. She was first married to William J. Greer, of this township. She relates that her intended husband, and herself, travelled from Delaware township to Findley on horse-back—both on one horse—through the almost trackless wilderness, where

Soil—Timber—Water. 239

they obtained a license, and then in the same manner went to the residence of Joshua Hedges, a Justice of the Peace, three miles west of Findley, where they were married, and returned to their homes. The trip occupied three days. What do my fair readers think of that style of wedding tour?

The soil of this township is generally a black sandy loam, intermixed with clay in some parts. The Blanchard River traverses the township from south to north, and with its fertile bottom lands, and numerous creek bottoms, makes it one of the best agricultural districts in the county. Many of the most beautiful farms in the county are to be found here. The lands—as in all parts of the county—were heavily wooded, and the improvements we see here are the result of the most arduous toil. The fruitful fields have been redeemed from the wilderness, only by the most patient industry and economy.

The timber here found is of the usual kinds, indigenous to the country, such as sugar, beech, elm, white and black ash, the different varieties of the oak, walnut, hickory, hackberry, buckeye, etc.

The township is well watered by the Blanchard River, which crosses it, and by the creeks and runs tributary to it. The most considerable creek is in the eastern part of the township, and called Potatoe Creek. Good drinking water can be had in all portions of the township, by sinking wells from ten to thirty feet.

The first school house was built in 1830, near the center of the township, on the farm now owned by J. A. Rose. The first school was taught by John Wolford. The school population was not large at that time, and were easily accommodated in the log school house. The enumeration of school age in this township, in 1880 was 355, outside the town of Mt. Blanchard. There are now eight school houses in the township, one graded and seven common or ungraded.

The first church was built in 1838 by the Methodist Episcopal denomination, in the town of Mt. Blanchard. But it must not be supposed that the people were without religious services up to that time. The school houses and private houses had been the churches. There are now seven churches in the township, three Methodist Protestant, two Methodist Episcopal, one Baptist and one Presbyterian.

Godfrey Wolford built a flouring mill on the Blanchard River in 1830, near the center of the township. The mill is now known as "Fahl's Mill." And Felix Miller built a saw mill—the first in the township—on the Blanchard River, near the south line of the township.

The only still-house ever in the township was built in 1833, by Abner Bell. It was run but a short time, and was then sold to Samuel Thornton, and removed to Jackson township, where it was operated for several years.

The first white child born in this township, was John B. Elder, and it is believed to be the first white child born in the county. Marian Greer was the first white female born in the township. Nancy Williams, wife of Nathan Williams, was the first white person who died in this township.

The first election for township officers was held in 1832. R. W. Hamlin, Harvey Smith and John Rose were elected Trustees, Godfrey Wolford, Clerk, and D. O. Hamlin, Treasurer.

The first couple married were Asa M. Lake and Charlotte M. Greer, and the second couple, William J. Greer and Rosanna Elder. Both couples were married by Joshua Hedges, J. P. of Findley.

Mr. Simpson Harris, long a resident of the township, and to whom I am indebted for much valuable information, relates the following incidents:

"In 1828, or 1829, as John H. Greer, M. S. Hamlin, J. Greer and D. O. Hamlin were out at play, they came to where a tree had been blown out by the roots, and in falling had left bare the skeleton of an Indian. Upon examination they found a large amount of jewelry, consisting of finger rings, ear and nose rings, wristlets, breast plate, necklace, and quite a large nugget, which they supposed to be copper, all engraved with some French characters. They, supposing the rings to be nothing but tin, and of no particular value, divided them equally between themselves, as near as they could.

"There was a trading post established in what is now Wyandotte County, the agent of which, hearing of their finding, sent word that if they would bring them to him he would pay them all they were worth. M. S. Hamlin sent his portion of the rings, etc., for which he received seven dollars in money. The nugget laid around for a long time, pieces being frequently hacked off, and it was finally lost. This was afterwards supposed by some to have been gold."

"In 1830, John Greer and M. S. Hamlin, two lads, concluded they would take a hunt, and with their guns and ammunition, on a beautiful morning, they started on their way. After spending some time in the sport, and securing what game they wanted, they started on their way homeward. After travelling sometime, and not reaching home, it became evident that they had lost their way.

"After a few moments of consultation they agreed on the direction they would take, when travelling until late in the afternoon, they came to an opening or clearing. At this they rejoiced to think they would soon rest their weary limbs. But their hopes were doomed to disappointment, for they had landed at Upper Sandusdy.

"But they did not allow this discovery to entirely discourage them. They concluded to try it again, but by a surer road this time. They struck off on the old Indian trail. To reach home that night they knew was impossible, but determined to go as far as they could. The afternoon being well spent, some preparation must be made for the night. Just as the sun was setting they came to an Indian wigwam. The old Indian and his squaw kindly took them in, administered to their wants, and they had a good night's rest. The next morning the old Indian pointed out the old trail to them, bade them God speed on their road home, where they arrived the same day."

MT. BLANCHARD.

In October, 1830, Asa M. Lake, one of the very earliest settlers of the county, laid out a town of fifty-three lots on a part of the west half of the north-west quarter of section 1, and the east half of the north-east quarter of section 2, and called it Mt. Blanchard. It is situated on the bluffs, or high grounds on the east bank of the Blanchard River. The location is a good one, surrounded by beautiful and rich farming lands. The town is regularly laid out in squares, the streets and alleys crossing at right angles. The buildings are mostly of wood, and the dwellings are commodious and respectable. The town was incorporated in 1865. Dr. John Foster was the first Mayor, since which time the following persons have held the office: H. C. Pickett, J. W. Turnpaugh, J. W. Wingate, W. W. Hughes, A. F. Naus, J.

W. Pickett, Jacob Harris and R. W. McVary, present incumbent.

A Post Office was established here in 1834, with John P. Gordon as first Post Master, since which time Elijah Stradley, Chester Cook, W. W. Smith, J. Lafferty, J. Patterson, L. A. Baldwin and Henry Greer, who now holds the office, have been Post Masters.

The Methodist Episcopal denomination built the first church in the town. It was a frame building and built in 1838. The Rev: Thomas Thompson and Rev. Gavit, then Missionaries at Upper Sandusky, were the first Methodist preachers. They organized a Society at the residence of Father Greer, one half a mile east of Mt. Blanchard, on the banks of Potatoe Creek, where they continued to worship until a hewed log school house was built on a corner of the Greer land, in 1833 late in the fall, worshipped there until they built their frame house in town in 1838, where they met about twenty years, then moved into their present house, south part of town.

The first school house in the town was of the then prevailing style, built of round logs, with huge fire place, clapboard roof and other peculiarities not now known to builders. The Union School of Mt. Blanchard was organized in 1868, and their present building was erected in 1873. It is a commodious, two story brick structure, the style and finish of which gives it a commanding appearance. There are three large school rooms, besides smaller ones for recitations, and other purposes. The building and grounds cost $8,000. In 1880, there were 151 children of school age in the district.

The business of the village is quite extensive for an inland town, with no railroad, or other transportation facilities.

There are two large dry goods stores, one by J. H. Biddle, and the other by W. S. Shoemaker & Co. These stores keep a full line of goods, and are doing a large and lucrative business. By keeping an assortment of standard articles, they are able to control the trade of the surrounding country for many miles.

The drug business is successfully carried on by Dr. W. M. Yost, and Henry Greer. Both of these gentlemen carry a full line in trade, and by fair dealing, and attention to business have been enabled to command a very fair trade. Both being experienced druggists, they have and deserve the confidence of the entire community.

Two family groceries supply the inhabitants with such articles as are needed in that line. One saloon supplies that want. The hotel "entertains man and beast," as the old signs used to read. This hotel is kept and conducted in such a manner as places it above the average of country hotels. Three blacksmiths are kept busy at their work, and two wagon shops supply the town and surrounding country with work in their line, built of the best materials, and in the best style of workmanship. There are two boot and shoe stores well stocked and well patronized. One butcher shop supplies the people with fresh meats. Such is the business of this thriving village.

The Odd Fellows organized a lodge here in 1858, and have a healthy membership of fifty. A Masonic lodge was organized here in 1878, and now numbers twenty.

The population of this village in 1880 was two hundred and eighty-six.

The following is a list of persons who have held the office of Justice of Peace, with the date of their election.

Asa M. Lake—1828, 1831, 1834.

Justices of the Peace.

Godfrey Wolford—1834, 1837, 1840, 1843, 1846, 1849.
John Lafferty—1835, 1838, 1841, 1844, 1847, 1850, 1853, 1856, 1859, 1862, 1865.
Benjamin Corbin—1847.
Robert Taylor—1855.
John Rose—1856.
Thomas Miller—1859.
Harvey Smith—1841.
Robert Park—1862, 1865, 1868.
E. A. Sheffield—1868.
Jacob Bridinger—1870.
Jacob Harris—1870, 1873, 1876, 1879.
Geo. W. Beard—1871, 1874.
Josiah Fahl—1877, 1880.
Balser Hauman—1880.

An exhibit of the number of acres, and number of bushels of grain, and number and value of live stock in this township, as returned to the Auditor in 1881.

Wheat,	3,771	acres.	70,073	bushels.
Oats,	286	"	7,949	"
Corn,	2,547	"	104,570	"
Flax,	114	"	1,069	"
Hay,	568	"	624	tons.
Horses,	574	number.	$30,070,	value.
Cattle,	1,223	"	14,270,	"
Sheep,	3,676	"	7,500,	"
Swine,	2,435	"	5,670,	"

EAGLE TOWNSHIP

Tp. 1, S.   R. 10, E.
AREA 23,040 ACRES.   POPULATION 1,309.

The Commissioners' records of the 3d of December, 1832, read: "A petition was presented by sundry citizens of the original township No. 1, south, in range 10 east, praying to be organized. Township 1 south in range ten east was accordingly set off, and formed into a body politic and corporate, and the said township shall be called Eagle."

This township is bounded on the north by Liberty and Findley townships, on the east by Jackson, on the south by Madison and Van Buren, and on the west by Union, and takes its name from the creek of the same name which runs through it. It is situated in the first range of townships south of the base line.

The records of the Land Office show that the first land entered in this township was the west half of the northeast quarter of section 35, by John Woodruff, on the first day of June, 1827. On the 6th day of June, 1829, Elijah Woodruff entered the north-west quarter of section 13. This land is now owned by William Yates and J. Alspach. On the 7th day of August of the same year, Philip Heakes entered the lands now owned by the heirs of George Arnold in section twelve, and in November of the same year, Geo. Bishop entered the north-west quarter of section 24, now owned by John D. Bishop. The north-west quarter of section 9 was entered by Joshua Hedges, of Pickaway County, on the 28th of September, 1830, and on the 27th of November, in the same year, Shun Sager entered the west half of the south-west quarter of section 31. This land is now owned by I. Heldman. In the later part of the year 1831, entries were made in sections 5, 6 and 8 by Jacob Powell, Peter Powell and John Powell, all of Fairfield County, O., and by John Bright in section 21. Other entries followed, and much of the land in the township was speedily taken up.

The soil of this locality is much of it a sandy loam. In some parts a clay soil predominates. The bottom lands along Eagle Creek are exceedingly fertile, and many very valuable farms may be found here. The surface of the land is generally level, except along the creek, where it is somewhat broken, but not enough to prevent easy cultivation. Some parts of the township have been, and indeed are yet, occasionally subject to a disease known as "Milk Sickness." The cause of this disease has never yet been discovered, and is attributed to the character of the soil, to the water, to vegetation, either living or decaying, but each and all of these theories have been discarded as not giving a satisfactory solution of the cause. Certain it is, however, the cause of the disease, no matter what it may be, is found only in the uncultivated or unreclaimed lands. It is not known on cleared or cultivated fields. Hence, perhaps the most rational conclusion is that the cause is some species of vegetation, that disappears when lands are once cultivated.

The timber is of the prevalent varieties found elsewhere in the county, such as walnut, beech, ash, oak, maple and buckeye. The timber and vegetation thoughout the township was of a very rank growth.

Eagle Creek and Tiderashy, with their tributaries, furnish an abundance of stock water, and sufficient drainage in all parts of the township. Eagle Creek crosses the township from south to north, in the east part, and Tiderashy Creek follows the same course in the western part, thus pretty thoroughly watering and draining the entire surface. These streams of course are small, and yet Eagle Creek has furnished water power for mill purposes ever since the early settlement of the township.

The first settlement made in this township was by John Woodruff in the latter part of 1829, and by John Decker Benjamin Whitman, Conrad Line, Jacob Zoll, and R. W. McClellon in 1830. These pioneers were followed in 1831 by John D. Bishop, Elias Decker, Amos Crum and others. These first settlers were for the most part from Fairfield and Franklin counties. Whitman was from New York, and McClellon from Pennsylvania. The first settlements were made on or near Eagle Creek, on the east side of the township. The Nunamakers, Heldmans, and others very soon after made settlements in the west part, and the Powells and others located on Tiderashy Creek.

At the first election in 1833, when the township was organized, there were barely electors enough to fill the different offices. Benjamin Whitman, Conrad Line, George Bishop, John Woodruff and John Decker were voters at that election.

The first school house built within the limits of the township was in the Bishop district, in 1834. Mr. John D. Bishop informs me that himself and Benjamin Whitman were the only tax-payers in the district at the time. Rachael McBride taught the first school in this building. There are now nine school districts, each one supplied with a com-

First Church—First Mill. 249

fortable school building, and an enumeration in the township of four hundred and fifty-eight children of school age.

There were no church buildings in the township until 1840, although religious services had been held, and societies formed before that time. These societies met for worship in private families, or in the different school houses. In 1840 the United Brethren Church erected a building on the farm of John Woodruff, on the east side of the creek. It was of hewed logs, small in dimensions, but sufficiently large to accommodate the religiously inclined of the young settlement. Of the first members of this church we have the names of Mrs. Woodruff, Conrad Line and wife, and some of the Deckers.

The first mill was known as Decker's hand mill, and here by a great deal of muscular power, corn could be ground fine enough for mush making. It was, however, a slow, laborious process. In 1830 George Bishop erected a saw mill, and in 1833, a flouring mill, still known as Bishop's Mill. In 1854 John D. Bishop, the present owner of the mill, attached steam power, as the mill previous to that time had been propelled by water. But after a few years trial he became dissatisfied with this, and removed it, since which time water has again been used as the motive power. Perhaps no mill in the county has been of more real benefit, when mills were most needed, than has this one. Not only did the immediate neighborhood patronize it, but people from a distance came here.

This township is being rapidly developed. Already it can boast of some of the richest farms in the county. There are a large number of very fine residences, and some of the very best farm buildings in the county. The soil is rich and when the timber is removed, is easily cultivated. The peo-

17

ple are engaged in agriculture and stock raising. The number and character of the church and school buildings found here, speaks of its intelligence and morals. One in travelling over the township cannot fail to observe the steady, permanent improvements being made in all parts, and is struck with the air of thrift and contentment which seem to pervade.

MARTINSTOWN

Was laid out on the south-east corner of section 36, by Martin Hollobaugh, in September, 1836. There were, perhaps, never any lots sold, or streets laid out, as the site was at the cross-roads, and the record of the platting of the town closed up its existence, if indeed it ever had one.

CLEMENT POST OFFICE.

A Post Office of this name was established in 1850, with Amos Crum as Post Master. The office was located on the Bellefontaine road about six miles south of Findley. Mr. Crum was succeeded as Post Master by John Swank, who held the office until it was discontinued in 1864.

GEORGE W. ALSPACH.

In the latter part of April, 1834, Mr. Alspach, to use his own language, "landed in Hancock County, in Eagle township, at the house of John Powell." He at once engaged to work for Mr. Powell at $13 per month. In the fall of the same year he went back to his home in Fairfield County, but soon returned, and went to work for Jacob Zoll. He says however, "that he took time to select a lot of land, and go to the land office to enter it, but was too late, as it had already been taken up." After returning to the township, he selected and entered the south-west quarter of section

22. Mr. Alspach is now living on this same tract of land, which by his industry has been converted into a beautiful and valuable farm.

Mr. Alspach says he was married in March, 1835, built a cabin on his land, moved into it in May, without a door or window in place. A blanket served to close the door. This cabin stood in the woods, with wolves howling them to sleep at night. His nearest neighbor was Benj. O. Whitman, who lived one mile and a half distant.

The first settlers in this part of the township, as Mr Alspach remembers them, were the Woodruffs, Whitman, John Decker, Ebright, William Tanner and Jacob Powell previous to 1834, then came Jacob Zoll, Peter Oman, Moses Elsea, Henry Keel, John Powell, Daniel and Peter Fellers, and J. Alspach. Mr. Alspach said that at one time he was at a log rolling, or house raising, every day for three weeks. All the township offices have been filled by Mr. Alspach, including Overseer of the Poor, and Fence Viewer, and yet he never became wealthy holding office. Mr. Alspach is and always has been an honest, upright man and good citizen.

JOHN WALTERS

Was born in Rockingham County, Va., June 22d, 1814, and in his infancy his parents removed to Kentucky. His father died in Shelby County, Ky., in 1824, and the widow, and children, of whom there were six, removed to Fairfield County, Ohio, two years later. Here Mr. Walters, having received such an education only as could be had in a common school of that day, followed the occupation of a farm hand until 1841, having by his industry and economy saved money enough, he made entry of the land on which he now resides, and came to this township, his mother, and other members of the family having preceded him.

In 1842, Mr. Walters was married to Miss Penelope Woodruff, and at once moved into a cabin on his land, and commenced life in earnest, clearing up and cultivating a fine tract of land. Mr. W. was the father of seven children, six of whom are now living. His health is none of the best, but he seems to enjoy life in his old days. Mr. Walters united with the United Brethren Church in 1842, and has ever since been a consistent member, and was for twenty-five years a class leader, and for the past nineteen years has held a license to exhort. He enjoys the respect and friendship of all his neighbors, and is a good citizen.

The following named persons have held the office of Justice of the Peace, having been elected at the dates mentioned.

Benjamin Whitman—1833.

Jacob Powell—1836, 1839, 1850, 1853, 1860, 1863, 1866, 1869.

William Williamson—1839.

Jacob Miller—1842, 1845.

W. W. Hughes—1842, 1845, 1848, 1858.

John Miller—1848, 1851.

Henry Bishop—1853.

John Swonk—1853.

Peter Bender—1857.

John Wise—1857.

John Croft—1857, 1866, 1869, 1872, 1875, 1878.

Abraham Keel—1863.

Peter H. Powell—1872, 1875, 1878.

L. W. Scothorn—1879.

Jacob B. Smith—1881.

Crop Statistics. 253

An exhibit of the number of acres of grain sown, and the number of bushels produced, and the number and value of live stock in Eagle township, as returned by the Township Assessor in 1881.

Wheat, 3,905 acres.	68,530 bushels.	
Oats, 315 "	11,242 "	
Corn, 2,867 "	117,170 "	
Flax, 104 "	1,077 bushels.	
Hay, 814 "	937 tons.	
Horses, 648 number.	$32,210, value.	
Cattle, 1,576 "	20,260, "	
Sheep, 2,577 "	5,990, "	
Hogs, 2,705 "	7,000, "	

FINDLEY TOWNSHIP.

TP. 1, N. R. 10, E. TP. 1, N. R. 11 E.
AREA 15,360 ACRES. POPULATION 5,556.

From the preliminary organization of the County of Hancock in 1820, until 1823 the counties of Hancock and Wood formed one township, called Waynesfield. The Commissioners of Wood County passed the following order at their session, May 28, 1823; "Ordered further that so much of the township of Waynesfield as is included in the unorganized county of Hancock be set off and organized into a township by the name of Findley, and that the election for township officers be held on the first day of July, A. D. 1823, at the house of Wilson Vance, in said township."

The township so remained until after the permanent organization of the county, when in 1828, the townships of Amanda and Welfare—now Delaware—were organized from territory in the south-eastern portion of the township. In 1829 the township of Jackson was organized out of territory then belonging to Findley township.

At the session of the Commissioners held on the 6th day of December, 1830, we find this entry in connection with the division of the townships of Findley and Amanda, and the formation of Marion township; " * * * * and likewise in the next place commencing at the south-east corner of section 32, thence north to the north-east corner of section 5, in township 1 north, range 11, thence west to the north-west corner of section 2, in range 10, thence south to the south-west corner of section 35, in township 1 north, thence east to the south-east corner of section 32, to the place of beginning, which shall be a body corporate and politic, and retaining the name of Findley." Thus by successive acts of the County Commissioners was the boundaries of this township, once co-extensive with those of the county, reduced to less than those of an original township.

The first entry of land in this township was that of the east part of the south-east quarter of section 13, by Vance, Neil and Cory. In September of the same year John Brown entered the north-west quarter of section 19. The first mentioned tract is now that part of the town of Findley lying on the west side Main street, between the river and Sandusky street. The Brown entry is that part of the town south of Sandusky and east of Main, known as Byal's addition. On the 4th of October, 1821, John P. Hamilton made entry of the west part of the south-west quarter of section 17, now owned by Aaron Baker. The south-west quarter of section 30 was entered by Job Chamberlain, on the 4th of October, 1821. This land has been known in connection with that adjoining it as Chamberlain's Hill. In the same month John Simpson entered the east half of the north-east quarter of section 25. This is now the Ross Bennett farm, adjoining the County Fair Grounds. On the 14th of November of the same year the east half of the north-east quarter of section 24 was entered by McIlvain and Neil. This is now included in the town of Findley. Thomas Slight entered the land known as the old Johnny Patterson farm on the south side of the river. In 1822 Joshua Hedges entered about one half of the north-east quarter of section 11, and which has ever since been known as the Hedges' farm. It lies along the north bank of the Blanchard, from the late Judge Strother's farm, to the Liberty township line. George Hollenbeck in the same year took up the south-east quarter of section 12, the farm now owned by Samuel Howard, and Asa M. Lake entered the lands on which Maple Grove Cemetery is now located. Entries of the Didway farm by Rev. James Gilruth, and of the John Heck farm by Joseph Westenhaver, and of the Vance farm by Judge Strother, and of the Campbell Byal farm by his father, John Byal, and of the A. W. Strother farm, and of the lands on which North Findley in now located, and the Jacob Foster farm and the Jesse Whitney farm, and many others were made prior to the premanent organization of the county.

This township takes it name from the town, and is composed of sections 1, 2, 11, 12, 13, 14, 23, 24, 25, 26, 35 and 36 in township 1 north, range 10 east, and sections 5, 6, 7, 8, 17, 18, 19, 20, 29, 30, 31 and 32 in township 1 north, range 11 east. This township is situated almost in the center of the county, and divided almost in the center east and west by the Blanchard River. It is bounded on the north by Allen township, on the east by Marion, on the south by Jackson and Eagle, and on the west by Liberty.

The soil of this township is generally of a rich quality, and varied in kind. Along the north line the soil is generally clay, underlined with what is called a hard pan, and is adapted to growing of grass, and for grazing purposes. Along the river and creek bottoms it is of the usual rich quality, sandy loam. On the south side of the river the entire body of land is underlaid with limestone, and as a consequence the soil is of the most productive quality. As an agricultural region this township is not surpassed by any in the county. Being around the county seat, the improvements are perhaps more marked and more elaborate than in more distant portions of the county, and give to the surroundings of the town a most comfortable and cheerful look.

This whole township—except the water courses—was very heavily timbered with walnut of the very best quality, oak, ash, hickory, elm, beech, and a great abundance of the sugar maple. But at the time this timber had to be removed it was of no value, and it took no little amount of labor to remove it.

The Blanchard River passes through this township, furnishing an abundance of stock water, and also sufficient, a portion of the year, to run the mills on its banks within the boundary of the township; the Carlin Mill at Findley, and Byal's Mill, just over the line in Liberty township.

Besides the Blanchard River, we have its tributaries, Eagle Creek, Lye Creek, and Whitney's Run, all of them quite considerable streams, entering the river from the south. All of these creeks in common with the river, have limestone beds. The stone is abundant, easily quarried, and suitable for building foundations for buildings, the stone work for bridges, and for making lime. On the north, Strother's Run and Hedges' Run, both moderately sized water courses, enter the river. These creeks and water courses, in connection with the river, furnish excellent drainage in abundance. There are no springs of any consequence in the township, but an excellent quality of water can be obtained easily by digging, in any part of the township. In its primeval state, although situated so near the river, much of the land was very wet, not swampy, but low, deep vegetable soil, and in many places underlaid with a hard pan of clay, the water was prevented from sinking, and having no channels opened, the surface was necessarily wet. But this has all disappeared under an intelligent system of drainage.

The town of Findley occupies so much of the township, and so much of the history of the two is inseparably connected, that not much can be said of the township, which may not as well be said of the town.

Of course the first settlement in the township was made within the limits of the town, and yet settlements were made at a very early day—almost as early as in town—by John P. Hamilton, only a short distance up the river from the town. Job Chamberlain, sr., began opening up a farm on Chamberlain Hill, almost at the same time that improvements began in the village. At almost as early a date, John Byal commenced on the river bank two miles west of town, to open up what is now one of the most beautiful and valuable farms in the county, and even before this time Joshua Hedges had located on his lands on the north side of the river, next to the Liberty township line. Judge Strother began the making of his splendid farm just outside the corporation line. George Hollenbach, Jacob Foster, Benjamin Strother, Wm. Taylor, Robert Benham, Aaron Huff, and quite a number of others came into the township prior to 1830.

The first school house, and the first church in the township were both inside the limits of the present town of Findley. There are now seven school houses in the township—outside of the town—with an enumeration of four hundred and forty-four youth. There are two churches, one Methodist Episcopal, one Evangelical, one a brick, the other frame.

The first election, in 1823, was held by order of the Com-

Job Chamberlain, Sr.

missioners of Wood County for the purpose of electing two Justices of the Peace, and only thirteen votes were cast. Job Chamberlain, sr., William Moreland and Benjamin Chandler were the Judges, Wilson Vance and Mathew Reighly, Clerks, and Robert McKinnis and Wilson Vance were elected Justices of the Peace.

Of the men who were officers of that election, Job Chamberlain, sr., and Wilson Vance were citizens of the county up to the time of their decease. Of Mr. Chamberlain, I have the following facts from his son Job, who is yet a resident of Findley.

Mr. Chamberlain was born in the State of Connecticut, and was married there to a Miss Deborah Root, and with her removed to Cayuga Co., N. Y., where they lived for twenty-eight years. They then emigrated to the west, and settled at Lawrenceburg, Ind., where after a residence at that place of two years, they came to Urbana, Ohio, and after a year's residence, they in 1822, removed to this township, and settled on what is known as Chamberlain's Hill. At that time there were but six white families in the county, Benjamin Cox, Wilson Vance, William Moreland, —— Smith, John Simpson and George Lake, who lived at what is now Mt. Blanchard.

When Mr. Chamberlain arrived in the township, there were no buildings on his land, and he was compelled to unload his goods on the ground, but what few settlers were here, assisted him in building a cabin, and such was their expedition that Mr. Chamberlain occupied his new house on the third day from the time the building was commenced.

Mrs. Chamberlain died on the 8th day of January, 1829, and about a year afterwards Mr. Chamberlain married a Miss Sarah Criner, and removed about six miles west of

Findley, in Liberty township, dividing his old farm between his two sons, Norman and Job. Mr. Chamberlain died in 1848, and his wife in 1854.

William Moreland came to the county in 1822, and settled on the north side of the river, on what was afterwards known as the Taylor farm, and now a part of North Findley. Mr. Moreland entered eighty acres of this land, which he afterwards sold to William Taylor for $375, and removed to Van Buren township, and served as a Justice of the Peace for several years, when he sold out, and came back to Findley.

Mathew Riley—or Reighly—was long a resident of the county, and held several important offices in both township and county. He eventually removed to the west.

Of the earliest settlers in this township, we may be permitted to speak of Joshua Hedges, who was the first Treasurer of the county, and who lived on the north-east quarter of section 11, about two miles west of the town of Findley, and on the north side of the river. Mr. Hedges was a tall, muscular man, a little stooped, of good constitution, energetic and of strict integrity. He was a native of Virginia; hospitable in his feelings, he never allowed either white man or Indian to leave his house in want. Politically, he was a Democrat of the strictest sort. He was for many years a member of the Methodist Church, and was in his acts consistent with his profession. He died in 1845. He had a large family, only two of whom are now living—Mrs. Rachael Dulin, of Portage township, and Mrs. Elizabeth Huntwork, of Kansas.

John P. Hamilton was also one of the early settlers of the township. He entered and cleared up the farm just east of Lye Creek, now owned by Aaron Baker. Mr. Hamilton was a man of strong will, and determined in any matter he took in hand. He was one of the first Commissioners of the county, and in his official capacity took an active part in the public improvements of the county, in developing its resources, and in inaugurating those measures which have led to our present greatness. Mr. Hamilton died about the year 1860.

Robert Bonham came to the township at a very early day, and commenced clearing up a farm a little north-west of Findley, and upon which he resided up to the time of his death in May, 1877.

Mr. Bonham was an industrious, economical, and unassuming man. As a neighbor, he was kind and accommdating, as a citizen, he was true to the best interests of the people, as he understood them, as a Christian he was consistent. Purely domestic in his habits, he very seldom went farther from home than the village, and was never in a railroad car until less than a year before his death. He was a man of peculiar habits, but respected by all who knew him. Mr. Bonham was a native of Virginia, and was three times married.

The first election held in the township, as it is now constituted, was on the 4th day of April, 1831, when the following officers were elected: Isaac Jameson, Thomas Slight, and Isaac Baker, Trustees; William L. Henderson, Clerk; Squire Carlin, Treasurer; Supervisors, Bass Rawson and Jacob Foster, sr.; Fence Viewers, John Boyd and Leonard Tritch; Overseers of the Poor, James B. Moore and John Smith; Constable, John Bashore. The important offices of Fence Viewers and Overseers of the Poor, with all their honors and emoluments, have long since been abolished.

John Byal, one of the pioneers of the township, was born

in the city of Baltimore, Md., on the 25th day of July, 1791, and was the second son of William Byal, who died in Findley, in 1840. The Byal family removed from Maryland to Pennsylvania, first to Huntington, and afterwards to Westmoreland County. In 1809, the family came to Ohio, settling in Stark County, and here in 1816 Mr. Byal was married to Elizabeth Newstutter, and commenced life on a tract of land purchased of the General Government, in Sugar Creek township, in that county. In March, 1832, Mr. Byal sold his Stark County farm, and came to Hancock County, and settled on the Byal farm, just east of the Infirmary. At that time it was all woods, and only by the hardest of labor, and the most rigid economy, was it reclaimed, and converted into one of the handsomest and most desirable farms in the county.

In the same year—1832—Mr. Byal built a saw mill on the Blanchard, just east of the present bridge across the river at that place. In 1834 he built what is now known as the Teatsorth Mill, being the first frame building in the county for mill purposes. It was an old fashioned water mill, with monster water wheel, which went splashing in a lazy, continuous round, but with force and life enough to supply the neighborhood with flour and meal during the season in which it was or could run.

Mr. Byal was the father of nine children, five of whom are living—Henry, the oldest, resides in Findley, and is quite wealthy, and for his honesty and business qualities commands the respect of his fellow citizens. He has filled a number of offices, having been Justice of the Peace for three terms. Catherine resides at Kalida, Ohio, William in Iowa, and Nancy and Rachael in Kansas.

Mr. Byal was elected County Commissioner in 1834, and

served two terms. He was one of the principal movers in the building of the present Court House. He also served as Justice of the Peace.

Mr. Byal died July 13th, 1853, and his widow survived him about six years.

BARNA BEARDSLEY

Was the oldest of seven sons of Daniel Beardsley, and was born in Delaware County, New York, on the 9th day of March, 1797. His parents were from the State of Connecticut, and of course were Yankees. In 1803 his father came to Ohio and settled near Newark, in Licking County. When about fifteen years of age, Mr. B. left his home and went to Columbus, O., or rather to Franklinton—as there was no Columbus then—and during the war of 1812-15, he served part of the time as a wagon-boy, and part of the time as clerk in the office of the Paymaster. He was several times sent out as the bearer of important dispatches, to the officers in command of the different posts in northern Ohio. Dispatches were sent by him to Gen. Cass at Zanesville, to Gen. Harrison at Fort Meigs, and to the commander at Fort Croghan at Fremont.

After the close of the war, he went to the mouth of the River Rasin, and engaged in the carpenter trade. He also assisted in the erection of the first frame buildings in Sandusky City. After several years absence he returned to Licking County, where on the 9th day of April, 1820, he married Mary Boylan, the eldest child of Aaron and Beulah Boylan. From that time until 1834, he followed his trade as carpenter, and operated Hollister's Distillery until September, 1834, when he came to Hancock County, his father-in-law and one sister having preceded him, and took up his residence with his wife and seven children in a cabin on the present Infirmary farm. The country was then very new, and being almost without means, a struggle commenced for the support of himself and his young family.

Fortunately his services as a carpenter were in demand in the new settlement, and steady employment was had, at what was then deemed good wages. But as all materials for building had to be wrought out by hand, not many buildings could be erected in a year, and the work was of the most laborious kind.

In 1840, Mr. B. and his sons having farmed quite extensively in addition to his work as a mechanic, he purchased of Aaron Hough thirty acres of land in Findley township, and he and his family at once went to work clearing it up, and in the fall of 1841 had so far succeeded as to be able to move on it, in a cabin which had been erected.

Here his four sons, the eldest having obtained his majority, and went out to do for himself, carried on what farming was possible on so new a tract of land, and the father worked industriously at his trade, building many of the first frame buildings in the town, as well as in the country.

In September, 1847, the the wife of Mr. B. died, and soon after the family were dispersed, the oldest son going to California in 1849, and dying there in 1850, the others beginning life for themselves at different places.

In 1856 he sold his farm, and went to Iowa, where he remained for about fifteen years, engaged most of the time in mercantile pursuits. He then returned to Ohio, and made his home with his children, in this and Putnam Counties, until the 4th day of April, 1881, when he died at Columbus Grove, O., in his eighty-fifth year.

Mr. Beardsley was a man below medium size, but possessed of uncommon physical endurance, and the most robust health. No one perhaps in the whole settlement could perform so much hard labor with as little fatigue as he. An almost iron constitution enabled him to endure the greatest hardships and perform the greatest labor. Scarcely ever needing the assistance of medicine, he hardly knew what it was to be sick. Having been a frontiersman all his life, he was inured to all the privations incident thereto. His last years were years of great suffering, being afflicted with an incurable malady, yet they were endured without complaint.

Mr. Beardsley united with the Methodist Church when young, and was a member for more than sixty years. His house, in the early days of his residence here, was the home of the Methodist ministers, Conway, Hill, Allen, Heustiss, Wilson, Biggs, Tibballs, Seelay, Runnells, Breckenridge, Pope, and a host of other preachers have partaken of his hospitality.

He was the father of ten children, five boys and five girls, seven of whom are living. He lived long enough to see all his children married, and at his death had ten children, forty-five grand-children, and twenty great grand-children.

The citizens of this township had long felt the need of better roads. The roads were no worse than elsewhere, only to the extent that there was more travel over them, and of course they were more worn. An effort had been made to provide for the building of free turpikes throughout the entire county, and to this end an act had been passed by the Ohio Legislature, submitting to a vote of the electors of the county the proposition to levy a tax for that purpose. But the proposition was rejected by a large majority. This township thereupon petitioned the Legislature for the passage of a special act allowing a tax to be levied for the purpose of macadamiziug the roads within its limits. The act was passed with two provisions, one that the question should be first submitted to a vote of the people, the other that none of the money so raised for macadamizing should be expended within the corporate limits of the village of Findley.

The question was duly submitted, voted on, and agreed to by a large and almost unanimous vote. The township trustees, under whose direction the work was to be done, went to work at once, to build roads. In the absence of gravel, stone had to be used. The matter was vigorously pushed, and inside of the five years in which the levies were to be made, many miles of road were constructed. At the expiration of the operation of the law, there yet being many roads not completed, another petition was sent up to the Legislature asking for a re-enactment of the law, to be in force for five years more. The prayer was granted and the trustees are collecting and expending the money so raised by taxation, and hope to be able to complete the macadamizing of all the principal roads from the corporation line of the village to the township line.

There are many very fine farm residences in this township. The residence of Campbell Byal, on the old John Byal farm, near the Infirmary, is a fine two-story brick structure, pleasantly located on the south bank of the river, and overlooking the rich bottom lands on the opposite side.

The residence of Edwin R. Hay, a short distance southeast of the town is one of the finest dwelling houses in the county. It, too, is a brick structure, tin roof. and of modern architecture.

A. P. Byal, on the Lima road, has built a very commodius

Justices of the Peace.

two-story brick, tastefully finished, with grounds well arranged, and good substantial stone walks.

W. R. McKee, on the Tiffin road, just east of town, has quite an imposing brick dwelling, surrounded by ample grounds, and accommodated with fine farm buildings to match.

Just north of town, we have the fine frame residences of Samuel Howard on the west side, and that of Ancel E. Morvin on the east side of the road, both beautifully located and surrounded with fine orchards and ample out-buildings

The persons named below were elected Justices of the Peace at the dates given, all of which are subsequent to the permanent organization of the county, and all resided within the present limits of the township.

Joshua Hedges—1829.
William L. Henderson—1831, 1834.
Elias S. Bryan—1832.
John Byal—1833.
John Campbell—1836.
Price Blackford—1837, 1840, 1843, 1846, 1849.
A Daughenbaugh—1839.
Hugh Newell—1840.
John Patterson—1843.
Paul Sours—1846, 1851.
Geo. W. Galloway—1849.
Jesse Wheeler—1852, 1855.
Henry Byal—1854, 1857, 1860.
D. B. Beardsley—1858, 1861, 1864, 1867, 1870, 1873, 1876, 1879.
John H. Burket—1863.
Elijah T. Dunn—1866.
Ezra Brown—1869.

A. P. Byal—1872.
Oren A. Ballard—1874, 1877, 1880.

Exhibit of the acreage and production of grain, and the number and value of domestic animals, as reported in 1881.

Wheat,	2,067	acres.	41,744	bushels.
Oats,	304	"	10,700	"
Corn,	2,026	"	84,245	"
Flax,	50	"	529	"
Hay,	800	"	976	tons.
Horses,	857	number.	$36,640,	value.
Cattle,	1,018	"	13,993,	"
Sheep,	1,423	"	2,833,	"
Hogs,	1,563	"	4,011,	"

FINDLEY.

The town of Findley was first laid out in the year 1821, by Joseph Vance and Elnathan Cory, and in the autumn of the same year, Wilson Vance and family removed to the place. Mr. Vance was soon joined by Squire Carlin, William Taylor, John Patterson, W. L. Henderson, John Boyd, Reuben Hales and Parlee Carlin, with others, so that in a few years quite a village had sprung up.

In 1829 the town was replatted, and on the 26th day of September of that year, Joseph Vance and Elnathan Cory appeared before Judge McKinnis, one of the Associate Judges of the county, and acknowledged the platting of the town of Findley, consisting of one hundred and fifty-six lots. The town plat was located on section thirteen, in township one north, range ten east. The lands in this section—five hundred and ninety-eight acres in all—were entered in parcels of fifty-five acres by Vance, Neil and Cory, seventy-six acres by McIlvain and Neil, seventy-five acres by Asa M. Lake, eighty-eight acres by John Gardner, one hundred and twenty-seven acres by Elnathan Cory, seventy-nine acres by James Gilruth and eighty acres by Joseph Westenhover.

John Gardner received a patent for his, dated June 3d, 1822, signed by President James Monroe. He afterwards sold to Thomas and John Simpson, and they to Wilson Vance, March 14, 1828. This tract was the west part of the south-east quarter of section thirteen, and contained eighty-eight acres. The consideration by Vance to the Simpsons was three hundred dollars.

The east part of the south-east quarter, was owned by Vance, Neil and Cory, and was that part of the section on which the town was laid out.

The lots numbered on Main street, from north to south. The lot on which the residence of Squire Carlin now stands being numbered one, and the business room of J. S. Patterson, corner of Main and Sandusky streets, number sixteen, the then southern boundary of the town. In these numbers, from one to sixteen, the Public Square was not counted. There were seventy-six lots on the west side of Main street, the lot on the corner of Front and West streets, owned by Rev. M. Burkle, being the last numbered on that side.

Crossing over to the east side of Main street, the lot now occupied by the Sherman House, is numbered seventy-seven, and south on Main street to the lot on north east corner of Main and Sandusky streets, now occupied by S. D. Fray's Drug Store, numbered ninety-six. There were eighty lots on the east side of Main street, ending with number one hundred and fifty-six, owned by Mrs. W. C. Cox, and on the corner of Front and East streets. No part of the land between Front street and the river was laid out into lots at that time.

Attached to the town plat we find the following certificate of Wilson Vance, surveyor:

"1st. All streets and alleys cross at right angles due north and south."

"2d. Main street is one hundred feet wide."

"3d. Broadway (now Monument Park,) is one hundred and fifteen and one-half feet wide."

"4th. Main Cross street is eighty-two and one-half feet wide."

".5th. Crawford, Putnam, Front, Back, East and West streets are each sixty-six feet wide."

"6th. Farmers and Mechanics alleys are each thirty-three feet wide, and all other alleys are sixteen and one-half feet wide."

In the acknowledgement attached to the plat, the proprietors, Vance and Cory, use this language, which is now a part of the record:

"The Public grounds, streets and alleys, are to the best of our knowledge, correctly designated by the notes attached to said plat, and are appropriated as public ways for the benefit of said town, and to no other use whatever."

Certain lots—thirty-nine in all—were donated to the County Commissioners, in trust, to be sold, and the proceeds arising from such sale to be used in the construction of county buildings. The ground known as the Public Square was not named as one of the lots donated for county purposes, and by the terms of the acknowledgement above alluded to, was appropriated for public use for the benefit of the town, and it so remains, unless a subsequent contract with the proprietors, or the town authorities, placed it in the hands of the County Commissioners. I have not been able to find such a contract on record.

The records say, however, that "on the 10th day of October, 1829, the Commissioners of Hancock County, met for the purpose of taking into their care the proportion of the town lots of Findley, which were deeded to said Commis- ers, by Joseph Vance and Elnathan Cory, and said Charles McKinnis and John P. Hamilton, present, ordered that the aforesaid lots be offered at Public Sale, on the ninth day of

November next. It is further ordered, that the County Auditor advertise said sale."

November 9th, 1829, the Commissioners, Charles McKinnis and John P. Hamilton, present, and proceeded to sell the above mentioned lots, and the following sales were made: Lots 2, 8, 9, 13, 17, 26, 29, 32, 43, 46, 5], 61, 79, 86, 89, 92, 95, 98, 104, 105, 108, 111, 116, 142, 146, 148 and 156 sold for prices ranging from five dollars for No. 148, to two hundred dollars for No. 8 (the lot on the corner of Main and Main Cross street, now owned by Frank Karst, sr.). The aggregate received was $1,025.40.

The first frame house in the town, was built by Squire Carlin, and stood on the same lot on which his present dwelling is located. The same building was afterwards removed to the upper end of Main street, between Hardin and Lincoln streets, and is known as the Frank Klaber property.

William Taylor built the second frame building, which he occupied as a dwelling, hotel and dry goods store. This building stood on the lot immediately adjoining the Davis Opera House, on the south. A few years ago it was removed to west end of Sandusky street, and was burned down. The building was not more than twenty-five feet square, and one and one-half stories in height. A building no larger than that at the present day would be a rather close place for a dwelling, hotel and dry goods store all at the same time. Yet it seemed to be abundantly roomy for all at that early day.

Squire Carlin also built the first brick house in the village, which took the place of the frame. This was used by Mr. Carlin as dwelling and store room. In time this too, had to give way to a better structure, the present large and comfortable residence.

The first tavern was kept by Benj. Cox, in a log house, near where the dwelling house of the late Wilson Vance now stands, just south of the bridge. The town was a straggling village of log huts, without streets or alleys which were passable, and with no business, except traffic with the Indians.

As the population increased, and buildings multiplied, more room was wanted, and additions were demanded, land holders adjoining the old town, platted and offered for sale numbers of lots.

In February, 1830, William Byal's addition of twenty lots was laid out. This addition was on south side Sandusky street, east of Main.

In 1837 Joseph Vance and Elnathan Cory laid out an addition of forty lots.

In 1840, John C. Howard laid out eleven lots, Jonathan Parker eight lots. Cory's addition of thirteen lots was laid out, and Baldwin's addition of twelve lots, and Vance and Cory's addition of seventy-eight lots were laid out in 1848. S. & P. Carlin's addition, on south side of East Sandusky street was made in 1848, and consisted of thirty-nine lots; and in 1852, they made another addition of twenty-eight lots.

An addition of fourteen lots was made in 1854 by Nathan Miller. A sub-division of out lots was made by J. M. Coffinberry, and Wilson Vance made an addition of one hundred and thirteen lots in 1854. Hurd's addition of four lots, and the Western Addition were laid out in 1855. Byal's second addition was made in 1860, and Vance's second addition of one hundred and eleven lots was made the same year. Cory's addition to Vance and Cory's addition was laid out in 1863. The continuation of Vance and Cory's of forty-four lots was made in 1866. E. Barnd made an addition in 1868. Another continuation of Vance and Cory's was made in 1869. Jones and Adam's addition was laid out in 1873, and in 1875 P. Carlin made an addition of seventeen lots.

These several additions were soon sold, and are now improved, many of them by beautiful residences or fine business houses. Pleasant streets, substantial sidewalks, beautiful grounds, all tell of the energy and industry of the owners. This tract of land so occupied by these additions, was at the early settlement of the place scarcely more than a swamp or swail, worth at most no more than government price, is now worth hundreds of thousands of dollars, covered as they are by the happy homes of so many of our citizens. But the old town, and these many additions, do not comprise the whole of the town of Findley.

East Findley—an addition to Findley—was laid out by James H. Wilson, in August, 1847, on the north part of the west half of the north-east quarter of section nineteen, and comprised but forty lots. In 1863 the proprietor laid out an addition of thirty-five lots, and thirteen out-lots, which he designated as the continuation of East Findley. In October of the same year, Cory's addition to East Findley, consisting of eleven lots, was laid out, and in 1866 Cory laid out nine lots more, and in 1873 he added nineteen additional lots.

This addition, or suburb of Findley, comprises all that part of the town east of Eagle Creek. It is pleasantly located, and the principal streets running east and west,

Stone Quarries—Manufactories.

correspond with like streets of the main town. There are a number of comfortable residences here. The streets are wide and bordered with shade trees. There are several manufacturing establishments, here, which are noticed elsewhere in this work. The children of this part of town attend school at the Central Building, only about two squares distant from the creek at west side. Eagle Creek, which divides this from the main town, is spanned by three bridges, one at Main Cross street, one at Sandusky street, and one at Lincoln street.

Along the creek are numerous stone quarries, from which a very large portion of the stone used for building and other purposes is taken. There are also several lime-kilns located along the creek.

In this part of the town are located the "Eagle Mills," "Fiudley Woolen Mills," "Findley Flax Mill," and Moore's Saw Mill, all of which are noticed elsewhere. East Lawn, the beautiful residence of M. B. Patterson, Esq., is also located on east end of Sandusky street. It is a most charming place. The building, a two story frame, with basement, built in the latest style of architecture, surrounded by ample grounds, highly ornamented with shrubbery. The grounds also contain a large green-house, filled with the rarest plants and flowers, also a beautiful island, surrounded by an ample fish pond. The whole is being surrounded by a nicely trimmed hedge.

Just across the street is the magnificent home of Capt. H. H. Albon, a fine three story structure, with basement, situated as it is on an eminence, it commands an extensive view of the town and surrounding country. The grounds are new, but when entirely completed, it will be one of the handsomest homes in the county.

There are a number of well arranged and comfortable private residences in this part of town. The ground on which the town is located is high, slightly rolling, with a warm sandy soil. A great many of the business men of the town reside here, amongst whom are Uncle Ben. Huber, J. M. Huber, the Druggist, D. C. Fisher, of the Findley Planing Mill, John Altman, Builder and Contractor. Here are also located the extensive Nurseries of Robinson and Moyer, and M. B. Patterson, also the Foundry and Machine Shops of Yocum and Hallowell, as well as the Pottery Establishment of Martin Hiersher.

Eagle Mills, the extensive flouring establishment under the management of McConnell & Kirk, are located here, and do a very large business, in the way of merchant and custom work. These mills have long been one of the industries of the town, and under whatever management they have been, their work has always been satisfactory.

Immense amounts of wheat is here floured, and shipped to eastern markets, and has always been considered of the best brands.

The town also has a fire engine house here, in which is kept one of the engines of the town, under the management of an efficient volunteer company.

NORTH FINDLEY.

Wiliam Taylor, one of the first settlers of the county, and for more than forty years a resident of Findley, laid out the town of North Findley in 1854. It is on the north side of the river, and is a part of the town of Findley, and known as the First Ward. It never had a separate existence as a town. The plat of the original town of North Findley is in the south-west corner of the west half of the north-west quarter of fractional section eighteen, and consists of forty-seven lots.

Lot number one is on the north-east corner of Main and Center streets (or Tiffin road), and the plat from thence extends north and east. The lots in the original town are nearly all occupied by good substantial dwelling houses, and public buildings,

In July, 1857, A. F. and D. M. Vance, of Urbana, Ohio, laid out an addition of sixty lots on the west side of Main street. This plat had some very desirable building lots, and although at that time, considered a good distance from the main town, yet lots sold readily, and were soon occupied as dwelling places. Just south of this addition was quite a body of land used at that time for farming and pasturage purposes, which was the property of William Vance, of Urbana. Mr. Vance, yielding to the demands for platting and selling this tract, in September, 1859, divided this ground into sixty-two lots, with the necessary streets and alleys. At the sale, lots sold readily, and at very good prices.

Judge D. J. Cory owned the land on the east side of Main street, between the river and the Tiffin Road, and as this tract separated the new town of North Findley from the old town, he, in March, 1861, laid out nineteen lots, one tier facing on Main street and one on Center street. These lots were in immediate demand, sold readily, and almost every one now boasts of a good dwelling house. Such is the beauty of the location of these lots, and the character of the improvements thereon, that Main and Center streets in North Findley, have long been acknowledged as one of the very pleasantest promenades in the town.

Edson Goit having purchased the lands adjoining on the north of A. F. and D. M. Vance's addition, laid out twenty-seven lots in October, 1860, and in June, 1864, he added thirty lots more. William B. Taylor and Aaron Hall became the owners of a parcel of land directly west of Goit's addition, and laid out fifteen lots in 1866. In November, 1874, Judge Cory laid out sixteen lots fronting on Center street, and east of his first addition. About the same time P. and M. Taylor laid out an addition on east side Main street, north of the original plat, and Gray and Patterson laid out lots fronting on Center street, and on the north side of that street.

Thus by successive additions, each addition to satisfy purchasers, has North Findley become quite an important part of the town of Findley.

The town is regularly laid out, the streets and alleys crossing at right angles. The streets east of Main, commencing at the south, are Center, Cherry and Walnut. Those on the west are Fair, High, Donelson, Corwin, Fillmore and Howard. Running parallel with Main, are Cory and Center.

Lake Erie and Western Railway passes through this part of the town, North Findley is connected with the main town by two iron bridges, one across the mill race and the magnificent river bridge on Main street. The town, with one exception—that of Bacherer's Bottling Works, is occupied exclusively as residences. The Union School District of which this is a part, have erected a fine school building, forty-four by sixty-four feet in size, two stories and a basement in heighth, surmounted by Mansard roof and tower. The building has four rooms, and is in every way comfortable and convenient.

The city authorities built an engine room near the railroad on Main street, and also a cistern. A very efficient volunteer fire company have charge of the hand engine, one of L. Button's Second Class, and are prepared to do good service. E. Bacherer's Bottling Works and Carlin's flouring mill are both in this part of town, but are noticed elsewhere.

Whilst there are no pretentions to grandeur in achitectural design, or magnificence in finish, yet there are very many tasty and comfortable dwellings in this part of town.

E. Bacherer, Dr. Waltman, Mrs. J. C. Powell, W. P. Dukes, Carter Heck and James Seeds, each occupy neat and commodious brick residences, with ample grounds surrounding. Whilst Wm. Edwards, John Poe, Frank Reynolds, E. C. Palmer, Jacob Foster, Samuel Howard and others have equally neat and tasty frames, with as beautiful grounds.

The streets are beautified by hundreds of shade trees, principally maple, and when in leaf, they present a cool and inviting appearance. Main street is supplied with gas lamps, and nearly all the streets have either brick or plank sidewalks.

The population of this suburb is about one thousand souls.

E. Becherer has quite extensive Bottling Works on Main street, and his bottled small beer and cider are known and appreciated all over the country. He is also the owner of two ice houses, and has for years supplied the town with ice. He is an enterprising citizen, and live business man.

Carlin's Mill, on the site of the first mill ever built in the county, is located here. It is a first class flouring mill in the quality of its work. When water power is not sufficient it is run by steam. It is kept in good repair, and has always had a fair share of custom.

The streets of Findley, as certified in the plat, are laid out north and south, and east and west, crossing each other at right angles. The streets running north and south beginning on the east, are named respectively, East, Mechanics Alley, Main, Farmers Alley, West, Liberty and Western Avenue. Those running east and west, commencing on the north, are Findley, Washington, Front, Main Cross, Crawford, Sandusky, Hardin, Lincoln, Lima and Hancock. Main street is one hundred feet wide, including sidewalks on either side, of twelve feet each. The walks in the business part of the street, are of Berea stone, and others are of brick. The street is nicely graded, with a sewer at either side, and is substantially McAdamized with stone. It is acknowledged to be one of the finest streets in Ohio.

Nearly all the commercial business of the town is transacted on this street. Its sides are lined with comfortable business rooms, the buildings being mostly two stories in heighth. The street presents a busy sight, with its immense trade in every department of commerce. There are very many very fine buildings on the street, and the inferior ones are fast disappearing, and being replaced by those of modern architecture and modern conveniences.

We find on this street, the *Sherman House,* Davis Opera House, Commercial House, Court House, Masonic Hall, Wheeler's Hall, Odd Fellow's Building, Joy House, First Presbyterian Church, and the new Lutheran Church.

Near the First Presbyterian Church, we have the celebrated wells of "natural gas." The old Court House, now the residence of Ex-Mayor Carr, has been lighted by this gas for years, and produces a light of excellent quality. The supply seems to be unlimited. From a small reservoir, Mr.

Carr uses the gas in the mechanical part of his business—dentistry—also to light the building, and for cooking purposes in the summer season. There is a portion of the town through which this vein of gas passes, in which the water is almost entirely unfit for use, on account of its presence.

The first settlements made in the town, and the first buildings erected, were on this street between Main Cross street and the river, and that part of the town for many years was the business center, but of late years business has gradually moved up street, until now very much of it is done between Sandusky and Main Cross streets.

Main street is now built up almost solidly from the north corporation line, to the south line of the town, a distance of nearly two miles.

Front street, running east and west, has no business houses. but has some very tasty residences and beautiful grounds. The sides of the street are lined with shade trees, and is a cool and inviting promenade in a warm day. Monument Park extends from this street to Main Cross street, and the church buildings of the German Lutherans, and the Church of God are situated on the west end of the street, as also the passenger depot of the L. E. & W. Railway.

Main Cross street is the second principal street in the village. The Public Square, on which is situate the Court House, is on the south-west corner of this and Main street. Monument Park faces on this street, and directly west of it is the new jail. On the west side of the Public Square and about one hundred feet south of this street, is the Congregational Church. On this street west of Main, are the large Carriage and Wagon shops of A. W. Ray and Buck, Reymond and Seyfang, the furniture establishment of A. Deitsch & Co., the Findley Foundry and Machine Works, the Steam Elevators on the L. E. & W. Railway, and the Catholic Church. There are also numerous fine residences. On the east of Main street, and on the south-east corner of the two streets, is the *Commercial House*, on the site of the old "Caravansary by John Reed," of ye olden time. An iron bridge spans Eagle Creek on this street, beyond which are the Findley Woolen Mill, Findley Flax Mill, and Moore's Saw mill. The German Reformed Church is also on this street.

Crawford street comes next in order. On the east of Main street, we have the large Livery Stables of W. J. Edwards and William Messenger, the Carriage Factory of A. R. Kridler, the Undertaking Establishment of J. R. Clark, the Furniture Establishment of D. Rummel, the Findley Oil mill, Findley Rake factory, and depot of the C. S. & C. Rail Road.

On the west of Main street, is the Carriage Works of May, Kuntz & Bryant, Fire Engine House and City Prison, Findley Bent Works, Lutheran Church, Findley Planing mill, and the new west end school building, and United Brethren Church.

After leaving Main street on Sandusky street, there are no business buildings or manufacturing establishments, except the *Handle Factory*, on the west end, and the foundry of Yocum & Hallowell, on east end. The Creek—Eagle—is also spanned by an iron bridge, just beyond which is the East Findley Fire Engine House, and the Eagle Flouring mill. Between Main street and the creek, we have the Evangelical Church, the Central School Building and the Findley Gas Works. On the west of Main street we have the First Methodist Episcopal Church.

Many of the finest residences and most beautiful grounds

in the city are on this street. The sides of the street are lined with a continuous row of maple shade trees, which give a most charming effect to the view. On the east we have the splendid residences of Dr. L. Firmin, Henry Byal, Ezra Brown, Mrs. Harsh, W. R. Carnahan, the heirs of H. P. Gage, E. P. Jones, S. D. Frey, Wm. Anderson and Mrs. Judge Palmer, whilst on the north side of the street is Isaac Davis' fine residence, also those of Hon. W. H. Wheeler and Moses Bullock. On the west are the residences of T. Carnahan, J. H. Wilson, Mrs. Glessner, John Ruthrauf, J. G. Hull, L. Fitzpatrick, Hawkins, Geo. Hall, J. W. Zeller, J. F. Burket, G. W. Kimmill, Henry Brown, W. E. Snyder, Peter Hosler, H. F. Winders, A. Kimmons and Mrs. Neibling.

At the north-west corner of Main and Hardin streets, we find the marble works of M. Louthan & Co., and on the north-east corner of the same streets stands the First Presbyterian Church. There are no business houses or manufacturing establishments on this street. It is built up almost solidly however, with comfortable dwellings. On the east end are the dwellings of Col. Bope, Rev. Meeks, Dr. F. W. Firmin, S. D. Houpt, Jos. Gutzwiler and L A. Baldwin, and on the west, Dr. Ruhl, Henry Swartz, D. Cline, C. Chadwick, L. McManness, J. W. Davis, and others.

Lincoln street is one of the best paved streets in the town. On this we find the Number 9 School Building, and Parker's flouring mill. On the south-east corner of Main and Lincoln is the new Lutheran Church. This street is occupied as residences. There is an iron bridge across Eagle Creek on this street.

Lima street is comparatively a new street, and occupied exclusively by residences. At the corner of this and Main street is the residence of Judge Whiteley, one of the finest in the city, surrounded by the most beautiful grounds. South of Lima on Main street, are fine residences of Judge Huffman, A. R. Belden, H. B. Green, G. W. Myas, J. S. Patterson, M. Gray and B. F. Kimmons.

All these streets are well shaded with maple trees, and have good, substantial brick walks, and present a home-like appearance, which adds much to the beauty of the town.

A post office was established at this place in 1821, and named Finley, which name it retained until within the last few years, when by order of the Postmaster General, it was changed to Findley, that the orthography might correspond with that of the name of the town. Wilson Vance was appointed Postmaster. The mail arrived once a week, the roads and streams permitting. Many of the old settlers remember Old Sammy Gordon, as he was called, the mail carrier from Urbana to Perrysburg, by way of Bellefontaine and Findley. This was the only mail route to Findley, and was travelled by the carrier, often-times on foot, frequently compelled to swim rivers, and sleep in the woods at night. Father Gordon, after a long and active life, full of privation and adventure, was reduced to such extremity in his old age, that he died in the Logan County Infirmary.

Mr. Vance was succeeded as Postmaster, by Jno. C. Wickham, who, after a few months, gave way to Squire Carlin, who held the position for about nineteen years. It certainly could not have been a very lucrative office at that time, for it is said that upon the arrival of the mail, the post master would put the papers and letters received for delivery in his hat, and as he met those to whom they belonged, he would deliver them. Mr. Carlin imforms me that at the time he took the office, there were but four newspapers received by subscribers, and as letters were received in the same proportion the above story does not seem improbable.

In 1849 Mr. Carlin, having made arrangements to go to California, resigned, and was succeeded by his brother, Parlee Carlin, who held the office for a short time, when he was succeeded by Robert Coulter, who was at the same time publishing a newspaper in the town. Mr. Coulter held the office a few years, when he was succeeded by William Taylor, and shortly returned to Urbana, where he died. Mr. Taylor removed the office to the corner of Main and Main Cross streets in the building now occupied by Frank Karst, sr. Abel F. Parker followed Mr. Taylor, and he in turn gave way to Oliver Munger, who held the office two or three years, and was succeeded by James Robinson.

Upon Mr. Lincoln assuming the Presidency in 1862, the Republican patrons of the office decided by vote, who should be recommended as Mr. Robinson's successor. The choice fell on Joseph B. Rothchild, and he was appointed. On the 1st of July, 1865, this office was made a money order office. When Andrew Johnson assumed control of the Government, after the assassination of President Lincoln, he removed Mr. Rothchild, and as the Senate would not confirm a successor, he appointed the late Col. J. M. Neibling Special Agent of the Post Office Department, and placed him in charge of the Findley Post Office. Upon the election of Gen. Grant, Amariah Ballou was appointed Postmaster, who after holding the office about two years, died, and was succeeded by Thomas E. Adams.

Mr. Adams held the office for a term of four years, and was then succeeded by Eli G. DeWolfe, the present incumbent. During Mr. Rothchild's term of office, Isaac Davis built a one story brick building on the north side of Sandusky street, just in the rear of his business house, and into this the post office was moved, and remained until Mr. De-Wolfe took possession, when he removed it to the Jeffersonian Building, south side Public Square, where it yet remains.

The money order business has been rapidly increasing, and there has been a greater number of orders issued in the past five years than there was in the first ten years after its establishment. The money order business now transacted through this office amounts to $50,000 annually. There have been 28,500 orders issued. The other business done at this office amounts to about seven thousand dollars annually.

On the 17th day of March, 1838, the Legislature of Ohio passed "An Act to incorporate the town of Findley, in Hancock County." The first section of that act provided that "So much of the township of Findley, in the County of Hancock, as herein described, to-wit: The S. E. part of the S. E. quarter of fractional section number thirteen, township one north, of range ten, also the S. W. part of the S. W. quarter of section eighteen, township one north, of range eleven, so far east as the bank of Eagle Creek; also the east half of the N. E. quarter of section twenty-four, township one north, of range ten, and also what territory of the N. W. quarter of section nineteen, as is situated south-west of Carlin's mill race, be and the same is hereby created a town corporate, and shall be hereafter known by the name of the town of Findley."

Section 2 provides for an election at the Court House, on the first Saturday in April next, to elect a Mayor, Recorder and five Councilmen.

"An Act to repeal the charter of the town of Findley,"

City Government.

was passed March 13, 1843. Why, or by what influence this last act was passed, we are unable to say.

The Legislature, on the 4th of March, 1845, passed another act, entitled "An Act to repeal the act entitled 'An Act to repeal the charter of the town of Findley, passed March 13, 1843, and to declare in force the act incorporating said town, passed March 7th, 1838.'" Then follows the sections of the act, in accordance with the title.

It will be impossible, on account of the loss of the records to give the names of those who held the office of Mayor, consecutively prior to 1858. The business of laying out opening up and improving streets, was carried on through the different administrations, and economy in expenditures, and a freedom from indebtedness, has always characterized the conduct of our municipal affairs. Whilst we may not have made as rapid improvement as some neighboring towns have done, we have never incurred a debt that was not promptly paid, and we are now, as we always have been, almost entirely free from debt.

The following persons held the office of Mayor previous to 1858, but as before remarked, we cannot give the exact order in which they were elected. John Adams, W. L. Henderson, Abraham Younkin, U. A. Ogden, N. Y. Mefferd, Josiah S. Powell, Jacob Carr, and perhaps others.

In 1858 Charles Carroll Pomeroy, late of Kentucky, and a most eccentric young man, was elected, but resigned before the end of his term, and was succeeded by Ezra Brown.

History of Hancock County.

In 1859—Ezra Brown, Mayor. S. F. Gray, Recorder.
    1860—Israel Green, " Wm. Klamroth, "
    1861—G. W. Twining, " H. S. Shannon, "
    1862— " " J. P. Dennis, "
    1863-- " " Sam. Huber, "
    1864—Jacob Carr, " B. F. Kimmons, "
    1865— " " " "
    1866— " " " "
    1867—N. W. Filkin, " J. C. Martin. "
    1868—J. A. Bope, " D. H. Pugh, "
                                                 E. G. DeWolfe, "
    1870—G. F. Pendleton, " Lem. McManness, "
    1872—D. B. Beardsley, " J. W. Davidson, "
    1874—Wm. Gribbon, " Jesse Wheeler, jr. "
    1876—Jacob Carr, " J. A. Meeks, "
    1878—Wm. Vance, " W. T. Platt, "
    1880— " " " "

    The city owns as yet but a small amount of real estate, but sufficient for present purposes, when completed. Having accommodations for the Fire Apparatus, and an office for Mayor, Mayor's court room, police headquarters and city prison.

    In 1880 the city was divided into four Wards. The first ward includes all of North Findley, and so much territory on the south side of the river and east of Main street, as lies between the river and Crawford street and west of Eagle Creek.

    The second ward includes all the territory lying between the river and Putnam street, and west of Main street.

    The third ward includes all the territory west of Main street and south of the second ward.

    The fourth ward comprises all the territory on the east

side of Main street, and south of the first ward, and all of East Findley.

These wards are very nearly equal in population.

In addition to the Central Fire Engine House, the city has an engine house in North Findley, and one in East Findley. The town supply of water for fire perpose, is taken from public cisterns, of which there are now about fifteen, all of large capacity.

The town was located on a flat piece of land, and consequently was subject to much inconvenience from rains and wet weather, and no doubt but it was rendered unhealthy from this almost continual dampness. No cellars could be built, and streets, and even lots in some places, had to be filled up, to make them at all comfortable. The surface drainage did not suffice to relieve the ground of surplus water, and it became a serious matter as to what should be done.

At last the city authorities inaugurated a system of sewerage. The town was divided into sewer districts, and Main street was at once thoroughly drained, by putting in a sewer of twenty inch pipe on either side, just outside the gutter line. Throughout the length of West street a large open ditch had been dug for carrying off the water. This for a time answered the purpose, but as the street become more of a thoroughfare, and buildings were erected along the line of the ditch, from the many obstructions continually occurring, the ditch became a nuisance, and the residents of the sewer district petitioned Council to deepen and sewer it, which was done.

Sewers have been constructed in Hardin, Lincoln and Lima streets, in North and East Findley, in the west part of the town, emptying into the river near the cemetery road.

And now by this system of drainage, cellars can be constructed in almost any part of the town.

The health of the town has been greatly improved, and the comfort of the citizens has been immeasurably increased.

In 1865 the city authorities arranged for the lighting of the streets by gas. They had for a number of years previously been lighted by coal oil lamps. There are now about one hundred and twenty-five street lamps in place, surmounted by large and beautiful globes, and lighted by gas, to the great convenience and comfort of the citizens.

PROFESSIONAL MEN OF FINDLEY.

The following named persons are located in and practice their profession in Findley:

ATTORNEYS.

Ballard, O. A.
Beardsley, D. B.
Bitler, J. C.
Blackford, Aaron
Blackford, Jason
Bope, J. A.
Brown, Ezra
Brown, Henry
Burket, J. P.
Carlin, W. L.
Dunn, E. T.
Graber, Alfred

Gribben, Wm.
Hamlin, J. M.
Johnston, J. H.
Mungen, Wm.
Pifer, Peter
Poe, John
Pendleton, Geo. F.
Shafer, M. D.
Shafer, A. B.
Strickler, J. C.
Totten, Theo.
Whiteley, W. H.
Whiteley, M. C.

PHYSICIANS.

Barnhill, T. G.
Carlin, C. R.
Firmin, L.
Firmin, F. W.
Hurd, Anson
Kimmel, J. A.
Knapp, F. H.

Minuti, J.
Oesterlin, C.
Pierson, J. W.
Rawson, Bass
Ray, Miss E. J.
Tritch, J. C.
Waltman, Wm.

Woodworth, T. F.

BIOGRAPHICAL SKETCHES.

WILSON VANCE

Was the son of Joseph Colville Vance, and Sarah, his wife, whose maiden name was Wilson. Mr. Vance's father was born March 24th, 1759, and was married April 10th, 1781, in Loudon County, Virginia. He emigrated to Pennsylvania in 1783. Mr. Vance's parents were both what was called Scotch Irish Presbyterians. They emigrated to Kentucky in 1788, where Wilson Vance was born January 19, 1796, in Mason County. The family came to Ohio in 1800, and settled in Old Town, Greene County. In 1804 they removed to Urbana. In 1816 Mr. Vance and his brother William went to Fort Meigs, on the Maumee River, where for a time they clerked for their brother Joseph, who was afterwards Governor of Ohio.

On the 14th of March, 1820, he was married to Sarah Wilson, by Rev. John Thompson, in Champaign County, and returned with his wife to Fort Meigs, where they remained until the fall of 1821, when with his wife and one child, and all their earthly possessions on an Indian pony, he came to Findley, himself walking the distance. He moved into the old fort until his log cabin was completed. The next season he erected a two-story log house, and kept a tavern. These buildings were situated on the south bank of the river, on the east side of Main street.' Mr. V. also farmed the bottom lands along the river, and by industry and economy laid the foundation of his future prosperity.

In 1830 he built a one-story frame house with five rooms, and in 1831, he in company with John W. Baldwin opened up a dry goods store, using the south room of the house as a business room. This is the same building now occupied by G. C. Barnd, in rear of the Sherman house. In 1837 Mr. V. bought out the interest of Baldwin, who went to New York City. Vance was engaged actively in mercantile pursuits up to 1852, when he sold out his stock at auction.

He however did not wholly retire from business, but was a partner with his sons, Miles W. and William, at Bluffton, Ohio, up to the date of his death.

Mr. Vance was one of the first Justices in the county, and officiated at the first marriage in the county. He was the first Clerk of the Court of Common Pleas, and the first Recorder of the county. He was Surveyor of Wood County, Treasurer of Hancock County, and the second Post Master at Findley. He superintended the building of the first flouring mill in the county. The structure was put up in 1825, and belonged to Elnathan Cory, and was on the site of the present Carlin Mill. His wife did all her own work, and that which was necessary in the boarding of the sixteen men employed in putting up the building, digging the race, and building the dam, although at that time she had three little children to look after and care for.

Mr. Vance and his wife were of the first membership of the Presbyterian Church, and I believe both were still members at their decease. The Church was organized at his house in December, 1831. He was always ready to do his part in sustaining the church, and contributed liberally to its various objects.

Mr. Vance was a good neighbor, an upright citizen and an honest man. He was a man of stong convictions, not easily swerved, and whilst honest in his opinions, and determined in his actions, he of course made some enemies for the time being, but no one questioned his motives. Mr. Vance was the father of twelve children, eight sons and four daughters, all of whom are dead but three, William, Horace M., and Bridget. Wilson Vance died March 1st, 1866. His children were all born in this county except Joseph, who was born at Ft. Meigs, and Miles W., who was born in Urbana. William was the second male child born in the county.

JONATHAN PARKER.

From an address delivered before the Pioneer Association by Mr. Parker, we learn that he was born in Louden County, Virginia, and that his grandfather was a soldier in the Revolutionary war. His father, with a wife and six small children, emigrated to Ohio in 1813, and settled in what Mr. Parker says he thinks is the poorest county in Ohio—Morgan. At the age of fifteen years, Mr. Parker was apprenticed to the trade of carpenter and joiner, at which he served for six years.

At the age of twenty-one, with one suit of clothes and seventy-five cents in money, Mr. P. says he started out on a tramp to hunt work. After two years time, and having saved $200, he became acquainted with the late Frederich Henderson, who had been to Findley, and purchased property, and intended to remove there in the fall. Mr. P. at once made arrangements to accompany him.

On the 18th of October, 1831, they started from Blue Rock township, Muskingum County, Ohio. Mr. Parker says: "We had four horses, and an old wagon, which latter broke down before we had gone ten miles. We then, after procuring another wagon, got along very well until we arrived at Upper Sandusky. There having been rain for several days the roads were in a terrible condition. When not far from where Carey now stands, the bottom fell out of the roads, and we were fast. Mr. Henderson made his way to Capt. Brown's for help, and I made my way to a cornfield to purchase some corn for our horses, which I did of a man by the name of Ogg. Mr. Henderson returned with a yoke of cattle, by the aid of which we were soon placed on firmer ground, and that night we lodged with Judge Smith.

"The next day a young Mr. Smith was hired to accompany them with a yoke of cattle, by the help of which they reached the residence of Peter George, at what was known as the old Ashery. The rains having so swollen the river that it could not be crossed with teams, the party hired a canoe from a Mr. Gipson, and Mr. George, and a Mr. Hewitt, piloted them down the Blanchard. There were in the canoe four men, one woman and one child. In this manner we made the voyage to Findley, where we arrived on the 28th of October, 1831.

"On our arrival in Findley, Mr. Henderson took lodgings in a log cabin near where the old jail on the Park stands. At that time there were but twelve families in the town, these were Wilson Vance, Allen Wiseley, Squire Carlin, Parlee Carlin, William Taylor, Thomas F. Johnston, Barnabus DeWitt, Bass Rawson, Laquina Rawson, George Flenner, John Basehore, William L. Henderson, being about fifty persons in all."

Mr. Parker says that when he came to the town, "the water"—for it had rained nearly all the season—" covered the ground from Main Cross street to Chamberlain's Hill." That when they landed, "they wanted to go to the residence of William L. Henderson, which stood on the ground now occupied by the store of Kurz & Morrison, and could only get there by cooning it on logs across the public square, and on through that part of town." Mr. Parker did much, very much, during his long residence here, to make Findley what it is to-day. Public spirited, industrious, honest and trusted, he helped to give tone and character to the place. In his death, which occurred but a few years ago, the town lost one of its most enterprising citizens, and the community a most valuable member. The close of his long christian life was peaceful and serene.

DR. BASS RAWSON

Was born April 17th, 1799, in the town of Orange, Franklin County, Massachusetts, and was one of the five sons of Lemuel Rawson, a tanner of Warwick, Massachusetts. In 1836, he removed to Bath, in Summit County, O., but died at the residence of his son, Dr. L. Q. Rawson, at Fremont, Ohio. Dr. Rawson—the subject of this sketch—and his four brothers left Massachusetts at an early day, and settled in Ohio. Four of the five brothers were physicians. The Doctor is of the sixth generation of the Rawson family, in direct descent from Edward Rawson, who was Secretary of the Massachusetts colony from 1630 to 1636. His mother's maiden name was Sarah Barrows. In his boyhood, Dr. Rawson worked on a farm, and attended a country school. He afterwards learned the trade of a hatter, at which he worked until he was about twenty years old. His health then failing, he quit farming to engage in the study of medicine. He attended the Academy at New

Salem for several terms, teaching school to defray the expenses of his education.

At the age of twenty-five, he married Amanda Blackmer, and removed to Ravenna, O., but after a few months he went to Otsego, N. Y., and located at Richfield. Here he taught school, and pursued the study of medicine with Dr. Thomas. In the winter of 1826-27 he attended medical lectures at Dartmouth College, N. H., and at the close of the term went to New Salem, and pursued his studies under Dr. Brook, of Oswego. In June, 1828, he emigrated to Ohio again, and practiced his profession with his brother in Medina County for about a year.

In September, 1829, he came to Findley, where he settled permanently in the practice of his profession. He was the first practicing physician in the town. When he came here there were but twelve white families in the place, the Indians were more numerous than were the whites. Here he has practiced for fifty years, and has always been able to command a large practice, and his successful treatment of cases has given him a wide reputation. The Doctor is a large land owner, and one of the wealthiest men of the county. He has always been economical in his style of living, having always all the comforts, and many of the luxuries, without the extravagancies. He is now, and has been a member and supporter of the Presbyterian Church for more than forty years.

The Doctor and Mrs. Rawson had but one child, Harriet E. A., who married Dr. W. D. Carlin. As Surgeon of the 57th O. V. I., Dr. Carlin died at Vicksburg, Miss.

CHARLES W. O'NEAL.

Mr. O'Neal was born in Middletown, Frederick County,

Maryland, January 19th, 1811. In 1833, he came to Zanesville, Ohio, where in 1834 he married Miss Amy J. Baldwin. In July of the following year he came to Findley, and studied law with Edson Goit and A. F. Merriam. He was admitted to the bar in 1838, and from that time to within a few years of his death he practiced his profession. Mr. O'Neal was a practical surveyor, and as such located many of the roads in the county. He also taught school a number of terms, and there are men and women residing here now who were his pupils.

Mr. O'Neal, by his industry and intelligence impressed upon the early settlers his worth as a citizen, and he was many times intrusted with responsible positions. He was Auditor of the county one term, and in 1844 was elected to the State Senate. In his profession he took high rank. As an advocate, although neither fluent or eloquent, he was terse, forcible and convincing. As a counselor, he was thorough and always safe. He was cautious, dilligent and methodical in his practice, and in his business transactions. In his profession he was dignified, truthful, and a despiser of petty fogging tricks, courteous and gentlemanly in all his relations to the court and bar, considerate towards witnesses, and persuasive before a jury.

At the age of sixteen he united with the Methodist Church, and remained an acceptable member until his decease. His attachment to the church of his choice was very strong, and he watched her interests with a jealous care. He died at Findley, Ohio, December 20th, 1879.

DR. W. H. BALDWIN.

Doctor Baldwin was born in Champaign County, Ohio, January 16, 1810, and came to Findley in 1832. Having studied medicine and attended lectures before he came to Findley, he at once commenced the practice, and rose to a high rank in his profession, and his practice became very large, extending into adjoining counties. An extensive practice at that day meant hard labor, long rides through a country in which there were but few roads, and no bridges. But none of these discouraged the faithful physician in his untiring efforts to relieve the afflicted.

But all these could not be endured without producing their legitimate effects. The strong and healthy constitution of Dr. Baldwin became impaired, and he became prematurely old and feeble. His last years were years of suffering, borne however, without complaint.

In April, 1835, Dr. Baldwin was married to Miss Mary Jane Patterson, who survived him some ten or twelve years. Four of the Doctor's children yet survive. He left to his widow a comfortable home, and to his children an unsullied name. In all the relations of life he was considerate, respectful and just, and enjoyed the highest esteem of the community. In 1842 he united with the Methodist Church, and retained his membership until his death.

In 1836 Dr. Baldwin was appointed Clerk of the Court of Common Pleas, for this county, which position he held for seven years, discharging all the duties with promptness and intelligence.

PRICE BLACKFORD.

Mr. Blackford was born in Pennsylvania, in 1803, and came to Ohio when but a boy, and with his parents located in Wayne County, but the family afterwards removed to Stark County. In 1834 Mr. Blackford, with his family, came to Findley, and he at once commenced the manufacture of fur hats, a trade which he had learned of his father. No professional man, and scarcely any young man considered himself dressed properly unless he was crowned with one of Blackford's hats.

Perhaps no man ever lived in Findley who enjoyed a greater share of the respect and confidence of the people than did Mr. B. His honesty was proverbial, and his dealings were all characterized by courtesy and fairness. He held the office of Justice of the Peace for fifteen years, and "Blackford's Decisions" were regarded as almost infalliable. He was a member of the Baptist Church for more than thirty years.

He had a family of six children, three of whom are living. Aaron and Jason are both practicing attorneys in Findley, and Albert is in business in Clinton, Mo. Mr. Blackford died in 1851, at the age of forty-eight years, and universally lamented.

SQUIRE CARLIN.

Mr. Carlin was the second of eight children, and was born in Cayuga Co., N. Y., December 25th, 1801. His parents came to Ohio when he was about six years old, and located at the mouth of Huron River, in Huron County, there being but one other white family in the county. Here his father commenced farming, but after a residence of about a year at this place, he removed to Michigan, near the site of the present town of Monroe. Here he remained but a few months, when he returned to Ohio, and located on the Maumee River, at the present town of Maumee City. Mr. Carlin's father being a blacksmith, he was employed by the Government to work for the Indians.

Mr. Carlin's family remained here, Squire working on a

farm, until the war of 1812 broke out. After Hull's surrender, the family went to Urbana for safety. They travelled through the wilderness country of Wood, Hancock, Hardin and Logan Counties. All the goods that Mr. Carlin was able to save in his flight, were packed on two horses, and with these, and his wife and four children, he made the perilous journey. When the family passed Findley, the Fort was occupied by soldiers.

After about two years, and before the close of the war, the elder Mr. Carlin and Squire returned to the Maumee. When the war closed the family returned to their old home. Mr. C. was employed about the farm, and in 1821 was married to Sarah Wolcott. He had made numerous trips to Findley, buying furs and stock, or whatever was for sale, and in 1826, with his wife and oldest child, William D., who was about four years old, he took up his residence here permanently. When Mr. C. first came, there was but one white family in the place.

Mr. Carlin's ancestors were Welsh, and were always noted for strong constitutions, and great powers of endurance; and Mr. C. himself has been a man of iron constitution, and has endured innumerable hardships and privations.

He followed trading with Indians, and made many excursions to their camps in the wilderness, sleeping on the ground, travelling in all kinds of weather, laying under the trees in winter, obliged to shake the snow from his blankets to prevent being entirely snowed under. Mr. Carlin built the first frame house, and also the first brick house in Findley, both on the lot on which he now resides. In 1826 he opened a dry goods store, and in 1828 his brother, Parlee, became connected with him. This partnership existed between these two brothers until 1852. The firm of "S. & P. Carlin" was known all over the country.

In 1849 Mr. Carlin was carried off by the California fever, and was one of the first who crossed the plains to that El Dorado, and endured the hardships of that long and severe trip equally well with the younger members of the company. The journey occupied about six months. After a residence of three years in California, without a day's sickness, he returned and continued in the dry goods trade until 1852. Mr. C.'s wife died in 1850, whilst he was yet in California.

Mr. Carlin was elected Treasurer of the county in 1830, and by successive elections served eight years. He was a voter at the first election held in the county for county officers. Mr. Carlin was also Post Master for nineteen years. Of an active energetic disposition he delighted to be out doors. The brothers were for years the proprietors of a flouring and saw mill. Mr. C. united with the Methodist Church in 1844, and has been a member ever since.

He has been extensively engaged in farming and railroading since he quit the mercantile business. He has lived here long enough to witness the rise and fall of many business firms. He has outlived nearly all his cotemporaries, and is about the sole link between the past and present. In 1854 Mr. C. married Mrs. D. B. Gardner, with whom he still lives. He was the father of thirteen children, ten by his first, and three by his last wife. Of the first there are but two, Elliott and Mrs. G. W. Myers, and of his second, Fred, who lives in Findley. Dr. W. D. Carlin, son of Mr. C., died at Vicksburg as Surgeon of the 57th Regiment.

HENRY LAMB.

Mr. Lamb's ancestors were of German descent, and he was born in Fairfield Co., O., August 16th, 1807, and remained in that county until 1830. He was the oldest of nine children, and was occupied as farm hand. In 1830 he came to Findley, then but a very small village, and commenced clearing up the farm now owned by William Stevenson, just north of the Strother farm, in this township. Just previous to his emigration to this town, and in the same year, he was married to Mary Pefler, who still lives to cheer his old age. During the first seven years of Mr. Lamb's residence in the county, he lived north of town in the country.

In 1837 he moved into the village, and engaged in the dry goods business, in which he continued for about five years. In 1840 he bought of John McCurdy the frame hotel building on the south-west corner of Main and Sandusky streets, known as "White Hall," and kept "tavern" there until 1849, when the building was burned down. Mr. Lamb then returned to farming, but subsequently engaged for a number of years with his son, Jacob, in the grocery business.

Mr. Lamb is the father of six children, five of whom are yet living, and all reside here except one. No man in the town, perhaps, has experienced so many changes in business life, as has Mr. Lamb. He has passed through all the ups and downs of pioneer life, and has seen many and great changes wrought in our county. Nearly all his early associates are gone.

JOHN H. MORRISON

Was born in Uniontown, Pa., and came to Perry Co., O.,

with his parents whilst quite young. At the age of fifteen years he lost his right arm by an accident. Mr. M. had a good common school education. He was a lawyer by profession, having studied with Philemon Beecher, at Lancaster, Ohio. He first commenced the practice in Bucyrus, Ohio.

In 1836 he moved to Findley, and at once offered his professional services to those of the new settlements who were so unfortunate as to have serious disagreements with their neighbors. Mr. Morrison soon gained a wide reputation as an active and fearless practitioner, and had his full share of clients. He was indefatigable in the interests of his clients, and left nothing undone to gain success. He was aggressive in his conduct of a case, and showed no mercy to opposing counsel. Fluent of speech, often eloquent, always sarcastic in his criticisms of counsel and witnesses, he had a powerful influence with juries.

Many of his professional acts were marked with an eccentricity that would scarcely be tolerated by courts of this day. His presentations of a case to a jury, and his comments on the evidence of witnesses was presented with a bluntness which often bordered on rudeness, and his treatment of courts was sometimes of an impetuous kind.

Yet Mr. Morrison was a kind-hearted man, social in his feelings, warm in his friendships, and honest in all his dealings. He was a man of more than ordinary ability, and in his day stood high as a lawyer, never deserting a client, never refusing to aid any one who appealed to him for counsel or advice. He had as compeers in his profession at the bar here, such men as J. H. Godman, C. W. O'Neal, Edson Goit, A. F. Parker, Jude Hall, W. M. Patterson, A. H. Bigelow, M. C. Whitely, E. Brown, J. E. Rosette, Count Coffinberry, Wm. Gribben and some others.

Mr. Morrison died in April, 1854, leaving a wife and five children, who still survive him.

JAMES H. WILSON

Was the son of James Wilson, and the third son of five children, and was born in York Co., Pa., where he resided until August, 1832, when he came to Findley. On the next day after his arrival here he bought the lots on which the Commercial House now stands, together with an unfinished two-story frame building thereon, for the sum of seven hundred dollars. This same frame building afterwards became the celebrated " Western Caravansary " tavern, and was the immediate predecessor of the Commercial House.

For about a year after Mr. W. came here he worked at the carpenter trade; he then engaged as clerk in the dry goods store of S. & P. Carlin. After an experience of eighteen months in this line, he put up a frame building on the present site of the Carnahan Block, having exchanged his first purchase for these corner lots, and went into the mercantile business on his own account, in which he remained for eighteen years. In the meantime, in 1848, he put up a large three story brick building—the largest building then in the town, except the Court House—and known as the Melodeon Building, which has just been torn down and removed, to give place to the magnificent block of T. & W. R. Carnahan. In this building were two store rooms on first floor, offices on second floor, and a public hall on third floor. In this building Mr. Wilson had his business room until he retired from the trade.

After retiring from mercantile business, Mr. W. was for

many years engaged in farming, and looking after his real estate interests, owning quite an amount of valuable lands. In 1847 Mr. Wilson laid out into lots, an eighty acre tract of land on the east side of Eagle Creek, which he called East Findley. The entire plat of the eighty acres, except five lots, has been sold, and nearly all the lots built upon.

Mr. Wilson, whilst engaged in the dry goods business made many trips to New York City for goods. The travel was made in wagons to the lake at Sandusky City; thence to Buffalo by lake, by stage to Lockport, by canal to Albany, and by the Hudson to New York City, occupying from nine to twelve days each way. Goods shipped at New York would arrive in Findley in from two to four weeks, if there was no delay en route.

When Mr. Wilson came to Findley, there were about a dozen white families here, amongst whom were Squire and Parlee Carlin, Dr. Rawson, Frederick Henderson, Jonathan Parker, William Taylor, W. L. Henderson, Mathew Reighly, Wilson Vance, Christian Barnd and John W. Baldwin. In 1840, Mr. W. married Susan E. Hutchison, who deceased July 8, 1880.

Mr. Wilson has for the past sixteen years been connected with the First National Bank, of Findley, as a stock-holder and director, and has practically retired from business. For many years after he came to the county, his business was such as to extend his acquaintance, and he perhaps knew every grown person in the county.

Mr. Wilson united with the Seceder Church when about fifteen years of age, and is still a member of that organization, which is now known as the United Presbyterians. After his removal to Findley, there being no society of his church here, he united with the church at Cannonsburg, of which he is still a member. Mr. Wilson, by industry and economy, has amassed a fortune, and is quietly enjoying it.

HENRY BYAL

Is the oldest son of John Byal, and was born in Stark County, Ohio, on the 23d of March, 1817. His father's family were of French descent, and his maternal grandfather, Conrad Newstetter, was a Hessian, and was one of Gen. Burgoyne's life guards. Mr. Byal came to this county in 1832, his father was a miller and farmer, and on his emigration to this county, settled on lands adjoining the present Infirmary Farm. Mr. B.'s father erected a saw mill on the Blanchard in 1832, and in this mill Henry worked for seven years. When not water enough to run the mill, he worked on the farm. He had only a common school education, and taught school one term.

In 1842 Mr. Byal was married to Doratha Comer, daughter of the late Isaac Comer, and immediately removed to the farm now owned by Conrad Renninger, and commenced life in the woods. In a few years, by the untiring industry of himself and wife, he had cleared up a large tract of land, and had an elegant new farm. After five years residence here he rented his farm, and in company with the late Edson Goit, he removed to Ottowa, in Putnam County, and engaged in the dry goods business. In this business he remained seven years, in the towns of Ottowa, Gilboa, and Pendleton, all in Putnam Co., O He returned to Findley in 1853, and went into the store of the late Edson Goit.

In the spring of 1854 he was elected a Justice of the Peace in Findley township, and held the office for three consecutive terms. Mr. B., although still living in Findley, claims to be a farmer. He is dealing quite extensively in lands in this, Wood, and Henry Counties, owning now about one thousand acres, the care of which occupies nearly all his time.

Mrs. Doratha Byal having died in 1860, Mr. Byal married Miss Mary Lamb in 1862, who is still living.

In 1866 Mr. Byal united with the Presbyterian Church in Findley, of which he has ever since been a member, and is at present a ruling elder. He is the father of four children, only one of whom—Mrs. S. D. Houpt—is now living.

WILLIAM L. HENDERSON.

Mr. Henderson was born in County Donegal, Ireland, in 1797, and with his parents came to this country, and settled at Mt. Eaton, Ohio. He had the advantages of a good education for his day. He came to Findley in 1829, and at once assumed a prominent place amongst the early settlers. In 1838 he was elected Auditor of the county, which office he held for four years, and then resigned. In 1842 he was appointed Clerk of the Common Pleas Court, which office he held for six years. In 1830 he was appointed Surveyor of the County, which office he held for eight years. Thus for *eighteen* consecutive years he filled a county office, and always acceptably to the people.

He was a man of strong constitution, and robust health. He had most decided convictions, and was not slow in defending any opinion he may have formed. He was not easily swerved from any course hs had marked out. After a long and active residence here, he went to Kansas, where he died in 1861, at the age of sixty-four years.

DR. DAVID PATTON

Was born at Steubenville, Ohio, in 1800, and when about

twenty-one years of age, began the study of medicine. He was a man of more than average ability, and had in addition a very fair English education, all of which enabled him to direct his energies to the best advantage.

After finishing his medical course, he practiced in Carrolltown, Carroll Co., O., for several years. In 1837 he came to Findley, and at once opened up an office, and announced himself as ready to render his professional services to any who might need them. Dr. Patton was a man well read in his profession, and soon succeeded to a fair practice, which increased as time went on. After a number of years practice here, he removed to Tiffin, but remained there only a short time, when he returned to Findley, and again went into practice.

Some years later he went to Iowa, where he remained, however, but a few years, when he returned to Ohio, and located near Cleveland, where he died in 1878. The Dr. was of Irish descent, a whole-souled, brusque sort of a man. Social, good-natured and jovial, he always had hosts of friends. He was somewhat literary in his tastes, and for a time was editor and proprietor of the Western Herald. In religious belief he was a Presbyterian.

HUGH NEWELL

Was the youngest of thirteen children, of Hugh and Margaret Newell, and was born in Washington Co., Pa., April the 8th, 1804. His father was a farmer, in which business young Hugh was reared. The elder Mr. Newell was a soldier in the Revolutionary war. Such was his hatred of the tories, that he would not permit his children to associate with their children. No wonder then that with the teachings of such a father, that his son Hugh was in all his life, the firm friend of freedom, and always loyal to the government, and a lover of his country. In 1814, Mr. Newell came to Ohio and located at Mt. Vernon, in Knox County. He was engaged in selling goods, and in manufacturing fanning mills. In December, 1826, he was married to Sallie Thrift, and came to Findley ten years later.

Upon his arrival in Findley, he went into the store of Green & Reed, and remained with them for about a year. He and Frederick Henderson then were engaged in the manufacture of bedsteads. In 1838 he went into the mercantile business on his own account, and was engaged in that occupation for about eighteen years, a portion of that time in partnership with the late Frederick Henderson. By industry, economy and fair dealing, he always controlled a large trade, and was enabled to accumulate quite a large property.

Mr. Newell made quite a number of trips to New York for goods in that early day. Such a trip meant hard travel for two or three weeks, by wagon, lake, canal and river; no palace cars, no restaurants, no comfortable hotel rooms. When goods were shipped at New York they were expected at Findley in about three weeks.

Mr. N. has been a member of the Methodist Episcopal Church for about forty-six years, and his life has always been consistent, and his example has been worthy of imitation. He has always been a leading member in the church. He is the father of three children, all living. Hannah is the wife of Henry Brown, Esq., of Findley, and Margaret is the wife of Rev. Samuel Mower, a travelling Methodist minister, and his son Starling resides in Indianapolis, Indiana.

FREDERICK HENDERSON

Was a native of Muskingum County, O., and came to this town with his wife and Jonathan Parker, in October, 1831. Mr. H. was a tall fine looking man, very courteous in his manner, and affable in conversation, and considerate of the feelings and opinions of others.

He was a cabinet maker by trade, and carried on that business for a number of years. In 1840 he and Mr. Newell formed a co-partnership in the dry goods trade, and occupied the room on the corner of Main and Main Cross streets, now occupied by Frank Karst. This partnership lasted for six years. Mr. Henderson then withdrew from the firm, and went into business alone. He occupied a frame building on the site of the present room of W. S. Hall, on Main street.

Mr. H. was one amongst the earliest members of the Presbyterian Church in Findley, and in 1837 he was chosen one of the elders. He remained a member until his death. He was a very successful business man, and accumulated a large property. Dying he left a wife and four children.

JUDGE DAVID J. CORY

Is a native of Warren County, Ohio, and was born April 17, 1801. His parents were of Dutch descent, and came to Ohio, the *North-West Territory*, in 1796, and settled eight miles above Cincinnati. Mr. Cory's father was a farmer and stock raiser, and also a large land dealer. Indeed the Judge says that his father invested all his money in lands, for the reason as he said, that water would not drown it, and fire would not burn it, hence it was safer than any other kind of property. The Judge himself has been a farmer and dealer in real estate ever since his boyhood.

In 1803 the family moved to Honey Creek, in the vicinity of Dayton, in which locality they remained until 1834. The Judge was married in April, 1827, to Mrs. Martha Meek, and with her he removed to Williams County, in what is now a part of Henry County, on the Maumee River, about eighteen miles above Perrysburg. Here he remained until November, 1848, when he came to Findley. He had passed through this county in 1816, with a drove of cattle, and had slept in the old Fort. When the Judge's family removed from Dayton to the Maumee, they did so with teams, passing through on Hull's Trail, and were fifteen days on the road, or rather in the woods, as there was not much that could be called a road on the entire route.

When Mr. C. came to Findley, he engaged in farming and real estate transactions, his father having been one of the proprietors of the town, left a valuable landed estate to look after. The Judge was also a large stockholder in, and President of the *Bank of Findley*, the first institution of the kind organized here. He was also one of the leading spirits in the projection, location, and building of what is now the Lake Erie & Western Railroad, and was for many years a Director in that organization. Indeed there were but few public enterprises that he was not prominently identified with, and took the lead in. Liberal, just, honorable and far-seeing, he was always a safe leader.

He signed the petition to the Legislature praying for the formation of the new county of Henry, and helped to organize the same, and was appointed one of the first Judges of the Common Pleas Court of that county. His associates were Pierre Evans and —— Waite, a brother of the present Chief Justice of the United States. On his emigration to the Maumee, he found but very few families in the present bounds of Henry County, but during his fourteen years residence there, much of the county was improved, roads opened and numerous settlements made all over the county, and especially along the river.

He had only the advantages of a common school education, but being a man of more than ordinary natural ability and good judgment, he has been a most successful business man, and has added largely to the fortune left him by his father. He is, perhaps, the largest land owner in the county, holding *twenty-three hundred* acres of land in this and Wood County, together with quite a considerable valuable town property. The Judge's public benefactions to churches and schools and charitable objects, amounts to thousands of dollars. His liberality in gifts to all worthy objects is proverbial.

He is now and has been ever since 1842, a member of the Methodist Church, to the support of which he has contributed more than any other man in the county.

Mrs. Martha Cory died February 26th, 1868, and in September 1869, the Judge married Miss Ann M. Wright, of Urbana. He is now in his declining years, quietly looking after his business interests, and enjoying life pleasantly.

WILLIAM TAYLOR

Was born in Mifflin County, Pa., May 12th, 1798. His early life was spent on a farm, and his chances for obtaining an education were very limited, and his want of education was a defect which he deplored, and in after life, by a patient application, he to some extent overcome. On the 25th day of April, 1826, he was married to Margaret Patterson, in Bedford County, Pa., and in the same year came to Richland County, Ohio, and located about eight miles from Mansfield, and followed farming. In 1828 he came to Findley, the county having just been organized, and the town having been designated as the seat of Justice.

Here he at once entered into mercantile pursuits, keeping on hand a general assortment of such goods as were the most in demand in a new settlement. He was also quite extensively engaged in the fur trade with the Indians and trappers, who were numerous. This trade was a profitable one. Many of my readers will remember the small frame building which stood just south of and adjoining Davis' Opera House, long known as Mefferd's Shop, and afterwards occupied by Dr. Detwiler as a residence. That building Mr. Taylor put up, and occupied as a dry goods store, tavern and family residence.

Mr. Taylor was naturally energetic and industrious, with good judgment and great discernment, of pleasing manner, and with these qualities, he soon commanded a good business, and accumulated quite a fortune, becoming the owner of much valuable property in both town and country. He took an active part in the early life of the county, being called upon to fill the important offices of County Surveyor, School Examiner, Commissioner and Postmaster of Findley; also Bank Director. In all these positions he ever acquitted himself with honor, discharging every duty with fidelity.

He united with the Presbyterian church at Perrysville, O., before his emigration to this county, and in December, 1831, assisted in the organization of the society in this place, and soon after was elected a ruling elder, which office he held at the time of his death.

Mr. Taylor was the father of five children, four of whom are living. Patterson makes his home in Missouri, Charlotte, wife of Milton Gray, and Minerva, wife of J. S. Patterson, reside in Findley, and Milton is in business in Toledo, Ohio.

EDSON GOIT, SR.,

Was born in Oswego County, State of New York, in 1808, and whilst yet in his infancy, lost his father, and during his boyhood he had but little time or opportunity to improve his mind, but such as he had he made the best possible use of, and by the time he was twenty years old, he taught a district school, and soon thereafter started for the western country. Ohio then, without railroads or canals, and but few wagon roads, was a long journey from New York, and the first appearance of young Goit after he left his native state with his bundle of raiment tied up in a handkerchief, was at Tiffin, in Seneca County.

He taught school in Tiffin and Fremont, then unpretentious villages, and in the mean time pursued the study of law with Abel T. Rawson. In due time, he was admitted to practice, and in looking around for a location, selected Findley, then but a village, but a new county seat, as the scene of his future efforts. Mr. Goit made the journey from Tiffin to Findley on foot, staying the first night with a farmer near the present town of Fostoria, and on the second night at the present site of Van Buren, and on the third day reached Findley. He made his home in the family of the late L. Q. Rawson, and waited patiently for six months for a client, but none came.

There was no other Attorney in the place. Mr. Goit was the pioneer of the profession in Findley. Being discouraged and disheartened at his lack of business, he announced at the breakfast table, that he would leave the place. But while yet at the table, a rap was heard at the door, and the inquiry was made: "Does a young lawyer board here?"

The visitor was a man from the east, desiring to collect a claim held against one who was teaching school not far away, and who was the owner of forty acres of land.

Mr. Goit drew up the necessary papers, the man collected his claim by taking the land, the teacher left the place, and Goit was employed to teach the remainder of his term of school.

Business brightened up, clients came, and he abandoned the idea of leaving the place, and went to board with Wm. Taylor, who was keeping tavern.

Mrs. Taylor's sister, Miss Jane Patterson, and her brother had come from Pennsylvania, making the trip on horseback, and took up their residence with Mr. Taylor. Mr. Goit and Miss Patterson were married in 1835.

No man in the county did more to develop its resources, and to assist the struggling community in its efforts towards wealth and prosperity. He engaged extensively in mercantile business in Findley, Bluffton, Gilboa and Ottowa. He was engaged in almost every public enterprise in town and country.

He was a man of unbounded generosity, and had great confidence in his fellow men. He was seldom appealed to in vain. But like all men of his kind, he became the victim of misplaced confidence. He indorsed notes, and went bail for almost every one who requested him to do so, and the usual result followed—embarrassment, importunity of creditors—and failure. But he neither made an assignment or went into bankruptcy, but took off his coat, went to work and assured his creditors that they should not loose a penny by him, but that if life was spared him, he would pay every dollar he owed. Life was spared, and he nobly redeemed his promise.

As an Attorney, Mr. Goit was a successful practitioner. He was Treasurer of the County, and also Prosecuting Attorney. Whetever faults Mr. Goit may have had, and he no doubt had some—for who has not—dishonesty was not one of them. His reputation for honesty was never questioned, even in his darkest hour. One of the great comforts to him in his last sickness, was the fact that he should die square with the world, as he expressed it.

Mr. Goit's social qualities always insured him a ready welcome in society. He died in October, 1880, at Bowling Green, Ohio, of which place he had been a resident for several years.

INDUSTRIES OF FINDLEY.

FINDLEY LINSEED OIL MILL.

In August 1865, James T. Adams, William Anderson and Calvin A. Cronninger purchased the frame building on the north side of Crawford street, originally the Presbyterian Church, but recently the Findley Woolen Mills, and placed in it the necessary machinery for the manufacture of Linseed Oil. The first year in which it was in operation, not more than three thousand bushels of seed were used. The proprietors loaned to farmers for sowing, about three hundred bushels.

In February 1868, Mr. Cronninger sold his interest to his partners, and retired from the business.

In 1873, the proprietors built a fine two story brick fire proof warehouse, or seed house in front of the frame building, and flush with the street. In this building, in addition to storage, is the office of the company, consisting of two rooms, paved with flagging, heated by a grate, and supplied with desks, safes and other office conveniences.

In August, 1877, Mr. Anderson sold his interest to Mr. Adams and Milton Taylor, of Toledo, and he, too, retired from the business.

In 1880 the old frame part was torn down and a fine brick structure took its place. This new building is occupied by machinery, and storage in second story, and it is fitted up with all the latest conveniences. The building and machinery are valued at $24,000. The annual consumption of seed is thirty-five thousand bushels. About three-fourths of this seed is produced in Hancock County, and the balance is brought from the west.

The oil is marketed at home and in Boston. The oil cake is sold in Philadelphia, for Pennsylvania. For the last twelve years C. H. Cummings, of Philadelphia, has purchased all the oil cake made at this mill.

FINDLEY WOOLEN MILL.

William Anderson and John D. McKibben purchased the old Presbyterian Church building on Crawford street in 1858, and after remodeling and fitting it up, put in four looms and two hundred spindles, together with the other necessary machinery, and commenced the manufacture of woolen goods.

In 1862 Mr. McKibben sold his interest to Mr. Anderson.

In 1865 Mr. Anderson sold the old building, and erected the present large buildings on Main Cross slreet, east of Eagle Creek. The building is of brick, forty feet wide by eighty feet long, and three stories in heighth. The rooms are large and well lighted. There is a one story brick addition or wing, twenty by forty-five feet, occupied as an office and sales-room. There is also a large Dye House and other necessary buildings, all of brick. The buildings cost about nine thousand dollars, and the machinery about sixteen thousand dollars.

There are eight looms, four hundred spindles, twe setts cards, and such other of the most approved machinery as belongs to an establishment of this kind. The capacity of the mill is 50,000 pounds of wool per annum. Cassimeres

Sattinetts, Blankets, Flannels and yarns are manufactured. The market for the goods is in the county.

FINDLEY FOUNDRY AND MACHINE WORKS.

In 1857 Augustus Sheffield erected a brick building, thirty by one hundred feet, on the south side of west Main Cross street, into which he put the necessary machinery for carrying on a foundry and repair of machinery.

In 1859 Jesse Wolf and Simon Willhelm purchased the entire property, having previously carried on the old Jackson Foundry, and operated under the name of Wolf & Willhelm until 1864. In 1863 William France took an interest in the business, which he retained until 1864.

In the latter year, R. S. Mungen became a partner by the retirement of Mr. Willhelm, and the firm name was changed to R. S. Mungen & Co.

In 1865 Louis purchased on interest, and the firm name became Adams, Mungen & Wolf.

Jesse Wolf sold out to Mungen and Adams in 1866, but after being out about a year returned. During this time the business was carried on under the name of Adams & Mungen.

Mr. Wolf retired finally from the establishment in 1868, by disposing of his interest to Vincent H. Coons, and Adams sold his interest to Cyrus Vail. The firm name was now Mungen, Coons & Vail.

In 1868 Vail resold his interest to Adams, and Mungen also sold to Adams, and Adams & Coons carried on the business until 1872, when Adams retired and John W. Davis, Wm. L. Davis, Jas. T. Adams, and Newton M. Adams became interested, since which time the firm name has been Coons, Adams & Co.

In 1880 William L. Davis having died, the others partners bought of the heirs his interest.

In 1873 an addition of brick, forty by one hundred feet, two stories high, was built, facing on Main Cross street, also an engine house.

This company have buildings valued at ten thousand dollars, and machinery valued at eight thousand dollars. They manufacture stationary and portable engines, saw mills, and mill machinery, and all kinds of castings. They employ twenty hands.

Vincent H. Coons, John W. Davis, James T. Adams and Newton M. Adams now compose the company.

FINDLEY FLAX MILL.

In 1870 the Delaware Bagging Company put up a frame building on east Main Cross street, east of Eagle Creek, into which they put machinery for the purpose of manufacturing tow from flax straw. The linseed oil mill having created a market for flax-seed, the cultivation of flax had become quite general.

In June 1872, J. T. Adams and William Anderson purchased the mill, and in 1877 Mr. Anderson, by the purchase of the interest of Adams, became sole owner.

The buildings are valued at three thousand dollars, and the machinery at two thousand dollars. About seven hundred tons of straw is worked up annually. Until the last year, the market for the tow, has been at St. Louis, Mo., and Louisville, Ky. The entire product of last year was sold in Lima, O.

A. W. RAY—CARRIAGE SHOP.

In 1860 Karr & Sprau came to the place and at once commenced wagon making and blacksmithing on a small scale, on the south side of Main Cross street, west of the Court House. After remaining here about two years, they disposed of the business to John M. Fergeson. Not long afterwards P. B. Morrison purchased an interest, and the business was carried on in the name of Fergeson & Morrison.

In 1866 Morrison disposed of his interest to S. C. Moore, and he after a year sold to George Heck. This firm of Fergeson & Heck put up a two story frame building thirty by sixty feet, fronting on Main Cross street, which was and is now used as a sales room below, and paint shop above.

In 1870 Mr. Fergeson retired, and was succeeded by J. L. Linnville, and the business was carried on by Heck & Linnville, until Mr. Heck sold to William Biggs, who in turn sold to Charles Fritcher, and he shortly after disposed of his interest to A. W. & J. K. Ray, and L. Fitzpatrick, and the new firm assumed the name of Linnville, Ray & Co. Two years later, Mr. Linnville retired, and Ray, Fitzpatrick & Ray become the firm.

In 1877 J. K. Ray died, and a few months afterwards A. W. Ray bought the entire establishment, and the business has ever since been conducted in his name.

Carriages and wagons of all styles are manufactured and are unsurpassed in material and workmanship. The business amounts to not less than $12,000 annually. Twelve hands are employed in the different shops, and the business of Mr. Ray is steadily increasing.

FINDLEY RAKE FACTORY.

In May, 1873, Andrew Bushon, Horace M. Vance and C. E. Seymour built a frame building, thirty by fifty feet, and two stories high, on the west side of Main street, in North Findley. This was the first Rake Factory, and all kinds of handles were also made. The firm was Bushon & Seymour. In December, 1873, an addition of fifteen by fifty feet was built.

Mr. Bushon retired from the firm in 1874, and the business was carried on under the name of Vance & Seymour until 1876, when Vance sold out to P. J. Sours, the firm then being Sours & Seymour until July, 1878, at which time Mr. Seymour became sole proprietor by the purchase of the interest of Mr. Sours.

On the 21st of May, 1880, the building was burned, together with the machinery and stock, at a loss of about nine thousand dollars.

In June, 1880, Mr. Seymour commenced the erection of a brick building, on the north side of Crawford street, on the site of the old Jackson Foundry, and completed it in November. The building is two stories in heighth, fifty by sixty-eight feet. It is supplied with the latest and most approved machinery, valued at six thousand dollars, the building being worth three thousand.

This establishment manufactures nothing but hand rakes. It gives employment to twenty-five hands, and make 15,000 dozen of rakes annually.

CARRIAGE SHOP—BUCK, REIMUND & SEYEANG.

In 1859 Daniel Buck built a small frame building on the north side of west Main Cross street, which he occupied as a wagon and blacksmith shop. About two years later, he took in a partner, Stephen Seyfang, a practical blacksmith. The business was carried on by the two, until 1866,' when Adam Reimund, a wood worker purchased an interest, and the business was carried on under the name of D. Buck & Co. This firm in 1868 erected a frame building on the same ground, which was used as a wood and paint shop.

In 1875, having previously purchased ground on the south side of Main Cross street, running south to Putnam street, the old buildings were removed to the new location, and a fine two story brick building, *thirty-five* feet wide and *eighty-five* feet long, facing the street, was erected. The first floor was finished up for and is used as an office and sales room, and the second floor as a paint shop. The building presents an imposing appearance, and is commodious in its arrangements.

The company manufacture wagons and carriages of the most approved styles, and all of first class materials. They employ *twenty-five* hands in the various departments, and their annual sales amount to not less than $25,000. The buildings and machinery is valued at $10,000. The members of the firm are Daniel Buck, Adam Reimund and Stephen Seyfang.

FINDLEY CARRIAGE BENT WORKS.

In November, 1879, Y. Bickham and Charles Wright leased the large two story brick building on west Crawford street, known as the *Novelty Works*, and with a capital of $10,000, under the management of Mr. Wright, commenced the manufacture of Carriage Bent Goods, such as shafts, poles, bows, felloes and sawed stock for carriages and wagons, under "Wright's Hot Form Process." The business was conducted for about one year in this way, when in January, 1881, Mr. Bickham retired from the firm, Mr. Wright purchasing his interest.

The concern is now known as the Findley Carriage Bent Works, C. Wright, Proprietor. The timber used is ash, oak and hickory, of which about two hundred thousand feet are used annually. The buildings occupied by the works are valued at $7,000, and machinery at $6,000. Twenty-five employees are required to operate the premises.

DIETSCH'S FURNITURE ESTABLISHMENT.

The firm of A. Dietsch & Co. in 1860 erected a frame building on west Main Cross street, one and a half stories high, and commenced the manufacture of furniture. In 1875 and 1876 they put up a two story brick building thirty feet wide and one hundred and thirty long. Such has been their increase in business, that during the last year it exceeded $16,000, more than half of which was of their own make.

All kinds of furniture is made, and all sales are by retail only. The firm consists of Charles Dietsch and his two sons, Edward and Anthony.

FINDLEY STAVE AND HANDLE FACTORY.

In 1872 D. C. Fisher, John K. Wise, A. Bushon, H. F. Winders, John M. Hamlin and Samuel C. Moore formed a partnership for the purpose of manufacturing barrel staves and farm tool handles, and at once commenced operations near the railroad, on west Sandusky street. In December of the same year, Mr. Fisher disposed of his interest to the remaining members of the firm and retired. Mr. Wise died in 1873, and his interest was purchased by the firm.

Mr. Bushon sold his interest to Messrs. Hamlin & Winders of the firm, in February, 1873. Soon after this, the establishment was destroyed by fire, at a great loss to the owners, but with commendable pluck and energy, and the assistance of friends, they immediately rebuilt, and enlarged the capacity of their establishment.

In 1875 Mr. Moore disposed of his interest to Henry Hellenkamp, and in 1878 Mr. H. sold to Hamlin & Winders who have since been the sole owners.

The machinery and grounds are worth $8,000, and oak staves, headings and all kinds of farm tool handles are made, for which a market is found throughout the United States, Canada and Europe. The business is constantly increasing, and now the demands for their work exceeds the capacity of the establishment. The present proprietors are John M. Hamlin and Henry F. Winders.

FINDLEY GAS LIGHT COMPANY.

This company was incorporated July 7th, 1871, by virtue of the laws of the State. The incorporators were William Anderson, William L. Davis, Samuel D. Frey, J. J. Wheeler and Chas. E. Niles. On the 26th day of August, 1874, the village council passed an ordinance granting the Gas Light Company the privilege of using streets and alleys, and of erecting suitable works.

In September of the same year, the company assigned all their privileges, benefits and franchises to R. T. Coverdale, who at once erected works, laid down mains, and in December the town was lighted.

In 1865 Mr. Coverdale sold to the Findley Gas Light Company, composed mainly of resident stockholders, who elected S. D. Frey, President, J. J. Childs, Secretary, Geo. W. Myers, Charles E. Niles and R. T. Coverdale, Directors.

Saddlery Establishment. 327

The works were sold to the new organization for $28,000, and were under the management of R. T. Coverdale until January, 1877, when they passed into the control of Y. Bickham, thence into the hands of the present company, composed of J. G. Hull, C. E. Niles, S. D. Frey, W. Anderson, G. W. Myers, Jennie E. Bickham and Y. Bickham. The officers are J. G. Hull, President and Treasurer, Y. Bickham, Secretary, E. B. Phillips, Superintendent.

The company have laid over seven miles of pipe, and one hundred and twelve street lamps, and about three hundred private consumers are supplied with gas. The business of the company is generally increasing, and a good article of gas is produced.

RUHL'S SADDLERY ESTABLISHMENT.

In 1876 John S. and George W. Ruhl purchased the two story brick building on the east side of Main and north of Sandusky street, and removed the saddlery shop of George W. Ruhl into the same. They at once commenced business in their line on a large scale, manufacturing all kinds of harness, and especially collars.

In 1880 they patented and improved a pad, called the "Ohio Team Pad," a very valuable improvment in the construction of harness.

The Messrs. Ruhl are now doing an extensive wholesale business in all kinds of saddlery goods, and are manufacturing largely. They have already sold over two thousand pairs of their team pad. One of the firm is on the road nearly all the time, making sales and looking after the interest of their establishment.

They employ twenty-four workmen, and they estimate their business at $50,000 a year. They have a building worth $5,000, and a large stock on hands, with a steadily increasing business.

EAGLE FOUNDRY AND MACHINE SHOP.

In 1871 W. K. Marvin removed the two story frame building, corner of Main Cross street and Mechanics alley, to the south side of east front street, and fitted it up for a foundry. The business was carried on for ten years, when the old building was torn down, and there is now in process of erection on the site, a brick building one hundred feet long and thirty feet wide, with an eight foot basement, and a eleven foot story above, with a large moulding room. Into this Mr. Marvin is placing all the necessary machinery for carrying on his business. He is largely engaged in the manufacture of portable engines, and all kinds of mill gearing, as well as making all kinds of castings.

His building and machinery are worth not less than $10,000. The members of the firm are W. K. Marvin and his sons, Russell and Demy.

RUMMEL'S CABINET AND CHAIR FACTORY.

This establishment is situated on the south side of east Crawford street. The building, which is a large two story frame, was built by Moses Bullock, in 1855, and occupied by him as a furniture manufactory, until September, 1856, when the business of Porch & Wheeler, in the same line, was consolidated with Mr. Bullock's, and carried on under the firm name of Porch, Bullock & Co., until the spring of 1858. Mr. Wheeler then retired, and David Rummell became a partner.

The new firm of Bullock & Co. continued until the fall of 1859, when Mr. Porch withdrew, and Bullock & Rummell carried on the business, until the latter part of the year 1862, when Rummell sold his interest to Mr. Bullock, and retired.

In the fall of 1875 Mr. Rummell purchased the entire stock of furniture from Mr. Bullock, and since that time has been sole proprietor.

The business of this establishment has steadily increased year by year, and notably so since Mr. Rummell's ownership, until it is now a first class institution. All work done is of the best quality. Mr. R. being a practical and intelligent workman himself, uses the knowledge gained by his long experience in the business, in the selection of all materials used by him, and all finished work which he handles. He keeps his sales-rooms filled with an assortment of goods in his line, from the cheapest to the very finest and richest of articles in his trade. His workmen are skilled mechanics, and this establishment is now regarded as one of the permanent and valuable industries of the town.

FINDLEY PLANING MILL.

In 1864 D. C. Fisher and W. H. Wheeler purchased the four lots on west Crawford streets, known as the old ashery lots, and put up a two story frame building, and completed it for the purpose of manufacturing sash, blinds and doors, and dressing lumber, and removed to it the business of D. C. Fisher from East Findley. The building cost about three thousand dollars. The firm was Fisher & Wheeler.

Whilst this firm was in existence, C. E. Seymour purchased a third interest and became a partner, the firm name was D. C. Fisher & Co. Wheeler soon afterwards sold his interest to John Shull, and without change in name, this firm existed until 1867, when Fisher disposed of his interest to William Anderson, and retired from the business. Under the new arrangement, the firm was John Shull & Co.

In 1869 Anderson and Seymour sold to G. W. Myers and S. D. Frey the John Shull manufactnring company was incorpated.

This company carried on the business until 1877, when D. C. Fisher and John Shull purchased the interest of Myers and Frey, since which time the firm is known as Shull & Fisher.

During all these years, and amid all these changes, the property has been greatly improved, and the business constantly increasing. The building now has an iron roof, a brick shaving room, and the most improved machinery has been introduced. The building is worth $4,000, and the machinery about $10,000. There is also quite an extensive lumber yard connected with the establishment, and the amount of lumber handled will amount to 2,000,000 feet annually. The manufacture of sash, doors and blinds, and finishing of all kinds of wood building materials exceeds $60,000 in value. Twenty men are employed in the different departments. The members of the firm are John Shull and D. C. Fisher.

CHURCHES.

METHODIST EPISCOPAL.

The Rev. Elam Day formed the first class in Findley in January, 1833. The first members were Catharine Swapp—now Mrs. H. M. Mosier—Sarah Carlin, wife of Parlee Carlin, Sarah Carlin, wife of Squire Carlin, William Dewitt and others.

The Rev. Thomas Thompson and Rev. Elanthan Gavitt were the first regular preachers. When Findley was made a mission circuit Elam Day was preacher in charge and B. Allen, assistant, and were appointed by the Ohio Conference. In 1833 they reported three hundred and eight members. The meetings were held in the school house and court house.

The first church building was erected in 1835 on the east end of Main Cross street, Whitman and Breckenridge then being the pastors. The building was a frame, and cost *Fourteen Hundred Dollars*. The membership was only *Fifty*.

This house was used continually until 1851 when a brick building, much larger and more substantial than the old frame, and at a cost of seven thousand dollars, was erected. The Sabbath school numbered one hundred and eighty-five, and the membership one hundred and eighty. The Rev. W. S. Lunt, pastor. The next year

Findley was made a station and Rev. Lunt was returned.

The present church edifice on west Sandusky street was erected in 1867-68 at a cost of $38000, including parsonage. It is a fine brick building with stained windows, slate roof, and a spire one hundred and eighty feet in height. The first story, or basement, more properly speaking, is used as lecture room, Sunday school and class rooms. The audience room on second floor, has a seating capacity of about *seven hundred*, with a gallery at one end. The desks, seats for choir and organ room are at the north end of the room. The organ is a good one, purchased at a cost of $2,000. The Rev. Isaac Newton was in charge of the station at the time of the building of the church, and was very active and efficient in his work. The Rev. Francis Davies is now in charge, with a membership of *three hundred*, and a Sabbath school of two hundred and eighty-five, under the superintendency of H. F. Winders.

Those pioneers of Methodism, Bigelow, Gurley, Runnells, Allen, Breckenridge, Heustis, Biggs, Wilson, Pope, Gavitt, Hill, Whiteman and others equally eminent, have traveled the wilds of this and adjoining counties proclaiming the truths of the gospel, with eloquence and zeal.

THE ENGLISH LUTHERN CHURCH.

In the fall of 1838 the Rev. M. Cortex, a German, was sent as a missionary to Hancock County and preached in Findley for about two years. In 1840 the Rev. Charles Wisler came, and remained until the latter part of 1841. He was followed in 1842 by the Rev. Barney Huffman, who labored here for three or four years, holding services in the court house.

English Lutheran Church.

In August, 1846, a meeting was held and preliminary steps taken to organize a society. On the 19th of September, 1846, another meeting was held at which Isaac Teatsorth presided, and the organization was perfected by choosing Samuel Snyder, George Welker and Samuel Reber trustees, and the organization was named "The English Lutheran Church of Findley, Ohio."

The Rev. J. Livengood was present when the society was organized, and soon thereafter the Rev. George Hammer became pastor of the Church.

The church building on Putnam street was erected in 1847. The pastor, Rev. Hammer, with his own hands, made and carried much of the mortar used in plastering the building. The North Ohio Conference of the Methodist Episcopal Church held its session in this building in 1849, it being then the best church building in the town.

In 1871 the congregation purchased two lots on the south-east corner of Main and Lincoln streets, and soon after built thereon a frame parsonage building. There is now in course of construction on these two lots a fine brick building for church purposes, which, when completed, will cost not less than $15,000, and will be a handsome structure, with a seating capacity of five hundred. The successive pastors of this church were the Revs. Geo. Hammer, J. Livengood, Thomas Officer, A. J. Imhoff, S. A. Ort, H. B. Belmer, Rev. Kinsel, P. S. Hooper, G. W. Miller, C. S. Sprecher, and J. W. Goodlin, the present one.

FIRST PRESBYTERIAN CHURCH.

The following historical sketch of this church has

been kindly furnished by Milton Gray, Esq., long an influential member:

"The Presbyterian Church of Findley was organized December 21, 1831, by Rev. P. Monfort, at that time acting as a missionary in North Western Ohio. The first meeting was held at the residence of Wilson Vance. The names of the members as they appear on the records are: William Taylor, Margaret Taylor, Phebe Henderson, Asa Lake, Chloe Lake, Ebenezer Wilson, William Coen, Sarah Coen, Mary Gibson, Wilson Vance and Sarah Vance. Ebenezer Wilson and William Coen were elected and ordained ruling elders.

During the first year or two after the organization services were occasionally held at the residences of some of the members, but afterwards were held quite regularly in the court house until the year 1836, when the first house of worship was erected.

The old church building, the first erected, was but recently torn down, it having been used for some years by J. T. Adams & Co. as a linseed oil mill.

The present church edifice was erected in 1857, and was dedicated December 27, 1857, the Rev. W. T. Finley, of Springfield, Ohio, preaching the sermon. The cost of the building was $8,888.88, as reported by the building committee.

The several ministers who have been pastors of this church are as follows: Revs. P. Monfort, T. B. Clark, —— Bellville, George Van Emon, R. H. Hollyday, J. A. Meeks, J. M. Cross, A. B. Fields, Eben Muse and R. R. Sutherland. The congregation is now without a pastor.

FIRST CONGREGATIONAL CHURCH.

On the 21st day of October, 1865, a number of persons met in Gage's Hall in Findley for the purpose of organizing a Congregational Church. Rev. Robert McCune, of Kelly's Island, presided, and J. A. Bope acted as clerk. A society was organized and officers elected as follows: Deacons, Paul Sours, John Eckles, James Davidson, Aaron Hall. Treasurer, James S. Ballentine. Clerk, James A. Bope. And Rev. J. A. Meeks was elected pastor.

In March, 1866. ground was purchased on the west side of the Public Square, on which to erect a Church building, and in June, 1867, the building was commenced, and under the superintendency of Paul Sours, assisted by J. P. Kerr, Jessie Guise and J. C. Powell, was completed in the December following. The building is of brick, covered with slate and surmounted by a tower. The size is forty-five by ninety feet, with projection in front for tower, and a recess in rear for organ. The cost of the building and furnishing was $18,000.

Of those who were members at the organization are the names of John Eckles and wife, Aaron Hall and wife, G. W. Neeley and wife, Paul Sours and wife, J. S. Ballentine and wife, C. J. Eckles and wife, J. A. Bope and wife, Rev. J. A. Meeks and wife.

The pastors have been Rev. J. A. Meeks, W. S. Peterson, —— Kutz, Thomas Gordon and D. T. Davies.

GERMAN LUTHERAN.

In 1858 Charles Deitsch, Ernst Kempf, Charles Hahn, Peter Roszman, Henry Lannert, Henry Hahn, Philip

Crouse, Valentine Wagner, and a few other members of this denomination met at the court house, and under the direction of Rev. M. During, organized a society and a Sunday school. The congregation met once in two weeks at the court house, and were under the ministrations of Rev. During.

The society feeling the want of a house of worship of their own, bought a lot on West Front street for three hundred dollars, and in 1862 erected thereon a brick building thirty-five feet wide and sixty feet long, at a cost of twenty-five hundred dollars. The building committee was Charles Deitsch, Charles Hahn and Henry Lannert. The church building was dedicated on Whit-Sunday in 1863, by Revs. During, Lang and Crownenwitt. The building has been greatly improved since by the putting up of a fine bell, the purchase of an organ and the laying down of carpets. The congregation has also purchased parsonage property for which they paid nineteen hundred dollars, so that the property belonging to the church is worth not less than six thousand dollars.

The present membership is one hundred and forty. There is a flourishing Sunday school of about eighty-five scholars connected with the church. The ministers employed since the organization of the church were Rev. M. During, Rev. M. Buerkle, Rev. J. T. Groath and Rev. J. B. Webber, the present incumbent. The present officers are Wm. Tribolet, Christian Schmidt and Daniel Buck, Trustees; C. Ritter and Fred Groath, Elders. C. Ritter is also superintendent of the Sunday school.

EVANGELICAL ASSOCIATION.

At the annual Conference of this association held in

Evangelical Church.

May, 1870, in the town of Findley and vicinity was taken up as an English mission and consisted of the following appointments: Findley, Fellers, Porters and Union Chapel on the Tiffin road, and the Rev. E. B. Crouse was appointed to the mission, with Rev. E. Peer as colleague, but the health of the latter failing the whole charge of the mission was left to Rev. Crouse. The services at this time were held in the United Brethren and Church of God buildings.

On the 11th of July, 1870, the society in Findley met to consult together on the propriety of building a house of worship. It was decided to build. A lot was purchased on east Sandusky street, extending back to Crawford street, and a brick building 38 feet by 62 feet was erected at a cost of about six thousand five hundred dollars. The building is neatly finished and furnished. It is surmounted by a tower, in which a good bell has been placed. The congregation deserves much credit for providing themselves with so comfortable a house. It was indeed a great undertaking for so weak a society, but the untiring energy and industry of the Rev. E. B. Crouse made it a success.

Amongst the early membership we find the names of John Powell and wife, John Crites and wife, George Jacobs and wife, Elizabeth Bolander, Rev. L. W. Hankey, Rebecca Miller, Sarah Miller, Paul Kornorer and wife. The ministers have been Rev. E. B. Crouse, Rev. W. Whitington, Rev. W. A. Shesler, Rev. S. Cocklin, Rev. James Hensel, Rev. C. L. Crowthers and Rev. C. E. Dresbach. There is a flourishing Sabbath school connected with the church.

CHURCH OF GOD.

This society was first organized in January, 1858, by Elder G. M. Harn. The meeting was held in the old Presbyterian church. The first members were J. C. Sherrick and wife, George M. Graul and wife, Jacob Grose and wife, John T. Grose and wife, Amanda Geyer and Elizabeth Cunningham, now Mrs. H. Shuler. Prayer meetings were held at private houses, with occasionally a sermon, until 1861, R. H. Bolton was appointed to Findley circuit. The meetings were then held in the North Findley school house until 1863. W. P. Small was appointed to succeed Rev. Bolton, and in 1863 to 1866 the meetings were held in the United Brethren church.

The society resolved to build a house of worship, and commenced work in April, 1866, and finished and dedicated the same in December of the same year. It is a brick structure forty feet by fifty feet, and cost about four thousand dollars. The building is conveniently located on the south side of west Front street. It is plainly but comfortably finished. The number of members is one hundred and thirty. From the first organization to the present time one hundred and forty-five persons have been baptized.

In 1879 the congregation bought a lot on Main street in North Findley, and built on the same a parsonage at a cost of about twelve hundred dollars. A Sabbath school was organized in 1867, and it is in a flourishing condition. The several ministers appointed here were R. H. Bolton, W. P. Small, G. W. Wilson, I. H. Deshirie, J. M. Cassell, J. W. Auckerman, S. Kline, J. V. Updyke, W. P. Burchard and S. Dickerhoff.

UNITED BRETHREN.

This society was organized in 1854. Amongst the first members we find the names of Joel Pendleton, Jacob Powell, Robert Owens, John Hibbitt, Solomon Moore, and Nicholas Weaver. Prior to the erection of a church building the society met in the brick school house on Front street. In 1854 the society purchased a lot on west Crawford, and erected thereon a house of worship. The house is of brick and neatly finished.

The society is in a flourishing condition and its present membership is one hundred and six. The Sabbath school numbers sixty, and much interest is manifested by teachers and pupils.

The following named ministers have supplied the church since the organization: Chester Briggs, M. Long, William Mathers, J. French, L. Moore, R. French, Wm. Glancey, T. J. Harbaugh, James Long, T. D. Ingle, Alvin Rose, A. W. Holden, I. Crouse, G. P. Macklin and E. A. Starkey.

ST. MICHAEL'S CATHOLIC CHURCH.

The first Catholic society organized here was in 1845, and met at the residence of John S. Julian. In 1850 the congregation erected a frame church building on west Hardin street, in which they worshipped until the winter of 1855–56, when it was burned down. They sold the lot and bought property on the west end of Main Cross street, and immediately commenced the erection of another house. The building is of brick, plainly furnished and cost $6,000. The present membership is about *five hundred souls*. At the first organization of the society the meetings were held but once a month, now they are held regularly in accordance with the usages of the church.

This society numbers among its members some of our best business men and most esteemed citizens. The following named persons have officiated in the capacity of priests to this congregation: Father Raetzer, Father Burns, Father Vattman, Father Deachan, Father Flemming, Father Pitts, Father Young, Father Rudolph and Father Doesner.

SCHOOLS OF FINDLEY.

UNION SCHOOL.

Until as late as 1854, the village of Findley was divided into four sub-districts for school purposes. In 1840 the four districts conjointly built a large two story frame building, with four rooms—one for each district—on the corner of Crawford and East streets. This same building is now known as the west end school building. In addition to this, each district had a smaller building for the use of the younger pupils.

In 1854 the Legislature passed what is generally known as the *Union School Law,* which authorized villages or separate school districts to organize as independent or *special school districts.* The matter of the formation of such special districts was considered by the people of the village, and three of the village districts availed themselves of its provisions, but the fourth refused, and subsequently was organized under the amendment to the Akron School Law, and has ever since been known as District No. *Nine.* The school building, by agreement became the property of the Union District, and schools were taught there for years.

In 1865 it was removed to the west end of Crawford street, on grounds purchased for school purposes, and has been so used to the present time.

August 10th, 1865, the Board of Education decided "that in their opinion it is necessary to purchase a site and erect a school building thereon." A meeting of the citizens of the district was called for September 2d, 1865, to whom was submitted the question of levying a tax of $18,000 for building. At that election, there were *two hundred and nineteen* votes cast, of which *one hundred and fifty-six* were for the tax. At a meeting of the Board May 4th, 1866, H. P. Gage, Isaac Davis and E. P. Jones proposed to sell to them the tract of land lying between the C. S. & C. Depot grounds and Sandusky street, for the sum of $2,000, which proposition was accepted by the Board.

In September of the same year, the Board made contracts for material and labor in the erection of the building. The building was originally intended to be two stories in heighth, but in August, 1867, it was changed to a three story building.

The building being completed, September 7th, 1868, was fixed upon as the time for its formal opening, at which time the patrons of the school assembled in Columbia Hall, as the hall in the building was named, and quite an interesting programme was carried out with much ceremony.

The wants of the town increased with its growth, and more school room was needed, and the Board of Education in January, 1877, ordered that the Clerk advertise accordin to law, for a meeting of the qualified voters on Monday, February 12th, 1877, to vote upon the proposition to authorize a levy of $5,000, for the purpose of building a school house in North Findley. At that election there were *three hundred and five* votes cast, all of which were in favor of the tax except *thirty-nine*.

On the 16th of March, 1877, bids were opened, and the contract for the building let to S. H. Kramer, for $5,547.41. This building is forty-four feet wide and sixty-five feet long, two stories in height, with basement and mansard roof, surmounted by a tower. There are two rooms on each floor, separated by a wide airy hall. The rooms are completed in the latest style, and will accommodate about fifty pupils each.

The Board have now under contract, the erection of a new building at the west end of Crawford street. The structure will be *sixty-five* feet wide, and *eighty-five* feet long, two stories in height, with a basement, and when finished, will be an imposing building, and add much to the beauty of the town. The contract has been awarded to Joseph Fleming, of Toledo, O., at the price of $13,012, and to be completed by the 1st of January, 1882.

Although organized under the Union School Law, the system of graded schools was not introduced until 1868, under Superintendency of Ephriam Miller, and not perfected until W. S. Wood had succeeded him. Prof. Wood was succeeded by C. E. Palmer, of Columbus, and he by the present Superintendent, J. W. Zeller.

The enumeration of youth in this district, is 1,216, and twenty teachers are employed.

DISTRICT NO. NINE.

This District includes the territory included within the boundary, commencing at the Old White Corner on Main street, running thence west to West street, thence south to the old corporation line, thence east to Main street, and has an enumeration of about two hundred children. It includes within its boundary many business houses, and the residences of some of the wealthiest citizens of the town.

For many years they occupied the Jonathan Parker building on Sandusky street, on lot now known as Patterson's corner. A lot was afterwards bought on west Hardin street, on which was erected a comfortable brick school building.

In 1865 the Directors purchased an acre of ground on west Lincoln street, then almost out of town, upon which they erected a building, the construction, re-modeling and furnishing of which cost about twenty thousand dollars. The district has a fine two story building above the basement, surmonted by towers and mansard roof. Their grounds are ornamented with numerous shade trees, which give them an inviting appearance, and the whole is surrounded by a neat fence.

The schools, four in number, are graded, and the higher branches are taught, and diplomas awarded to graduates from the High School Department. The schools are well conducted by an efficient corps of teachers, and pupils make such progress, and become possessed of such an education as is acquired at other graded schools. This Dirtrict was one of the four districts into which the town was originally divided, and at the formation of the Union School District, it refused to join the other three, and has ever since, whether wisely or unwisely, been an independent district.

BENEVOLENT SOCIETIES.

ODD FELLOWS.

Hancock Lodge, No. 73 I. O. O. F., was instituted August 17, 1846, with Abraham Younkin, Jacob Carr, Edson Goit, Abel F. Parker and James H. Barr as charter members. The Lodge has always been in a flourishing condition, and its finances have been well managed. Its relief fund has been liberally, but judiciously expended.

In 1872 the Lodge erected a fine three story brick, metal roof, building, on their lot, on east side of Main, between Sandusky and Crawford streets. The building was put up under the direction of a committee of five members of the Lodge, to-wit: William M. Detwiler, James T. Adams, G. C. Barnd, Charler E. Niles and Jacob C. Powell. The cost of the ground on which it stands was $1,600, and of the building $9,000. The first floor is occupied as a book store by D. C. Connell, the second floor by the Public Library, and the third floor as a Lodge room. The present membership is one hundred and fifty-nine.

On the 21st day of June, 1866, Golden Rule Encampment was instituted under a charter granted to L. G. Thrall, Charles E. Niles, Sylvester M. Geyer, William McKinnis, Charles J. Krause, William L. Glessner, Henry B. Green and George W. Neeley. The Encampment hold their meetings in the Lodge room, and now have a membership of ninety-nine.

FINDLEY LODGE, NO. 227 F. & A. M.

In the month of January, 1852, a Dispensation was granted by the Grand Master of the State, for the organizing of a Lodge of Masons at Findley, and on the 16th day of the same month the organization took place, and continued under Dispensation until October of same year.

On the 22d day of October, 1852, the Grand Lodge of Ohio, then in session at Chillicothe, granted a charter to Abraham Younkin, Abel F. Parker, Edwin Parker, David Patton, J. M. Coffinberry, George Arnold, Adolphus Morse, E. S. Reed and C. B. Wilson as charter members, with Abraham Younkin as W. M.; J. M. Coffinberry, S. W.; and Geo. Arnold, J. W. On the 29th day of November, 1852, James A. Kellum, as Proxy of the Grand Master of the State, duly instituted the Lodge and installed the first officers as follows: Abraham Younkin, W. M.; George W. Springer, S. W.; W. L. Henderson, J. W., E. S. Reed, Treasurer; David Patton, Secretary; Thomas McKee, S. D.; J. E. Rosette, J. D., George Arnold, Tyler.

The meetings were for a number of years held in the second story of a frame building on the north side of Sandusky street, now occupied by Patterson's dry goods house. The Lodge subsequently removed to the third story of the building now known as "Old White Corner," just south of the Public Square, where the meeetings were held until 1863, at which time removal was made to a room in third story of the present "Joy House Block," on Sandusky street, which was prepared and occupied by the Lodge until 1878, at which time an arrangement was made with G. W. Kimmell, who was remodelling his building on Main street, by which the third story was to be so arranged as to fit it for use as a Lodge Room.

In this building the fraternity have a Lodge room, ɑ four other smaller rooms—the Lodge room being twer seven feet wide and fifty-two feet long—all finished and ɪ nished at a cost of more than *sixteen hundred dollc* making one of the most beautiful and convenient Lo rooms in northern Ohio. The present membership is ab one hundred and thirty.

FINDLEY CHAPTER, NO. 58 R. A. M.

Abraham Younkin, James A. Kellum, William L. H derson, Ben Metcalf, S. T. Heffner and George Arnold tained a charter from the Grand Chapter of the State their session in Chillicothe, October 16th, 1854, empower them to open a Chapter of Royal Arch Masons, in the tc of Findley, which was done with James A. Kellum as H Priest; Abraham Younkin, King; and W. L. Henderɛ Scribe. The Chapter has always held its meetings in sɑ room with the Lodge. Its membership is now about fo

FINDLEY COUNCIL, NO. 50 R. & S. M.

A charter was granted October 12th, 1862, by the Gr Council of Ohio, in session at Cincinnati, to James Wilɪ H. D. Ballard, B. F. Kimmons, W. E. Snyder, D. B. Beaɪ ley, J. M. Muber, William Anderson, M. B. Patterson Isaac Bonham authorizing them to form a Council of Rɪ and Select Masters. The late Dr. B. S. Brown, with R Cook, C. M. Nichols and J. A. Aull, all of Bellefontaine, direction of Grand Council, instituted the new Council der the name of Findley Council; James Wilson, First Il trious Master; H. D. Ballard, Dep'ty Master; and B

Kimmons, Principal Conductor of Work. The Council meets in the Lodge room, and the membership is about twenty.

KNIGHTS OF HONOR.

On the 11th day of September, 1878, the Supreme Council of Knights of Honor, in session at Wooster, Ohio, granted a charter to D. C. Connell, H. B. Green, F. W. Entrekin, Ernst Bacherer, W. H. Shuler, H. W. Bleecher, J. M. Beelman, G. H. Wheeler, E. G. DeWolfe, Wm. Edwards, J. C. Bushan and Tim Fellers to open a Lodge at Findley The Lodge was instituted accordingly. The meetings are held on the second and fourth Fridays of each month, in their hall on the south-east corner of Main and Crawford streets. The membership is twenty-one, and one death, that of Geo. H. Wheeler, has occurred since their organization.

ROYAL ARCANUM.

P. L. Teeple, as Deputy Supreme Regent, instituted a Council of this order in November, 1878, with thirty-four charter members. Hancock Council, No. 187, hold their meetings in Knights of Honor Hall, on the second and fourth Wednesdays of each month. Two members have died, Capt. John Wescott and Dr. T. C. Ballard. The present membership is forty, and the numbers are increasing. The present officers are D. B. Beardsley, Regent; B. F. Kimmons, Vice Regent; J. W. Zeller, Orator; F. B. Lay, Secretary; A. A. Dillinger, Treasurer; and Wm. Edwards, Collector.

AMERICAN LEGION OF HONOR.

A Council of this order was organized in May, 1881, by T. C. Garrison, Deputy Supreme Commander, with a membership of twenty-two. Present membership about thirty. The Council holds its meeting on the second and fourth Mondays of each month, at Knights of Honor Hall. There have been no deaths since its organization. The officers are J. M. Huber, Commander; Dr. T. G. Barnhill, Vice Commander; D. B. Beardsley, Past Commander; Dr. T. F. Woodworth, Orator; C. E. Seymour, Secretary; B. F. Kimmons, Treasurer; and C. M. Humason, Collector.

ST. MICHAEL'S BENEVOLENT SOCIETY.

This society was organized in ——, and has now twenty-eight members. It is connected with St. Michael's Catholic Church, and its members must be members of that church, males between the ages of twenty-one and sixty years only being eligible. Members are entitled to care, attention and assistance when sick or disabled, and also a stated sum of money as weekly benefits. The society, though small in numbers, has expended quite a sum in sick benefits, and is in a prosperous condition. Frank Karst, sr., has been President of the society ever since its organization.

NEWSPAPERS.

HANCOCK COURIER.

The Democratic Courier was established November 10th 1836, by Jacob Rosenberg, and edited aud published by him until January 17th, 1839. The paper was then 18x26 inches in size.

Mr. Rosenberg was born in Bedford County, Pennsylvania, October 13th, 1811, and was raised and reiceved a good common school education at that place. At an early age he went to Millersburg, Ohio, where he learned the printing business in the office of the *Farmer*. He came to Findley on the 29th day of September, 1836, and started the paper shortly afterwards. He was a very strict party man, and very popular with the masses, and was at one time elected Sheriff.

A discussion arose in the Democratic party in 1840, as to the best method of making nominations of candidates, one faction in favor of the delegate system, and the other in favor of nominating by popular vote. Mr. Rosenberg started a paper in the interest of the delegate system, which he called the *Hancock Farmer*. So great was the feeling that in 1844 there were two Democratic tickets put in the field, and by this division, the Whigs were enabled to elect some of the officers.

Mr. Rosenberg was a plain, terse, and forcible writer. He was a man of strong impulses, and nothing could swevre him from what he believed to be right. He died in Findley in 1844, and was buried in the old grave yard, but his remains have since been removed to Maple Grove Cemetery.

On the 24th of January, 1839, Mr. Henry Bishop purchased the *Courier* and published it until July 1st, 1845. We can ascertain but little about the private life of Mr. Bishop. He was born and raised in Franklin County, Ohio. He received a good English education, and was a man of sound practical common sense. He was rather an eccentric character, and when he went to take his seat as a member of the Ohio Legislature, to which he was elected in 1851, he wore a hunting shirt and leggins. He was not a remarkable writer, his productions being rather illogical. After disposing of the office in 1845, he removed to his farm in Eagle township, and was drowned in Eagle Creek, June 18th, 1855.

On the 1st of July, 1845, Mr. William Mungen purchased the *Courier*, and conducted it until November, 1849, when he rented it to W. M. Case, (better known as "Mood Case,") for one year. But as Mr. Case was one of those good-natured, worthless fellows, Mr. Mungen was obliged to do most of the writing during that time. Mr. Mungen, then after control of the paper for a short time, rented it to B. F. Rosenberg, and in the spring of 1851, sold one half to Henry Brown, and shortly after sold the remaining half to A. Blackford.

Mr. Mungen was born in Baltimore, Md., May 12th, 1821, came to Ohio in 1830, received a common school education, and studied Latin and German and physical sciences to some extent at home. Studied and practiced law, was elected Auditor of Hancock County for two terms, and to the Senate of Ohio in 1851. Entered the Union Army in

1861 as Colonel of the Fifty-Seventh Regiment of Ohio Volunteers. During the time he has resided in Ohio he has held several local offices. He was elected to the 40th and 41st Congresses of the United States. Mr. Mungen was a clear, forcible, logical writer. He is at present practicing law in Findley.

Henry Brown entered into partnership with Mr. Mungen in the publication of the *Courier* in the spring of 1851. On the 1st day of January, 1851, Aaron Blackford purchased Mungen's interest, and continued until the fall of 1854, when Mr. Brown sold to Blackford, and at the end of one year Mr. Brown assumed the entire control of the paper, and edited it until January 1857.

Henry Brown was born in Albion, Orleans County, N. Y., and was educated at the Albion Seminary. He came to Ohio when about seventeen years of age, and taught school for several years. He then read law with W. P. Noble, at Tiffin, O. He was elected Auditor of Hancock County in 1854. He is a nervous, excitable man, and a hard worker. He was a prolific writer, and carried conviction at his pen's point. He has held the office of Prosecuting Attorney several terms, and is now practicing law in Findley.

In January, 1857, Benjamin Franklin Rosenberg purchased the *Courier*, and conducted it successfully until July 18th, 1861. Mr. Rosenberg was born in Bedford, Pa., and at the age of two years came with his parents to this place, where his father, Jacob Rosenberg, established the *Courier* in 1836. In 1847 "Frank" commenced an apprenticeship to the art of printing with H. K. Knapp, in the office of the *Kalida Venture*, in Putnam County. Mr. Knapp sold the *Venture*, and established the *Standard* at Ashland. "Frank" went with him. From there he went into the office of the *Seneca Advertiser*, published by John G. Breslin, in Tiffin, O. In the same office was W. W. Armstrong, now one of the editors of the *Cleveland Plain Dealer*. Finishing his trade he returned to Findley and was engaged with Mr. S. A. Spear, on the *Home Companion*, in the capacity of foreman. In 1854 when A. M. Hollabaugh started the *North-West* at Napoleon, Ohio, "Frank" went with him. Sometime afterwards he established the *Sentinel* at Ottakee, the pioneer paper of Fulton County. He then went into the office of the *Shelby County Democrat*, which Mr. Hollabaugh had just purchased. He succeeded Mr. Brown in the ownership and management of the *Courier*, which he sold to Mr. Hollabaugh in 1857. Mr. Rosenberg died in Findley, October 4th, 1869.

On the 25th day of July, 1857, the *Courier* passed into the hands of Mr. Hollabaugh, who edited it until March, 1861.

Alpheus M. Hollabaugh was born in Frederick County, Md., October 16th, 1832, and came to Findley in 1837, where he received a good common school education. He learned his trade as printer with John G. Breslin, Tiffin, O. Before his connection with the *Courier*, he had edited and published the *North-West*, at Napoleon, and the *Shelby County Democrat* at Sidney, Ohio, and in 1865 was connected with a paper in Gallipolis, Ohio, and also at Van Wert. He was a good printer, and possessed some ability as an editor, but wss more windy than logical. He died in Findley of consumption on the 4th day of February, 1871.

In March, 1861, Messrs. L. Glessner & Son assumed charge of the *Courier*, and continued until January 1st, 1865.

Lewis Glessner was born in Somerset County, Pa., September 1st, 1811, and when six years old moved to Columbiana County, Ohio, and settled in the woods, where he remained at farm work. He learned his trade in New Lisbon, and removed to Delaware, O., in 1833. He came to Findley in the spring of 1861. He in connection with his son, W. L. Glessner, published the *Courier* until January 1st, 1863, when he sold out, and removed to Newark, O., where he took charge of the *Newark Advocate*, which he purchased. In May, 1866, he again took control of the *Courier*.

W. L. Glessner was born at Delaware, O., September 27th, 1840, and at the age of eighteen entered the office of the *Shield and Banner* at Mansfield, Ohio. In 1861, in company with his father, L. Glessner, he entered into the business of editing and publishing the *Courier*. In 1865, he took entire control of the paper, which he held until May 1866. Shortly after disposing of the *Courier*, he purchased the *Toledo Record*, but failing in this, he went to the *Wheeling (Va.) Register*, and finally to New York City. In 1868, in company with C. C. Stone, he purchased the *Clinton (Ill.) Register*, and is yet publishing that paper.

In May, 1866, Mr. L. Glessner again took charge of the *Courier*, which he continued until his death, March 13th, 1869, since which time the *Courier* has been published by his widow, Mrs. Georgiana Glessner, under the editorial control of F. H. Glessner.

Mr. L. Glessner was a strong partisan, a most estimable and genial gentleman, a fine writer, a correct business man, and scrupulously honest in all his dealings.

When the *Courier* came into his hands in 1866 it was a thirty-two column paper printed on a hand press. In 1868 the paper was enlarged to a thirty-six column, a Campbell Power Press put in the office, to which, in a short time, steam was added. Just previous to his death, Mr. G. had finished a fine block on east Sandusky street, into a part of which he had removed the office, and the paper has now in connection with the newspaper press, ample job rooms, where all kinds of plain and fancy job work is done neatly. The present circulation of the *Courier* is about seventeen hundred copies weekly.

(The foregoing facts are extracts from an article by F. H. Glessner, at their anniversary, ten years ago, with the addition of more recent facts by the AUTHOR.)

WESTERN HERALD.

On the 1st day of January, 1845, John T. Ford issued the first number of this journal, of which he was editor and proprietor. In politics the *Herald* was devoted to the interests of the Whig party. The office of the *Herald* was in the second story of the frame building on the south-east corner of Main and Sandusky streets, now occupied by L. A. Baldwin, as a produce store. Under Mr. Ford's management the *Herald* obtained a circulation of four hundred. This was doing pretty well in a county where the Democracy had a majority of more than a thousand votes in a voting population of not much exceeding three thousand voters. The *Herald* was a weekly journal, and was a rather spicy sheet.

The paper was under Mr. Ford's control until November, 1845, at which time he sold one half interest to James M. Coffinberry, of Maumee City, under the condition that Mr. Ford should be the publisher, and Mr. Coffinberry should take editorial charge. In the spring of 1846 Mr. Ford disposed of his entire interest in the *Herald* to Mr. Coffinberry. Whilst Mr. Ford was connected with the paper, William F. Gilkeson and Gideon R. Nightingale did the composition and press-work, and William L. Howell and Pat G. Duncan, son of Gen. Andrew Duncan, were the first boys employed in the office.

Mr. Ford was long a resident of Hancock County, but never engaged in the newspaper business after he disposed of the *Herald*. Mr. Ford assisted Engineer Weeden in locating the Branch Railroad; he also assisted the Contractor Beach in its construction. A track-layer from the main line by the name of French, ironed seven miles of the road, and under the direction of Engineer Swigart, Mr. Ford completed that part of the work, and drove the last spike on its completion. He was five years clerk in the depot at Findley, and eleven years conductor on the road, succeeding N. E. Childs, who was the first who held that position. The travelling public remember Mr. Ford as the patient, good-natured, accommodating conductor on the old "strap iron" road. He is now residing on a farm near Chillicothe, Mo., enjoying the peaceful life of a farmer.

In November, 1845, J. M. Coffinberry became part owner of the *Herald*, and the name was changed to *Findley Herald* about a year later. Mr. Coffinberry purchased the interest of Mr. Ford, and conducted the paper for about three years, when he in turn sold to Dr. David Patton. The circulation at this time was about five hundred copies. Judge Coffinberry says that at the time he purchased the paper, and whilst Mr. Ford was connected with it, it was printed on an old wooden Ramage press, but that he subsequently purchased a second hand press of John C. Gilkeson, of Mansfield.

Judge Coffinberry.

Judge Coffinberry was born at Mansfield, Ohio, in 1818. He studied law with his father, the old "Count," who at the time was located at Perrysburg, and on his admission to the bar, practiced law with his father in Maumee City. He was elected and served as Prosecuting Attorney of Lucas County. After he severed his connection with the *Herald*, he resumed the practice of law in Findley.

In 1855 he took up his residence in Cleveland, where he at once took a front rank at the bar, and such was his reputation for legal ability, that in 1861 he was elected one of the Common Pleas Judges of that city, which office he filled with credit to himself, and to the entire satisfaction of his constituency.

As a writer and editor, he was clear, comprehensive, and incisive, as a lawyer, he was learned, eloquent and logical, as a Judge, he was upright, clear and forcible in his rulings and decisions. As a citizen, he is held in the highest esteem, and as a business man, he has been entirely successful.

This paper changed proprietors and name very often, and we are only enabled to give the names, without vouching for the accuracy of the order in which they are given. Dr. Patton was succeeded in his proprietorship by W. P. Reszner; then came Robert Coulter, who changed the name of the paper to the *Journal*. A man by the name of Lyon —his initials I do not remember—became owner, and the paper was then called the *Home Companion*, and was a literary newspaper. Mr. Samuel A. Spear became proprietor, and during his ownership the name was changed to the *Jeffersonian*.

Mr. Spear was a thoroughly educated gentlemen, a fine writer, firm in his convictions of right, and bold to defend them. D. R. Locke became proprietor, and whilst conducting the paper here, commenced writing the "Nasby Letters," which have made him so famous. The paper passed into the hands of L. G. Thrall, who disposed of it to Locke's —C. N. & O. T.—and I. S. Chamberlain. Chamberlain retired and W. G. Blymire succeeded him. This firm sold out to W. P. Miller & Co.—the Company being E. G. DeWolfe, present Post Master and one of the publishers of the Republican. During the time that the Lockes' published the paper it was called the *Hancock Jeffersonian*, but Mr. DeWolfe changed it to the *Findley Jeffersonian*. Mr. Miller sold out to O. J. DeWolfe, and the paper was conducted by DeWolfe Bro.'s, until they in 1877 sold out to A. H. Balsley, the present publisher.

THE DAILY JEFFERSONIAN.

On November 15th, 1880, the initial number of the "*Findley Daily Jeffersonian*" was issued by the proprietor of the *Weekly Jeffersonian*, without however any fixed idea of making it a permanent publication, but rather as an experiment. The interest with which it was received and the success with which it was met, determined the proprietor to continue it, and it has now completed its first year, with a promise of long continuance.

Its present circulation is six hundred copies, about four hundred of which are circulated in the city, and nearly all of the balance at the various Post Offices in the county. The paper is a spirited little sheet, and gives a large amount of local news, as well as a synopsis of the latest telegraphic dispatches.

A. H. Balsly, the proprietor, was born in the city of Pittsburg, Pa., December 15th, 1828, and whilst a resident of

The Findley Republican.

that city, acquired a thorough knowledge of the art of printing, and his first practical experience as an editor was in a subordinate position. His first venture for himself was as editor and proprietor of the *Grand River Record*, at Painesville, O. He then became editor of the *St. Clairsville Independent*. Afterwards for thirteen years he published the *Plymouth Advertiser*.

After disposing of this, he in 1868 went to Fremont, O., and became proprietor of the *Fremont Journal*. This paper he sold in the fall of 1875, and in May 1876, he purchased and took charge of the *Findley Jeffersonian*, to which he added the *Daily Jeffersonian*. Besides these two papers Mr. Balsley is interested in the publication of the *Milan Advertiser*, and the *Carey Times*.

Mr. Balsley is a practical printer, a good business man, and a ready and forcible writer.

THE FINDLEY REPUBLICAN.

The first copy of the *Republican* was issued as a seven column folio, February 5th, 1879, by J. M. Beelmon and J E. Griswold, editors and proprietors. On the 18th of July, 1879, Griswold retired from the firm, disposing of his interest to J. M. Beelmon, who enlarged the paper to an eight column folio. On the 1st of January, 1881, a partnership was formed by and between J. M. Reelmon, E. G. DeWolfe, formerly of the *Jeffersonion*, and Jason Blackford, and an improved 32x50 inch Campbell Press, and other material purchased, making it one of the best equipped newspaper and job offices in the county, and the paper was issued as a nine column folio.

On the 17th of October, 1881, Mr. Blackford wishing to devote his entire time to the profession of the law, disposed of his interest to his partners, who are the present proprietors. The paper is Republican in politics, and is fast winning its way to public favor, by its fearless independence in local, as well as in State and National politics. As an advertising medium it is already recognized. Its circulation is increasing, and it bids fair to prove a successful newspaper venture.

Eli G. DeWolfe, editor of the Republican, was born in Centerville, Butler Co., Pa. In 1850, he commenced to learn the printing business in the office of the *Butler Whig*, and completed his trade in the office of the *Prospect Record*, at Prospect, in the same county. Owing to poor health he was compelled to relinquish the business until 1862, when he became editor of the *Pike County Republican*, published at Waverly, Ohio. He, however, sold that office to accept the position of foreman in the *Ohio State Journal* office at Columbus, O., in 1866, and in September, 1868, he assumed editorial control of the *Findley Jeffersonian*.

He disposed of the *Jeffersonian* office in 1868, and was appointed Post Master at Findley by President Grant, and was re-appointed by President Hayes in 1880. In 1881 he assumed the editorship of the *Findley Republican*. As a political writer Mr. DeWolfe is bold and aggressive, freely criticising the acts of officials, and pointing out any defects in their conduct of public affairs. His articles on all subjects are fairly written, and in ability compare with the best efforts of the average newspaper man.

There were several other newspaper ventures in the town, amongst which was a German paper by Zwanzie, but it only lived about a year, and was then removed to Lima. The Barnd Bros. engaged in the newspaper business, independent at first, but afterwards espoused the cause of the Granger movement. This however failed, and the paper became an advertising medium, under different names, such as *Reporter*, *Property Journal*, etc., and has finally been removed to Fostoria.

HOTELS.

"JOY HOUSE."

This hotel occupies the two south first floor rooms, and the entire second and third stories of the building on the south-west corner of Main and Sandusky streets. The building was built by a joint stock company, and when finished, two rooms on first floor, and a part of the second and third stories was opened up by the late S. T. Heffner, as a hotel, called the "Dixon House." Indeed the entire block covering a square, of two hundred feet each way was called the "Dixon House Block."

There were four business rooms on the first floor facing on Main street, which with the two occupied as hotel, made six ground floor rooms. Heffner was succeeded as landlord by Dick Ellis, and he by John Fisher. Stewart Sprague leased the house and conducted it for many years. Finally A. & D. Joy, of the Gault House, at Carey, purchased the two south rooms of H. P. Gage, in whose hands it was, and opened up the "Joy House." They have very materially enlarged its capacity as a hotel, by the addition of quite a number of parlors and sleeping apartments. It is a first class hotel in every sense of the word, and merits and receives a full share of patronage.

This building stands on the site of the old White Hall Tavern, kept by Henry Lamb, and which was burned down many years ago.

COMMERCIAL HOUSE.

This is a three story brick building, fifty feet wide, and two hundred feet long, situated on the south-east corner of Main and Main Cross streets, on the site of the old " Findley Caravansary, by John Reed," and the present building was formerly the " Reed House."

This hotel is in one of the most eligible and convenient locations in the city, being directly opposite the Court House, and in the immediate vicinity of many business houses. With the additions lately made to it, it has become one of the largest and most imposing buildings in the town. After the death of Eli S. Reed, the builder, the property passed into the hands of Samuel Renninger, who, after conducting it for some years, leased it to Henry Guntner and Truman Woodworth, who were succeeded by E. B. Belding, and he by Jasper Constable. Mr. Renninger then sold the premises to Henry C. Deitsch, the present proprietor.

Mr. Deitsch has made many valuable improvements, the most considerable one being an addition on the east along Main Cross street, one hundred feet long, and thirty feet wide. The first floor, facing on Main Cross street, will be occupied as business rooms, and sleeping apartments will be arranged in the second and third stories. When entirely completed, it will be one of the best arranged and convenient hotels in the country. Mr. D. is getting a full share of the traveling public.

SHERMAN HOUSE.

This is the building known as the " Schwab House," in *ye olden times*. It is a three story brick, situate at south-east corner of Main and Front streets. It has changed hands several times since the death of Mr. Schwab, and is now owned by T. J. Stackhouse, who, after occupying it for several years, leased it to a Mr. Edmunds, the present landlord.

The hotel has always had the reputation of being a good stopping place for the hungry, who desired a good square meal. It is very extensively patronized by the country people, and is a good stopping place for any class of people.

BANKS.

THE FIRST NATIONAL BANK OF FINDLEY.

This Bank was organized in the spring of 1863, and it capital stock—fifty thousand dollars—was all subscribed for and invested in bonds of the United States. This was prior to the decisive battles of Gettysburg and Vicksburg were fought, and at a time when many of the shrewd and careful capitalists of the State were timid, fearing the final results of the war, and hesitated in taking National Bank Stock, knowing that the same would be invested in United States securites.

E. P. Jones, the President, and Chas. E. Niles, the Cashier of the Bank, were original subscribers to the stock, and have held the offices named, ever since its organization. During, and for several years succeeding the war, this bank was the designated depository, and Commercial Agent of the United States, for the Fifth Congressional District of Ohio, and as such received and disbursed millions of dollars of government money, without the loss of a cent to the government or the bank.

The bank has ever enjoyed the reputation of strength and solidity, having never in all its career suspended for one moment the payment of its deposits, not even in the panicky times of 1873. It has loaned hundreds of thousands of dollars, to our stock dealers, grain merchants, business men and farmers, and has thus aided materially in the great commercial interests of our town and county.

The present Directors of the bank, are E. P. Jones, C. E. Niles, J. H. Wilson, J. F. Burket and G. W. Kimmel, names which should be a sufficient guarantee that the business of the bank will continue to be carefully and safely managed.

FARMERS BANK.

This Banking institution was organized by G. W. Hull, Peter Hosler and J. G. Hull, and commenced business in the room lately occupied by the defunct Hancock Savings Bank, on the first day of January, 1880. Peter Hosler is President, G. W. Hull, Vice President, J. G. Hull, Cashier, J. C. F. Hull, Assistant Cashier, and Will. Hosler, Teller. It is a bank of deposit and discount, with a capital of $60,000.

The President, Peter Hosler, was for four years Treasurer of the county, has been a most successful farmer, and is the owner of a very large tract of valuable lands in the county and town. G. W. Hull, the Vice President, is also Prsident of the Crawford County Bank, at Bucyrus, O. The Cashier was a farmer until he entered the bank here.

The well known character of these men, gives the bank a reputation for solidity and fair business transactions, which commends it to public favor.

FINDLEY FIRE DEPARTMENT.

The Village Council passed an Ordinance, April 27th, 1856, for the establishment of a Fire Department, section one of which ordinance provided that "The Fire Department shall consist of one Chief Engineer and two Assistant Engineers, and one Captain for each regularly organized company, or engine house."

The first engine was a small affair, called the "Tom Thumb," and was, from its diminutiveness, of but little consequence at a fire. The village authority disposed of this and bought a second hand engine, called "Jenny Lind," which from its awkard construction and mammoth size, was so unwieldy as to be of but little more use than was "Tom Thumb." It was known as a double decker, the men who worked being placed on top of the engine, and working in a row boat fashion.

In 1856 a new second hand engine of the then mondern style was purchased, with the necessary hose and reels. This was one of the most approved patern of hand engines, and has done most efficient service on more than one occasion. In 1859 another hand engine was purchased of the L. Button manufacture, and named after the maker. About this time the "Jenny Lind" was dismantled, and the running gears were converted into a hook and ladder truck, and a company formed to operate it. The L. Button is a second class machine, and proved to be a valuable addition to the fire apparatus of the town.

In 1871 the town authorities purchased a Silsby Rotary Steam Fire Engine, at a cost of seven thousand three hundred dollars, including two hose reels and one thousand feet of hose. A volunteer company was at once formed and took charge of the apparatus.

In 1877 another steamer of the Silsby patern was purchased, which, including two hose reels and one thousand feet of hose, cost three thousand seven hundred and forty dollars. The whole force of the department is volunteer, and is composed of five companies, two steamers, two hand engines and one hook and ladder. After the purchase of the second steamer, the city authorities built an engine house in the first ward, North Findley, in which they placed the L. Button engine, in charge of a company, and also one in the fourth ward, East Findley, in which they placed the "Citizen's Gift" hand engine, also in charge of a volunteer company.

The entire department is volunteer, and now consists of not less than two hundred active, efficient members. The value of the fire apparatus is about $20,000. There are thirteen public cisterns, in different parts of the town, which have cost the tax payers about $8,000. Fortunately, the department is not called out very often on duty, as the town for the past thirty years has been singularly free from fires.

MAPLE GROVE CEMETERY.

On the 25th day of December, 1854, the following named persons filed papers for the incorporation of a company to be called "The Maple Grove Cemetery Association," to-wit: D. J. Cory, William Taylor, Hugh Newell, Jesse Wheeler, A. H. Bigelow, Benj. Huber, J. B. Hull, Parlee Carlin, G. H. Crook, Henry Porch, Dr. W. H. Baldwin, H. P. Gage, John Ewing, F. Henderson, M. C. Whitely, Dr. D. Goucher, G. W. Galloway and J. H. Wilson. The first election for officers was held at the office of M. C. Whiteley, on the 22d of June, 1855, at which time John Ewing, H. P. Gage and Parlee Carlin were elected Trustees, and William Taylor, Clerk.

About twenty acres of land on the west bank of the river just outside the west corporation line, was bought of George Biggs, and laid out into lots. A main avenue extends through the center of the grounds from east to west, and on either side of this avenue, there were two hundred and fifty-two lots laid out, making in all, five hundred and four lots, through which passed two other avenues, one on either side of the main one, and parallel with it. The lots are laid out in rows, and are eight feet wide and twenty-four feet long. August 3d, 1860, after many of these lots had been sold, the association proposed to the town and township, that if they would avail themselves of the provisions of an act of the Legislature, providing for the joint ownership, by Incorporated Villages and Townships, of cemeteries, and assume the amount still due upon the purchase of the lands, they would transfer the grounds to them. This was accordingly done, and Dixon Stansberry, William Mungen and William Church, as Trustees, deeded the lands to the town of Findley and Findley Township, and the name of "Maple Grove Cemetery" was adopted.

In 1872 the authorities purchased of Jasper Lytle, for $2,200, a tract of 22 acres adjoining their grounds on the south. In 1865 a further addition of two hundred and eighty-six lots, was laid out in the rear of the first platting of lots.

In 1878, under the direction of L. A. Baldwin, C. B. Hall and Henry Brown, Cemetery Trustees, a very fine and imposing Mortuary Chapel was built, at a cost of two thousand dollars. This chapel is used for the reception and retention of bodies before burial, at the request of the friends of the deceased. The trustees deserve much credit for the erection of so tasteful a building, in this city of the dead.

The entire occupied part of the grounds, is profusely planted with evergreen and shade trees, whose beautiful foliage, and inviting shade, dispel much of the gloom naturally surrounding such a place. A wide shady driveway extends the length of the grounds on both sides. There are many very beautiful and costly monuments, marking the resting place of friends.

The families of Jesse Wolf, W. C. Cox, Wm. Taylor and F. Henderson have very pretty vaults erected for the reception of their dead.

The grounds are situated on the high banks of the Blanchard, and are thoroughly underdrained. A public highway passes along the river bank, in front of and between the cemetery grounds and the river. A beautiful iron fence is built along the entire front. The whole is in charge of three trustees, elected by the village, but who are under the control and direction of the council of the village. The village council and the trustees of the town meet in joint session in May of each year, and determine on the amount of money to be raised, and the rate of taxation.

Maple Grove Cemetery is fast becoming one of the most beautiful burial places in the country. The present Board of Trustees is L. A. Baldwin, J. R. Clark and J. L. Kenower.

JACKSON TOWNSHIP

Tp. 1, S. R. 11, E.
AREA 19,200 ACRES.   POPULATION 1,338.

The Commissioner's Record of December 7th, 1829, Charles McKinnis, John P. Hamilton and Mordica Hammond, Commissioners, reads: "A petition presented by sundry citizens of Amanda and Delaware Townships, praying for a new township, to be set off as follows, to-wit: Number one, range eleven, south of the base line, into a body politic and corporate, and to be named Jackson, which was agreed to by said Board."

At the December session of the Commissioners in 1836, it was "ordered that an election be held in Jackson township, to elect a Treasurer and three Trustees for section *sixteen*, on the 20th day of December, 1836, and that notices thereof be set up in three of the most public places in the township, after having been satisfied by the inhabitants of said township, that there are twenty electors in said township, at the usual place of holding elections." It was also ordered "that sections 3, 4, 5 and 6 in township one south, range twelve, (now Ridge township) and sections 1, 12, 13, 24, 25 and 36, in range number eleven, township one south, (now Jackson township) be attached to Amanda township."

Jackson township now comprises sections 2, 3, 4, 5, 6, 7, 8, 9, 10, 11, 14, 15, 16, 17, 18, 19, 20, 21, 22, 23, 26, 27, 28, 29, 30, 31, 32, 33, 34 and 35, in township one south.

Peter George made the first entry of land in the township on the 21st day of November, 1823, which entry was

Land Entries—First Settlement. 373

the east half of the north-east quarter of section thirty-five, (now owned by G. W. Krout).

December 10th, 1823, Wm. Greer entered the east half of the south-east quarter section thirty-five, (now owned by heirs of T. G. Hammond).

On the 18th of May, 1827, Mordica Hammond entered the west half of north-east quarter of section thirty-five.

David Egbert entered the east half of north-east quarter of section two, and in September of the same year Alpheus Ralston entered the south-west quarter of section seven, upon which he soon after settled, and upon which he still resides. In November of the same year George Bishop, of Franklin County, took up the south-east quarter of section seven. These entries were followed by others made by Levi Williamson, William Newell, John Swank and others.

This township was named in honor of Gen. Andrew Jackson, who was then President of the United States. Its boundaries are, on the north, Findley and Marion townships, east by Amanda, south by Delaware and Madison and west by Eagle.

The first white man who settled in the township, was Judge Mordica Hammond, whose widow, Mrs. Tillie Hammond, is, I believe, still living. Judge Hammond came here in 1827, and settled on the Blanchard River, in section thirty-five, there being no neighbors nearer than Mt. Blanchard. Indeed but a very small portion of the lands in the township had been entered at that time. The Judge resided upon the same tract of land at the time of his death, which he had reclaimed from the wilderness, and converted into a beautiful farm.

But Judge Hammond was not long without neighbors. Peter George, Wm. Greer, the Egbert's, Ralston, Williamson, Newell, the Missmores, the Treeces, and others quickly followed.

The timber of this part of the county is oak, elm, walnut, beech, maple, buckeye, &c., and heavily wooded the whole face of the township.

The soil is rich and productive, especially so along the water courses. The population is a purely agricultural one, there being no manufacturing establishments of any moment in the township. There are many valuable farms and beautiful farm buildings here, and the township is one of considerable wealth, and its people are industrious and energetic.

The township is well watered by the Blanchard River—which passes through from south to north—and its tributary creeks and runs. Wells, which are easily dug in any part of the township, furnish a supply of good wholesome water.

This part of the county never having had the advantage of railroads, is comparatively new, but when once improved, will be a beautiful part of the country.

The first school house was built in 1832, and the first school was taught by the now venerable Aquilla Gilbert, Esq., of Vanlue. At the time Mr. Gilbert taught the school there were no public school funds, and the compensation was one dollar and fifty cents per scholar, paid by voluntary subscriptions. The district included all of Jackson and Amanda townships, and if the "school-master boarded around," as was then the fashion, he certainly had to spread himself over a good deal of territory.

The first church was built in 1833.

A hand mill owned by Godfrey Wolford, was the first in the township, and Mr. Gilbert says that he and Judge

First Birth—First Death.

Hammond with whom he resided during the winter of 1828-29, used to go to mill every other day to grind enough meal to support the Judge's family. The first flouring mill was built in 1835 by Michael Missmore, but as it was propelled by water, it was rather uncertain as a means of procuring bread. This mill was the first frame building erected in the township.

The market for the first settlers was Portland and Sandusky City. But as was said by one of the old pioneers, it made but little difference to them where the market was, as they had but little to sell.

Aquilla Gilbert and L. P. Hamblin were the first couple married in the township, Asa M. Lake Esq., of Mt. Blanchard, officiating. Capt. Dan. Gilbert, their son, and now of Vanlue, was the first white child born here. Capt. Dan. has grown up with the county, and doubtless remembers with pleasure his boyhood days, spent in clearing, and the old log school house, long since replaced by the neat brick or frame.

The first death was that of Mrs Margaret Williams, wife of an old hunter and pioneer. Her remains were interred in what is now the Mt. Blanchard Cemetery.

There are many fine farms and farm buildings in this township, and it is fast becoming a wealthy locality. The fine residences of John Doty, Rev. Asa Ellis, Thompson Myers, David Bibler, Geo. Treece, Moses Elsea, jr., Henry Bowers, Alpheus Ralston and Peter Struble, are as modern in construction and comfortable in finish, as any in the county. The out-buildings on these farms are of the most convenient, ample kind.

This township is peopled by a quiet pastoral population. Thrifty, neighborly and hospitable. Much attention is paid to the common schools, and the necessary school buildings, and school apparatus is provided, and competent teachers employed, to the end that all the youth may have an opportunity of acquiring a good common school education.

LEVI SAMPSON

Was one of the early settlers of this township. He was a man of limited education, but possessed a large stock of good common sense, sterling integrity, and a perseverance that overcame all obstacles. His life, whilst it was one of labor and toil, and in the early years of his residence here, one of privations, was so good naturedly enjoyed by him, and so cheerfully did he meet all the hardships and disappoinments of pioneer life, that he was known amongst his neighbors as "Sunny Sampson." He became quite wealthy, and had a well improved farm and good buildings.

In 1851, just previous to the adoption of the present State Constitution, he was appointed Associate Judge, in place of Michael Price, resigned. Judge Sampson died a number of years ago, regreted by his neighbors.

ALPHEUS RALSTON

Was the son of William Ralston, and was born in Rockingham County, Va., in June, 1801. Whilst quite young, his parents removed to Wood County, in the same State, but now West Virginia, where he remained until his twenty-fourth year.

In 1826 he came to Ohio, settling in Picakway County, and in the same year was married. After a residence here of about four years, he sold out his possessions and came to Hancock County in 1830, and took up his residence in this township, on the same tract of land on which he now resides.

At that time his nearest neighbor on the north, was Mr. Chamberlain, three miles distant, and Mr. Woodruff, on the south, about the same distance. No neighbors on the east nearer than the river, six miles away, and Philip Cramer on Tawa Creek, seven miles distant, was the nearest family west.

The Perrysburg and Bellefontaine road was not yet located or opened up, only a wagon track led to Findley. Mr. R. was at the first election in the township, and with Aquilla Gilbert, Mordica Hammond, the Beards, and others effected the organization of Jackson Township. His first neighbors were the Williamsons

Mr. R. is the father of eight children, four of whom are living. The farm upon which he resides is one of the most valuable in the township, and he is enjoying his declining years, surrounded by kind neighbors and friends, and with a sufficiency of this worlds goods. He has always retained the good will of his acquaintances, and has been noted for his industry, honesty and fair dealing. He speaks with pleasure of his early associates in the settlement of the township.

JOSEPH NEWELL

Was born July 6th, 1808, in Shenandoah County, Va. and when six years old, came with his parents to what is now Fairfield County, Ohio. Here he remained until 1836, and where he married. In that year he came to this township and took up his residence on lands entered by him a few years previously. Mr. N. was one of the pioneer Methodists of the township. The year preceeding his emigration here, a society had been organized by a Methodist itinerant, of which Mr. Newell's brother James, and two sisters and a Mrs. Bond were members. His wife became a member of the same society the year after they came here, and Mr. N. a few years later.

The first church in the township was built on Mr. N.'s land, and there has been a church building here ever since, and a regular preaching place.

Mr. Newell has raised a large family, and provided liberally for them. He has won and retained the friendship of his neighbors, and been an honest citizen, a warm friend and a consistent christian. The early ministers, no matter to what denomination they belonged, always found a welcome at his house, and a cordial invitation to its hospitality.

GEORGE TREECE

Was born in Pickaway County, Ohio, January 9th, 1827, and in November of the same year came to this county, his father's family locating in this township.

Mr. Treece is one of the largest farmers and land owners in the township. He has always followed the occupation of a farmer, and by his industry and intelligence, has made it a success, and he in now the owner of many of the best cultivated acres in the township.

At an election held in this township in October, 1833, there were *ten* votes cast.

The first company muster was held at the house of Aquilla Gilbert, and the company—about fifty men in all—was composed of men from Amanda, Delaware, Richland and Jackson Townships, under the command of Capt. Godfrey Wolford and Lieutenants R. W. Hamblin and Josiah Elder.

Capt. Wolford having been promoted to Major, the command of the company devolved upon the Lieutenants, and one who was there, has suggested that had they been at the first Bull Run fight, the fortunes of the day would have been very different.

Wild game was plenty in all parts of the township, and the hunting of it was a source of profit as well as pleasure, and the table of the backwoodsman was scarcely ever without a supply of venison or bear steak, or a squirrel pot pie.

There are now eight school buildings in the township, nearly all of which are brick, and the enumeration of youth of school age, amounts to *four hundred and seventy-one.*

In 1863 a post office was established on the road from Findley to Mt. Blanchard, about six miles from Findley, and called *Ewing's Corners*, with Jesse Ewing as postmaster. The office was, however, discontinued after about eight years. Mr. Ewing was the only postmaster.

NORTH LIBERTY.

This village was laid out in April, 1853, by J. F. Houk, on the north-west part of the west half of the north-west quarter of section 27. Fifteen lots were platted.

In 1867 John Douty and A. M. Houk made an addition of twenty-eight lots, and in 1859 six more lots were added by Jacob Hoy.

The place never assumed very large proportions or very much importance. It never advanced beyond a cross roads village, and its business was entirely local, being confined to the trade of the immediate neighborhood. Its location is in the midst of a rich agricultural district, but remote from railroads.

Its business was confined to one grocery store, one wagon shop, one blacksmith shop, one shoe shop, one saw and shingle mill. There is one church and one school building, and one physician. The town, so far as improvements in the way of new buildings are concerned, is at a stand still. Population in 1880 was one hundred and eighteen.

In 1855 or 56, a post office was established here, under the name of Houcktown, and the postmasters have been as follows: Robert Davidson, J. R. Babcock, John Garst, Israel Sampson, Eli Gorsuch, John Ebaugh and David Beagle.

The following named persons have been elected Justices, at the dates mentioned:

Aquilla Gilbert, 1830, 1833, 1836, 1839, 1842.
George Henry, 1835.
Joseph Tromney, 1839, 1842, 1845, 1851, 1854.
Arthur Russell, 1844, 1847, 1850.
Charles O. Mann, 1845, 1848, 1851, 1854.
Andrew W. Houk, 1856.
John Teems, 1855.
D. W. Engle, 1857, 1863, 1866.
Joseph S. Struble, 1857.
James Waltemire, 1859.
Henry Bowers, 1859, 1863, 1866, 1869, 1872, 1875, 1878, 1881.
Thomas Waltemire, 1862.
Eli J. Shelden, 1869, 1872, 1875, 1878.
Israel Sampson, 1880.
John C. Hayes, 1881.

Stock and Crop Statistics.

Statistics of the number and value of live stock and acres and bushels of grain produced, as reported to the Auditor of the County, in 1881.

Horses, 547 number.	$75,140,	value.
Cattle, 1,205 "	14,150,	"
Sheep, 3,023 "	5,995,	"
Hogs, 2,137 "	5,050,	"
Wheat, 3,416 acres.	59,820	bushels.
Oats, 416 "	13,270	"
Corn, 2,655 "	106,055	"
Flax, 67 "	600	bushels.
Hay, 879 "	979	tons.

LIBERTY TOWNSHIP.

TP. 1, N.   R. 10, E.
AREA 15,360 ACRES,   POPULATION, 1,101.

From the organization of the county in 1828, until December, 1830, this township was a part of Findley township. At the session of the County Commissioners held in that month, present, Mordica Hammond, John P. Hamilton, and Charles McKinnis, it was determined that it was necessary to divide the townships of Findley and Amanda into three townships, after the following manner: Then follow the boundaries of Findley and Marion, and this order in relation to Liberty township, " and in the next place commencing at the south-east corner of section 34, in township 2 south, range 10, thence north to the north-east corner of section 3, in township 2 north, thence west to the north-west corner of section 6 in range 9, thence south to the south-west corner of section 31, in township 2 south, thence east to the place of beginning, in which bounds shall be made a separate township, and become a body corporate and politic, and be known and designated by the name of Liberty."

This township comprises sections 3, 4, 5, 6, 7, 8, 9, 10, 15, 16, 17, 18, 19, 20, 21, 22, 27, 28, 29, 30, 31, 32, 33, and 34 in township 1 north, and range 10 east, and is bounded north by Portage township, east by Findley, south by Eagle, and west by Blanchard. It is situated in the cen-

First Entry of Lands and Settlement.

ter of the county north and south, and just west of the east and west center, which location gives it some advantages over its neighbors.

The first entry of lands in this township was made July 3d, 1821, by Vance, Neil and Cory, of the south-west quarter of the south-east quarter of section 8.

On the 20th of December of the same year, Robert McKinnis entered the east part of the north-west quarter of section 7, and Charles McKinnis entered the west half of the north-west quarter of section 7. John Gardner entered the north half of the north-east quarter of section 10, and on the 27th day of the same month Jacob Poe entered the west half of the south-west quarter of section 8. September 5th, 1825, Thomas Wilson entered the east half of the south-east quarter of section 9, and in August 1828, R. L. Strother entered the north-east quarter of section 21, and these were followed by entries made by Alfred Hampton, John Hobbs, Richard Watson, Isaac Comer and others.

The first settlement was made in 1821, in the spring, by Jacob Poe, and in the fall by Robert McKinnis and his sons, Charles, James, Philip and John. Judge McKinnis settled on the farm now owned by Oliver P. Shaw, James on the farm owned by Solomon Swarts, and Poe on the farm now owned by his son Nelson. The sons of Charles McKinnis now reside on the lands on which he first located.

These men were followed by Fishel and his sons John, Michael and Daniel, and some grown up daughters, Johnson Bonham, John Boylan, Judge Ebenezer Wilson, Richard, William and George Watson, Barna Beardsley, William Fountain, Isaac Strother, Nathan Frakes, Isaac Comer, Povenmire, John Price, the Radabaughs, Solomon Lee, Abraham Bails, and others.

This township was heavily timbered with walnut, ash, beech, sugar, oak, cottonwood, sycamore, and the inevitable buckeye. No part of the land was clear of timber, and the immense forests of walnut which were destroyed, burned up to make way for the plow, would now be of incalculable value.

The soil of this locality is variable. Along the river it is warm and sandy, and on the ridges, sandy with a mixture of gravel. Between the ridge and the river it is a rich vegetable loam, in places partially mixed with clay. On the north of the river the prevailing soil is clay. The rich bottom lands are adapted to corn, the sandy gravelly soil to wheat, and the clay or up lands are used for grazing purposes. The principal crops are wheat, corn, oats, flax and grass.

The Blanchard River crosses this township from east to west, furnishing an abundance of water not only for stock purposes, but during a good portion of the year enough to propel the two flouring mills located upon it. The river bottom lands are exceedingly rich and productive, but are subject to occasional overflows, by which crops and fences are damaged more or less.

On the north side we have Watson's, Wilson's, Grassy and Worden's runs, small wet weather streams, whose channels furnish good drainage for the adjacent lands. There are several springs along Watson's and Wilson's runs, which keep them supplied with water the year round.

On the south side Comer's run enters the river on the Dye farm, and is the only creek of any importance on that side. None of these creeks furnish water power now. There was for a number of years a saw mill on Comer's run, on the old Povenmire farm, just south of the Findley and Kalida State road, but that has long since been abandoned. On the farm of Nelson Poe, and some forty or fifty feet from the river is what the people in the neighborhood call a sink hole, that is the water dissappears in the ground, and is not seen again until it is emptied into the river.

Blanchard Church, on the Ewing farm, on Defiance road, built by the Presbyterians in 1850, was the first church building in the township. The congregation, however, previous to that time, held services in private houses, and in the school house in the neighborhood. The society was organized in 1832 by Rev. Peter Monfort. The first stated minister, the late Rev. Geo. VanEmon, was at the same time pastor of the church in Findley. Of the first membership we find the names of Judge Wilson and wife, William Coen, wife and two daughters, Jacob Poe and wife, and Mrs. Judge McKinnis.

As a proof of the strictness of church rules, and their enforcement, in years gone by, it is related to me by a friend that the late William Taylor, of Findley, was once reported to the congregation that met at the house of Jacob Poe, as having been guilty of violating the rules regarding the keeping of the Sabbath day, which violation occurred in this wise:

At that day the means of transportation of produce and other barter to a market, was by floating it down the Blanchard, Auglaize and Maumee, to Perrysburg or Toledo. Mr. Taylor was in trade at Findley, and desiring to make a trip, had his fleet of canoes loaded, waiting for a rise in the river, and a favorable time to set out on his voyage. After waiting a few days, the favorable time to start came on Sunday; and Mr. Taylor being impatient by delays, shoved off his canoes, and silently, perhaps, floated down the peaceful

Blanchard, never intending any disrespect to the day or the church. But the church dignitaries could not overlook so flagrant a breach of church regnlations, and Bible commands, and Mr. Taylor was cited to appear and answer, and to show cause why he should not be visited with the penalties of his disobedience. My friend says he came, answered, confessed, and was forgiven.

In 1832 the first school house was built in the township, on the farm now owned by John Reed, Esq. Richard Wade was the first teacher. There are now eight school houses in the township, the most of which are commodius buildings. The youth of school age number three hundred and seventeen.

There are one Evangelical, one United Brethren, one Christian Union, and one Presbyterian Church building, in the township. Each of these churches has a flourishing Sunday School attached, under the charge of efficient and zealous superintendents.

The first mill, or rather mills—for there were a flour, and lumber mill both—was butilt by John Byal, and is near the Infirmary. The flour mill was run by water. The machinery was moved by a large overshot wooden wheel, which kept plashing and creaking all day, and about which there was to us boys always a charming atmosphere of coolness, and a capital place for fishing. The water pouring over the dam, not in a rush, but slowly and at times almost noiselessly, the slow but continued movement of the old wooden wheel, the long drawn-out screech of the wooden machinery of the mill, the quiet movements of the miller, all had a lazy feeling inseparably connected with them, which I guess was contagious, for when we boys got sprawled out on the grassy bank of the river, near the old mill, we were sure to be infected with such feelings, and it required something tolerably exciting to fully arouse us.

In about 1844 Miller Johnson built a saw mill at the site of the Holden Mill, and in about 1853 Amos Hartman, now of Iowa, built a flouring mill at the same place, both of which mills are now standing.

When the township was first settled wolves were very plenty, and also very destructive, killing the sheep, hogs, and even young cattle of the settlers. Near where the Blanchard Church now stands Mr. Poe had some young cattle killed by the wolves. Numbers of wolves were killed for their scalps, for which the State paid a bounty.

In this township is the Indian Green, Plum orchard, and Indian burying ground. Of the Indian Green, as it was called, is said by the early settlers, that quite a considerable tract of land on the north bank of the river, had been partially cleared up, on which the Indians had a burying ground, and perhaps a village, and certainly some kind of fortifications or earth works, of which I have heretofore spoken. In addition to this there were several acres of lands along the river bottoms which had not only been cleared, but cultivated as every indication plainly showed. Whether the presence of so many plum trees was the work of the Indians, or of that eccentric person already alluded to—Johnny Appleseed—will perhaps never be known. The fact however remains that they were here, and among them were also a number of apple trees.

The Indian burying ground was frequently visited by members of their tribe—the Ottowas—and at one time a white man by the name of Ellison, with his family, settled on this ground. Ellison dug up quite a number of skeletons, and opened graves for such trinkets as were buried with the dead. This coming to the ears of the Indians, they visited the place, and were so emphatic in their denunciation of the vandalism, that Ellison thought it prudent to quit the premises, which he did. This plum orchard and burying ground covered some twelve acres or more.

Of the earliest settlers of this township, I have already spoken of the McKinnis family. Nelson Poe, a descendant of that family, resides upon the old farm of his father, Jacob Poe, who came to this part of the county with the McKinnis.' Jacob Poe was a hardy specimen of the backwoodsman. He was a relative of the celebrated Indian fighters, Adam and Andrew Poe, and was possessed of the physical strength and courage attributed to the celebrated brothers. He lived to a good old age, respected and honored.

John Boylan, for more than forty years a resident here, came from near Newark, Licking County, Ohio, in 1832. He was one of the first school teachers in the county, and for many years taught "the young ideas how to shoot," and how to shout too, for that matter, for I have a very vivid recollection of the energetic manner in which he swung the birch.

Mr. Boylan was a local preacher of the Methodist Church, and one of its earliest members in the connty. As a minister he was fervent and touching in his appeals, and powerful in his exhortations. After his long residence here he went west, and is now a resident of Iowa.

Richard Watson and wife are both dead, and all their living children but one are now residents of the county. Mr. Watson was a good neighbor, an enterprising citizen, and honest in all his dealings. He died, leaving to his children a fine farm, which he had reclaimed from the wilderness. Mr. Watson, though a strong partisan of the

Democratic school of politics, did not attempt to impertinently intrude his opinions on others. He held the office of Coroner of the County for one or two terms.

Isaac Comer came to this township from Fairfield County, and located on the farm now owned by J. B. Wagner, about four miles west of Findley, on the Benton road. Mr. Comer was one of those large, jolly, good-natured men that we occasionally meet. Frank in all his sayings, kind and generous in his acts, honest and prompt in his dealings, he was universally liked, aud his death was sincerely regretted.

The Rev. Geo. Van Emon, one of the purest men who ever lived, may well be claimed by this township, as nearly all his life in this county was spent here. As a minister he was sincere, and his words carried conviction with them. As a christian he was blameless. As a neighbor he was kind and hospitable. As a citizen he was one whose example might be safely followed.

William Fountain, or the *old man Fountain*, as he was familiarly called, came to the county in 1830, and settled in this township, on lands on which he resided for nearly fifty years, and up to the time of his death. Of an unassuming and retired disposition, attentive to his own affairs, taking little part in public matters, his acquaintance was never very extensive. But no man in his neighborhood was more highly respected, or considered more trustworthy. Mr. Fountain came from Franklin County, and lived to be almost a centenarian.

Mr. F. was born in Caroline Co., Md., January 6th, 1784. He was of Irish descent, and was the second of three brothers. In 1824 he came to Franklin Co., Ohio, and settled in Plain township. In 1809 Mr. F. was married to Sarah Barton, by whom he had five children. Mrs. F. died in 1821, and Mr. F. married Mrs. Rebecca Smith, with whom he lived until the time of her death, a period of more than forty years. Mr. F. sold his farm in Franklin, and came to Hancock, taking up his residence on the farm on which he died. At the time of his death he was the oldest person in the county.

DANIEL CUSAC

Was born in Mifflin County, Pa., in January, 1790. His parents were natives of Ireland, and were married before leaving that country. Mr. Cusac came to Perry County, Ohio, when quite a young man, and there married Sarah Sellers, who died in October, 1881, at the advanced age of eighty-eight years, having survived her husband about fourteen years. Mr. Cusac came to this county in 1838, and took up his residence in this township, on the farm on which he died. He had ten children, nine of whom are still living. John and Mrs. Judge Cooper, two of the children, reside in Portage township. Two of them, Capt. Isaac Cusac and Mrs. Mulford, are in Pleasant township. The others, William, James, Mrs. John Reed, Mrs. James Cooper and Mrs. Robert Poe reside in Liberty township. Mr. C. had a limited common school education, but was a man of good strong common sense. He was a consistent member of the Presbyterian Church for fifty years, and led an upright, honest life, respected by all who knew him.

Unassuming and domestic in his habits, he made no figure in public, and although his counsel and advice was sought for, it was given with modesty and fairness, and for the best interests of those desiring it. He died at a good old age, loved and respected, and left to his children a good name, and to his wife a good home.

PHILIP MCKINNIS

Was the second son of Judge Robert McKinnis, one of the very earliest settlers of the county, and was born in Butler Co., Pa., January 9th, 1801. He came with his father's family to Ross Co., O., when young. In 1822 the family came to this township, and settled on the river, near the present site of Cronninger Mills.

In 1827 he married Susan Dukes, and commenced life on the farm now owned by Conrad Renninger. He was a man of strong constitution, scarcely knowing what it was to be sick. He had a limited common school education, but was a man of good hard common sense. He had a family of eleven children, nine of whom are living. Mr. McK., after a long residence in the county, sold out and removed to Putnam County in 1855, near Gilboa, and finally to near Leipsic, where he died in 1868, his wife surviving him some two years. Their remains now rest in Maple Grove Cemetery.

Mr. McKinnis was a fair specimen of the frontiersman. Possessed of great endurance, courage and industry, backed by the strictest honesty, he won and held the respect of all who knew him. His word was as good as his bond; he punctually fulfilled all his engagements, redeemed all his promises, and faithfully discharged every duty. He was a member of the old School Baptist Church for over thirty years. His son William, who resides in Findley, is the only one of the family now living in the county.

NELSON POE

Came to this township when he was but three months old, having been born in Ross Co., O., September 4th, 1822. He was the third son of Jacob Poe. His mother was a daughter of Judge McKinnis. His paternal ancestors were of German extraction, whilst his mother's people were Scotch Irish. The father of Mr. Poe settled on the farm now owned and occupied by the subject of this sketch. At the time of his coming here there were but a very few families in the county, but the Poe family was possessed of that kind of pluck which never gave way before difficulties, or became discouraged at privations.

On his father's side, Mr. Poe is distantly related to the celebrated historical fighting brothers, Adam and Andrew Poe, and also to the eminent divine, Rev. Adam Poe. Farming has always been the leading occupation of Mr. Poe, although during the winter seasons of thirty years, he taught a country school. He is a man of fair education, and has always been regarded as a successful educator. He may well be termed a self-educated man, for his school privileges were very limited. He is a member of the Presbyterian Church at present, and has been a church member for the past sixteen years.

In 1846 he was married to Mary Lytle, who still lives to add to his enjoyment. They are the parents of three children. The eldest son was killed during the late war. The second son—Luther—resides in Fostoria, and the youngest, a daughter, is at home with her parents. Mr. P.'s school days were passed in the old log school house, under the instruction of such primitive teachers as Richard Wade, Benj. Cummins and others.

Mr. Poe has resided in the county longer than any other person, with the single exception of Job Chamberlain, of Findley. He has witnessed the steady but great transformation of a wilderness into fruitful fields; has seen the dense forests disappear, and in their places spring to life;

Farm Buildings. 393

beautiful fertile fields; has lived to see an uninhabited country settled by an industrious, thrifty, wealthy, happy people, with school houses and churches in every neighborhood; to see railroads built, traversed by the iron horse drawing the trains well laden with the products of this rich county; to see telegraph wires stretched all over the land. And in this great work he has been no idle spectator.

This township contains some of the finest farm buildings in the county. Amongst them is the fine brick residences of W. C. Watson, R. W. Boyd, Elijah Gowdy, Cornelius Ewing, John Hart and Samuel Mosier, and the very substantial frame dwellings of Joseph Wilson, Jacob Grubb, Wm. Renninger, C. C. Harris, all on the north side of the river, whilst on the south side, Crondall Watson, Henry Sherrick, Henry Rudisill, John Radabaugh, Joseph Barnhill, David Bish, J. M. Moorehead and others living on the south side have equally tasteful dwelling places. The farms are well improved, and supplied with the best of out-buildings.

JUSTICES OF THE PEACE.

Below we give the names, with the dates of their election of those who have held this office.

Benjamin Cummins—1831, 1834.
Johnson Bonham—1834, 1843.
Merriman Price—1836.
James H. Barr—1841.
Van Burton—1841, 1844.
John Smith—1842.
William S. Burkhead—1844.
Aaron Hall—1845, 1848, 1851.
Levi Taylor—1837, 1840, 1853.
John Radabaugh—1847, 1880.

Thomas H. Taylor—1853, 1856, 1859, 1862.
Alexander Philips—1850, 1868, 1872, 1875.
John Hall—1853, 1856, 1859.
W. H. Fountain—1860, 1863, 1866.
J. E. Dresbach—1865.
Joseph Wilson—1872.
John Reed—1873.
Henry Rudisill—1877, 1880.
R. W. Boyd—1877.

Table showing the number and value of live stock, and the number of acres of grain sown, and bushels produced, as returned by township Assessor in 1881.

Horses,	472 number.	$24,470, value.
Cattle,	1,120 "	14,070, "
Sheep,	2,310 "	4,980, "
Swine,	1,675 "	4,580, "
Wheat,	2,709 acres.	52,884 bushels.
Oats,	225 "	7,325 "
Corn,	2,539 "	112,030 "
Flax,	31 "	235 "
Hay,	509 "	613 tons.

First Land Entries.

MADISON TOWNSHIP.

Tp. 2, S., R. 10, E. Tp. 2, S., R. 11, E.
Area 15,360 acres. Population 1,235.

At the June session, 1840, of the County Commissioners, it was "Ordered that sections No. 1, 2, 11, 12, 13, 14, 23, 24, 25, 26, 35 and 36 in township 2 south, range 10 east, and sections 5, 6, 7, 8, 17, 18, 19, 20, 29, 30, 31 and 32 in township 2 south, range 11 east, be set off and constituted as a new township, called Madison." Those sections in range 10 were a portion of Van Buren township, and those in range 11 were a part of Delaware township.

This township was named in honor of James Madison, fourth President of the United States. It lies on the south side of the county, and is bounded on the north by Eagle and Jackson townships, on the east by Delaware, on the south by Hardin County, and on the west by Van Buren township.

On the first day of June, 1829, Abel Tanner made entry of the west half of the north-west quarter of section 23, and on the same day William Y. Woodruff entered the north-east quarter of section 2. These were the first entries of lands in the township.

Squire Carlin on the 9th day of July, 1829, entered the west half of the south-west quarter of section 11. John Longwith, of Pickaway County, entered the east half of the north-east quarter of section 5, on the 5th of May,

1830, and in September of the same year, Chaney Rickets entered the east half of the south-west quarter of section 2. In November, 1832, the north-east quarter of the south-east quarter of section 5, was entered by Alexander Grant, of Franklin County.

In October, 1834, Robert Hurd and Robert Shaw, both of Portage County, made entries of lands in section 7, and Henry Imhoff, of Stark County, entered the west half of the north-west quarter of section 6. Other entries speedily followed, and settlements were made in many portions of the township.

The timber in this part of the county is maple—sugar and soft—beech, hickory, ash. The different varieties of oak was abundant in all parts of the township. Black walnut, blue ash, and red elm is found along the streams. On the wet lands are black ash and sycamore. This part of the county was very heavily timbered.

The soil for the most part consists of a compact yellow clay subsoil, covered with a vegetable mould. Along the streams may be found small areas of alluvial lands, which are very fertile. The soil on the wet lands consists of a deep black loam, which is very productive when properly drained. Generally speaking the lands of this township can be considered as only moderately fertile.

Although the township is well watered, there are but few streams of water, and they are not of much importance as water courses. Eagle Creek, which is formed by the junction of what is called the east and west branches, which unite about eighty rods north-east of the south-west corner of section 14, and thence take their course as one creek. Flat Branch is so called on account of the small amount of fall it has. It drains the south-eastern part of the township, and is a tributary of the East Branch. Buck Run is in the north-eastern part, and empties into Eagle Creek near the north line of the township. The West Branch of Eagle Creek rises in the *Hog Creek Marsh* in Hardin County, and the East Branch rises near the Hardin County line.

"The weight of authority," writes Dorillas Martz of this township, "is that Simeon Ransbottom was the first to settle in this township, though Abel Tanner and Abner Hill came the same year." Tanner came in February, 1825, from near Kenton, Ohio, where he had resided for three years previous. He and his wife were both natives of Rhode Island. He located on the banks of the West Branch of Eagle Creek, near the camping ground of Gen. Hull, as he passed through in 1813. Mr. Tanner died in 1833, aged forty-two years, and his wife died three years later.

Simeon Ransbottom settled on the west bank of Eagle Creek, two miles below Tanner. He was a native of Virginia. His wife was born in Ireland. Mr. Ransbottom died in 1851, his wife having died many years previously.

The family of Abner Hill consisted of himself, wife, and step-daughter. He resided in the township for several years. He committed a burglary by breaking into Carlin's Mill at Findley, for which exploit he was sent to the Ohio Penitentiary, and was the first representative to that institution from this township, if not from the county.

Settlements were very soon after made by Jacob Helms, Benjamin Sparr, Andrew Rickets, John Diller, N. B. Martz, J. W. Williams and others, and farms were opened up all over the township.

Mr. N. B. Martz says that when he came to this township in 1834, he found a man by the name of John Diller living in section 11, on lands which he had bought of a Mr. More-land, who claimed to have purchased the lands of Simeon Ransbottom. Mr. Martz adds that his impression is that Ransbottom was the first settler within the present limits of Madison township, and that John Tullis came with him perhaps. Mr. Martz says that from the appearance of the buildings, clearings, and fruit trees when he first visited the Diller's and other places, he is led to believe that the first settlement had taken place at least ten years before that visit.

The first church building erected in the township was by the Methodist Episcopals at Arlington, in 1858. It must not be supposed that religious worship was unknown prior to this time, or that no minister had visited this region. Here as elsewhere the school houses and private houses were used as places of worship. There are now four church buildings in the township; two Methodist Episcopal, one Protestant Methodist, and one Disciples.

The first school house built in the township was on the land now occupied as the German Lutheran Cemetery, at the west line of the township. It was of the usual style, of logs, with clapboard roof. There are now eight school buildings, all comfortable and commodious. The enrollment of youth is two hundred and twenty-three males, and one hundred and ninety-five females, making a total of four hundred and eighteen.

The first hotel, or tavern as such places were then called, was kept by John Diller, and was located on the west bank of Eagle Creek, at the place now known as Waterloo. This tavern was called *The Cross Keys*.

The people of this township devote themselves to agricultural pursuits, and are a peaceable, quiet and thrifty community. Education and religion command the respect and attention of all. The first settlers are principally from the eastern part of the State and from Pennsylvania. There are, however, quite a number of Germans, and their descendents.

John. W. Williams, one of the early settlers, and proprietor of the village of Williamstown, died but a few years ago, at a ripe old age, and was perhaps at the time of his death the oldest person in the township. Mr. Williams was Post Master for many years, and was ten times elected Justice of the Peace. He commanded the confidence and respect of his neighbors, and had many friends.

Christian Welty, a resident here, was one of those substantial men, who early sought a home in the west. He was a man of good judgment, sound mind and strict integrity.

Andrew Rickets, after a long and useful life, died but a few years since, leaving his family a goodly heritage, accumulated by industry and frugality. His widow, a very estimable lady, and a fair specimen of the goodly dames of the early years of the township, now resides in Findley, respected by all who know her.

Mr. Rickets, besides holding several township offices, was for two terms, a Commissioner of the county, and filled the office with both ability and fidelity.

Robert Hurd, who came to this township in 1839, was born at East Haddam, Conn., March 16th, 1785, and emigrated to Portage County, Ohio, in 1820, and settled in Twinsbnrg township, as agent for the brothers, Aaron and Moses Willcox—twins—from whom the township derived its name. Mr. Hurd made extensive entries of lands in and about the site of the present town of Arlington, in 1834, and his sons, William B. and Lorenzo, and son-in-law, Joseph Fitch, at once settled on part of these lands, then all a wilderness. Mr. Hurd laid out the town of Arlington, and was active in the formation of the township of Madison, from parts of Delaware and Amanda townships. For a number of years Mr. Hurd held the office of Justice of the Peace. He frequently appeared in Justice's Courts as an attorney, conducting his cases with much ability. Mr. Hurd died at Arlington in 1861.

NAPOLEON B. MARTZ

Was the son of Michael Martz, and was born in Rockingham County, Va., in November, 1809, and came to Hancock County in 1834, and settled on the farm now owned by his son, Dorillas. He was married in November, 1830, to Hannah Nicholls, who still accompanies him in the journey of life. Mr. Martz was a resident of the county *forty-one* years, when he got the western fever, and went to Douglas County, Ill., where he now resides.

Mr. Martz' grand-parents were from Bavaria, hence his German extraction. He is a man of good morals, although not a church member. He has a fair English education, and good strong common sense. His opinions were the result of careful thought, and his advice was sought by his neighbors. Honest, intelligent, sociable and accommodating, he easily won, and always held the esteem of his neighbors.

The following persons have been elected to the office of Justice of the Peace.

Solomon Watkins—1840.
Joseph Leslie—1840.
Thomas Reese—1843.
N. B. Martz—1843.

J. W. Williams—1846, 1849, 1852, 1855, 1858, 1861, 1864, 1867, 1870, 1873.
Joel Markel—1849, 1852.
L. P. Wing—1855, 1858.
Robert Hurd—1859.
David Wardwell—1861.
L. D. Wiseman—1864.
Philip Wilch—1867.
Peter Wilch—1869.
E. Longworth—1870.
J. C. Clingerman—1873.
Jonas Huff—1876, 1879.
T. H. Bushong—1876.
D. Martz—1878.

WILLIAMSTOWN.

This town was laid out in 1834, and named in honor of John W. Williams, the proprietor. It is located on part of the north-west quarter of the north-west quarter of section 31, and the north-east quarter of section 36. In originally contained *forty-eight* lots, and as remarked by a resident, "it commenced small, and has held its own exceedingly well." At the time the town was laid out, there was no family within three miles of it.

Mr. Williams opened a store and tavern in the place, and travel commenced along the range line, now the Bellefontaine State road. In about 1837, Christain Welty also opened a store, and a Dr. Smith located here for a short time, being the first in the township. He was succeeded by Dr. A. F. Burson, now of Mt. Blanchard, famous for his success in treating the "Milk Sickness," then prevalent in this part of the county.

The village is about fourteen miles directly south of Findley, and about three miles from the Hardin County line. The business of the town consists of one steam saw, shingle and lath mill, by William Heacock; a wagon and carriage shop, by Joseph Phillipi; a shoe shop, by William Knight; a blacksmith shop, by William Vanscoich; two grocery stores, one by J. B. DeHaven, and one by Cramer & Crabill, and one physician. Population 128.

A Post Office was established here in 1835, and Christian Welty was first Post Master. The office was called "Eagle," but in 1866 it was changed to Williamstown. The Post Masters have been Christian Welty, J. W. Williams, B. D. Evans, John DeHaven, and again Dr. B. D. Evans, the present incumbent.

WEST UNION.

This place was laid out by Andrew Sheller, in January, 1835, in the south-east corner of section 36, in lands now owned by A. Woods, and comprised forty-eight lots. It has no other history.

ARLINGTON.

In November. 1854, Robert Hurd, Esq., laid out the town of Arlington, on the south-west part of section 6, and the south-east part of section 1. The town originally contained seventeen lots, but since its first platting, successive additions have been made, until now it is quite a village.

Its business interests are not very extensive. There is one wagon and carriage shop, operated by Julius Dorney. Eli Bowman has a blacksmith shop, and Huff & Cramer are the proprietors of a steam saw and planing mill. There is one shoe shop; one pump factory. Woods & Co., and Joseph Huff each have a dry goods and grocery store, and Dr. L. S. Lafferty keeps a drug store in connection with his practice as a physician. There are also two saloons. A tile factory is in successful operation, owned by Brothers & Son.

The population of Arlington in 1880, was one hundred and thirty-six.

Upon the establishment of a Post Office here in 1846, Dr. B. Beach was appointed Post Master, and has been succeeded by L. P. Wing, E. B. Vail, W. K. Drake, Thomas Stark, Philip Wilch, L. S. Lafferty, E. P. Lease, and C. F. King.

An exhibit of the number of acres and bushels of cereals, and the number and value of live stock, as returned by Township Assessor in 1881.

Wheat, 2,814 Acres.	45,188 Bushels.
Oats, 443 "	13,263 "
Corn, 1,605 "	70,040 "
Flax, 103 "	927 "
Hay, 467 "	459 Tons.
Horses, 459 number.	$18,140, Value.
Cattle, 1,007 "	8,580, "
Sheep, 2,097 "	4,060, "
Swine, 1,816 "	2,420, "

MARION TOWNSHIP.

Tp. 1, N. R. 11, E.
Area 15,360 acres. Population 987.

The Commissioners at their session on the 6th day of December, 1830, caused the following record to be made: "It appearing to this Board necessary to divide the townships of Findley and Amanda into three townships after the following manner, to-wit: Beginning at the south-west corner of section 31, in township 1 north, in range 12, running thence north to the north-west corner of section 6 in township 2, in range 12, thence west to the north-west corner of section 4, in range eleven, thence south to the south-west corner of section 33, in township one north, in range 11, thence east to the place of beginning, which boundary shall be a separate township, and become a body corporate and politic, and shall be known and designated by the name of Marion."

The township was named in honor of the dashing South Carolina Ranger, Francis Marion, of Revolutionary notoriety, and is bounded on the north by Cass township, on the east by Big Lick, on the south by Amanda and Jackson, and on the west by Findley, and comprises sections 1, 2, 3, 4, 9, 10, 11, 12, 13, 14, 15, 16, 21, 22, 23, 24, 25, 26, 27, 28, 33, 34, 35 and 36, in township 1 north, and range 11 east.

Elnathan Cory made the first entry of lands on the 28th

Soil—Timber—Water.

day of November, 1822, of the north-east quarter of the north-east quarter of section 21.

On the 24th day of October, 1825, Alexander Robertson entered the south part of the north-east quarter of section 23. Jonas Hartman, of Pickaway County, entered the south-east quarter of section 24, on the 28th of April, 1830, and on the 15th of October, of the same year, Rezin Ricketts, of Seneca County, entered the west half of the south-east quarter of section 15. December 28th, 1830, Allen Wisely entered the east half of the south-west quarter of section 14.

Other entries were made by Jacob Iler, of Pickaway County, Joseph Orwig, Daniel Egbert and Major Bright, of Fairfield, Nimrod Bright and John Leeder, of Pennsylvania, Isaac Jones, of Richland, and others.

Walnut, oak, ash, beech, sugar, elm and buckeye are the prevailing kinds of timber.

The soil in the north part of the township is clay and sand. The river bottoms are exceedingly rich and productive, being a vegetable soil, and the south portion of the township has a soil of loam, very rich.

The township is well watered by the Blanchard River, and its tributaries, the outlet of the Prairie on the north, and Deer Creek on the south. On the farm of Allen Wisely are sulphur springs or deer licks, at which places the hunters of the early day laid in wait for the unsuspecting game. Good water may also be obtained by sinking wells. The river and creeks form a perfect system of drainage, and heretofore furnished water power for several mills.

Marion, though one of the smallest, is yet one of the wealthiest agricultural townships in the county. There are very many valuable farms and farm buildings.

The first settlers were Asher Wickham, Joseph Sargeant, and Othniel Wells. These parties settled near the western line of the township, Ashar Wickham on the George Burns farm, Joseph Sargeant on the T. J. Burns place, and Wells on the Charles Thomas farm. Very shortly after, Allen Wisely, Major Bright, Edward Bright, Joseph Baker, Lewis Thomas, and others commenced improvement in different parts of the township.

Major Bright became the owner of a large tract of valuable land. He at one time held the office of Associate Judge for this county. Several of his children reside in this and Big Lick townships, and are quite well off. Mr. Bright was long a resident of the township.

Lewis Thomas is still a resident of the township, owning a fine farm on the banks of the Blanchard, with good buildings and pleasant surroundings. Mr. Thomas, though well up in years, is vivacious, and loves to recount the incidents of his pioneer life. He is an earnest christian, an honest farmer, a good neighbor, and a valuable citizen.

No man in the township perhaps is better known, or more generally respected than is Allen Wisely. He owns a very valuable farm, well improved and delightfully located. Mr. Wisely has lived in the township long enough to see it change from an unbroken wilderness to fruitful fields; the rude log cabin replaced by the elegant frame and brick residences of the prosperous and happy farmers.

The old Baptist Church at William Davis' was the first one erected in the township. It has long since been replaced by a fine frame structure called the Union Bethel, in which any orthodox denomination have a right to worship. There are three United Brethren and one Methodist Episcopal Church buildings in the township,

The first school house was built on William Marvin's farm in 1836, and the first school was taught by Adam Robinson. There are now six good school buildings in the township, with an enumeration of three hundred and twenty-two youth of school age.

The first election was held in April, 1831. Asher Wickham, Joseph Sargeant, Allen Wiseley, —— DeWitt, Lewis Ward, Joseph Johnston, Joseph Baker, Major Bright, Adam Beard, Justin Smith, —— Powell, Edward Bright and O. Wells, thirteen in all, were the voters. The emigrants to this township came mainly from the eastern portion of Ohio.

In 1837, Daniel Opp put up a frame building on the farm now owned by Edward Wiseley, and commenced tavern keeping. A Post Office was also established at his place, and called Crow, and Mr. Opp appointed Post Master. After about two years Mr. Opp died, and the Post Office expired with him, since which time there has not been a Post Office in the township.

The office of Justice of the Peace has been filled by the following named persons:

Willis Ward—1831.
Major Egbert—1831.
Charles Thomas—1833.
David Egbert—1832, 1853.
Adam Heisley—1835,
Albert Ramsey—1838, 1841, 1844.
Allen Wiseley—1838, 1859, 1862, 1865, 1868.
Rezin Rickets—1841, 1844, 1847, 1850, 1853, 1856.
William Marvin—1847, 1851.
William Davis—1853, 1856, 1859, 1862.
Daniel Alspach—1863.
B. J. McRill—1866.

Isaac Davis—1869, 1872.
Michael Glenner—1871, 1874.
Amasa Buckingham—1875.
James Wilson—1877, 1880.
Andrew Bish—1878.
C. S. Johnston--1880.

WILLIAM B. MILLER.

Mr. Miller was born in Fairfield County, Ohio, February 11th, 1825, and is the son of Martin Miller, who was a farmer. Mr. M. has always followed the business of farming. He has a good common school education, and taught school a number of terms. He is perhaps above the average farmer in intelligence, owing to his better educational advantages, and is in every sense of the word a progressive man. He keeps well up with the times, availing himself of the latest and best improvements and information in his business; keeps himself not only thoroughly posted in all that pertains to agriculture, but is perfectly conversant with the politics of the country, and with what interests the people in State and National affairs, and is possessed of comprehensive and at the same time conservative views on the subjects. His neighbors have the most implicit confidence in his intelligence and ability, and he has on more than one occasion been put forth as the exponent of the principles of his political party, and on every such occasion he has received a generous support.

Mr. Miller was married in 1845 to Jane Martin, and in 1847 he came to this county, and settled in this township, on the farm on which he resides. He is now, and has been for the past seventeen years, a member of the United Brethren Church. His daily life has been such that his example has gone very far towards shaping the morals, and consequent prosperity of the community. His honesty is proverbial, and his counsels safe.

WILLIAM MARVIN, SR.

Was the son of Zera Marvin, and was born in Luzerne County, Pa., July, 1798. Mr. Marvin's father had a variety of occupations; dealing in merchandise, farming a little, and preaching occasionally. He was a minister of the Baptist Church. Mr. Marvin was a carpenter by trade, and followed that nearly all his life, although he owned quite an extensive lot of land.

In 1818 he married Mabel Roberts, who came to Ohio with him, and to this county, and died August 25th, 1852 Mr. Marvin came to Ohio in 1823, and resided in Wayne County for eleven years. He came to Hancock County in October, 1834, and bought in this township, in the June following, on the same lands he occupied up to within a year before his death. The first winter that the family were in the county, the families of William and Mathias Marvin— seventeen persons in all—lived in one cabin, twenty feet square.

Mr. Marvin was the father of sixteen children, fourteen of whom are living, and all married and heads of families. At the time of his death his children, grand-children, great-grand-children, and great-great-grand-children numbered not less than three hundred and fifty persons. He was a man of extraordinary endurance, good constitution, strong will, firm in his convictions, and determined in his actions He was a member of the Baptist Church for more than sixty years. He came to Findley about a year before he died. His decease took place in May, 1880. Of industrious, frugal habits, he was enabled to assist his children in their start in life, and they are all now in easy circumstances.

WILLIAM DAVIS

Was born in 1808, in the State of Maryland. His father was a native of Wales. Mr. Davis emigrated to Ohio in 1833. In 1830 he was married to Margaret Lafferty. He was one of the early settlers of the township, and owned a very large tract of land, which was improved by his industry and good management, and became very valuable. Mr. Davis was a man of untiring industry, and energy. No obstacle was so great that he did not overcome it. No labor was too severe for his performance. No duty was left undone. No promise unredeemed. He settled in the wilderness, and commenced life with a determination to succeed, if industry, economy and fair dealing would bring success, and he did succeed, as the broad acres of rich lands under a high state of cultivation, with good farm buildings, fully attest.

Mr. Davis had a family of eleven children, seven boys and five girls. All of his children who are now living, reside in the county. Mr. Davis joined the Baptist Church in 1842, and was a member at the time of his death. Although possessing but a limited common school education, Mr. Davis was always the friend and patron of schools and churches. His influence and his means were always in their favor.

Mr. Davis enjoyed the confidence of his neighbors for his intelligence and integrity, and by their votes he held the office of Justice of the Peace for a number of years, and was also a County Commissioner for three years, although the political party to which he belonged was greatly in the minority. He lived to see the county, in which he spent more than thirty years of his life, become prosperous and wealthy; dotted all over with the richest of farms, and with beautiful and substantial farm buildings. He was for many years one of the largest dealers in live stock in the county, and by his liberality in prices, and his prompt payments, he relieved many a poor family from want, if not from actual suffering. Perhaps no man in the county had a more general acquaintance with all classes of people, or who was more respected. Mr. Davis died in 1863.

Table of statistics, showing crops, and stock, as returned to County Auditor by the Township Assessor in 1881.

Wheat, 2,797 acres.	53,449 bushels.
Oats, 304 "	9,782 "
Corn, 2,436 "	95,100 "
Flax, 121 "	1,156 "
Hay, 1,018 "	1,135 tons.
Horses, 505 number.	$25,750, value.
Cattle, 1,199 "	14,710, "
Sheep, 1,998 "	3,450, "
Hogs, 2,259 "	5,390, "

ORANGE TOWNSHIP.

Tp. 2, S.   R. 9. E.
  Area 23,040 acres.   Population 1,451.

December 6th, 1836, the Commissioners of Hancock County ordered as follows: "That the original surveyed township number two, south of range nine, in Hancock County, Ohio, be set off into a separate township, politic and corporate, and named Orange. Ordered that the voters be notified thereof, to meet on the third Tuesday in December, A. D. 1836, to elect township officers."

This township is in the south-west corner of the county, and retains its original limits of thirty-six sections. It is bounded on the north by Union township, on the east by Van Buren, on the south by Hardin county, and on the west by Allen county.

Henry L. Dally, of Tuscarawas county, made the first entry of lands in this township, being that of the south-east quarter of section nineteen. This entry was made May 1st, 1834.

On the 12th of June, 1834, William Bryan, of Richland county, Ohio, entered the south half of section six—now owned by B. Ewing, R. Greer and A. Kimmel—and David Thompson, of Stark county, entered the north-east quarter of twenty—now owned by Asa Battles—and Sam'l Thompson, of Columbiana county, entered the west part of the south-east quarter of section twenty-two.

In September of the same year, George McManima, of Richland county, entered the south half of the south-east quarter of section seventeen. In August of the same year, John Stump, of Seneca county, took up the north-west quarter of section eighteen—now owned by Thomas Murray, of Bluffton.

In October, 1834, John Carnahan, of Putnam county, entered the west half of the south-west quarter of section seven, and Henry Atler, of Penn., entered the south-east quarter of section eighteen, and Joseph Morrison, also of Penn., entered the north-east quarter of section nineteen, and in November, 1834, Simeon Dudgeon, of Knox county, entered the south east quarter of section twenty-one. These entries were followed by others, and in a very few years all the lands in the township were taken up.

The face of the country in this township is generally level, although it has quite sufficient undulation to render drainage easy and abundant.

The soil is varied, but very fertile. In the northern part is what is called the "marsh," a low, wet tract, utterly unfit for cultivation, or in fact, for any purpose almost, until by the expenditure of vast sums of money, it is being ditched and drained, when it becomes one of the richest tracts in all the county. In other parts of the township the soil is of loam, or clay, or sand, and sometimes of all combined. But in no part of the township is the soil of a poor quality. The crops produced are of the principal cereals and vegetable, and of the best quality, thus showing the varied richness of the soil, which adapts itself to these productions.

The township is watered by Riley Creek and its tributaries. This stream crosses the township from east to west, and furnishes a supply of water for stock during the year. Although a considerable stream, it is of little consequence, except for drainage and stock purposes. The smaller creeks and runs which lead into this, are means of drainage to the adjacent lands.

In 1833, as I am informed by an old resident of this township, Henry L. Dalley, David Thompson and William Bryan came here and were the first settlers of the township. At that time, and for several years afterwards, the Wyandotte Indians claimed the county as a part of their hunting grounds, and were quite frequent visitors to the cabins of the *pale-faces*, but as they were peaceably disposed and honest, they were welcome.

The first settlers were soon followed by Stump, Shaw, the Battles, the McKinleys, the Marshalls, John Hasson, Wm. Agin, E. S. Crawford, J. T. McConnell, James Reed and others, who formed settlements in various portions of the township.

James Reed built the first frame building in the township, and J. T. McConnell built the first brick.

The first election was held by order of the Commissioners, in the fall of 1836, at which election there were fourteen votes cast.

The first school house was built in 1837. The pioneers of this township early appreciated the blessings of education, and were not unmindful of the moral and religious training of their children, and as a consequence, churches and school houses followed close in the wake of the settlements. Next to shelter for themselves and families, they provided these other necessaries to civilization, good order and prosperity. There are now nine school houses in the township, with an enrollment of four hundred and ninety-one youth.

The first church building in the township was built by the

First Mill. 415

Episcopal Church of North America, in 1837. There are now quite a number of places of worship in the township.

The first marriage was that of George McManima, and a Miss Morrison, both of whom are now dead. David Thompson was the first white child born in Orange township, and a Mrs. Ivers, who died in 1838, was the first person who deceased within its limits.

John Stump built the first mill, and there was a general rejoicing amongst the inhabitants at its completion, as previously facilities for obtaining flour had not been the best.

The reading of that day was confined principally to the bible, common school books and occasionally a newspaper. These, however, were quite sufficient to occupy their leisure hours, which were but few, so busy were they building cabins, and preparing their clearings for cultivation, and in assisting their neighbors.

Teachers in the common schools received one dollar per week, and boarded around, and were expected to sleep with the children, and have control of them from the time they left home in the morning until they returned at night.

JOHN MCKINLEY,

One of the pioneers of Orange township, was born in Westmoreland County, Pa., September, 23, 1801, and at the age of two years crme with his father, Wm. McKinley, to Trumbull County, Ohio, then on the frontier.

On the 13th of March, 1823, he was married to Mary Marshall, and in August, 1836, he and his family came to Hancock County. The country was entirely new, or at least destitute of roads, and Mr. McK. had to cut his way through the woods to the place where he now resides, camping at night in the wilderness through which he passed.

Not in the least discouraged, he at once went to work, and with the assistance of his boys and encouragement of his good wife, he soon opened up a good farm. He is still living on this same farm, one of the best in the township, and endeared to him, not only by the recollection of many weary years of toil, but by many of the very pleasantest days and memories of his life.

Mr. McKinley, although four score years mark his age, is a stout, healthy man, and bids fair to live many years yet. He performs but little hard work, but employs much of his time looking after the affairs of his farm. He has always borne the reputation of being honest in his dealings, frugal, but not stingy, and hospitable alike to neighbor or stranger,

Mr. McK. was present at the organization of the township, at which time there were but fifteen voters, and each voter was elected to an office. He held the office of Justice of the Peace twelve years, and the office of County Commissioner six years.

HENRY L. DALLY

Came to this township from Tuscarawas county in 1833, and his was the first family which settled in this part of the county. The family consisted of himself, wife, four sons and four daughters. The country was entirely new, and they had no neighbors within three or four miles.

Mr. Dally was a tall, muscular man, inured to hardships, industrious and honest in all his dealings, and a good neighbor. He and most of his family were members of the Disciples Church. He located on and cleared up the farm now owned by J. W. Shaw.

After remaining here for nearly twenty years, he becam

restive, and finally, in 1850, he emigrated to Iowa, and again he became a frontiersman. His family, or those of them who are yet living, are somewhere in the west.

ISAAC THOMPSON

Was the second of ten children of David Thompson, a farmer, who came here from Stark county. Isaac was born in Marlboro township, in that county, February 25th, 1828, and when about five years of age, was brought to this township by his father's family. This family was the second to locate here.

Young Thompson commenced life in the woods, and all the ups and downs of a frontier residence. He has always followed the independent occupation of a farmer, and now owns a very valuable farm of two hundred and eighty acres, well improved and very productive.

Mr. Thompson has a fair common school education, although his entire attendance at school, was only about *fifteen* months, and that after he was fifteen years of age. He is a man of good natural ability, good business tact, and safe counsellor, and his advice and assistance in business matters, is sought after by his neighbors, with whom he stands high.

In October, 1850, he married Louisa McKinley, by whom he had six children, all living. Mr. Thompson is a member of the Disciples Church, and has been for about fifteen years. His Christian life has conformed to his profession. He is very punctilious in all his business transactions. Honest, conscientious and faithful in the discharge of all his duties. Firm in his convictions of right, not easily turned aside from what he deems to be right.

Mr. Thompson has resided in this township continuously

since he first came here in 1833, and has never been absent from it more than a month at a time. He has been present at every election held in the township, the first of which were held at his father's house. Such is the confidence reposed in him by his neighbors, that he has been called up to fill almost all the offices in his township. On his father's side, his ancestors were of the old Puritan stock, and on his mothers side, they were from Ireland.

JOHN T. M'CONNELL.

Mr. McConnell was born in Penn. in 1809, and came to this township In 1838, and at once commenced clearing up the farm on which his son, D. J. McConnell now resides. He resided for some years in Jefferson County, Ohio, where in 1830, he was married to Eliza Dunlevy. Mrs. McConnell died in February, 1862. Mr. McConnell was the father of twelve children, seven of whom are now living, only two of whom, however, are living in this county. Mr. McConnell always followed the occupation of farming.

He had a fair common school education, and was a member of the Presbyterian Church for more than thirty years, and was one of the first members in this township. He was a man of strong constitution; never sick. He was a man of strong convictions, slow to yield a point, and tenacious in his belief. He was a good neighbor, and an honest man At his death, he left a beautiful farm of one hundred and sixty acres of land, well improved, all by his own labor and industry. His first neighbors were John McKinley, E. R. Burns, William Ivers, Benj. Marshall, James McConnell, Willard Boutwell and Thomas Walls, all of whom are dead except McKinley and Burns.

On the farm which he cleared up, are to be found some

Ancient Mounds.

interesting relics of the past. About the center of the farm is a mound or ridge, which from its formation, was no doubt built as a defense against enemies of some kind. The earth is thrown up in the shape of a mound or ridge, about thirty feet wide at the top, and scooped out or excavated, forming a rude fortification, commanding the surrounding country In and around this the timber was evidently removed, as the present growth is not more than eighteen or twenty inches in diameter.

About twenty rods east of this was a mound higher than any other portion of the ridge, and from bones and other articles found there, is evidently the burial place of the dead of those who built the mounds. In the neighborhood are other mounds of similar character, all no doubt built by the same parties.

The following list comprises the names of those who have been elected to the office of Justice of the Peace.

William Morrison—1837, 1840, 1843.
John McKinley—1837, 1840, 1843, 1846.
James Reed—1846, 1849, 1855, 1858.
Wm. M. Marshall—1849.
James Cummings—1852.
John A. Ewing—1852, 1855.
Jonathan Dunlap—1858, 1861, 1864.
N. Mains—1860.
James L. Henry—1863.
Isaac Thompson—1866, 1869.
W. M. McKinley—1867, 1870, 1873, 1875.
M. C. Palmer—1872, 1875, 1878.
Joseph Henry—1879.

A table giving the number of acres of grain sown and the number of bushels produced, and also the number and value of live stock, as returned by the Township Assessor in 1881.

Wheat,	2,792	acres.	48,376	bushels.
Oats,	571	"	17,635	"
Corn,	2,449	"	95,360	"
Flax,	211	"	1,981	"
Hay,	1,177	"	1,344	tons.
Horses,	661	number.	$32,990	value.
Cattle,	1836	"	21,420	"
Sheep,	5230	"	6,530	"
Hogs,	2820	"	7,230	"

PLEASANT TOWNSHIP.

Tp. 2 N.   R. 9 E.
AREA, 23,040 ACRES.   POPULATION 1,866.

John Byal, John L. Carson, and John Rose, commissioners, at their session March 2, 1835, "Ordered that the original surveyed township number *two* north, in range *nine* east, be laid off and formed in a body politic and corporate, and designated Pleasant township." Previous to this date it had been a part of Blanchard township.

This township lies in the northwest corner of the county, and is bounded on the north by Wood County, on the east by Portage township, on the south by Blanchard township and on the west by Putnam County. It derives its name no doubt from its pleasant location and scenery, and is an original township of *thirty-six* sections.

John Algire, of Fairfield County, made the first entry of land in this township. The northeast quarter of section thirty-one being bought by him March 15, 1833. On the 20th day of April, same year, Alexander Kilpatrick, of Hardin County, entered the northwest quarter of the southeast quarter of section thirty-one. Edward Steveson, of Franklin County, entered the west half of the northeast quarter of section twenty-seven, and on the same day John J. Needles of the same county entered the east half of the northeast quarter of the same section. On the 19th day of October 1833, John McCulloch, of Jefferson county and William Woods, of Washington

County, Pa., entered lands in section twenty-eight, and on the same day Eliakim Crosby entered the west half of section twenty-nine. Jacob Lamb, of Fairfield County, entered the southeast quarter of section thirty, and George Kalb entered the west half of the northeast quarter of section twenty-six, on the 2d day of November, 1835.

In 1834 entries of lands were made by Henry Hemry Nathan Fidler, John Kalb, Benjamin Cummins, Anthony Wilcoxson, Robert Fletcher, Robert Sherrard, Alexander Amspoker, Benjamin Todd, Bennet Kiger, Michael Price and others.

The first settlement in this township was made in 1833 by Edward Steveson, Benjamin Todd and John J. Needles, at and near where the village of McComb now stands. In the following year William and Alexander Kilpatrick, George Algire, John Kalb, Alexander Amspoker, came to the same neighborhood. In 1835 Robert Morrison, John Bartholomew, Charles Blakeman, Michael Price, David Wright, Jacob Thomas and others reinforced the new settlement.

Benjamin Todd came from Franklin County, O., and settled on the present site of the village of McComb. He was the first Justice of the Peace in the township, having helped to organize the township, and has held various offices since, discharging the duties of all with honesty and fidelity. He was also a member of the first church organization in the township, and has ever since led a consistent Christian life, and now, at the age of ninety years, and having raised a large and respectable family of children, he resides in the village of McComb, surrounded by the triumph of himself and compeers, over nature, loved and respected by all who know him, almost the last of the hardy pioneers of this part of the county.

John J. Needles emigrated from Franklyn County also, and redeemed from the wilderness a beautiful farm. He was a rather impulsive, eccentric kind of a man, but withal a kind neighbor and a good citizen. He removed to Iowa in 1856 and there died about six years ago.

William Kilpatrick, after a residence of a number of years, moved to Defiance County in 1859, and his brother Alexander, followed him after having made this township his home for nearly half a century. Both were honest men and good citizens.

George Algire still resides here, on the same lands he cleared up and beautified, one of the oldest residents of the township. A small wiry man of good constitution, untiring energy and industry, he has accumulated a competency, and enjoys it in the society of his friends. He has been a minister of the Methodist Episcopal church for more than forty years. As a minister he is fervent and zealous, of considerable ability, he plainly points out the way as he understands it. As a christian he has led a consistent life. As a man and neighbor he commands the greatest respect.

John Kalb, another of that noble band, after a long and useful life closed up his earthly career on the first of March, 1872. In his death the community lost a valuable member. Mr. Kalb was a member of the Methodist church for many years, and two of his sons, John S. and and Isaac N., were ministers of that church. Father Kalb was a fine speeimen of the frontiersman, and contributed his full share in clearing up the county.

Charles Blakeman is still living, and a resident of McComb. He, too, was a farmer, and a man of probity and industry, and has always enjoyed the esteem of his neighbors. He is now in his old age, quietly enjoying the fruits of his labor.

David Wright, Sr., still resides on the old home farm, made pleasant and valuable by his own industry and economy. He is passing the declining years of his life surrounded by his family and friends, beloved by all.

The soil of this locality is a rich black loam, on a clay subsoil. On the ridges, or higher lands, the soil is much mixed and made up of sand and gravel. The entire body of land in this township is rich and very productive.

The timber does not vary much from that of other parts of the county, being principally walnut, ash, oak, elm, maple and beech.

The head waters of Portage River, with some small tributaries, are sufficent, with wells, which are from ten feet to twenty feet deep, to supply all the water necessary.

The first election was held in 1835 and Benjamin Todd, George Algire, Charles Blakeman, Michael Price, John Kalb, John J. Needles, Alexander Amspoker, Robert Morrison, Robert Fletcher, Benjamin Cummins, David Wright and Jacob Thomas were the voters. The officers elected were Benjamin Todd, J. J. Needles and Alexander Amspoker, Trustees: Benj. Todd, Clerk; George Algire, Treasurer; Benj. Todd, Justice of the Peace.

The first church organization was in the year 1835. The Rev. Thrap, of the Methodist church, at that time organized a class, of whom Benj. Todd and wife, and John

Kalb and wife were the members. Services were held in private houses, and in the school house until 1850, when the Methodists erected a church building, which was the first in the township.

The first school house was built in 1838 at the present site of McComb. It was of the then approved style, round log, clap board roof, mud chimney order of architecture. There are now eight good school buildings in the township, and an enrollment of *four hundred and forty-four* children of school age.

The first flouring mill was built by Thomas Pickens in 1845 on Pickens' Run. Previous to that time a hand mill owned by William Todd, was the only means of making bread-stuff in the township. In 1841 George Algire built a saw mill on Algire's Run. Its capacity for manufacturing lumber was *three hundred* feet per day. The first steam saw mill was built in 1850 by Tipton & Porter, and the first steam flouring mill was built by Capt. Isaac Cusac in 1857.

Thus has this part of the county been developing little by little, with the hardest of labor, the greatest of patience, and most persevering industry, until to-day Pleasant township is one of the most populous, wealthy and beautiful in the county. Her farms, and farm buildings, will compare favorably with those of any other part of the county, whilst in honest thrift, intelligence and true hospitality her people are surpassed by none.

List of persons who have been elected to the office of Justice of the Peace:

Benjamin Todd—1835, 1838, 1843, 1846, 1849.
George Hemry.—1838.

Renjamin Cummins—1850, 1853, 1856, 1859.
Thomas B. Kelley—1855, 1874.
Charles Pursey—1856.
Samuel McBride—1859.
Isaac H. Myers—1862, 1865.
Daniel High—1862.
J. E. Creighton—1864.
Jackson Crites—1865, 1868.
S. H. Fairchild—1868.
A. R. Bechtel—1869.
Elisha Todd—1870.
Joseph C. Brown—1872.
William H. Todd—1873.
Jacob Priest—1876.
Isaac Cusac—1877, 1880.
W. S. Kelley—1880.
F. F. Parker—1880.

OLNEY.

In April 1857, Isaac Fairchild laid out the town of Olney on the southwest quarter of the northwest quarter, and the west half of the southwest quarter of section fifteen, which comprised forty lots. The platting of the town was as far as it ever progressed, and it was only a town on paper. The lands on which this town was to have been built are now owned by J. B. Williams.

MCCOMB.

Benjamin Todd laid out a town on the northeast part of the west half of the northeast quarter of section twenty-six, in 1847, and called it Pleasantville. The town originally comprised only eighteen lots. Afterwards successive additions were made by Mr. Todd, Ewing, Rawson and others. The town is pleasently situated on the ridge running from Tiffin to Ft. Wayne, and about ten miles from Findly. The village is the largest in the county, outside of Findley, and being situate in a fine farming country, and having good railroad facilities, bids fair to become a place of some importance.

This town was incorporated in 1858, when the name was changed from Pleasantville to McComb,

The first Mayor was William Chapman. For some years the town waited and watched for the completion of the Continental Railway, which had been graded for miles, both east and west of the village, alternately between hope and fear, the energies of the place became paralyzed, business gradually fell off, and everything came to a stand still, and a state of retrogression was setting in. The people, however, appreciating the situation, roused up and procured the building of the McComb and Deshler Branch of the Dayton and Michigan Railroad, and thus obtained communication with the outside world, and, as if fortune was now determined to smile upon them, the Continental changed hands and under the name of N. Y. C., and St. L. Railroad, has already more than fifty miles of road completed, beginning at Arcadia and running west through McComb. To say that the long expectant people of this village are jubilant, but tamely expresess the situation.

A post office was established here in 1847 with William Mitchell Postmaster. He has been succeeded by Zelotus Barney, James Porter, Eliza Fisher and Mrs. Margaret Barney, present incumbent.

The Odd Fellows have a flourishing lodge here, established in 1859, called McComb Lodge No. 354.

The business of this place is rapidly on the increase. A number of good business houses have recently been erected, as well as many residences. There are already *two* well stocked dry goods stores, *two* hardware stores, *two* neat well filled drug stores, *one* clothing store, *two* grocery and provision stores, *two* meat markets, *one* furniture store, *two* harness shops, *four* blacksmith shops, *one* jewelry store, *one* gunsmith shop, *two* wagon and carriage shops, *two* saw mills, *one* steam flouring mill, *two* shoe shops, *one* undertaker, *one* livery stable, *one* pump factory, *two* hotels, *five* physiciasn, *one* attorney, and *one* news paper, the "McComb Herald," by a Mr. Darke, and *three* churches, one Methodist Episcopal, one Presbyterian and one Disciples.

There are a number of very tasty dwellings, many of them surrounded by beautiful grounds. Altogether the village has an air of thrift and rapid growth, which is very encouraging to its people, and the beauty of its location, its healthfulness, and intelligent society, are sources of just pride to the inhabitants. Four hundred and twenty-three was the population in 1880.

There is here a fine brick school building, and three teachers are employed to conduct the schools. There is an enumeration of one hundred and eighty-one youth in the district.

The following named persons held the office of Mayor of the village:

William Chapman.
Benjamin Cummins.
S. H. Fairchild.
W. J. Sholty.
Charles Blakeman.
J. R. Turnpaugh.
A. R. Bechtel.
E. Todd.
I. H. Myers.
A. Bennett.
J. T. Smith.
Isaac Crusac.
W. H. Conine.
S. A. Cooper.
H. W. Hughes.

PORTAGE TOWNSHIP.

TP. 2, N.   R. 10, E.
AREA 15,360 ACRES.   POPULATION 914.

The County Commissioners at their session in March, 1835, "Ordered that original surveyed township No. 2 north, range 10 east, be set off into a separate township, politic and corporate, and named Portage. Ordered that the voters be notified thereof, and to meet the first Monday in April to elect township officers."

In 1850, on the formation of Allen township, two tiers of sections on the east side of this township were detached and made a part of that township, so that Portage township now includes only sections 3, 4, 5, 6, 7, 8, 9, 10, 15, 16, 17, 18, 19, 20, 21, 22, 27, 28, 29, 30, 31, 32, 33 and 34.

This township derives its name from a branch of the Portage River, which runs through it. It lies on the north line of the county, and is bounded on the north by Wood County, on the east by Allen township, on the south by Liberty, and on the west by Pleasant.

The first entry of land was made by Jacob Lamb, on the 13th of October, 1831, of the south half of section 19. Henry Culp, of Fairfield County, entered the north-west quarter of section 20, on the 24th day of September, 1830. The east half of the north-west quarter of section 15 was entered on the 21st day of April, 1831, by William Cromlish. July 24th, 1832, John Thompson entered the west

First Settlers.

half of the north-west quarter of section 22, and on the 19th of August, 1833, John Moorehead, of Stark County, entered the north-east quarter of section 27, and Samuel Moorehead entered the south-east quarter of section 22. On the 18th of June, 1833, Samuel Howard, of Richland County, entered the north-west quarter of the south-east quarter of section 4.

The first settlers in this township were John Thompson, on the farm now owned by James Deter, and George McClay on the farm just north of him, Charles Crist, John and Amos Cooper in 1833, George Taylor, Ezra Hazen on the Edgington farm, Robert Walters, Samuel and John Moorehead, John Reed, sr., and a little later Sandford F. Dulin, George Mitchel, Mahlen Morris, Switzer and John Norris.

A number of these old settlers still reside on the lands they entered and cleared up with so much labor. Samuel Moorehead resides here with his son, John E. John Cooper is still a resident of the township, and relates many incidents in pioneer life.

Sanford F. Dulin is one of those early settlers who always had faith in the future of this township. He has cleared up and now occupies, with his aged wife, a valuable farm, and although well up in years, is as jovial and light-hearted as in his younger days. Just at his farm, are a good brick school house, and a comfortable frame church, in the success of both of which Mr. Dulin has always felt a deep interest.

John Thompson, after a residence of many years in the township, got the western fever, which took him off, and I believe he is not now living. He was a most excellent man, and respected by his neighbors for his intelligence and his honesty.

John Moorehead, who attained a ripe old age, and by industry and honesty accumulated quite a property, passed peacefully away only a few years ago, surrounded by a number of his children, and in the midst of many friends.

John Reed, sr., too, is dead. After improving one of the tracts of land in the township, and rearing quite a large family, he died almost in the prime of manhood, lamented by all who knew him.

Mahlen Morris was one of nature's noblemen. Honest, industrious, intelligent, he was called upon by his neighbors to look after the affairs of the township, in more than one responsible station. He was four times in succession, elected a Justice of the Peace, and filled the office faithfully.

In 1846 he was elected to the office of County Treasurer, and with his family removed to Findley. In 1848 he was re-elected, and in 1849 he died of an attack of typhoid fever. His loss was universally lamented. Such had been his conduct of the affairs of the office that he had won the confidence of all the people of the county.

The first school house was built near Pleasant Hill, but the exact date I could not learn, perhaps in 1834. The second school house was built in Judge Cooper's district, and the first teacher was Miss Rebecca Hedges. There are now six good substantial school buildings in the township, and valued at $2,440, and an enumeration of three hundred and four youth.

The first church was built by the Presbyterians on Sand Ridge, near where Miles Wilson now lives. Amongst the first members were Miles Wilson and some of his family, John Norris and wife. The second church was built by the United Brethren, on Ten Mile, in 1836. Treat Demming and wife, and Samuel and Henry DeRhodes were of the first membership. There are now three churches in the township; two Methodist Episcopal and one United Brethren. These buildings are valued at $1,834.

The first marriage in the township was that of Amos Cooper and Elizabeth Poe. The first child born was Allen Cooper, son of the Judge, and the first death was that of a child of John Norris. There are many well improved farms, and many good, substantial and comfortable farm buildings in this township.

On the farm of Geo. Mitchell are very fine farm buildings; the same may be said of those of Judge Cooper and Adam Crumrine. John E. Moorehead, G. W. Montgomery, T. F. Edgington, John Lewis, and a number of other residents have fine dwellings and substantial out buildings. The roads and farms generally are in good condition, and thrift, industry and valuable improvements are seen every where, sure indications of the intelligence and prosperity of the people.

The soil in the north part of the township is of sand and loam; the sandy portion is known as the Sand Ridge. The south part has a predominance of clay, of a yellowish hue. This clay in some places is mixed with sand and gravel, but all is easily tilled, and exceedingly productive. More than one-third of the land in the township is wood land, primeval forest.

The timber in the north part is sycamore, elm, hickory, and oak. In the south poplar, oak, ash, walnut, beech and sugar principally. The whole surface of the township was heavily wooded.

This township is watered by the west branch of the Portage River, and by numerous springs along Sugar Ridge, and other points in the township.

There was a Post Office established in this townsiph in 1860, with Jarvis Humphrey as Post Master. Upon the removal of Mr. Mumphrey from the township, Joseph Johnston succeeded him, and held the office until his faculties became impaired by age, so that he was unfit to further discharge the duties, when Mrs. G. W. Montgomery, the present incumbent, was appointed.

There are 15,443 acres of land in this township divided as follows: Plow land 6,623, meadow and pasture 2,646, uncultivated and wood 6,174, all appraised at $386,515. Houses appraised at $33,940, mills $600, other buildings at $21,650, total lands and buildings $442,105.

JOSEPH JOHNSTON

Was a native of Virginia, where he was born on the 4th day of April, 1801. His father—Isaac Johnston—moved from Boutetot County, Va., to Ohio, in 1811, and settled at Portsmouth, in Scioto County. The elder Johnston was a potter by trade, and followed that business whilst in Portsmouth.

The subject of this sketch has been a farmer all his life. In 1827 the family came to this county, and took up their residence in the village of Findley. Mr. Johnston was married in 1832 to Susan George, and removed to what is now Marion township, and in the same year was elected Sheriff of the county, which office he filled acceptably one term. He had for neighbors in this township, such men as Asher Wickham, Charles Thomas, E. S. Jones.

In 1853 Mr. Johnston sold his Marion township farm, and removed to this township, where he still resides. He had a family of fourteen children, twelve of whom are living. He is of English descent, had but limited educational facilities, and was compelled to depend upon his own resources in that direction. He helped build the first school house in Marion

Joseph Johnston. 435

township, helped to organize, and was a voter at the first election held in that township. He was prominently connected with the early history of the county, and his industry and energy, with his good common sense, gave him quite an influence with the early settlers.

He has lived long enough to see the vast improvements made in the county, and to enjoy the fruits of his labor. His wife died in 1850, and he afterwards married Jane Dudgeon, who died in 1879. In 1863 he was appointed Post Master at Portage Center, which office he held about sixteen years. In 1870 he united with the Methodist Episcopal Church, and is still a member. His family has become separated, some reside in Michigan, some in Indiana, and some in this county. Few men have passed through so checkered a life as has Mr. Johnston, coming to the county at an age when new scenes would be most vividly impressed on his mind, and when the surroundings would be most heartily and most fully appreciated. He remembers with pleasure those who were his companions in that half century ago, many of them long since dead. Mr. Johnston, although in feeble health from old age, and past hardships, still retains his memory, and loves to talk of those days and scenes, and people of long ago.

JUDGE JOHN COOPER

Was a native of Fayette County, Pa., where he was born April 25th, 1811. He is the oldest son of James Cooper, who came to Pennsylvania from New York. Mr. Cooper's ancestors on his father's side were Scotch, and on his mother's side were Low Dutch. His father was a farmer, in which business the Judge has been engaged all his life, and very successful has he been. In 1812 the family came to

Perry County, Ohio, and settled near Somerset. That part of the State was but sparsely settled, and the land which the Judge's father had entered had to be reclaimed from the wilderness, and here the Judge labored until 1832, when he came to this township, bringing with him his young wife, Jane Eliza, daughter of Daniel Cusac, whom he married in 1830. There were but seventeen families in the township, which included Portage and the west half of Allen, when he came here. He at once located on the same land on which he now resides. Mr. and Mrs. Cooper celebrated their *Golden Wedding*, at the fiftieth anniversary of their wedded life, and all their children were present.

His first neighbors in the township were John Thompson, Robert Walters and John Howard, and they were about the only residents of what is now Portage township. The Judge has held important offices in the township and county. In 1849 he was appointed one of the Associate Judges of the county, and held that office until the adoption of the present constitution. In 1862 he was elected County Commissioner, and served six years as such. He was also one of the first Directors of the County Infirmary.

Mr. Cooper had no other educational advantages than those furnished by a common country school. He is not a member of any church, but in religious belief has a leaning towards the old school Baptists. He has always been a friend to schools and churches, and has taken an active interest in both. He is the father of nine children, six of whom are living.

SAMUEL HOWARD

Is the son of a farmer, and was born in Westmoreland County, Pa., December 7th, 1814. He was brought up on a farm, and has followed that vocation all his life. When but a few months old his parents came to Richland County, Ohio. Mr. H. is the oldest of eleven children, of whom eight are yet living. He came to this county in 1833, and settled on what is called "Ten Mile Creek," in this township. They were surrounded by the forest; Indians plenty; game in abundance. Mr. Howard said that when they got up in the morning, and wanted to kill a turkey, they were at a loss to know which direction to go, as they were gobbling all around. Mr. Howard said that his father had fifty dollars in money when he came here, and that he borrowed of him to enter forty acres of land, on the condition that he should keep the family in provisions for one year, and as there were eleven of them in the family, he said it required a great deal of hard labor on his part to do so, especially as flour was sixteen dollars per barrel, and corn one dollar and a half per bushel. The settlers then had to go to Tiffin to mill, and to the village of Findley to trade.

In December, 1837, he married Elizabeth Carroll. with whom he now lives, and built a cabin in the woods, and commenced life, full of hope and energy, determined to succeed. In 1850, having been elected Treasurer of the county, he sold his land and moved to Findley. He served two terms as Treasurer. He then purchased the old Trout farm, at Van Buren. After residing here for some years he sold out, and bought the Hollenbeck farm, joining the north corporation line of Findley, where he resided until about one year ago, when he moved into the town.

Mr. Howard was Captain of Co. G, 118 Regiment, O. V. I., in the late war, and was with that Regiment in all its marches and battles until the spring of 1864. In 1863 Capt. Howard was detailed to go to Boston to assist in organizing the drafted men of Massachusetts. He remained there for three months, when he rejoined the Regiment and went to Eastern Tennessee. In the spring of 1864 he had the misfortune to get his leg broken, and was discharged.

He is the father of eleven children, six of whom are living. Mr. Howard has always been noted for his public spirit and liberality. He has been prominent in many of the enterprises which have so greatly benefited our county.

Such is the confidence in which he is held by the people of the county, that he was again elected Treasurer of the county in 1878, and re-elected in 1881.

SAMUEL MOOREHEAD

Was born in Westmoreland County, Penn., in 1798, and came to Ohio with his father's family in 1814, and settled near Massillon, Stark County. Mr. M. lost his mother before leaving Pennsylvania, and his father married again soon after he came to Ohio. He is a farmer, reared to the profession by his father, who followed the same business. In 1821 he married Mary Edgar, and in 1834 came to this county, and settled in Portage township, on the farm now owned by his son, John E. His parents were of Irish descent. The Mooreheads are generally large muscular men, endowed with great physical endurance, and industrious, frank, open-hearted, liberal and hospitable. Their genial, good nature is notorious.

Mr. Moorehead has been a member of the Presbyterian Church for more than fifty years, and was one of the pioneers of that denomination in this part of the county. He is the father of but two children, one son—John E.—who resides on the home farm, and one daughter—Mrs. W. K. Leonard—who resides in Big Lick township. His wife died about 1854, and he never re-married. He accumulated quite a large property, which he and his children are now enjoying. Mr. Moorehead, though now in his eighty-fourth year, retains his mental faculties almost wholly unimpaired, and is the same jovial, kind-hearted man he was in his younger days.

LAFAYETTE.

Jacob Andre laid out a town on the north part of the east half of the north-west quarter of section 15, on lands now owned by Daniel Warner, and called it Lafayette. It comprised seventy-two lots, and had great expectations. But here ends its eventful history.

The office of Justice of the Peace for this township has been held by the following named persons, who were elected in the year indicated;

Peter Heller—1833, 1836.

Mahlen Morris—1836, 1839, 1842, 1845.

John Edgington—1837, 1840, 1862, 1865.

Samuel Howard—1847.

John Kelley—1844, 1847, 1850.

Henry B. Wall—1850, 1851, 1854, 1857, 1860.

Adam Crumrine—1850, 1853, 1856, 1859, 1862, 1865, 1868, 1871, 1874.

Charles R. Thomas—1868.

William M. King—1870, 1873, 1876, 1879.

Thomas F. Edgington—1877, 1880.

A table showing the number and value of live stock and the number of acres and bushels of grain raised in this township, as returned by Township Assessor in 1881.

  Horses, 388 number. $18,490, value.
  Cattle, 998 " 10,610, "
  Sheep, 3,582 " 7,170, "
  Swine, 1,610 " 3,680, "
  Wheat, 2,219 acres. 45,570 bushels.
  Oats, 338 " 10,010 "
  Corn, 2,030 " 79,670 "
  Hay, 679 " 879 tons.

UNION TOWNSHIP.

Tp. 1 S. R. 9 E.

AREA 32,040 ACRES.   POPULATION 1,623.

The record of the County Commissioners of the 4th of June, 1832, says: "There was a petition presented by sundry inhabitants residing in the original surveyed township No. one south, in range *nine*, praying to be set off as a township, under the name of Union, which petition was favorably considered, and they were accordingly set off under the above name.

Union is bounded on the north by Blanchard township, on the east by Eagle, on the south by Orange, and on the west by Putnam county. It is an original township of thirty-six sections.

The first entry of land was made on the 16th of October, 1829, by Philip Powell, being the north-east quarter of section two.

April 2d, 1830, John Bright entered the north-west quarter of section twenty-two, and in October of the same year, Philip Cramer entered the south half of section one. The west half of south-east quarter of section twelve was entered by John Baker, January 30, 1832, and the same year Richard M. Carson, of Pickaway county, entered the east half of the north-east quarter of section four, and Rudolph Snyder entered the east half of the south-east quarter of section thirty-six.

About the same time the south-west quarter of section four was entered by Daniel Tussing, of Fairfield county, and a little later, Abraham Rose of the same county, entered the north-west quarter of north-east quarter of section thirty-six.

The first white settler in this township was Philip Cramer, who settled on Tiderishi Creek, in section one, in November, 1830. His sons Jacob and Daniel now reside on the same premises. When Mr. Cramer came, he had to make his own road through the forest to their lands. No neighbors, no clearing, all strange solitude.

In the spring following, Nicholas Folk settled on what is now known as the Teatsorth farm, on Ottawa Creek, and in the fall of the same year George Burket and Wm. Lytle, with their families, settled farther up the creek.

Other families were not long in finding their way into this section of the county, attracted by the location and richness of the lands. Two or three families of the Wades settled near the center of the township. John Flick, Daniel Fox and others along the creek. Levi Showalter, James Burns, Pancoast, Gibson and Taylor in the western part, and Benj. Marshall, James West and others in the south part of the township.

Philip Cramer lived to a very old age, and was the pioneer minister of the United Brethren Church. He was a man of some ability, zealous in his "Master's work," a good neighbor, honest in all his dealings, and much respected by all his acquaintances.

Wenman Wade was of that class of robust and pushing frontiersman, who pave the way for a better civilization and prosperous country, by boldly pushing out into the wilderness, and enduring the hardships and privations of pioneer life uncomplainingly. Honest, industrious and contented. Mr. Wade was one who enjoyed the confidence of the community in which he lived. He held the office of Justice of the Peace, and in entitled to the distinction of being the first person in the county whose election was contested, as the following notice will show:

"To the Clerk of Hancock County:—You are requested to withhold the return of the election of Union township, wherein Wenman Wade was elected Justice of the Peace, and the election is contested, and the said contest is to be tried on the 13th of September, 1838.

WILLIAM ROLLER,
A Associate Judge."

September the 5th day, 1838.

It does not appear who the contestant was, or the grounds of contest. I infer that Mr. Wade established his claim to the office, for in 1841 he was again elected.

Levi Showalter still resides in the township, a hale, hearty old man, with the same frank, brusque manners, sterling honesty and neighborly spirit of old. Respected and trusted by all who know him, his path on the downhill side of life, seems a pleasant one.

James Burns, one of the best of citizens, industrious honest, after years of toil, accumulated a competency for himself and family, died surrounded by kind friends and neighbors, regretted by all.

George Burket was born in Berks County, Pa., and emigrated to Fairfield County, Ohio, at which place he was married to Mary Fox. In 1831 he came to Hancock County with his wife and two children. He settled on the farm afterwards owned by his son Jacob. Mr. Burket was a tall slender man, and of rather delicate health. With the help of his family, he cleared a very valuable farm, at which plaec he died about eighteen years ago.

Jacob Burket, son of George, was born in Fairfield county, in December, 1811, and when about five years of age, his parents removed to Perry county, where he remained until 1831, when he came to this township.

When Mr. Burket came, there were but two other families in the township Philip Cramer, who resided where his son Jacob now does, and Nicholas Folk, who then lived on what is now known as the Teatsorth farm.

Mr. Burket was present and voted at the first election in the township. He says that at that election, Philip Cramer, Nicholas Folk and George Burket were elected Trustees, and Wenman Wade, Clerk.

Mr. Burket was married in 1832 to Sarah Cramer, by Esq. John Cramer. This was the first marriage in the township. Mrs. Burket died in 1850, and he was again married this time to the widow of Philip Cramer, jr.

After a long and active life on his farm, Mr. Burket removed to the village of Rawson, where he is quietly enjoying his declining years. He has always enjoyed the esteem of his neighbors, and has a host of friends.

Nicholas Folk came from Fairfield County, and took up his abode on the Tawa Creek, on what is known as the Teatsorth farm, which he entered. Mr. Folk was a small man, rather feeble in health, but succeeded in clearing up the farm on which he lived and died. He was respected by all who knew him.

REV. RICHARD BIGGS

Was born on the 12th day of November, 1806, in Columbia County, Pa., and died at his home in the town of Rawson, Ohio, on the 18th day of July, 1880.

In 1829 he united with the Methodist Church in Northumberland County, Pa. He shortly afterwards removed to Summit County, Ohio, where in July 1836, he was licensed to preach.

In 1838 he removed to Hancock Co., and settled near the present town of Rawson. Two years later he was admitted to the North Ohio Conference at its session in Norwalk, and for more than thirty years was an itinerant minister, and having the following charges: Findley, Kalida, Defiance, Clarksfield, Amherst, Dalton, Congress, Chesterville, Marcellus, Millersburg, Shaneville, Pleasantville, Mt. Blanchard, Adrian, Arcadia, Bluffton, Bettsville and McComb.

Mr. Biggs was left an orphan when but six years of age. His educational privileges were very limited, yet such was his dilligence in his studies, that he began teaching at the age of sixteen. He was always a close student, and kept up with the times. He was a man of unyielding rectitude, and pure in his life, modest and retiring in his disposition, yet faithful in the discharge of every duty. He commenced the ministry when it meant hard labor, little pay; the country being new, the appointments were long distances apart, and the people scattered and poor, yet he earnestly and uncomplainingly toiled to lay the foundations of good society, good government and good morals. His wife still survives him, as also four of his children.

The principal timbers found in this township, do not differ from those elsewhere in the county, being walnut, oak, elm, ash, beech, maple, hackberry, hickory, sycamore and buckeye.

The soil along the creek bottoms is of a sandy nature, but the uplands are of loam or clay. The soil in all parts of the township is exceedingly productive, and when once entirely cleared of stumps and roots, is easily cultivated. The principal crops are wheat, oats, corn and grass.

The township is well watered by Ottawa and Tiderashy Creeks. And these creeks also furnish good drainage for the lands adjacent, and by the numerous small tributaries that empty into them, assist in the drainage of the whole township.

In 1845 Edson Goit, Esq., erected a flouring mill on Ottawa Creek, Thomas Pickens doing the millwright work. This was perhaps better known as the *Teatsorth Mill* It was a water mill, but after its sale by Goit to James Teatsorth, steam power was attached. The mill was a great convenience to the surrounding country, and its loss—for it was torn down and removed some years ago—was seriously felt by the community.

The first church in the township was built by the United Brethren, and is known as the *Clymer Church*. There are now eleven church buildings in the township, which certainly speaks well for the morals of the inhabitants. They are owned as follows: United Brethren two, Evangelical two, United Presbyterian one, Methodist Episcopal one, Methodist Protestant two, Christian Union two, Church of God one. These buildings are all substantial, and many of them really tasteful in their construction and finish.

The first school house was built at the center of the township, and a school has been kept there ever since. There are now ten school buildings in the township, all of them, I believe, of brick, and finished and furnished in modern style The schools in this township have the reputation of being amongst the very best in the county.

The enumeration of youth of school age is three hundred

and thirty-six males, and two hundred and ninety females, total six hundred and twenty-six.

The first settlers of this township were from the eastern and interior counties of the State, very largely from Fairfield county.

The following persons have held the office of Justice of the Peace:

John Kramer, 1833.
Wenman Wade, 1835, 1838.
Ephraim Moody, 1839.
Thomas Dewese, 1841.
Henry Stover, 1842.
Thomas Stratton, 1842, 1845, 1851, 1854, 1862.
Samuel Dewese, 1845.
C. F. Malahan, 1847, 1850, 1853.
John West, 1848.
John McConnell, 1856.
Wm. Stratton, 1857.
Rial Beach, 1859.
James Burns, 1861.
Charles George, 1862.
D. W. Cass, 1864.
John Stratton, 1865.
Peter Reckert, 1866, 1869, 1872, 1875, 1878, 1881.
George W. Mull, 1867.
S. J. Nowlan, 1872, 1875, 1878.
A. J. L. Hartman, 1872.
G. W. Burket, 1881.

RAWSON.

The town of Rawson, on the Lake Erie & Western Railway, was laid out in 1855 by Frederick Keller and G. J. Kelley, on the north-west corner of the south-west quarter of section thirteen, and the north-east corner of the east half of the south-east quarter of section fourteen, and originally comprised but fifty-four lots. The town was named in honor of L. Q. Rawson, of Fremont, Ohio, who was then President of the railroad.

The principal streets running east and west are named Vance, Kelley, Henderson and Boalt, and those running north and south are Main and Gale.

The town started out fairly, and soon quite a number of buildings were erected, but as the railroad, the locating of which had called the town into existence, was not built, and for years there seemed to be but little hope that it would be, the town came to a halt, and was of but little significance in the history of the township. A few mechanics had invested all their means in property in the prospective town, and could not sell it again. The town perhaps could always boast of a small country store and grocery combined, but for years it was a desperate struggle to keep life in the place.

Finally the long looked for time arrived. The railroad was finished, the whistle of the locomotive was heard, and business revived. Real estate changed hands, buildings were put up, stores were opened, the buzz of machinery was heard, and all was bustle, business and speculation, and streets were opened up to accommodate prospective trade.

Of course the keen edge of excitement wore off and the inhabitants gradually settled down to every day life, and although to the stranger there appears but little life in th place, yet quite an amount of business is carried on, and the business of the town is gradually increasing.

Additional lots have been laid out by Fred. Keller in 1859, by Jacob Burket in 1873, by C. J. Kelly in 1874, and by Benj. Stringfellow.

The Methodist Epicopal and Methodist Protestant have each a comfortable church building here, and the United Brethren have a society but no building; they worship in the Methodist Protestant Church.

A post office was established here in 1863 and named Rawson, with James C. Benham as postmaster. Since that time the office has been held by Jackson Miller, James Woods, T. E. Woods and Nicholas Watson, the present incumbent.

An Odd Fellows Lodge was organized here in January, 1875, and is in a flourishing condition, having a good working membership.

The railroad was completed and the first train ran through in December, 1873. There is now a large grain warehouse located convenient to the track, and from whence great quantities of grain are shipped.

There is one dry goods and grocery store, T. B. Gilbert; one drug, grocery and queensware store, Woods & Co.; one drug, grocery and provision store, G. W. Burket; one grocery and notions, J. B. Sorbie.

A first class flouring mill has just been completed and put in operation. Radabaugh & Crossley are manufacturers of hard wood lumber, and planing mill attached. H. J. Blymire operates a saw and shingle mill and handle factory. Nowlan and Miller have blacksmith shops. G. F. Folk carries on the furniture business, and Eli Brallyer is engaged in shoe making. Population in 1880, 227.

CANNONSBURG.

Benjamin Marshall, Franklin Ballard, Wm. McConnell and James C. Marshall were the proprietors of this town. It was laid out on the east part of section thirty-five, and the west part of section thirty-six, and consisted of 36 lots, with the principal steets crossing each other at right angles. Cannonsburg was at one time a place of some neighborhood importance, but never rose to the dignity of other than a small country village. Railroads came just near enough to it to ruin what little trade it had. There is now one general store, one saw mill, one wagon shop, one blacksmith shop, and one undertaker's establishment, and these include all the business places.

A post office was established here in 1841, with Thompson Bartel as postmaster, since which time E. P. Leslie, H. P. Eaton, D. W. Cass, Fuller Ballard, Henry Lue, J. D. Buss, J. A. Combs, sr., J. F. Stienman, Lydia A. Rossman, and J. A. Combs, jr., have held the office. Population in 1880, ninety.

CORY.

This town is also situated on the Lake Erie & Western Railway, and was laid out in November, 1872, by Mathias Markley and Samuel Kemerer, and is located on a part of the west half of the south-west quarter of section twenty-two, and when laid out consisted of thirty-two lots. To these additions have since been made by Kemerer, Markley and John C. Smith.

The lots were readily sold, and quite a number of buildings erected, and as the town is located in the midst of a rich agricultural district, the place has become one of some importance, and quite an extensive business is carried on. There are a number of neat and comfortable dwelling houses, mostly of wood, and several large and well arranged business houses.

There is a large and convenient school building, for the accommodation of the children of the district. The Evangelical Association own a church building, and the Methodist Protestant Church also have a fine frame building. A flourishing Sunday School is attached to each.

The business places are two dry goods stores, in which are kept an assortment of standard goods; one drug store, one grocery and provision store, and a meat market.

The manufacturing interests are a pump manufactory, and one wagon and carriage shop, one blacksmith shop, one flouring mill, one saw mill, one handle factory, one undertaking and furniture establishment. There is one physician, and David Comer has an office in which he attends to the business of Notary Public and conveyancer.

A post office was established here in 1873, called Mt. Cory, with Benjamin Wildemuth as postmaster. The office has been filled by Alfred Longbrake and the present incumbent, W. J. Stauler. The population of the town is two hundred and sixty.

Table showing the acreage and bushels of grain produced in 1880, and the number and value of animals as returned by the Township Assessor in 1881.

Wheat, 4,050 Acres.   68,641 Bushels.
Oats,   410   "   13,261   "
Corn,   3,342   "   133,420   "
Flax,   146   "   1,289   "
Hay,   998   "   1,164 Tons.
Horses,   804 number. $27,730, Value.
Cattle, 1,653   "   15,000,   "
Sheep, 2,546   "   3,670,   "
Swine, 3,011   "   5,560,   "

VAN BUREN TOWNSHIP.

Tp. 2, S. R. 10, E.
Area 15,360 acres, Population, 1,011.

At a session of the County Commissioners held March 7, 1831, this entry was made on the records:

"A petition of sundry inhabitants of Hancock County was presented for setting off the original surveyed townships, numbered one and two, in range 10 south of the base line, into a township, which was accordingly set off, to be known and designated by the name of Van Buren."

At the March session of 1834, the Commissioners ordered that township 2 south, in range 9, be attached to Van Buren township for corporate purposes.

In June, 1840, at the formation of Madison township, sections 1, 2, 11, 12, 13, 14, 23, 24, 25, 26, 35 and 36 of Van Buren were made a part of the new township, so that this township is now composed of sections 3, 4, 5, 6, 7, 8, 9, 10, 15, 16, 17, 18, 19, 20, 21, 22, 27, 28, 29, 30, 31, 32, 33 and 34 in township 2 south.

This township, which was named for President Van Buren, is situated on the south line of the county, and is bounded on the north by Eagle township, on the east by Madison, on the south by Hardin County, and on the west by Orange township.

The first entry of land was the north-west quarter of section 27, on the 4th of January, 1831, by Benjamin Sparr.

In April of the same year, Samuel Green entered the east half of the south-west quarter of the same section, and in July, James West entered the east half of the north-east quarter of section 23.

May 16th, 1833, John Diller entered the north-east quarter of the south-east quarter of section 10, and in December of the same year Solomon Bergman, of Licking County, entered the west half of the south-west quarter of section 17. Peter Pifer and C. Price, both of Pennsylvania, on the 20th of May, 1834, made entries of land, the one took up the north-east quarter of section 8, and the other the east half of the north-east quarter of section 9.

In October, 1834, Robert Shaw, of Portage County, Peter Foltz, of Fairfield County, Isaac Ashburn, of Knox County, Joseph Smith, of Columbiana County, Henry Freed and Daniel Besserman, both of Stark County, Ohio, made entries of lands here. Other entries speedily followed, many of them by newly arrived emigrants from Germany.

The first settlement was made by Nicholas Essinger, Adam Gassman and Peter Pifer, as early perhaps as 1833. Not far from the same time Adam Reddick, Peter and Henry Heldman came in, and were quickly followed by Philip Heldman, Michael and Peter Wilch, all from Germany. Soon the Stinemans, the Freeds, the Bessermans, the Hassons, the Barmouths, the Prices and others, nearly all Germans, followed and began to open up farms. These pioneers were industrious, thrifty, honest and moral, and their robust health, the result of frugal living, their energy and solid strength, backed up by a fixed determination to succeed in the land of their adoption, soon enabled them to open up valuable farms, and to-day we have not a more industrious, honest, peaceable and contented people than those found in this township.

The timber found here consists principally of walnut, the different varieties of oak, ash, maple and elm, with beech, sycamore and buckeye. It required much time and great labor to remove this great mass of timber in clearing up the land and preparing it for cultivation.

The soil in the low lands is a black loam, on the uplands clay, but all so mingled and enriched by other substances as to be very fertile.

This township is watered by Ottowa and Riley Creeks, both of which have their sources here. Good drainage can be had anywhere in the township by these and their small tributaries.

Log school houses, the first built in the township, were at Fulhert's and John Tilles', and were erected about the same time. The school houses here, as elsewhere in the county, followed close on the settlements, and these were perhaps built as early as 1834. There are now six school houses in the township with an enumeration of youth amounting to three hundred and twelve.

The German Reformed Church building at Jacob Traucht's was the first erected in this township. There are now one Methodist Episcopal, one Dunkard, one German Reformed, and one German Lutheran Church building in the township.

The emigrants to this place were many of them directly from Germany.

This table exhibits the number and value of live stock, and the acreage and bushels of cereals, as returned to the County Auditor, by the Assessor of the township in the year 1881.

    Horses, 448 number. $18,004, value.
    Cattle, 1,238 "   11,474, "
    Sheep, 1,524 "   2,570, "
    Hogs, 2,155 "   3,172, "
    Wheat, 2,502 acres.   42,304 bushels.
    Oats, 714 "   21,539 "
    Corn, 1,653 "   56,252 "
    Flax, 172 "   1192 "
    Hay, 449 "   414 tons.

The following named persons have been elected Justices of the Peace at the dates named:

John Bollenbaugh—1832.
Charles Bradford—1834.
Christian Welty—1836, 1839.
Andrew Rickets—1837.
Thomas Morrison—1840.
Henry Hull—1840, 1843.
Michael Besserman—1843, 1846, 1849.
George Rinehart—1846.
Alex. Hodge—1846, 1849, 1852, 1855, 1858.
Benj. Sparr—1852.
John B. Pugh—1858, 1861, 1864.
Eliab Hasson—1861, 1864, 1867, 1870, 1873.
Adam Stineman—1867, 1870, 1873, 1876.
Christ Shaller—1876.
William Montgomery—1881.

WASHINGTON TOWNSHIP.

Tp. 2, N. R. 12, E.
Area 23,040 acres. Population 1,941.

At the meeting of the County Commissioners, on the 5th day of March, 1832, Charles McKinnis and Robert L. Strother, two of the Commissioners being present, the following record was made: "It appearing to the Board of Commissioners necessary, they have set off the original township two north, in range twelve east, which shall be a body corporate and politic, and known by the name of Washington Township."

This township was named in honor of the "Father of his country," and is situate in the north-east corner of the county, and is bounded on the north by Wood County, on the east by Seneca County, on the south by Big Lick Township, on the west by Cass Township. It contains thirty-six sections of land, of six hundred and forty acres each.

The first entry of land in this township was made November 24th, 1830, by Joseph Long, of Fairfield County, Ohio, who made entry of the west half of the north-west quarter of section four, and on the same day, Caleb Roller, of the same county, entered the east half of the south-east quarter of section five.

December 1st, 1830, John Gersuch, of Wayne County, Ohio, entered the north-east quarter of section five, and on the 17th day of the same month, he made entry of the north-east quarter of section one. On the 17th day of December, 1830, James Connelly, of Richland County, Ohio, entered the west half of the north-west quarter of section three.

On the 17th day of March, 1831, the east half of the north-east quarter of section two, was taken up by John Norris, of Wayne County. Thomas Kelley, also of Wayne County, on the 16th day of April 1831, made entry of the north-west quarter of section one, and on the 7th of May in the same year, Richard Cole, of Columbiana County, entered the west half of the south-west quarter of section one.

These entries were followed in the same year by those made by Wm. Norris, of Seneca County, James G. Wiseman, of Perry County, William Wisely, of Fairfield County, Michael and Liverton Thomas, of Wayne County, Alexander Work, of Jefferson County, John Mackrill, of Richland County, James Beeson, David Peters and others.

The first settlement was made in the township by John Gorsuch, who commenced on the north-east quarter of section one, in April, 1831. The next settler was James Sweeney, who located on the south-east quarter of section four, in the same month, and John Norris settled on the north-east quarter of section two about the first of May; and in the same month, James Wiseman located on the north-west quarter of section twelve.

Mr. Sweeney and Mr. Wiseman having come to the township in the prime of manhood, and endured all the hardships of frontier life, both lived to a ripe old age, and died but a few years ago on the farms they first settled on. Mr. Gorsuch is also dead, I believe, but when or where he died

I am unable to say. Mr. John Norris, I believe, still lives in Portage township in this county, on section thirty-two, and is the only survivor of the four pioneers of this township.

In 1832 several more families settled in the township, among them those of Jacob Heistand, Elijah McRill, Wm. Eckles, Wm. Ferrel, James Bryan, Liverton Thomas, Joel Hales, Elijah R. Anderson.

This township, like almost all the others in the county, was very heavily timbered, indeed, was a dense forest. The principal kind of timber were white, red, burr and swamp oak; white, red and hickory elm; white, black and blue ash; white and black walnut; wild cherry; hard and soft maple; beech, shellbark and white hickory, basswood, cottonwood, sycamore and buckeye. In the early settlement of the township, nearly all this timber was valueless except for fencing, and was regarded as a serious drawback in improvments, but such is the demand for timber at this day, that such as was then destroyed, utterly wasted, would now bring fortunes to the lucky owners.

The soil of this locality is somewhat varied. The entire part of the township, except the north tier of sections, is a heavy clay soil, with patches of vegetable mold in the depressions and along the streams, and occasionally some sand and clay mixed on the higher points. The north tier of sections from one to six inclusive, has a gravel ridge running through them, covering about one half the sections, with a narrow strip between the ridge and the Wood County line, of a deep, rich, black vegetable mold. Near the foot of the slope of the gravel ridge, is a strip of red clay, not more than four or five rods in width, but very productive. The surface of the whole township slopes gently to the north.

to the summit of the ridge, from thence to the north line of the township the declination is more abrupt.

This township is watered by the east and middle branches of the Portage River. These branches are now known by the names of Arcadia and Fostoria Creeks, one passing through the town of Arcadia, and the other one through Fostoria. The east branch has its source in section twelve, in Big Lick Township, running in a north-easterly direction, entering this township in section thirty-five, running across the township in a north-easterly course, leaving it near the north-east corner of the county. The middle branch rises at the south line of the township, about four miles south-east of the village of Arcadia, crossing the township, leaving it near the north-west corner.

These streams are of little consequence, except that they afford an outlet for the surface water of almost the entire township. The middle branch drains about three-fourths of the township. It has more and larger tributaries than the other branch, and runs through a deep valley. The bluffs where this stream crosses the ridge, are probably forty feet in heighth.

The first school house was built in this township in 1833 or 1834, and was located on the north-west quarter of section twelve, on the farm of James Wiseman, and now owned by Gov. Foster. The first school in that house was taught by Isaac Wiseman, and was the first school in the township. There are now nine school houses, with eleven school rooms. The enumeration of youth of school age is three hundred and twenty-seven males, and three hundred and seven females, total, six hundred and thirty-four.

The United Brethren have an Academy in that part of Fostoria which is situated in this township. The schools of the township are at present in a healthy and flourishing condition, and much interest is felt in their success by the patrons. The school buildings are as a whole, comfortable houses.

The first church in this township was built in 1832, at the center of section five, by the Methodists. Although the building was erected at this time, yet for some reason it was not occupied for church purposes until some years later. The first church in which worship was conducted, was on section one, near the north-east corner of the county, now West Fostoria, and was built by the Methodists. It was a hewed log building, about twenty-six by thirty-two feet, and probably seven feet between the floor and ceiling, and was covered with lap shingles.

There are now seven churches in the township. Two Methodist Episcopal, one Evangelical Lutheran, one Presbyterian, one German Reformed, one German Baptist and one United Brethren.

The first election was held in the fall of 1832, when Gen. Jackson and Henry Clay were candidates for the Presidency. There were twelve votes cast. The names of the electors were John Norris, John Gorsuch, Silas Gorsuch, Nelson Gorsuch, James Sweeney, James Wiseman, Liverton Thomas, Jacob Heistand, Elijah McRill, William Ferrall, James Bryan, William Eckles. The vote stood, as now remembered, Clay eight, Jackson four. Liverton Thomas was elected Justice of the Peace, and was the first elected in the township.

The Lake Erie & Western Railroad runs across the township in a diagonal direction from north-east to south-west. It enters the county near the south-east corner of section one, and leaves it in the north-east part of section thirty. What was called the old Continental Road, graded some fifteen years ago, but recently changed hands, and is now called the New York, Chicago & St. Louis Rail Way, and being rapidly completed, runs in a strait east and west line across the township, a little south of the center. Both these roads run through the village of Arcadia.

Hon. Henry Sheets, of whom I obtained the greater portion of the foregoing relating to the township, relates the following incident of pioneer life.

When Jacob Heistand came to this township from Wayne County, he brought with him several head of cows and young cattle, and not having any inclosure in which to keep them, allowed them to roam at large in the woods. He took the precaution, however, to put a bell on one, that he might be able to find them when wanted. But one evening when he went for them, he found they had strayed farther away than usual, he did not find them until dark, and on his return, in passing around one of the large swails in the neighborhood, he lost his way, and the cattle not being very particular as to the course they took, went in an opposite direction from home. Mr. Heistand followed until late in the evening without coming to his or any other clearing. The woods were infested by wolves, which now began to howl close by him; the cattle gathered close about him, through fear of the wolves. Mr. Heistand concluded that he would stay with the cattle, and procured a cudgel, with which to keep the wolves at bay. But they becoming more bold, and howling fiercer, he concluded to start on again, hoping to strike some clearing, which he happily did in a few minutes but about four miles from home. The clearing was that of James Wiseman, with whom he remained during the night.

JAMES G. WISEMAN

Was born in Greenbrier County, Va., in August, 1790. He served in the war of 1812 as a cavalryman, under Capt. Lewis. Mr. Wiseman was married to Elizabeth Summers, in 1814, and in September, 1817, removed to Ohio, settling in Madison County. He and his wife made the trip from Virginia to Ohio, a distance of more than four hundred miles on horseback. After two years residence he removed to Perry County, which place was his residence until the spring of 1831, when he came to Washington Township.

Mr. Wiseman was a medium sized man, rugged and hardy, just the kind of a man to endure the hardships and privations of a frontier life. He was passionately fond of hunting, and was expert in the use of the rifle, but he never allowed this fondness for sport to interfere with the real business of life, that of making a comfortable home for himself and family. He cleared up a large and rich farm. He was an honest, genial whole souled man, ever ready to assist the needy, and no man more fully enjoyed the confidence of his neighbors.

Mr. Wiseman died in 1873, and his wife survived him about seven years. They were the parents of thirteen children, and lived to see all of them become married men and women except two, one of which died quite young, and the other was killed in the late war.

WILLIAM CHURCH

Is the oldest of the eight children of Collis and Elizabeth Church, and was born in Potsdam, St. Lawrence County, New York, February 4th, 1818. His father was a farmer, and William followed until he was twenty-one years of age, at which time he commenced learning the trade of blacksmith, and although he is now and has been for a number of years a farmer, he has not forgotten how to swing the sledge and weld the iron, and does all his own smithing, besides occasionally a job of repairing for his neighbors.

Mr. Church came to Ohio almost fifty years ago, the family and household goods making the trip in a wagon. On their arrival in the state, they located in the northern part of Wayne County, near the village of Jackson. Here Mr. C's mother died.

In 1834 the family came to the county and located on the land on which the town of Rawson now stands. Mr. Church came to the village of Findley and learned his trade with David Webster.

In 1840 he married Martha J. Teatsorth, and followed his trade for thirteen years. He then purchased the farm in Liberty Township, known as the Burkhead farm. After a residence here of a few years, he sold out and removed to the farm on which he now resides in the township. Mrs. Church died in 1873.

Mr. Church is the father of four children, three of whom are living. He has always been a man of strict morals, but never united with any church organization. He owns one of the finest farms in the county, on which are very tasteful and substantial buildings. He has always been noted for his honesty and industry. He practices economy without penuriousness, and hospitality without extravagance.

CHARLES E. JORDAN

Is the third child of Charles Jordan, and is a native of Richland Township, Belmont County, Ohio, where he was born May 23, 1800. His father was a farmer, and emigrated from Penn. to Ohio, in 1797. The family left Belmont County in 1828, going to Tuscarawas County.

Mr. Jordan was married in Belmont County February 11, 1826, to Margaret Moore, who lived until May, 1873, dying at Arcadia, Ohio.

Mr. Jordan by trade is a boot and shoe maker, but never followed the business but a very few years, since which time he has been a farmer. He came to this township October 2d, 1833, and settled on the lands immediately adjoining the town of Arcadia, on which his son John lately died. He found this land all in the woods, built his cabin, and went to work in earnest to make him a home, and his success is attested by the beautiful farm now occupying the place of the forest.

Mr. Jordan was the father of nine children, five of whom are yet living. He had five sons in the Union army in the rebellion, three of whom are now dead. James was killed in the engagement at Dallas, Ga. John and Charles both died since their return home. Robert lives in Iowa, and William near Arcadia, Ohio.

Mr. Jordan was amongst the first settlers in this township, and at once took a prominent place in the affairs of the township. At the first election he attended in the township, there were but fourteen votes cast. He has held several township offices, amongst them that of Justice of the Peace. He has been a member of the Lutheran Church for about fifty years, and assisted in the organization of the first Lutheran Society in the township.

Mr. J. has a fair common English education, although he never attended school more than two months in his life. Mr. Jordan moved to Findley in 1874, and still resides there. By his economy and industry in his younger days, he is now enabled to enjoy his old age without being a burden to any one.

RISDON.

This town was laid out September 6th, 1832, by John Gorsuch, who certified "That the east half of the above town, comprising all the lots from number one to number thirty inclusive, in the west half of the north-west quarter of section six, township two north, range thirteen east, in the county of Seneca, and includes the east half of Main street, being the county line between Seneca and Hancock Counties. All the rest of the said lots, on the west half of said town, from thirty-one to sixty inclusive, are laid out on the east part of the north-east quarter of section one, township two north, range twelve east, in the county of Hancock."

This town, and the town of Rome, in Seneca County, were years ago united, and form the town of Fostoria. There is located here the College of the United Brethren, and some very handsome private residences. Quite a number of manufacturing establishments are also located here, and altogether it is a prosperous portion of the growing town of Fostoria.

A comfortable brick building for the public schools has been erected, and the enumeration of youth of school age amounts to one hundred and four.

ARCADIA.

In July 1855, David Peters and Ambrose Peters laid out this town, comprising one hundred and thirty-five lots, on the south part of the north half, and the north part of the south half of the south-west quarter of section twenty-two.

Other additions were made by William Wheelan and Charles E. Jordan.

The town is located about eight miles north-east of Findley, at the crossing of the Lake Erie & Western and the New York, Chicago & St. Louis Railroads, and has a population of about six hundred. The country surrounding it is rich and well improved, and there seems to be no good reason why Arcadia should not become quite a good point. Its inhabitants are intelligent and enterprising, and already quite a large trade is done here.

The business of the town is represented by two quite respectable dry goods stores, two drug stores, three grocerys, two hotels, three blacksmith shops, two wagon shops, two shoe shops, two cabinet shops, one cooper shop, one bakery, one restaurant, one tin shop, one flouring mill, one handle factory, one saw mill. There are here one Methodist, one Presbyterian and one Lutheran church, and a good brick school house. There are four physicians and one lawyer located here.

The Odd Fellows instituted a Lodge here in July, 1874. and now have a membership of *forty-four*.

The Lake & Western Railroad was finished through this place in the spring of 1859, and the N. Y., C. & St. L. Railway commenced laying iron here on the 28th of May, 1881, and on the 2d day of June the cars ran across Main street.

This town was incorporated in 1859, at which time Geo. W. Kimmell was elected Mayor, and Dr. D. B. Spahr, Recorder. The office of Mayor has since been filled by the the following persons: Jacob Peters, Joseph Dillery, E. B. Warner, C. E. Jordan, J. E. Beeson, A. D. Harbaugh, George Stahl and J. W. Fisher. Joseph Dillery has been five times elected Mayor, and J. E. Bowman was six times elected Recorder.

A post office was established here In 1859, with A. W. Fredcrick Postmaster, who has been succeeded by David Peters, Jacob Peters, William Karn, Joseph Smart, William Moffat and J. H. Beeson, the present incumbent.

The following named persons were elected Justices of the Peace in this township, at the dates named:

Liverton Thomas—1832.
James Wiseman—1835, 1838, 1841, 1844.
William Eckles—1835.
Oliver Day—1838.
Joel Hales—1841.
Michael Roller—1841, 1843, 1847, 1850, 1853.
Ephraim Peters—1844.
William Baker—1846, 1849, 1852.
Thomas Buckley—1847.
Charles S. Kelley—1854, 1857, 1860, 1863, 1866.
Wesley Bradford—1855.
Anthony Fox—1856, 1859, 1863, 1866, 1869, 1872, 1875, 1878.
Charles E. Jordan—1860, 1863.
Jacob Peters—1866, 1869.
James McCauley—1869, 1873.
Ezra B. Warner—1872.
Geo. W. Grubb—1874.
D. P. Lloyd—1876.
J. W. Fisher—1877.
C. German—1879.
Joseph Dillery—1880.

Crop Report.

Table of crop and stock statistics for the year 1880 as returned to the County Auditor by the Township Assessor in 1881:

Wheat,	3,894 acres.	86,932	bushels.
Oats,	950 "	31,230	"
Corn,	2,531 "	104,028	"
Hay,	572 "	496	tons.
Horses,	722 number.	$35,360	value.
Cattle,	1330 "	14,293	"
Sheep,	4856 "	8,995	"
Hogs,	2537 "	5,932	"

SOCIAL STATISTICS.

Table showing number of marriages, births and deaths each month in the year ending March 31st, 1880:

1879:	Marriages	Births.			Deaths.		
		Male.	Female.	Total.	Male.	Female.	Total.
April,	23	15	25	40	6	12	18
May,	17	29	28	57	5	13	18
June,	14	29	29	58	8	9	17
July,	12	27	16	43	9	13	22
August,	17	37	35	72	18	16	34
September,	23	41	39	80	15	13	28
October,	32	37	27	64	14	12	26
November,	26	24	34	58	10	8	18
December,	42	35	29	64	11	9	20
January,	15	39	43	82	12	11	23
February,	15	34	29	61	18	18	36
March,	19	37	52	89	18	18	36
Totals,	255	384	384	768	144	152	296

Of the number of deaths, 14 were above the age of 80 years, and 89 were under *one* year of age. Twenty-three were of foreign birth. The greatest mortality was of housekeepers 58, and farmers 44. Of those who died 180 were single, 91 were married, and 24 were widowed. Twenty-four died of diphtheria, eighteen of lung diseases, fourteen of brain disease, eleven of heart disease, and six by accident or violence.

Statistical Tables. 471

Table showing amount of taxes levied in 1880, on Grand Duplicate.

State,	$12,338.83
County,	19,172.23
Poor,	12,781.44
Bridge,	23,066.71
Building,	11,503.33
Road,	12,365.21
Indebtedness,	3,834.40
Township,	7,264.26
School,	42,214.31
Special,	23,117.35
Village,	13,488.82
Total,	$181,146.89

Table of Miscellaneous Statistics.

Acres land sold, 20,464.	Av. pr. acre	$53 50	
Town Lots,	25.	"	720.00
No. of Deeds Recorded,			535
No. of Mortgages Recorded,			409
Amount Secured,			$467,028
No. of Mortgages Cancelled,			139
Amount Released,			$236,978

Domestic Animals died of Disease.

Horses,	192	Value,	$12,045
Cattle,	280	"	6,239
Sheep,	622	"	1,741
Hogs,	1,922	"	6,486

Value of Manufactured Articles.

Wooden Ware,	$ 4,200	Carriages, Buggies,	$28,700
Wagons, Drays, &c.,	3,900	Other Artic's of W'd,	35,000
Saddles, Harness, &c.,	12,000	Tin, Copper, &c.,	6,000
Oils,	39,955	Cigars & Tobacco,	800
All other Manufact's,	44,800	Drain Tile,	3,560

Total, $178,915.

PRESIDENTIAL ELECTION, 1880.

A table showing number of votes cast for each candidate for President, and total vote in each election precinct:

Townships and Wards.	Garfield.	Hancock.	Weaver.	Dow.	Total.
Allen,	96	139			235
Amanda,	156	203	2		361
Big Lick,	146	145	1		292
Blanchard,	201	121		1	323
Cass,	97	92	5	1	195
Delaware,	202	151			353
Eagle,	104	200			304
Findley,	118	102	2		222
Findley, 1st Ward,	171	115	10		296
2nd "	112	156	1		269
3d "	193	104			297
4th "	174	130	2		306
Jackson,	106	198			304
Liberty,	134	117			251
Madison,	100	153		2	255
Marion,	131	112			243
Orange,	119	184			303
Portage,	105	114			219
Pleasant,	227	218		5	450
Union,	162	249			311
Van Buren,	57	127			184
Wash'ton, Fostoria Prec't	115	47	1		213
Arcadia "	98	123	9		230
	3,124	3,350	33	9	6,516

ADAM, 274
ADAMS, J T 321 334 James T 318 320 321 345 Jno 167 John 129 156 287 Louis 320 Newton M 320 321 Thomas E 285
AGIN, Wm 414
ALBAN, H H 129 153
ALBERTSON, Elizabeth 232
ALBON, H H 275
ALEXANDER, John 83
ALGIRE, 17 George 422 423 424 425 John 421
ALLEN, 39 265 332 B 331 Ethan 180
ALSPACH, Daniel 407 George W 250 251 J 246 251 John G 217
ALSPOCH, Adam 196 Daniel 165 Mrs 197
ALTMAN, John 276
AMSPOKER, Alexander 422 424
ANDERSON, Elijah R 459, John 103 104 W 327 W H 126 168 William 127 128 283 318 319 321 326 330 347 William H 124
ANDRE, Jacob 439
APPLESEEDS, Johnny 131 132 133 134 387
ARMSTRONG, Gen 159 Mrs 186 W W 353
ARNOLD, George 246 346 347
ASHBURN, Isaac 454
ATLER, Henry 413
AUCKERMAN, J W 338
AUGUSTUS, David 237
AULL, J A 347
BABCOCK, J R 380
BACHERER, 278 E 279 Ernst 348
BAILS, Abraham 383
BAIRD, George W 109
BAKER, Aaron 164 255 260 Charles 181 182 Isaac 75 261

BAKER (continued)
John 441 Joseph 406 407 William 468
BALDWIN, 110 273 293 Amy J 298 D M 214 David M 207 214 I J 167 John W 68 306 L A 243 283 355 370 371 Mary Jane 299 W H 167 298 299 369
BALLARD, Franklin 450 Fuller 450 H D 347 O A 291 Oren A 268 Philip 214 216 T C 348
BALLENTINE, James S 167 335 Mrs 335
BALLOU, Amariah 285
BALSLEY, A H 358 Mr 359
BAME, S M F 127
BANNING, Col 157
BAPE, J A 168
BARMOUTH, 454
BARND, 360 Christian 306 E 274 Elijah 50 167 G C 345 G W 191 Jacob 92 John 183 190 191 Mr 184 185
BARNEL, Adna 181 C G 158 Christian 167 181 Elijah 139 164 181 G C 181 Gamaliel C 168 Henry 181 J 167 Jacob 138 John 181 182
BARNEY, Margaret 428 Zelotus 428
BARNHILL, Joseph 393 T G 291 349
BARR, James H 118 167 168 345 393
BARROWS, Sarah 296
BARTEL, Thompson 450
BARTHOLOMEW, John 422
BARTON, Sarah 389
BASEHORE, John 295
BASHORE, John 66 261
BASKET, J F 128
BATES, 68 Curtis 109

BATTLES, 414 Asa 412
BAUMGARTNER, Leonard 226
BAYLESS, Henry 123 Richard 222
BEACH, B 403 Rial 447
BEAGLE, David 380
BEARD, 377 Adam 407 Amos 28 64 Geo W 245 James 29 195 John 63 66 195
BEARDSLEY, Barna 263 383 D B 125 166 267 288 291 347 348 349 Daniel 263 Mary 263 Mr 264 265 Mrs 264
BECHTEL, A R 426 429
BECK, 197 A S 127 168 Andrew 195 Michael 46
BEEK, A S 123
BEELMAN, J M 348
BEELMON, J M 359
BEER, Thomas 148
BEESON, J E 467 J H 468 James 229 458 Mr 183
BELDEN, A R 284
BELDING, E B 363
BELL, Abner 240 Gen 88
BELLVILLE, 334
BELMER, H B 333
BENDER, Peter 252
BENHAM, James C 449 Robert 258
BENNETT, A 429 Ross 255
BENSING, Mrs 124 125 Nicholas 124 125
BENTON, Thomas H 214
BERGMAN, John 128 216 Solomon 454
BERRY, Curtis 237
BESSERMAN, Daniel 454 Michael 456
BIBLER, David 127 375
BICKHAM, Jennie E 327 Y 324 325 327
BIDDLE, J H 244
BIG MEDICINE, 20 21
BIGELOW, 39 332 A H 304 305 Aaron H 121
BIGGS, 39 265 332 George 129 369 Richard 444-445 William 322
BISH, Andrew 408 David 126 393
BISHOP, George 246 248 249 373 Henry 110 111 252 351 J D 168

BISHOP (continued) John D 246 248 249
BITLER, J C 291
BLACKFORD, A 128 129 351 Aaron 291 300 352 Albert 300 Jason 291 Mr 359 Price 267 299 300
BLACKMER, Amanda 297
BLAKEMAN, Charles 422 424 429
BLANCHARD, 34
BLEECHER, H W 348
BLINN, Wm 226
BLOCKFORD, A 124
BLODGET, Selden 29
BLODGETT, Seldon 65
BLYMIRE, H J 449 W G 358
BOID, John 29 30 31
BOLANDER, Elizabeth 337
BOLLENBAUGH, John 456
BOLTON, R H 338
BOND, Mrs 378
BONHAM, Isaac 347 Johnson 383 393 Robert 261
BOOTH, Esther 234
BOPE, Col 283 J A 158 288 291 335 James A 335 Mrs 335
BOURNE, Sylvanus 177 178 179
BOUTWELL, Willard 418
BOWERS, Henry 123 375 380
BOWMAN, Eli 402 J E 468
BOYD, John 62 101 261 269 R W 393 394
BOYLAN, Aaron 263 Beulah 263 John 215 216 383 388 Mary 263
BOYLES, Hugh 122 John 122 126
BRACKLEY, Michael 110
BRADFORD, Charles 456 Wesley 468
BRAND, G C 293 Jacob 168
BRANDEBERRY, Andrew R 231
BRANDEL, Gamaliel C 68
BRAYTON, Elijah 218
BRECKENRIDGE, 39 265 331 332
BRENNER, Fred 197 Mrs 197
BRESLIN, John G 353
BRIDINGER, Jacob 245
BRIGGS, Chester 339
BRIGHT, Edward 406 407 James 226 John 247 441 Major 405 406 407 Nimrod 405

BRIGHT (continued)
  William 127
BROTHERS, 403
BROWN, A 201 B S 347 Capt 295
  E 305 Elisha 167 201 Ezra 267
  283 287 288 291 Geo W 227 H
  168 Hannah 310 Henry 94 124
  126 128 129 164 165 167 168
  283 291 310 351 352 353 370 J
  C 125 J H 201 James 230 John
  255 Joseph C 426 T P 112
BRUNDIGE, John 237
BRYAN, 187 Elias 181 Elias S 181
  182 267 James 459 461 William
  412 414
BRYANT, 282
BUCK, 281 Daniel 129 323 324
  336 Michael 237
BUCKINGHAM, Amasa 408
BUCKLEY, Thomas 167 468
BUERKLE, M 336
BULLOCK, Moses 283 328 329
BURCHARD, W P 338
BURGOYNE, Gen 307
BURKET, G W 447 449 George
  442 443 444 J F 124 283 366 J
  P 291 Jacob 443 444 John H
  267 Mary 443 Sarah 444
BURKHEAD, 464 William S 393
BURKLE, M 270
BURMAN, Catharine 231 John
  181 182 183 231 232 Philip 191
BURNAP, B F 200 201
BURNS, E R 418 Father 340
  George 406 James 442 443 447
  T J 406
BURSON, A F 401
BURTON, Van 393
BUSHAN, J C 348
BUSHON, A 325 Andrew 323
BUSHONG, A J 126 J 168 Jacob
  126 168 Simon 125 T H 401
BUSS, J D 450
BUTTON, L 279 367
BYAL, A P 164 165 166 167 266
  268 Absalom P 167 Campbell
  256 266 Catherine 262 Col 88
  Doratha 307 308 Elizabeth 262
  Henry 128 262 267 283 307-
  308 John 78 88 90 168 256 258
  261 266 267 386 421 Mary 308

BYAL (continued)
  Mr 263 Nancy 262 Peter 122
  Rachael 262 William 262 273
CAMPBELL, 183 David 83 107
  John 49 267 John W 83
CAPELL, O P 158
CARLIN, 16 279 397 C R 291 D B
  302 Dr 297 Elliott 302 Fred
  302 Harriet E A 297 P 94 273
  302 305 Parlee 55 90 111 112
  116 269 285 295 301 306 331
  369 S 77 164 273 302 305 Sarah
  301 331 Squire 22 29 38 45 62
  66 83 92 94 168 261 269 270
  272 284 295 300-302 306 331
  395 W D 155 302 W L 291
  William D 301
CARNAHAN, John 413 T 283 W R
  283
CARR, Jacob 55 287 288 345 Mr
  280 281
CARROLL, Elizabeth 437
CARSON, Dick 211 212 Jno L 168
  John L 210 212 216 421 Richard 210 Richard M 441
CASAD, Anthony 62 64
CASE, Mood 351 W M 351
CASS, D W 447 450 Gen 263
  Lewis 228
CASSELL, J M 338
CEASER, Mrs 122
CHADWICK, C 283
CHAFFIN, John 231
CHAIN, Jerry 130 Levi 130
CHAMBERLAIN, 16 19 Debora..
  259 I S 358 Job 22 24 29 31
  255 260 392 Job Sr 101 258 259
  Julia 115 Mr 377 Norman 260
  Sarah 259
CHAMBERLIN, Job 30 46
CHANDLER, Benjamin 29 259
  John 206
CHAPMAN, John 133 Jonathan
  134 William 427 429
CHARLES, Isaac B 126 127 John
  126 127 Malissa 126
CHESTER, Thomas 29
CHILDS, J J 326 N E 356 Nathaniel E 168
CHRISTMAS, C W 178 179
CHURCH, Collis 463

CHURCH (continued)
  Elizabeth 463 Martha J 464 William 370 463-464
CLARK, J R 282 371 T B 334
CLAY, Henry 461
CLINE, D 283
CLINGERMAN, J C 401
COBB, Alonzo H 231
COCKLIN, S 337
COCLE, Jeremiah 208
COEN, Mrs 385 Sarah 334 William 334 385
COFFINBERRY, 68 Andrew 122 Count 146 305 J M 273 346 356 James M 355 356 Judge 357
COLE, Aaron 123 Abraham 195 Elias 168 Richard 458 Thomas 64 195
COLEBAUGH, C W 229
COLLETT, John 177 178
COLLINS, George C 181
COMBS, J A Jr 450 J A Sr 450
COMER, David 129 451 Doratha 307 Isaac 307 383 389
CONINE, W H 429
CONKLE, 124 Adam 122 123
CONNELL, D C 345 348
CONNELLY, James 458
CONSTABLE, Jasper 363
CONWAY, 39 265
COOK, Abner Jr 148 Chester 166 243 Henry 216 R T 347 Rezin 214
COOLEY, James 106
COONS, Vincent H 320 321
COOPER, Allen 433 Amos 431 433 Isaac 127 James 435 Jane Eliza 436 C John 68 164 168 431 435-436 Judge 432 433 Mrs James 390 Mrs Judge 390 S A 429
CORBIN, Benjamin 245
COREY, Judge 94
CORTEX, M 332
CORY, 255 270 274 383 Abel M 112 Ann M 313 D J 128 164 277 369 David J 311-313 Elnathan 24 46 269 271 273 293 404 Judge 20 219 278 Martha 312 313
COULTER, Robert 164 284 357

COVERDALE, R T 326 327
COX, Benjamin 11 18 259 273 Hiram 164 J D 152 James 161 Lydia 19 Mrs W C 270 W C 165 370
CRABILL, 402
CRAIGHILL, W B 108 109
CRAMER, 402 Daniel 442 Jacob 442 444 John 444 Philip 377 441 442 444 Philip Jr 444 Sarah 444
CRAWFORD, Abner 231 E S 414 John 200 Robert 123
CREIGHTON, J E 426 Samuel 123 168 231
CRINER, Sarah 259
CRIST, Charles 431
CRITES, Jackson 426 John 337 Mrs 337
CROFT, John 252
CROMLISH, William 430
CRONNINGER, Calvin A 318 Henry N 129
CROOK, G H 369
CROSBY, Eliakim 422
CROSS, Charles 200 J M 334
CROSSLEY, 449
CROUSE, E B 337 I 339 Philip 335 336
CROWNENWITT, Rev 336
CROWTHERS, C L 337
CRUM, Amos 247 250
CRUMRINE, Adam 433 439
CRUSAC, Isaac 429
CULP, Henry 430
CUMMINGS, C H 319 James 419
CUMMINS, Benjamin 392 393 422 424 426 429
CUNNINGHAM, Elizabeth 338
CURRIE, Jackson 125
CUSAC, Daniel 390 436 Isaac 168 390 425 426 James 390 Jane Eliza 436 John 390 Sarah 390 William 390
CUSAD, Anthony 168
CUSAE, Isaac 112 153 John 127 128 166
DALLEY, Henry L 414
DALLY, Henry L 412 416-417
DARKE, Mr 428
DARRAH, Jefferson 159

DAUGHENBAUGH, A 267
DAVIDSON, J W 154 288 James 335 Robert 380
DAVIES, D T 335 Francis 332
DAVIS, 17 Alfred 125 206 208 Elijah T 62 Isaac 123 127 283 285 342 408 J W 283 Jeff 161 John W 320 321 Margaret 410 William 168 237 406 407 410-411 William L 320 321 326
DAY, David P 228 230 Elam 229 230 331 Oliver 468
DEACHAN, Father 340
DEBRILL, 161
DECKER, 249 Elias 247 John 248 251
DEHAVEN, J B 402 John 402
DEITSCH, A 281 Charles 335 336 Henry C 363
DELANY, 39
DEMMING, Mrs 432 Treat 432
DENNIS, J P 288
DENNISON, Jas 167
DERHODES, Henry 432 Samuel 432
DESHIRIE, I H 338
DESNEY, B A 190 Hannah 190
DETER, James 431
DETWILER, Dr 314
DEWESE, Samuel 447 Thomas 447
DEWITT 407 Barnabus 295 Joseph 29 38 62 Wm 65 William 331
DEWOLFE, E G 288 348 358 359 Eli G 285 286 360 O J 358
DICKENSON, Rudolphus 146
DICKERHOFF, S 338
DIDWAY, 256 Mrs Frederick 39
DIETSCH, A 325
DILDINE, Sampson 29 65 115 Sarah 115
DILLER, John 397 398 454
DILLERY, Joseph 467 468
DILLINGER, A A 348
DITWILER, William M 345
DIX, John A 148
DODGE, Henry H 148
DOESNER, Father 340
DORNEY, Julius 402
DORSEY, David 231

DOTY, John 375
DOUGHERTY, Campbell 161 Frank H 128
DOUTY, John 379
DOWNING, 17 210 David 166 212 213 214 George 212 216 Isaac 212 John L 116 Johnny 212 Mrs Wm 213 William 212 213
DRAKE, Robert B 158 Uriah E 225 W K 403
DRESBACH, C E 337 J E 394 John 201
DUDGEON, Jane 435 Simeon 413
DUDLEY, Benjamin 122
DUKES, 208 210 Eli 209 214 John 17 164 206 207 209 Lewis 17 206 Lewis Sr 206 207 Richard 17 206 Susan 115 391 W P 216 279
DULIN, Benjamin F 121 Rachael 260 Sanford F 431
DUNCAN, Andrew 356 Pat G 356
DUNKEN, Amos 226
DUNLAP, Jonathan 419
DUNLEVY, Eliza 418
DUNN, E T 123 129 291 Elijah T 267
DUNNING, Eli 216
DURING, M 336
DYE, 384
EATON, H 77 H P 450 Washington 123
EBAUGH, John 380
EBERLEY, Mrs 18 22
EBERLY, Mr 103
EBRIGHT, 251
ECKINLEY, John 168
ECKLES, C J 335 Charles 230 Esther 234 John 232 234 335 Mrs 335 William 229 459 461 468
EDGAR, Mary 438
EDGINGTON, Jno 168 John 439 Levi 237 Perry 122 Thomas F 439
EDINGTON, T F 433
EDMUNDS, Mr 363
EDWARDS, J P 227 W J 282 Wm 279 348
EGBERT, 374 Daniel 405 David 373 407 Major 407

EGBERT (continued)
   Uriah 196 218
ELDER, 16 Ephraim 28 John 28
   65 John B 240 Josiah 29 38 65
   68 237 238 378 Robert 64
   Rosanna 240
ELDRIDGE, Alpheus 229
ELLIOT, George 230
ELLIOTT, Cyrenius 149
ELLIS, Asa 375 Dick 362
ELLISON, 387 388
ELLSWORTH, John 103 104
ELSEA, James 164 Moses 251
   Moses Jr 375
ENGLE, 210 D W 168 380 Jacob
   211 214
ENSMINGER, George 181 182 191
   192 Michael 182 Miss 183
ENSPERGER, Christian 181
ENTREKIN, F W 348
EPLEY, 208 Henry 206
ERNST, Frederick 123 G W 127
ESSEX, Philip 218
ESSINGER, Nicholas 454
ETHERTON, B A 199 201
EVANS, B D 402 Pierre 312
EVERETT, James L 108
EWING, 385 427 B 412 Cornelius
   393 Jesse 379 John 68 92 369
   John A 419 Judge 150
FAHL, Josiah 245
FAIRCHILD, Daniel 78 90 168
   230 231 232 E C 230 Eleazer C
   229 S H 426 429
FARST, Frank 285
FELLERS, Daniel 251 Hugh 127
   Peter 251 Tim 348
FENSTENMAKER, John 197 Mrs
   197
FERGESON, John M 322
FERRALL, William 461
FERREL, Wm 459
FETHIAN, George 106
FIDLER, Nathan 422
FIELDS, A B 334
FILKIN, N W 288
FINCH, B 123
FINDLEY, James 12
FINLEY, 39 W T 334
FIRMIN, Edmund W 156 F W 283
   291 L 283 291

FISHEL, 16 210 Daniel 383 John
   29 38 383 Michael 208 214 383
FISHER, Catharine 231 D C 276
   325 329 330 Eliza 428 J W 467
   468 John 362
FITCH, Joseph 400
FITZPATRICK, L 283 322
FLAISEG, E N 161
FLECK, Joseph 125
FLEMING, Joseph 343
FLEMMING, Father 340
FLENNER, George 66 295
FLETCHER, Robert 422 424
FLICK, John 442
FOGLESONG, 210 Sol 208 Solomon 74 210 214
FOHL, G S 49
FOLK, G F 449 Nicholas 442 444
FOLTZ, Peter 454
FORD, Jesse 164 John T 355 356
   Philip 157
FOREMAN, Geo 152 153 160 John
   161
FOSTER, Andrew 121 Daniel 117
   Gov 460 Jacob 64 66 117 256
   258 261 279 John 242 Mr 187
   188 William 121 122
FOUNTAIN, Rebecca 390 Sarah
   389 W H 394 William 383 389
   390
FOX, Anthony 468 Daniel 442
   David 165 Mary 443
FRAKES, Mr 187 188 Nathan 19
   28 38 64 181 383 Susy 19
FRANCE, William 320
FRANKS, John 228 230 232 John
   Sr 234
FRAY, S D 270
FREDERICK, A W 166 468 Alfred
   W 168
FREED, Henry 454
FRENCH, J 339 R 339
FREY, S D 283 327 330 Samuel D
   326
FRICK, D 193 Daniel 193
FRITCHER, Charles 322
FROST, Charles 216
GAGE, H P 283 342 362 369
   Hanks P 112
GALLOWAY, G W 123 165 369
   Geo W 267 Mr 166

GARDINER, John 29
GARDNER, D B 302 John 24 46 115 180 269 383 John Jr 46 Susan 115
GARFIELD, Gen 157
GARNETT, J C 128
GARRISON, T C 349
GARST, John 380
GARTEE, Jacob 124 125
GASSMAN, Adam 454
GAVIT, Rev 243
GAVITT, 332 Elanthan 331
GEORGE, Charles 447 E 193 Henry 28 62 195 Peter 28 38 91 186 195 196 295 372 374 Susan 434
GERMAN, C 468
GERSUCH, John 457
GEYER, Amanda 338 Sylvester M 345
GIBSON, 442 J W 227 James 195 Mary 334 W H 154
GILBERT, Aquilla 78 118 168 195 196 199 201 374 375 377 378 380 Dan 375 Daniel 155 156 202 204 Jesse 195 L P 375 T B 200 201 449
GILCHRIST, Hugh 181 182 183 184 John 181 183 184
GILKESON, John C 356 William F 356
GILRUTH, Father 40 James 39 49 256 269
GITCHEL, David 29
GLANCEY, Wm 339
GLASGOW, John 179
GLAUNER, Michael 126
GLENNER, Michael 408
GLESSNER, F H 354 355 Georgiana 354 L 353 354 Lewis 353 Mrs 283 W L 354 William L 345
GODFREY, Charles M 111
GODMAN, 68 J H 304 Mr 64
GOIT, 68 278 Edson 138 164 167 168 277 298 304 307 345 446 Edson Sr 315-317 Jane 316
GOODE, Judge 150 Patrick G 147 149
GOODIN, John 109
GOODLIN, J W 333

GORDEN, Samuel 199
GORDON, John P 243 Sammy 284 Thomas 335
GORSUCH, Eli 380 John 458 461 466 Nelson 461 Silas 461
GOUCHER, D 369
GOWDY, Elijah 393
GRABER, Alfred 291
GRAHAM, 219 Geo W 227 James 222 John 168 218 227 Mary 218
GRANT, Alexander 396 Gen 285 President 360
GRAUL, George M 338 Mrs 338
GRAY, 278 Charlotte 315 M 284 Milton 315 334 S F 154 165 288
GREEAR, William 29
GREEN, 310 H B 160 284 348 Henry B 345 Israel 165 288 Samuel 454
GREER, Charlotte 115 Charlotte M 240 Father 243 Henry 166 243 244 J 241 John 241 John H 241 Marian 240 R 412 Rosanna 240 W J 237 William J 64 83 238 240 Wm 373 374
GREERS, 16
GRIBBEN, William 111 168 122 291 305
GRIBBON, Wm 288
GRISWOLD, J E 359
GROATH, Fred 336 J T 336
GROSE, Henry M 225 Jacob 338 John T 338 Mrs 338
GROUL, Jacob 123
GROVE, 17 Thomas 206
GROVES, L C 123 214 Thomas 206 209
GRUBB, Geo W 468 Jacob 393
GUISE, Jessie 335
GUNTNER, Henry 363
GURLEY, 39 332
GUTZINLER, J 167 Jos 283
HACKETT, William 218
HACKNEY, William 28 30 31 63 83 84 115 167 195 196
HADDOX, John 127
HAGGERTY, R J 130
HAHN, Charles 335 336 Henry 335
HALE, Reuben 29 30 Reubin 31
HALES, Baker 165 Joel 459 468

HALES (continued)
  Reuben 62 64 269
HALL, Aaron 164 165 278 335 393
  C B 167 370 Geo 283 James C
  111 112 John 394 Jude 168 304
  Lawrence W 147 Mrs 335
  Richard 73 199 W S 311
HALLOWELL, 276 282
HAMBLETON, Bleuferd 28 John
  P 30 31
HAMBLIN, Daniel 29 Don Alonzo
  48 66 68 84 L P 375 R W 378
  Reuben W 29 83 Rueben W 64
HAMILTON, 16 19 66 J P 168
  John P 28 46 48 62 65 67 83
  255 260 261 271 272 372 382
HAMLIN, D O 240 241 Don
  Alonzo 28 30 31 45 62 167 237
  J M 291 John M 325 326 M S
  241 R W 240
HAMLINS, 16
HAMMER, George 333
HAMMOND, Judge 38 374 375 M
  168 Mordica 28 31 62 63 68 83
  372 373 377 382 T G 373 Tillie
  373
HAMPTON, Alfred 383
HANCOCK, John 33 Vanrensalear
  65
HANKEY, L W 337
HARBAUGH, A D 467 T J 339
HARDY, Addison 190 231 Hannah
  190 John 189 230 232 Joseph O
  190 Martha 189 Oliver P 190
HARMON, Henry J 108
HARN, G M 338
HARRIS, C C 393 Jacob 123 243
  245 Simpson 241
HARRISON, Gen 263
HARRY, Samuel 230
HARSH, James 158 Mrs 283
HART, John 393
HARTMAN, A J L 129 447 Amos
  387 H C 193 J L 126 Jonas 405
  Rufus R 166 William 126
HASKINS, Mr 188
HASSAN, Eliab 125 126
HASSON, 454 Eliab 456 John 414
HATCH, C H 201 Charles 201
HAUMAN, Balser 245
HAWKINS, 283

HAY, Edwin R 266
HAYES, John C 380 President 360
HAZEN, Ezra 431
HEACOCK, William 402
HEAKES, Philip 246
HECK, Carter 279 George 125 322
  John 256
HEDGES, Joshua 29 30 31 38 62
  65 83 84 115 239 240 247 255
  256 258 260 267 Josiah 107
  Rebecca 432
HEFFNER, S T 347 362
HEISLEY, Adam 407
HEISTAND, Jacob 459 461 462
HELDMAN, 248 Henry 454 I 247
  Peter 454 Philip 454
HELLENKAMP, Henry 326
HELLER, Peter 439 S M 193 W L
  191
HELMS, 17 Jacob 397 Joseph 123
  Mrs Henry 238
HEMRY, George 425 Henry 422
HENDERSON, Charles 227 F 369
  370 F H E 156 Frederick 294
  Frederick 54 119 139 306 310
  311 Hiram E 155 Mr 295 Phebe
  334 W 167 W L 118 167 168
  269 287 306 3346 William L
  48 92 261 267 295 308 347
HENDRICK, John J 73
HENDRICKS, James 29 John J 63
  195 199
HENRY, George 380 J L 167
  James L 419 John 123 Joseph
  419 Sheriff 124
HENSEL, James 337
HEUSTIS, 332
HEUSTISS, 39 265
HEWITT, Jesse 29 John 195 Mr
  295
HIBBITT, John 339
HIERSHER, Martin 276
HIGGINS, David 146 Judge 147
HIGH, Daniel 426
HIGHLAND, Sarah 115
HILL, 39 265 332 Abner 397 John
  L 167 Mrs 397
HINEBAUGH, Henry 218
HISSONY, L J 193
HOBBS, John 383
HOCKENBERRY, Peter 182

HODGE, A 165 Alex 456
HOLDEN, A W 339
HOLLABAUGH, A M 353 Alpheus M 353
HOLLABOUGH, A M 165
HOLLENBACH, George 258
HOLLENBECK, 437 George 256
HOLLOBAUGH, Martin 250
HOLLYDAY, R H 222 334
HOLMES, Alex 177 178 179 James 177 Samuel 178 179
HOOPER, P S 333
HOPKINS, Mathew E 216
HORTZIE, Augustus 127
HOSLER, Peter 126 168 283 366 Will 366
HOUCHINGS, Hannah 209
HOUGH, Aaron 264
HOUK, A M 379 Andrew W 380 J F 379
HOUPT, Mrs S D 308 S D 283
HOWARD, Aaron 167 D W H 112 Elizabeth 437 John 436 John C 273 Jos 181 Samuel 158 164 168 256 267 279 431 436-437 439 William 125
HOWE, Henry 134
HOWELL, William L 356
HOXTER, Samuel 166
HOY, Daniel 126 Jacob 379
HUBBARD, James 108
HUBER, Ben 276 Benj 168 J M 276 349 Sam 157 288
HUFF, 402 Aaron 258 Abraham 31 58 59 61 62 64 195 196 200 Abram 28 Eliza 217 James 401 John 29 63 73 195 217 Joseph 402 403 Judge 38 63 68 101
HUFFMAN, Barney 332 Judge 284 Samuel 122 Samuel B 168
HUGHES, 210 H W 214 429 Hiram W 216 Owen 211 214 W W 168 242 252
HULBERT, Hiram 230 232
HULL, 301 G W 366 Gen 12 397 Henry 456 J B 369 J C F 366 J G 283 327 366
HUMASON, C M 349
HUMPHREY, Jarvis 433
HUNT, John E 109
HUNTER, John 24 46 64 66 205 206
HUNTINGTON, Anthony 125 Elijah 110 Samuel 183
HUNTWORK, Elizabeth 260
HURD, 273 Anson 291 Lorenzo 400 Robert 396 399 401 402 William B 400
HUTCHISON, Susan E 306
ILER, Jacob 405
IMHOFF, A J 333 Henry 396
INGLE, T D 339
INOPQUANAH, 20
IVERS, Mrs 415 William 418
JACKSON, Abner M 148 Andrew 373 Gen 461
JACOBS, George 337 Mrs 337
JAMES, John 186
JAMESON, Isaac 261
JOHNSON, Andrew 285 Isaac 29 30 31 64 66 Joseph 29 38 63 167 Miller 387 Squire 155 156 Thomas F 65 167 W A 205
JOHNSTON, 16 C S 408 Isaac 434 J H 291 Jane 435 Joseph 407 434-435 Susan 434 Thomas F 48 75 116 295
JONES, 274 E P 283 342 365 366 E S 31 434 Edmun S 28 Edmund S 38 Edwin S 29 62 83 84 168 Isaac 405 John 29
JORDAN, C E 467 Charles 464 465 Charles E 129 464-466 467 468 James 465 John 465 Margaret 465 Robert 465 William 465
JOY, A 362 D 362 David 113
JULIAN, John S 339
KAGEY, Jos R 167
KAGRY, Samuel 183
KALB, 17 George 422 Isaac N 423 John 422 423 424 425 John S 423 Mrs 425
KARN, Abraham 199 E 165 Elizabeth 232 Ezra 166 189 232 233 William 468
KARR, 322
KARST, Coroner 124 Frank 284 311 Frank Sr 128 349
KEASY, Christopher 157

KEEL, Abraham 252 Henry 251
KELLER, Frederick 448 449
KELLEY, Charles S 126 468 G J 448 John 185 439 Thomas 458 Thomas B 426 W C 158 W S 426
KELLUM, James A 346 347
KELLY, John 14 Thomas 168
KEMERER, P 167 Samuel 450
KEMPF, Ernst 335
KEMPHER, J 181
KENOWER, J L 226 371
KEPLER, Rachel 115 Samuel 115
KERR, J P 335
KIGER, Bennet 422
KILPATRICK, Alexander 421 422 423 W H 216 William 422 423
KIMMEL, A 412 G W 366 J A 291
KIMMELL, G W 346 Geo W 467
KIMMENS, B F 128
KIMMILL, G W 283
KIMMONS, A 283 B F 284 288 347 348 349
KING, C F 403 William M 439
KINSEL, Rev 333
KIRK, 276
KLABER, Frank 272
KLAMROTH, William 77 288
KLNE, S 338
KNAPP, F H 291 Frank H 128 H K 352 H S 150
KNEPPER, 210 214
KNIGHT, William 402
KNOWLTEN, Samuel 122
KORNORER, Mrs 337 Paul 337
KRAMER, John 447 S H 343
KRAUSE, Charles J 345
KRIDLER, A R 282
KROUT, G W 373
KUNTZ, 282
KUTZ, 335
LAFFERTY, J 243 John 91 164 168 245 L S 403 Margaret 410
LAKE, 16 Asa 29 46 62 64 65 66 334 Asa M 29 38 65 115 236 237 238 240 242 244 256 269 375 Charlotte 115 Charlotte M 240 Chloe 334 Edwin S 66 George 259
LAMB, Henry 164 303 362 Jacob 303 422 430 Mary 303 308

LANE, Ebenezer 64 146
LANG, Rev 336
LANNERT, Henry 335 336
LAPE, Capt 88
LASH, Joseph 231
LASKEY, George 111
LAY, F B 348
LAYTON, W V 124
LEADER, John 183
LEASE, E P 403
LEE, David 125 H L 201 J P 129 Jason 201 John 193 Solomon 383
LEEDER, John 405
LEIBER, Ephraim 129
LEONARD, A 165 Mrs W K 438 Robert 222 S B 127 Wm K 227
LESLIE, E P 450 Joseph 400
LEWIS, Capt 463
LEWIS John 433
LINCOLN, Mr 285
LINE, Conrad 248 249 Mrs 249
LINNVILLE, J L 322
LIVENGOOD, J 333
LLOYD, D P 468
LOCKE, D R 358
LOCKWOOD, Samuel 83 Samuel M 83 107
LOEHR, J H 193 Jacob H 123
LONG, Alexander 114 James 339 John 29 30 31 73 83 168 218 Joseph 457 M 339 Mr 220 Mrs 218 Robert 64 218 219
LONGBRAKE, Alfred 451
LONGWITH, John 395
LONGWORTH, E 401
LONGWORTHY, A 154 Albert 158
LOUTHAN, M 283 Moses 160
LOUTHEN, Moses 128
LOUTHON, H H 167
LOVELL, K Henry 152
LUE, Henry 450
LUNEACK, Louis 168
LUNT, Rev 332 W S 111 331
LYON, 357
LYONS, James 103 104
LYTLE, Jasper 370 Mary 392 Wm 442
MACK, Frederick 127
MACKLIN, G P 339
MACKRILL, John 458

MACULLY, Robbert 29
MADISON, James 395
MAINS, N 419
MALAHAN, C F 447
MANN, Charles O 380
MANSFIELD, Dr 130
MARION, Francis 404
MARKEL, Joel 401 John 129 165 166
MARKLEY, Mathias 450
MARSHALL, 414 Benjamin 418 442 450 Isaac W 166 James C 450 Mary 415 Robert 213 216 W M 168 Wm M 419
MARTIN, Gen 159 J C 288 Jane 408 John C 153 Robert L 226 Washington 123 William 165
MARTZ, D 401 Dorillas 397 400 Hannah 400 Michael 400 N B 397 398 400 Napoleon B 400
MARVIN, Demy 328 Mabel 409 Mathias 409 Russell 328 W K 328 William 407 409 William Sr 409-410 Zera 409
MATHERS, William 339
MATHIUS, Ephriam 216
MAY, 68 282 John B 155
MCANNELLY, Moses 109 222 224 226
MCBRIDE, Rachael 248 Samuel 426
MCCAHAN, D D 167
MCCAHON, D D 127
MCCAUGHEY, J W 191
MCCAULEY, James 468 John 148
MCCLAY, George 431
MCCLELLAN, Samuel 229
MCCLELLON, R W 248
MCCLISH, 208 James 206
MCCONNELL, 276 D J 418 Eliza 418 Hugh 127 J T 414 James 418 John 190 447 John T 418-419 Wm 450
MCCRARY, Thomas 140
MCCULLOCH, John 421
MCCUNE, L P 193 Robert 335
MCCURDY, John 136 138 139 303
MCILVAIN, 255 269
MCKEE, John L 231 Thomas 346 W R 267
MCKIBBEN, John D 319

MCKINLEY, 414 John 415-416 418 419 Louisa 417 Mary 415 W M 126 419 Wm 415 Wm M 112
MCKINNIS, 16 17 19 388 C 168 Charles 29 30 31 46 48 60 62 65 66 67 83 271 272 372 382 383 457 James 29 38 60 62 65 383 John 60 383 Judge 38 63 64 68 101 269 392 Mrs Judge 385 Philip 24 46 60 65 66 67 85 86 115 383 391 Rachel 115 Robbert 29 Robert 24 58 59 60 62 115 259 383 391 Susan 115 391 William 128 129 345 391
MCMAHAN, John 110
MCMANIMA George 412 415
MCMANNESS, L 283 Lem 288
MCMINNIS, Philip 29
MCMURRAY, Hugh 183
MCPHERSON, 14 162
MCRILL, B J 407 Elijah 459 461
MCVARY, R W 243
MCWHORTER, Henry 46 64 195 217
MEEK, Martha 312
MEEKER, Forest 114
MEEKS, J A 288 334 335 Mrs 335 Rev 283
MEFFERD, N Y 287
MERCHANT, M 214
MERRIAM, A F 298
MESSENGER, William 282
METCALF, Ben 347
MICHAELS, L 193
MILES, Col 157
MILLER, 181 449 Ephriam 343 Felix 240 G W 333 Jackson 449 Jacob 252 Jane 408 John 252 Martin 408 Mr 187 188 Nathan 273 Rebecca 337 Sarah 337 Thomas 245 W P 358 William 214 William B 408-409
MILLHAM, Daniel 215 David 208
MINUTI, J 291
MIRES, William 214
MISSMORE, 374
MITCHEL, George 431
MITCHELL, Geo 433 William 428

MOFFAT, William 122 468
MOFFITT, 17 John 208 Orlando 206 Thomas 208 216 William 208
MONFEST, Peter 116
MONFORT, P 334 Peter 385
MONROE, A A 161 Alex A 153 James 269
MONTGOMERY, G W 433 Mrs G W 434 William 456
MOODY, Ephraim 447
MOORE, 219 275 282 A J 221 James B 261 John 164 165 220 223 L 339 Margaret 465 Mr 220 Mrs 223 Mrs John 220 S C 322 Samuel C 325 326 Solomon 339 W R 168
MOOREHEAD, J M 393 John 431 John E 431 433 438 Martha 188 Samuel 431 438-439 183 Mary 438
MORELAND, 17 19 Jacob 29 46 115 John M 166 Julia 115 Mr 398 Sarah 115 Susan 115 William 24 29 46 62 66 73 115 259 260 William Jr 29 63 64
MORRELL, Joseph 123
MORRIS, Mahlen 431 432 439 Mahlon 168 Mr 213
MORRISON, 68 John H 150 303-305 Joseph 413 Miss 415 Mr 304 305 P B 322 Robert 422 424 Thomas 456 William 419
MORSE, Adolphus 346
MORVIN, Ancel E 267
MOSHER, G S 167
MOSIER, Catharine 331 H M 331 Samuel 123 393
MOTT, Chester R 147
MOWER, Margaret 310 Samuel 310
MOYER, 276 Samuel 129
MUBER, J M 347
MULFORD, Mrs 390
MULL, George W 447
MUMERT, A 193
MUMMA, Abraham 227
MUMPHREY, Mr 434
MUNGEN, Oliver 156 R S 165 320 William 110 122 155 164 167 291 351 352 370

MUNGER, Oliver 285
MURRAY, Thomas 413
MUSE, Eben 334
MYAS, G W 284
MYERS, G W 327 330 Geo W 326 I H 429 Isaac H 426 James 110 Mrs G W 302 Samuel 167 Thompson 375
NAUS, A F 242
NEEDLES, John J 421 422 423 424
NEELEY, G W 335 George W 345 Mrs 335
NEIBLING, J M 152 153 167 285 Mrs 283
NEIL, 255 269 270 383
NEWELL, 374 Hannah 310 Hugh 267 309-310 369 James 378 Joseph 377-378 Margaret 309 310 Mr 311 Sallie 310 Samuel 108 Starling 310 William 373
NEWHOUSE, John 227
NEWSTATTER, Elizabeth 262
NEWSTETTER, Conrad 307
NEWTON, Isaac 332
NICHOLLS, Hannah 400
NICHOLS, C M 347
NIGHTINGALE, Gideon R 356
NILES, C E 327 366 Charler E 345 Charles E 326 345 365
NOBLE, W P 352
NORRIS, John 431 432 433 458 459 461 Mrs 432 Switzer 431 Wm 458
NOTT, Dr 129 Henry K 128
NOWLAN, 449 S J 447
NUNAMAKER, 248 A J 129
O'NEAL, 68 Amy J 298 C W 167 304 Charles 297-298 Charles W 110
OESTERLIN, C 291 Chas 112 164 Dr 165
OFFICER, Thomas 333
OGDEN, U A 287
OGG, 295
OLIVER, William 13
OMAN, Peter 251
OPP, Daniel 407
ORAM, Nicholas 130
ORR, Martha 189
ORT, S A 333

484

ORWIG, Joseph 405
OVERHOLTZ, Abraham 127
OVIATT, Geo D 157
OWENS, John 114 Robert 339
PAGE, Andrew W 229
PALMER, C E 343 E C 127 279 John 123 M C 419 Mrs Judge 283
PANCOAST, 442
PARISH, John 120
PARK, Robert 245
PARKER, A F 165 168 304 Abel F 121 285 345 346 Edwin 346 F F 426 Jonathan 54 273 294-296 306 311 344 Lyman 110
PATTERSON, 278 J 243 J S 270 284 315 James 46 Jane 316 John 63 92 101 267 269 Johnny 255 M B 158 275 276 347 Margaret 313 314 Mary Jane 299 Minerva 315 W M 168 304 Wm M 121
PATTESON, 68
PATTON, David 308-309 346 356 Dr 357
PAXON, Eli 122 123
PAYNE, John 231
PEER, E 337
PEFLER, Mary 303
PENDLETON, Darius 158 G F 168 288 George F 126 291 Joel 168 339
PERKEY, John F 111
PETERS, Ambrose 466 David 458 466 468 Ephraim 468 Jacob 467 468 John 226
PETERSON, W S 335
PETTIS, James 63
PHIFER, Edwin 168
PHILIPS, Alexander 394
PHILLIPI, Joseph 402
PHILLIPS, Alex 112 164 Alexander 126 E B 327 Job 123
PICKENS, Thomas 425 446
PICKETT, H C 242 J W 242 243
PIERSON, J W 291
PIFER, Peter 167 291 454
PILLARD, James 148
PILLARS, James 123 Judge 126 127 129
PITTS, Father 340

PLATT, W T 288
PLOTTS, Ira 200 201 204 W L 201
PLUMB, Marquis Lafayette 237
POE, 16 Adam 40 388 392 Andrew 388 392 Elizabeth 433 George L 63 Jacob 24 29 38 46 62 383 385 388 391 Jane 63 John 279 291 Luther 392 Mary 392 Mr 387 Mrs 385 Mrs Robert 390 Nelson 383 385 388 391-393 Sarah 115
POMEROY, Charles Carroll 287
POOL, Philemon P 130
POPE, 265 332
PORCH, 328 Henry 369
PORTER, 425 James 153 428
POTTER, E D 112 Emery D 147 148 149 Emory D 110
POULSON, Andrew 223 Cornelius 218 Levi 218 226
POVENMIRE, 383 384
POWELL, 211 248 407 B B 168 Daniel 210 214 G W 168 J C 335 Jacob 210 214 247 251 252 339 Jacob C 345 John 166 210 214 247 250 251 337 Joshua 66 Josiah S 287 Mr 186 Mrs 337 Mrs J C 279 Oliver 127 P H 129 Peter 247 Peter H 252 Philip 441 T C 67 William 210 214 William H 215
PRATT, H 201
PREBLE, Joshua S 152 157 161 S W 167
PRICE, C 454 Daniel S 156 John 383 Judge 150 Merriman 393 Michael 68 376 422 424
PRIEST, Jacob 426
PUGH, D H 288 John B 456
PURSEY, Charles 426
RADABAUGH, 383 449 John 393 John M 216
RAETZER, Father 340
RALSTON, 374 Alpheus 373 375 376-377 William 376
RAMER, Fred 227
RAMSEY, Albert 407 Samuel 122 130
RANSBOTTOM, Mrs 397 Simeon 29 397 398

RATHBUN, John 14 15 Nelson 16
RAWSON, 68 427 Abel 64 Abel T
 315 Amanda 297 Bass 66 261
 291 295 296-297 Dr 306
 Edward 296 Harriet E A 297 L
 Q 296 315 448 Laquina 295
 Lemuel 296 Sarah 296
RAY, A W 281 322 J K 322 Miss
 E J 291
REAMER, Frederick 226
REBER, Samuel 333
RECKERT, Peter 447
REDDICK, Adam 454
REDFERN, P C 232
REED, 310 E S 346 Eli S 152 363
 James 414 John 63 123 127
 282 363 386 394 John Sr 431
 432 Mrs John 390 Rebecca 63
REELMON, J M 359
REESE, Thomas 400
REIGHLEY, Mathew 54 167
REIGHLY, Mathew 29 30 31 65 84
 259 260 306 Matthew 24
 Rachael 260
REIMUND, Adam 324
RENNINGER, Conrad 307 391
 Samuel 363 Wm 393
RESZNER, W P 357
REYMOND, 281
REYNOLDS, Frank 279
RICHARDSON, Joseph 23
RICKETS, Andrew 118 168 397
 399 456 Chaney 396 Jerry 227
 Rezin 405 407
RILEY, 19 Mathew 260 Mrs 20
RINEHART, G W 129 George 456
RITTER, C 336
ROBBINS, Jackson 166
ROBERTS, A S 201 Mabel 409
ROBERTSON, Alexander 405
ROBINSON, 276
ROBINSON, Adam 407 James 122
 167 L 167 Mr 285
RODER, Henry 183 Mrs 183
ROLLER, 219 Caleb 457 Michael
 468 William 68 117 218 222
 225 226 443
ROMICH, Jacob 159
ROOT, Deborah 259
ROSE, Abraham 442 Alvin 339 J
 A 239 John 168 217 237 240

ROSE (continued)
 421
ROSENBERG, B F 351 Benjamin
 Franklin 352 Frank 352 353
 Jacob 117 118 167 350 352
ROSETTE, J E 305 346 John E
 168
ROSS, Enoch 231
ROSSMAN, Lydia A 450
ROSZMAN, Peter 335
ROTH, Adam 123
ROTHCHILD, Joseph B 285
ROWSON, Bass 94
RUCKMAN, James 227
RUDISELL, Henry 127 Henry 393
 394
RUDOLPH, Father 340
RUHL, Dr 283 George W 327 John
 S 327 Marshal 124
RUMMEL, D 282
RUMMELL, David 328 329
RUMOR, Francis 183
RUNNELLS, 39 265 332
RUSSELL, Arthur 380 Timothy
 166 William 127
RUTH, Jacob 226
RUTHRAUF, John 283
SAGER, Shun 2477
SALTZMA,N Jos 168
SAMPSON, Israel 380 Levi 376
 Sunny 376
SANDFORD, Asa 83
SARGEANT, Joseph 406 407
 Samuel 64 224
SARGENT, 218 Joseph 28 66
 Samuel 28
SAUNDERS, J G 214 J H 214 T J
 214
SCHMIDT, Christian 336
SCHWAB, Mr 364
SCOTHORN, L W 252
SEEDS, James 279
SEELAY, 265
SEENEY, George E 147
SELLERS, Sarah 390
SEYFANG, 281 Stephen 324
SEYMOUR, C E 323 329 330 349
SHAFER, A B 112 124 168 291 M
 D 124 126 129 152 291 Solo-
 mon 167
SHALLER, Christ 456

SHANNON, H S 288 Jos C 167 Joseph C 116
SHAW, 414 George 29 38 91 118 168 206 208 209 J W 416 Oliver P 383 Robert 396 454
SHEARER, Michael 215
SHEETS, H 168 Henry 113 167 462
SHEFFIELD, Augustus 320 E A 245
SHELBY, John 106 107
SHELDEN, Eli J 380
SHELLER, Andrew 402
SHERIDAN, John L 200
SHERMAN, 153 154 162
SHERRARD, Robert 422
SHERRICK, Henry 393 J C 338 Mrs 338
SHESLER, W A 337
SHIPPY, D 229
SHOEMAKER, John 29 64 195 217 218 224 Mr 220 224 W S 244
SHOLTY, W J 429
SHOWALTER, Levi 442 443
SHUCK, Peter 201
SHULER, Fred 201 202 203 Henry 126 Mrs H 338 W H 348
SHULL, John 142 329 330
SIDDALL, Sylvester J 168 W W 167
SIMKINS, George W 28
SIMPSON, John 29 46 255 259 269 270 Thomas 269 270
SLIGHT, 19 Joseph 28 Thomas 28 30 31 46 65 83 255 261
SMALL, W P 338
SMART, Joseph 468
SMICK, J H 128
SMITH, 259 Chaples D 29 Darius 168 David 198 Dr 401 E 183 George 196 Gideon 231 Harvey 240 245 Hiram 92 J T 429 Jacob B 252 John 73 195 261 393 John C 450 Joseph 454 Judge 295 Justin 407 Kirby 158 L D 126 Mr 20 Rebecca 390 W W 243
SNAKE-BONE, 103 104
SNYDER, Rudolph 441 Samuel 333 W E 283 347 Wm 125
SORBIE, J B 449

SOURS, Mrs 335 P J 323 Paul 167 267 335
SPAHR, D B 467
SPARR, Benjamin 397 453 456
SPEAR, S A 353 Samuel A 357
SPEROW, Isaac 214
SPINK, J C 146
SPITLER, Noah 127 S 181 Samuel 168 181 187
SPONSLER, W A 204
SPRAGUE, Stewart 362
SPRAU, 322
SPRECHER, C S 333
SPRINGER, Geo 193 George W 346
STACKHOUSE, T J 364
STAFFORD, James 129
STAHL, George 467
STANSBERRY, Dixon 370
STARK, Thomas 403
STARKEY, E A 339
STAULER, W J 451
STEADMAN, James B 113
STEARNES, Joseph E 153
STEARNS J E 152
STEEDMAN, Samuel H 111
STEEKER, Jacob 231
STEVENSON, William 303
STEVESON Edward 421 422
STIENMAN, J F 450
STINEMAN, 454 A 167 Adam 125 456
STINSON, David 205
STONE, C C 354
STOUGH, Henry 231
STOUGHTON, D M 152 153
STOVER, Henry 447
STRADLEY, Elijah 243
STRATTON, John 447 Thomas 447 Wm 447
STRICKLER, J C 291
STRINGFELLOW, Benj 449
STROTHER, A W 165 256
STROTHER Benjamin 258 Isaac 383 Judge 164 256 258 R L 164 168 383 Robert L 68 217 457
STRUBLE, Joseph S 380 Peter 375
STUMP, 414 John 413 415
SUM-UN-DU-WAT, 102 103 104 105

SUMMERS, Elizabeth 463
SUTHERLAND, R R 334
SWAGART, George 29
SWAN, Charles J 112
SWANK, John 250 373
SWAPP, Catharine 331
SWARTS, Solomon 383
SWARTZ, Henry 283
SWEENEY, James 458 461
SWIGART, Engineer 356
SWONK, John 252
TANNER, Abel 29 395 397 Mrs 397 William 251
TAYLOR, 442 Charlotte 315 George 431 Henry D 126 John 29 L 168 Levi 168 393 M 278 Margaret 313 334 Martha 188 Milton 315 318 Minerva 315 Mrs 316 P 278 Patterson 315 Robert 245 Thomas H 127 394 Washington 188 William 49 54 62 63 64 73 92 101 117 136 164 168 188 258 260 269 272 276 285 295 306 313-315 316 334 369 370 385 386 William B 278
TEATSORTH, 444 I N 165 Isaac 333 Isaac N 166 James 446 Martha J 464
TEEMS, John 380
TEEPLE, P L 348
THARP, 10
THOMAS, 15 219 Arthur 12 14 Capt 13 16 Charles 406 407 434 Charles R 439 Dr 297 Henry 223 Jacob 422 424 James 223 Lewis 406 Liverton 458 459 461 468 Michael 458 Mrs 223
THOMPSON, 39 David 412 414 415 417 Isaac 417-418 419 Jacob 123 John 199 292 431 436 Joseph 216 Louisa 417 Rev 197 Sam'l 412 Thomas 28 46 63 195 199 209 243 331
THORNBERG, Robert 191
THORNTON, Samuel 240
THORP, 10
THRALL, L G 345 358
THRAP, J J 152 Rev 424
THRIFT, Sallie 310

TIBBALLS, 265
TILDEN, Daniel J 108 Myron H 147
TIPTON, 425
TODD, 17 Benjamin 422 424 425 427 E 429 Elisha 426 Mrs 424 W H 127 William 425 William H 426
TOTTEN, Theo 291
TRAUCHT, Jacob 455
TRAVIS, John 29
TREAT, Samuel 109
TREE-TOP-IN-WATER, 20
TREECE, 374 George 375 378-379
TRESSLER, W A 112
TRIBOLET, Wm 336
TRICHLER, George 155 156
TRIMBLE, Allen 23 83
TRITCH, J C 291 Leonard 261 Parlee C 167
TROMNEY, Joseph 380
TROUT, 437 Ephraim 186 George W 185 John 181 182 183 185 187 191 192 Miss 183 Mr 188
TULLIS, John 29 63 398
TUPPER, Edmund W 12
TURLEY, C L 165 166
TURNPAUGH, J R 429 J W 242
TUSSING, Daniel 442
TWINING, G W 288 Joseph 199
UPDYKE, J V 338
VAIL, Cyrus 320 E B 403 Edwin B 77
VAN BUREN, President 453
VANCE, 256 274 383 A F 277 Bridget 20 294 D M 277 Horace M 294 323 Joseph 83 269 271 273 292 294 Joseph Colville 292 Miles W 293 294 Mr 20 Mrs 20 Sarah 292 334 William 129 153 165 277 288 292 293 294 Wilson 16 19 24 28 31 38 40 46 47 59 62 64 83 85 86 92 114 115 167 168 254 255 259 269 270 273 284 292 292-295 306 334
VANEMON, George 182 334 385 389
VANHORN, J M 196 James M 166
VANLUE, William 168 199 200

VANSANT, Mr 203
VANSCOICH, William 402
VATTMAN, Father 340
VAUGHN, 161
VEAL, John 205
VICKERS, James 230 232 233
WADE, Mr 188 Richard 386 392
  Wenman 116 442 443 444 447
  William 29 62
WAGGONER, Samuel 109
WAGNER, J B 389 Valentine 336
WAITE, 312 Chief Justice 46 M
  R 46
WALKER, Geo F 152 153 M B
  154 Widow 186
WALL, Col 88 H B 168 Henry B
439 Richard 122
WALLS, Thomas 418
WALTEMIRE, James 161 380
  Thomas 380
WALTERNIRE, James 159
WALTERS, John 251 252 Lower
  122 Penelope 252 Robert 431
  436
WALTMAN, Dr 279 Wm 291
WAMPLER, J 178 179
WARD, Lewis 407 Willis 407
WARDEN, A C 129
WARDWELL, David 401
WARNER, Daniel 439 E B 467
  Ezra B 468
WASHINGTON, George 88
WATKINS, Solomon 400
WATSON, Crondall 393 George
  383 Nicholas 449 Richard 383
  388 Richard M 131 W C 393
  William 383
WEAVER, Nicholas 339
WEBBER, J B 336 Simon B 153
WEBSTER, David 464
WEEDEN, Engineer 356
WEGEHAH, 20
WELCH, John 230
WELKER, George 333
WELLS, E C 193 Mrs E 193 O
  407 Othniel 406
WELSH, John 109
WELTY, Christain 401 Christian
  399 402 456
WESCOTT, John 111 202 204 348
  Josiah N 11

WEST, James 442 454 John 447
WESTENHAVER, Joseph 256
  Joseph 269
WHEELAN, William 467
WHEELER, 328 Geo H 348 J J
  326 Jesse 77 110 267 Jesse Jr
  288 John W 155 156 W H 113
  283 329
WHETSTONE, Peter 182
WHITE, Joseph 46
WHITELEY, Judge 283 M C 110
  121 291 W H 291
WHITELY, Judge 46 122 M C 122
  305 369 Machias C 147 W H
  128
WHITEMAN, 332
WHITINGTON, W 337
WHITMAN, 331 Benj O 251
  Benjamin 248 252
WHITNEY, Jesse 256
WICKHAM, Asher 28 66 406 407
  434 J C 31 216 Jno C 284 John
  C 28 29 41 62 63 83 167 209
  216 Miner T 28
WILCH, Michael 454 Peter 401
  454 Philip 401 403
WILCOXSON, Anthony 422
WILDEMUTH, Benjamin 451
WILEY, James 182
WILKES, Wm 181
WILKINS, W A 113
WILKINSON, C S 193
WILLCOX, Aaron 399 Moses 399
WILLHELM, Simon 320
WILLIAMS, J A 153 J B 426 J W
  397 401 402 John W 399 401
  Margaret 375 Nancy 240
  Nathan 64 240
WILLIAMSON, 374 377 Levi 373
  William 226 252
WILSON, 39 265 332 C B 167 346
  Ebenezer 29 58 59 61 62 161
  334 383 Elias 125 G W 338
  George 166 H 164 165 283 366
  369 James 155 305 347 408
  James H 274 305-307 Jane 63
  Joel W 110 Jome 152 Joseph
  61 127 393 394 Judge 38 63 64
  101 385 Miles 160 432 Mrs 385
  Rachel 63 Rebecca 63 Sarah
  292 Susan E 306 Thomas 62 63

WILSON (continued)
 383 W P 203 204
WINCHESTER, Gen 12
WINDERS, H F 283 325 332
 Henry F 326
WINELAND, Joseph 231
WING, Alonzo D 167 L P 401 403
WINGATE, J W 242 Thomas 28
WINNELL, 124 James 122 123
WISE, John 252 John K 325
WISELEY, 219 Allen 219 407
 Edward 407 William 218
WISELY, Allen 405 406 William 458
WISEMAN, Elizabeth 463 Isaac 460 James 458 460 461 462 468 James G 458 463 L D 401
WISLER, Charles 332
WITTEMYER, A 216
WOOD, Amos E 109 110
WOLCOTT, Sarah 301
WOLF, Jesse 320 370
WOLFORD, Godfrey 29 30 31 83 237 238 240 245 374 378 John 239
WOOD, James 229 W S 343
WOODRUFF, 251 Elijah 246 John 246 248 249 Mr 377 Mrs 249 Penelope 252 William Y 395

WOODS, A 402 J T 158 James 230 449 T E 449 William 421
WOODWORTH, T F 291 349 Truman 363
WORK, Alexander 458
WORKMAN, Daniel M 107
WORTMAN, Jonn 216
WRIGHT, Ann M 313 Charles 324 325 David 422 424 David Sr 424
WYANDOTT, 19
WYANT, George 225 John 127 Peter 225
YATES, William 164 246 Wm M 167
YERGER, A 167 Abraham 129
YOCUM, 276 282
YOST, W M 244
YOUNG, Father 340 Robert 106 107
YOUNKIN, Abraham 287 345 346 347
ZARBAUGH, John 193 Sol 193
ZELLER, J W 283 343 348
ZOLL, Jacob 248 250 251
ZWANZIE, 360

www.ingramcontent.com/pod-product-compliance
Lightning Source LLC
Chambersburg PA
CBHW060233230426
43664CB00011B/1630